A Postcolonial Reading of the Acts of the Apostles

Biblical Hermeneutics Rediscovered

The Series as the name suggests will focus on Biblical Hermeneutics, i.e., literary works concerned with methods of interpreting the Old and New Testaments of Bible via different stream of topics like Literature & Poetry, Indigenous Philosophizing, Ethical response towards Ecology, Health & Healing, Science & Technology, Feminist Theology, Sociological approach towards Human Rights, Law & Politics, Arts, History of Ideas, Ancient Civilizations, Cultural Contiguity, Religious Cosmologies & Mysticism, Appraisal of various Theologians, World Peace & Harmony, Global Capitalism, Network Marketing, Cybertheology, Population & Demographics, Epigraphic Studies, Contextualized Education, and many others. We welcome a Mss. on any topic/s mentioned, whether they are original works, scholarly monographs, collections of conference papers, revised dissertations, or translations of historical documents. Through the Series we, the Publishers, are striving to put forward published works that may help Institutions, Academic Bodies, Researchers, Scholars and the World at large in furthering their respective knowledge and understanding on the concerned subject. We welcome your comments on our efforts and further suggestions on how we can enshrine new ray of analysing & explaining the written Texts through our upcoming books.

Biblical Hermeneutics Rediscovered - 12

A Postcolonial Reading of the Acts of the Apostles

Implication for Theological Education in India

Jose L

CWI

Christian World Imprints(TM)

First Published in 2018 by

Christian World Imprints(TM)
Christian Publishing & Books from India
H-12 Bali Nagar, **New Delhi-110015**
info@christianworldimprints.com
www.ChristianWorldImprints.com
Phone: +91 11 25465925

ISBN 13: 978-93-5148-254-3 ISBN 10: 93-5148-254-5

Cataloging in Publication Data--DK
Courtesy: D.K. Agencies (P) Ltd. <docinfo@dkagencies.com>

Jose, L., 1965- **author.**
A postcolonial reading of the Acts of the Apostles : implication for theological education in India / Jose L.
pages cm. -- (Biblical hermeneutics rediscovered ; 12)"... edited version of the doctoral dissertation submitted to the Senate of Serampore (Serampore University) in the year 2013"--Preface.
Includes bibliographical references.
ISBN 9351482545
ISBN 9789351482543

1. Bible. Acts.--Postcolonial criticism. 2. Theology--Study and teaching--India. I. Title. II. Series: Biblical hermeneutics rediscovered ; 12.

LCC BS2625.52.J67 2018 | DDC 226.606 23

Printed in India

Dedication

To the loving memory of my parents, Late Mr. Livingstone and Mrs. Baby Livingstone who were an example of simplicity and devotion to the Lord and Saviour Jesus Christ.

Contents

Foreword

I am delighted to write a foreword for the book entitled, "A Postcolonial Reading of the Acts of the Apostles" by the Rev. Dr. Jose L., Associate Professor of New Testament studies at New Theological College, Dehradun. Our friendship began in the early nineties when he joined for his BD studies at The United Theological College and later MTh studies. He has been an honest and transparent person with a lot of openness in accepting new ideas and conversations.

This book is a revised version of his doctoral dissertation. The uniqueness of this work is that Dr. Jose was able to identify the differences that exist among scholars in viewing the Acts of the Apostles either as a 'Pro-Roman' or as an anti-Roman discourse. In order to support his arguments, the author brilliantly sought the help of scholarly materials through rigorous and systematic library research. The most appealing hypothesis he argues is that in the first century, the socio-economic–political and cultural infrastructure of the empire was challenged by the nascent Christian ecclesia taking a postcolonial stand. The author systematically exposes the mode of resistance of the nascent Christian ecclesia against the Roman Empire. The endeavor indeed offers a new dimension to the study of the Acts of the Apostles from a postcolonial viewpoint.

The monograph also discusses the understanding of the heavenly ascent of the Roman Emperors and similar beliefs in the first century Greco-Roman world. I consider this analysis to be important in terms of developing a possible Christology for the emerging Christian communities in the early church. The exalted Christ has been a major theme discussed in the Acts. Dr. Jose meaningfully uncovers the cultural hybrid in Acts by addressing the radical position of Luke in locating the empire in Acts.

In my view, Dr. Jose indeed provides a new dimension to "the uninterrupted proclamators of the word of God in the midst of persecution and martyrdom" (P. 176). The very assumption about the unholy alliance between religion and politics in Roman Empire is very relevant in today's context. By addressing the issues of strategic essentialism against cultural essentialism by the subaltern community, the author offers a new and powerful hermeneutical tool for the study of the New Testament. As this book enters into the field of published resources, I am sure, it will pinpoint an eminently unique style in the interpretation of the scriptures. I trust this book will create new challenges in understanding the New Testament more meaningfully.

Rev. Dr. C. I. David Joy, Ph.D.
Professor, United Theological College
Bangalore

Preface

This book, "A Postcolonial Reading of the Acts of the Apostles," is an edited version of the doctoral dissertation submitted to the Senate of Serampore (Serampore University) in the year 2013. Not many changes have been made in the content except for some editing in order to make the book reader friendly. The book of Acts in the New Testament literature has been a fascinating book all through the ages, which people have interpreted it differently either as historical, theological or missional treatise. Recently, New Testament scholars have discovered the significance of the Roman colonialism and Jewish cultural nationalism in the text. However, they have placed it in polar opposite categorizations.

Taking the postcolonial methods of hybridity, mimicry, and ambivalence (strategic essentialism and transcultural hybridity), I have attempted to read the literature of the colonized community responding to its colonial experience beyond the anti and pro polarity. The first century ecclesia affiliates and distances simultaneously from both the Roman colonial powers and native Jewish religio-cultural nationalistic discourses of power in order to carve out a new space of identity. This is a very strategic position adopted by the persecuted ecclesia of the first century and the same position possibly applies in the Indian context where the minority community has been persecuted by the colonial powers.

Pauls trial scenes before the Roman and Jewish political authorities and his defensive speeches explain the postcolonial position of the Christian community in the first century colonial Rome. He affiliates himself with Imperial Rome by making one of the amenities of his Roman citizenship and appeal for trial before the Caesars court. The literature also addresses various features of postcolonial literature like ethnicity, border crossing, gender diversity, diaspora, and transcultural position of the minority. A postcolonial ecclesiology is formulated through this study to draw guidelines to the present day Indian ecclesia that faces enormous challenges from the Imperial powers.

The seed for a postcolonial reading of Acts was put into my heart by the Rev. Dr. Simon Samuel, principal of New Theological College. He introduced the Postcolonial methodology to the community in a faculty seminar paper, which became instrumental in drawing me to this field of research. Dr. Simon also helped me to chart out a proposal for my dissertation based on the Acts of the Apostles. I am grateful to him and also to his wife Mrs. Rajamma Simon for their encouragement during the course of my thesis writing. Dr. Simon walked so many extra miles with me so that I would complete my thesis on time. I want to express my sincere thanks to him for his brotherly love and concern.

I am indebted to Rev. Dr. Gnanavaram, my thesis guide and the principal of Tamilnadu Theological Seminary, Madurai for ably supervising my thesis not as a student but as a younger brother. He rendered all possible help in completing my initial work within 42 months of my research.

I am very grateful for the support I received from the founders of New Theological College, Rev. Dr. George and Mrs. Leela Chavanikammannil who stood with me as parental figures. I am grateful to them for their constant support. I am also thankful to the management of New Theological College, including Rev. George C. Kuruvilla for the spiritual and financial support during the course of my study.

I express my appreciation and thanks to Rev. Dr. David Joy for his meticulous reading of all the chapters of my thesis and for his valuable suggestions which were immensely helpful in the completion of my work on time. I express my sincere thanks to the staff of United Theological College library for their kind help in the use of the library and the UTC administration for the accommodation they provided for my stay.

I am grateful to Dr. Rohan Gideon (faculty, Tamil Nadu Theological Seminary, Madurai) and Dr. Roji T. George, my former colleague and currently faculty at SAIACS, Bangalore who rendered their help in the final stages of the thesis. I would also like to appreciate Dr. Biju Chacko, Dean of Academics (New Theological College) and my colleague, Dr. P. V. Joseph (faculty at New Theological College), for their assistance in editing the work and converting it into a book form. I must appreciate the help of Rev. Samuel P. Rajan and his family who arranged for the necessary materials from the UTC Library and made my stay comfortable while I was in Bangalore.

I am deeply indebted to my godly parents and in-laws who were an inspiration in my journey in Christian ministry and theological education. I am thankful to God for the legacy my parents left behind in the service of the Lord. Both of our parents are not with us today to share the joy of the great honour that I received in theological education, but I am sure that this honour is God`s covenantal faithfulness to my parents.

At the end, I express my deep appreciation to my beloved wife Kripa Jose and our daughter Phoebe Jose for their constant support and prayers, especially in the moments of my distress and difficulties. Finally, I want to extend my thankfulness and appreciation to Major V. I. Luke and the administrator Mrs. Starla Luke (India Bible College and Seminary, Kumbanadu, Kerala) for providing a home for my family and ministerial opportunity for my wife Kripa in the capacity as Assistant Librarian at India Bible College and Seminary. Within a short period of time, they became more than a family to us through their love and affection.

Introduction

Luke, in his historical narration, covers forty years of the development of the first-century Christian community where a small group of Galilean marginalized Jews formed the core of Jesus' movement. Later this group was relocated to Jerusalem to form a community of equals over against the oppressive structures of Jewish nationals and the Roman imperial government. From the beginning, the Acts of the Apostles depicts a typical postcolonial nature of the encounters of different cultures. The ambivalent nature of the first century Jewish-Gentile Christian minority towards the Roman colonial powers would give a clear picture of the postcolonial condition of the subjugated group. The community's interaction with the majority Jews in Jerusalem and the Greek nationalities of the Roman Empire seem to have shaped their socio-religious culture and their theological stand.

There are differences exist among scholars in viewing the Acts of the Apostles either as a 'pro-Roman'[1] or as an anti-Roman discourse.[2] However, the Acts of the Apostles presents much more than just the polarized views. Therefore, these multiple stances could be treated as Luke's discursive strategy towards Rome and Jewish nationalism, especially his both pro-Roman and anti-Roman posturing as

[1] The pro-Roman position defends either the newly formed church or Paul himself (Ac. 18:5; 25:8; 26: 31). *Apologia pro ecclesia* is a common perspective made by some of the prominent Lukan scholars. For them Acts is a defense for Christians (harmless, supportive, law-abiding, loyal or neutral towards Rome) against the charges brought by Roman officials. Robert Maddox, *The Purpose of Luke-Acts* (SNTS; Edinburgh: T & T Clark, 1985), 91-93; Philip F. Esler, *Community and Gospel in Luke-Acts*, (SNTS; Cambridge: Cambridge University Press, 1989). For Maddox, and Esler, Luke-Acts was written for Christians. Haenchen and Fitzmayer favour Lukan apology to Rome on behalf of the church. E. Haenchen, *The Acts of the Apostles. A Commentary* (Oxford: Basil Blackwell, 1982), 630 31; J.A. Fitzmyer, *The Acts of the Apostles: A New Translation with Introduction and Commentary* (New York: Doubleday, 1998), 58.

[2] Cassidy and Horsley observe the message of Luke-Acts as subversive and disrupting the existing order. They highlight so much on the anti-Roman passages. R.A. Horsley, *The Liberation of Christians: The Infancy Narrative in Social Context* (New York: Crossroad, 1989); R.J. Cassidy and P.J. Scharper, eds., *Political Issues in Luke-Acts* (New York: Orbis Books, 1983).

well as his affiliative and disruptive Jewish posturing in the first century colonial context. Such posturing could be a postcolonial ambivalence.

The Acts of the Apostles resonates the Roman empiric and the imperial cultic voices beginning with the narratives of the origin of early Christianity. However, traditional scholars of Acts seem to think that Acts has little to do with Roman imperialism and Jewish cultural nationalism.[3] For them, Acts is solely a theological, historical, and missiological treatise than a discursive and a disruptive response to native Jewish national and religious traditions and Roman imperialism. This polarity shows the rich complexity of Acts.

Students of Acts cannot avoid noting the relationship between the theme of Acts and the imperial cult.[4] The very nature of the Roman Empire reflected through political events and by political terms have a bearing on Acts. In addition, the complexity of Luke-Acts might lead people to interpret the political passages positively or negatively towards Rome.[5] However, positing with one set of passages and rejecting the other would impoverish readers of the rich complexity of the imperial cult and its influence in Acts. For instance, the liberal way of using the terms like 'the Lord', 'peace', 'judge' (ό κυρίος, εἰρηνη, κριτής) by Luke shows the relation between Lukan writing and the imperial cult.[6] Similarly, there seems

---

[3] For instance, Haenchen, *The Acts of the Apostles*; I.H. Marshall, *The Acts of the Apostles: An Introduction and Commentary* (England: IVP, 1988); F.F. Bruce, *Commentary on the Book of Acts* (London: Marshall, Morgan & Scott, 1972); Fitzmayer, *Acts*; Ben Witherington III, *The Acts of the Apostles: A Socio-Rhetorical Commentary* (Grand Rapids: Eerdmans, 1998). From here on Acts is used for the Acts of the Apostles.

[4] The socio-political dimensions of the Roman empire of the first Century Greco-Roman world is narrated by Luke in placing different political personalities in his two volumes. For example, King Herod of Judea (Lk. 1:5), Caesar Augustus, Quirinius (Lk. 2:1-2), Herod Antipas I (Lk. 23:7), Tiberius Caesar, Felix, Festus, while Caesar's name is unnamed. The peculiar political stance of Luke is clear from the beginning of Acts (eg., address to 'most excellent' Theophilus').

[5] C. Kavin Rowe, "Luke-Acts and the Imperial Cult: A Way through the Conundrum," *JSNT* 27/3 (2005), 287. There are positive passages: eg., Ac. 3: 13; 13: 7-8; 19: 31, 37 which show the positive attitude of Roman officials to the Apostles. On the other side, negative passages eg., Ac. 4: 12, 25- 26; 16: 21 (cf. Lk. 4: 5; 12: 30; 18: 32-33; 19: 38), critiquing the status quo of the Roman empire leading the relationship between Acts and the imperial cult in the opposite direction.

[6] Rowe, "Luke-Acts and the imperial Cult," 294. Luke uses the term κυριος- 100 times each in Luke and Acts. Luke uses the "absolute ό κυριος consistently and expansively for Jesus in his earthly Career (Lk. 7:13), 295. Acts frequently joins 'Ιησους and κυρίος; he is the κυριος οὐρανου και γης (Ac. 1: 21; cf. 4:33; 8:16; Ac. 17: 24 cf. Lk. 10:21). Peter's speech in Cornelius' house points to the reference of Jesus' role as the judge of the living and the dead where Caesar is considered to be the final judge of the living. Jesus is pointed to be the provider of peace- εἰρηνη δια 'Ιησου χριστου (Ac. 10: 36) when Caesar is considered to be the supplier of peace. J.R. Howell, "The Imperial Authority and Benefaction of Centurions and Acts 10: 34-43: A Response to C. Kavin Rowe", *JSNT* 31/1 (2008), 37. According to Gilbert, listing the name by beginning with 'Parthia' emphasizes the political force of the list because of its intolerance under Rome's reign even after its conquest. Gary Gilbert, "The List of Nations in Acts 2: Roman propaganda and the Lukan Response," *JBL* 121/3 (2002), 528.

to be some relevance to the Christian preaching about kingdom of God and about the Lord Jesus Christ (Ac. 1: 3; Ac. 28: 31) in the Roman imperial context.

Luke's use of irony to censure the imperial cult (Ac. 10:1-11:18; 12: 1-24) is note-worthy. He presents Jesus as the 'this one (Jesus) is Lord of all' (οὑτος ἑστιν παντων κυριος; Ac. 10:36) as opposed to the Roman emperor who was widely acknowledged as the 'lord of all' ('παντων κυριος').[7] There are also internal evidences to show the popular notion of the imperial cult when Festus addresses Emperor Caesar as 'to the Lord' (τῳ κυριῳ; Ac. 25:26). This seems to reiterate the connection between the lord of Acts and the Roman emperor.[8] Howell tries to find the ironical positive characterization of the Centurion in the Cornelius episode as an evidence (both in the text and in the ancient literary texts and inscriptions) to show verbal and conceptual connection in criticizing the imperial cult.[9] Similarly, is it the list of nations in Acts 2 that ironically challenges "Rome's position as ruler of the inhabited world and offers an ideology that counters Rome's universal rule with power and might?"[10] What is the purpose of Luke to depict the new found movement as the people of 'the way' (ἡ ὁδος), which expands its mission toward Rome? Is it a postcolonial strategy that counters the Roman colonial strategy of its expansion toward the East? Did Luke mimic the logic of the empire by One-God concept and criticize the colonial domination of the empire? Does the ideological concept 'the world' (οἰκουμενη) mimic the political and philosophical period of the Roman Empire?

Through the narratives, Luke probably questions the oppressive realities of the empire inequality, poverty, oppressive structures of the Roman political leaders, slavery and bribery etc. The slave girl's prophetic words "these men are

[7] Rowe, "Luke-Acts and the Imperial Cult," 291. The phrase οὑτος ἑστιν παντων κυριος (Ac. 10:36), "would likely make the verbal and conceptual connection with imperial cult" and its religious propaganda. Rowe gives importance to the pronoun οὑτος as it suggests a demonstrative purpose, meaning 'this one', which gives the importance of Jesus' lordship of all over against Caesar. He finds the presence of the Roman Empire keenly in the narration of the Cornelius episode in Caesarea (Ac. 10: 1-11:18). He also catalogues this truth in his essay by showing similar slogans that were used for the emperor in antiquity. For a similar view with certain differences, refer, Howell, "The Imperial Authority and Benefaction," 26.

[8] "[The] use of παντων in 10:36 precludes ultimate allegiance to the emperor on the part of the Gentile neophytes." Rowe, "Luke-Acts and the imperial Cult," 294.

[9] Howell, "The Imperial Authority and Benefaction," 25. The centurions were benefactors and judges of their provinces and more than that they were the tax-collectors and villains in ancient society. However, Luke mockingly portrays the positive features of a Centurion while the Lukan audience has a preconception of a Centurion, 39.

[10] According to Gilbert, the list of Nations in Acts 2 counters the Roman propaganda of a universal rule. He further proves his argument from the ancient writers such as Virgil, Horace, Pliny the Elder and Josephus who evoke the glory and power of the empire by their list of nations. He adds that "[the] use of geographic lists as a form of a political propaganda extolling Rome's universal rule persisted throughout the first century." Gilbert, "The List of Nations in Acts 2," 514, 516. Luke also promotes universalism (Ac. 1:8) in contrast to the ideology of the Roman Empire.

servants of 'the most high God' who proclaims to you the way of salvation," seem to mimic the colonial empire (Ac. 16: 17). Likewise, what is the purpose of Luke's portrayal of a long narration of Paul's trial as well as other imprisonment of the apostles that show the incompetence of Roman officials?

Does Luke visualize a new community of fellowship (koinwnia) in the context of Roman imperial cult that goes along with the strategic subjugation of the ethnic minorities, the diaspora Jews and the 'other' communities of the empire? Does he visualize a new community with certain socio-cultural values (e.g., impartiality- Ac. 10:35; παντων, ἐν παντι ἔθνει) that would counter the imperial values? Why does Luke use Stephen's speech on the Jerusalem temple to criticize the ethnocentric and nationalist definition? Does the Lukan theology attempt to correct the improper obeisance to human beings (Ac. 10:26; Ac. 14: 15)? Does the Lukan preferential option for Θεος in the Gentile context help to counter the imperial cult?[11] What was Paul's purpose to establish churches in Greco-Roman cities? Was there a postcolonial strategy in planting *ecclesial* units in the major part of Greco-Roman cities replacing 'the empire'?

In order to answer these questions there are basically two major trends that need to be analyzed for a Postcolonial reading of Acts.

i. Lukan discursive response to Rome.
ii. Lukan discursive response to native Jewish religio-cultural tradition.

The Eclectic Methodology Used to Read the Acts of the Apostles

This study employs Postcolonial Criticism (here after alternatively PC) to read primarily the Lukan response to Rome. Among the varying reading practices of PC, the researcher would prefer 'Strategic Essentialism' and 'Transcultural Hybridity' model[12] that employs the theoretical concepts of mimicry, hybridity and ambivalence. In addition to that the reading also recognizes the transforming power of liberation and feminist model of hermeneutics in dealing with the topic.[13] According to Fiorenza, this would be a critical liberation and feminist

[11] "The cities Luke and his first readers traveled were crowded with imperial cult, with statuary of humans representing themselves as gods, gods in human form whose faces sometimes resembled members of the imperial family, and with executions where criminals were made to represent the gods." Laura Nasrallah, "The Acts of the Apostles, Greek cities, and Hadrian's Panhellenion," *JBL* 127/3 (2008), 260.

[12] A model used by Samuel to read the gospel of Mark. The model is explained later in this thesis. Simon Samuel, *A Postcolonial Reading of Mark's story of Jesus* (London: T & T Clark, 2007).

[13] Postcolonial criticism, like the feminist criticism, attempts also to trace the voice of the voiceless in a discursive context. The feminist model of hermeneutics pioneered and outlined by Elisabeth Schüssler Fiorenza in particular is related to postcolonial criticism. In her words, it is a 're-articulated postcolonial criticism' from a feminist critical perspective, *The Power of the Word. Scripture and the Rhetoric of the Empire* (Minneapolis: Fortress Press, 2007), 113-129. Both models pay attention to the inscription (approximation or internalization) of dominant voices (patriarchy/kyriarchy in the case of feminist criticism and colonialism/imperialism in the case of PC) in the

hermeneutics.[14] These methods help the researcher to critically evaluate the economic liberation as well as women's emancipation. This inclusive methodology will enable the researcher to study not only the socio-cultural aspect of colonialism but also the socio-economic factors of colonialism. The postcolonial critical tool, like feminist criticism, is equipped to enter into this complex terrain of the text and explore the domineering and liberative dynamics of the text. Postcolonial theorists claim that this method is interdisciplinary and uses a wide range of methods; so it is eclectic. Complimentary and correlative dimensions of historical, literary, socio-cultural, contextual and postcolonial interpretation will definitely bring the prospective results.

The hypothesis for this research is that Christianity since its inception in its eastern sphere (both in Greco-Mediterranean world as well as in the Asiatic region, specifically in India) has been a persecuted powerless minority and not a dominating colonial religion. Thus, one would be able to see Acts as a postcolonial literature in the sense of the discursive traits of mimicry, hybridity and ambivalence.

The Trajectory of the Previous Research leads to the Postcolonial Reading of the Acts of the Apostles

For long the New Testament scholars have generally viewed Acts as a historical and /or theological treatise. For the recent years studies have been done in the socio-historical and cultural world of Acts. Few like Horsley and Cassidy have studied the text by analyzing the socio-political and the cultural discursive contexts of Acts. Scholars like Witherington have studied the text socio-rhetorically.[15] However, the political discourses in the narrative world of Acts lead scholars to interpret differently from traditional interpretations to postcolonial approaches. In Samuel's article "The Imperial Prison and the Irrupting Gospel as Discursive Symbols of Stewardship," uses mimicry to analyze the way Luke radically criticized the Slave system in Philippi (Ac. 16: 16-40).[16] In postcolonial language the slave girl is mockingly mimicking the slave system by her prophesy that the missionaries are '*slaves of the most high God'*/ Δουλι του θεοῦ τοῦ ὕψιστου and proclaimers of *salvation.* "[The] Roman governance failed to offer any salvation or safety

scripture and also attempt to recover the liberative voices of the silent subaltern women in the case of feminist criticism and of the colonial subject in the case of PC.

[14] Elisabeth Schüssler Fiorenza, "Transforming the Margin Claiming Common ground: Charting a different Paradigm of Biblical Studies" in *Still at the Margins. Biblical Scholarship Fifteen Years after Voices from the Margin,* edited by R.S. Sugirtharajah (New York: T & T Clark, 2008)," 35. She argues for a 'collaborative hermeneutics' between the three approaches. Fiorenza, *The Power of the Word*, 120-121.

[15] Witherington III, *Acts.*

[16] Italics used for emphasis to recognize postcolonial terms. Simon Samuel, "The Imperial Prison and the Irrupting Gospel as Discursive Symbols of Stewardship," *niyog-* NTC Magazine (2004), 39.

to a powerless, poor slave girl from being abused and exploited by her greedy masters."[17] Symbolically, Paul the apostle became the 'saviour' of the terrified Roman imperialism by responding to the 'saving call'- Lord, what is it necessary for me in order that I may be saved? (Κύριοι, τί με δεῖ ποῖεν ἵνα σωθω; Ac. 16: 30).[18] The Roman colonial opportunism was mocked by the valour of the Philippian prisoners along with Paul and Silas who did not run away for safety as deliverance came in the jail[19] from a divine initiative. Finally the Roman jailor and his family receive salvation/ *salus* which are promised by the Roman government. Similarly, Samuel's postcolonial reading of Mark is another promising starting point in this field.[20] He argues his case convincingly that the author of Mark narrates the story of Jesus neither as a pro-nor as an anti-Roman discourse but as a complex discursive strategy of affiliative and antagonistic towards Rome. In conclusion, he finds the discourses of the first century Christian community to be ambivalent.

Virginia Barrus' work on Luke- Acts in the Postcolonial Commentary is a milestone in the literary field of Acts.[21] She adopts the postcolonial theories of collaboration versus resistance, ambivalence, hybridity and boarder translations against the empire to understand Luke's ideological/cultural position. She projects God as the ideological superior in order to decolonize the dehumanized Roman imperial powers.[22] This leveler is used to smite the imperial, exploitative Agrippa I, as 'he was eaten by worms and died' (Ac. 12:23). For her, the novelistic genre of the literature itself shows the great potentiality (subversive as well as accommodative) of the postcolonial reading of the text.[23] She perceives this literature as 'a source of political critique' as well as a 'political possibility.'[24] The trial of Paul before the Roman governors (Felix, Festus) and King Agrippa shows the laxity and the greedy nature of the Roman imperial personalities. According to Barrus, Luke mocks and ridicules the atmosphere in the political capital where the Roman citizen is not able to see the face of the emperor which shows the instability of the center.

---

[17] Samuel, "The Imperial Prison and the Irrupting Gospel, 39.

[18] Samuel, "The Imperial Prison and the Irrupting Gospel, 40.

[19] Samuel, "The Imperial Prison and the Irrupting Gospel, 40.

[20] Samuel, *A Postcolonial Reading of Mark's story of Jesus.*

[21] Virginia Barrus, "The Gospel of Luke and the Acts of the Apostles," in *A Postcolonial Commentary on the NT Writings*, edited by Fernando F. Segovia and R. S. Sugirtharajah (London: T & T Clark, 2007), 133-155.

[22] Barrus, "The Gospel of Luke and the Acts," 137.

[23] The genre of Acts is a disputed issue because of its unique nature. Barrus, "The Gospel of Luke and the Acts," 145. The subjugated 'talked back' by telling stories questioning the hegemony of Rome or similar to any 'monolithic version of history.' The novelistic presentation is open ended.

[24] Barrus, "The Gospel of Luke and the Acts," 153.

It seems that Rome supersedes Jerusalem in Luke's narrative and it "has became less a 'place' than an unbounded space of expansive inclusiveness in which the distinctions between Jew and Gentile, emperor and subject, colonizer and colonized are finally rendered irrelevant."[25] By this portrayal "Luke- Acts carries a message of political subversion, it opposes the totalizing claims of one empire- 'the Roman'- with the totalizing claims of another- God's kingdom."[26]

Ruben Muñoz-Larrondo's unpublished Ph.D dissertation to Vanderbilt University, "Living in Two Worlds – A Postcolonial Reading of the Acts of the Apostles," is another milestone in the postcolonial biblical literature.[27] He also makes use of the postcolonial theories of hybridity and mimicry as an act of subversion. He values his diaspora identity as a similar point of confrontation of the first century hybrid Christian community (mainly Paul) who lived between the two worlds- the world of the Roman Empire and the world of the dominant Jewish center.

Muñoz-Larrondo's postcolonial reading starts with the episode of King Agrippa I (Ac. 12:20-23) and he uses type-scenes for the purpose of subversion-alterity reading of resistance. He gives detailed exposition of the bond between the Roman imperial cult and the socio-economic-religio-political life of the colonial subjects of the first century Greco-Roman world. Here the Jerusalem centered Jewish institutions with the Roman political establishment are in opposition to the followers of the way. According to him, the encounters the Apostles faced in Philippi, Thessalonica, Corinth and Ephesus are an act of subversion to the Roman colonial constituencies through postcolonial tool of mimicry. However, the conflicts with the Jewish dominant institutions in the first part of Acts (Ac. 1-12) are not given serious attention. Even the second part (Ac. 13-28) where Paul's trials before the Roman authorities are also not given adequate attention. Moreover, he did not attempt for a comprehensive reading of the Acts of the Apostles.

Muthuraj also studies certain texts that has socio-political and religious underpinnings (Ac. 4: 12; 12: 20-23; 17: 1-9) in the context of Roman colonialism and tries to project the anti-imperialist notions.[28]

The cultural and political discourse dimensions of Acts have been neglected for many years by the traditional interpreters. By seeking Luke's ideological

[25] Barrus, "The Gospel of Luke and the Acts," 139.

[26] Barrus, "The Gospel of Luke and the Acts," 139.

[27] Rubén Munñoz-Larrondo, *Living in Two Worlds-A Postcolonial Reading of the Acts of the Apostles,* Ph.D Dissertation submitted to the faculty of the Graduate School of Vanderbilt University, 2008, 107. MuozLarrondo.pdfetd.library.vanderbilt.edu/…/PhdDissertationRuben (5 Oct 2010).

[28] J.G. Muthuraj, "A Post-colonial Reading of Acts," in *Interweaving Methodology and Praxis-Exploring Disciplinary Options in Today's World,* edited by I.J. Mohan Razu (Bangalore: BTESSC/SATHRI, 2007), 84-85. Bruce, *The Book of the Acts*, 94; Witherington III, *The Acts of the Apostles,* 194. Witherington advocates for an inclusive salvation of spiritual, physical and social realms.

position, Barrus and Muñoz-Larrondo reflect the Roman imperial position which is a milestone in the interpretation of Acts. However, the postcolonial readings done on Acts by the contemporary New Testament scholars are not satisfactory because of the anti-colonial confrontational approach rather than the postcolonial ambivalence. Furthermore, there is no detailed study done in this line on Acts. So, the research will be an exciting and stimulating endeavor to give an in-depth study of Acts of the Apostles in this direction.

The Scope of Postcolonial Reading of the Acts of the Apostles

By the late twentieth century, some NT scholars (Richard Cassidy and R.A. Horsley) shifted our attention from the traditional interpretation to postcolonial approaches. However, a detailed postcolonial reading has not been done on Acts as yet. Thus, the researcher finds a possibility to incorporate the postcolonial methodology along with the existing socio-political methods in order to explore the wider cultural context of the Acts of the Apostles with specific reference to Roman imperialism and native Jewish cultural nationalism.

Reading Acts from a postcolonial method seems to give a fresh vantage point to interpret Acts from the traditional apologetic stance or the subversive and disrupting Roman ideology. So, the work seems to be an eye opener in the field of biblical scholarship that sees this literature either as pro-Roman or anti-Roman. This is possibly a groundbreaking endeavor in the New Testament field, except for a sketchy work done by Barrus in *A Postcolonial Commentary on the New Testament* and Munñoz-Larrondo's *Living in Two Worlds*. In this research, the study- through postcolonial lens attempts to explore the discursive responses of Luke towards both the native Jewish dominant traditions and alien Hellenistic and Roman power-discourses. The researcher further attempts to explore the nature of Roman imperialism and the responses of the native subject communities like Greeks, Jews and Christians towards Rome and to their own religio-cultural traditions.

As an Indian citizen, the presenter lives in the postcolonial context and the reading of the book of Acts most likely would influence the postcolonial experience. As a member of a minority (Christian) community, the reading of Acts in this line may help to express the struggles of the Christian minority which lives in the context of an internal 'colonialism' duplicated by religious fundamentalism, the self proclaimed 'empire makers'. As the first century imperial cult is so much associated with the society and culture of the Greco-Roman world, Indian society is also dictated by the majority religious traditions of the upper caste/ Brahmanism.[29] In this context, what is the response of the minority Christians who live in co-existence with the majority with a fear of religious imposition?

[29] For instance during Bhumi puja for laying the cornerstone of Government public buildings, the brahmanical deities are displayed and venerated, as also in public places (post offices, railway stations, government schools) as a religious-cultural imposition on the minorities.

In the first century, the socio-economic-politic and cultural infrastructure of the empire was challenged by the nascent Christian ecclesia taking a postcolonial stand. Through the postcolonial study of Acts, one learns how the marginalized/colonized get a new identity because political discourse is about the colonized 'other.' In addition, the transforming power of the postcolonial study on Acts will empower certain sections of the people who have been treated worse than slaves in 'free' India. The racial, cultural and political neocolonialism in India is very much analogous to the first century Christian experience of the Greco-Roman context where the subjects doubtless ask the question 'What must I do to be saved (Ac. 16: 30)?' The answer is not plain as one sees in the Acts of the Apostles. It is both theological as well as political.

Postcolonial interpretation is significant in a context where people have experienced Western colonialism and imperial domination for many centuries. Even today, the Indian majority experiences a complex nature of colonialism because colonialism is not only geographical but also cultural, ideological and perceptual. So, the Indian masses continue to suffer a 'wounded psyche,' because of the lingering experience of colonization by the fundamental religious communities. Postcolonial theory offers a space for the colonized and resurrects the marginal.[30] It is therapeutic in nature because it is "a disciplinary project devoted to the academic task of revisiting, remembering, and interrogating, a complex project of historical and psychological recovery."[31] Resistance of the colonized is found through the postcolonial reading which is applicable in other engagements of the present day neocolonialism (Liberalization, Privatization Globalization).

There are two major trends to analyze a Postcolonial reading of Acts, the first is mainly focusing on the Lukan discursive response to Roman imperial position (e.g., Ac. 1: 1-11; 2: 1-12; 2: 43-47; 4: 32-37; 8: 26-40; 12: 1-25; 16:11-40; 24-26; 28:17-31). The second is Lukan discursive response to native Jewish religio-cultural tradition would be taken up in relation to the first response (eg., Ac. 2:22-38; 3:17-26; 4:8-12; 5:28-32; 6:1-11:30; 13:1-52; 14:1-21:36).

As stated, Postcolonial methodology is used to analyze the Acts of the Apostles as a postcolonial literature in the complex situation of the imperial cult and Roman colonialism. So joining one stream of thought will lead the reader to miss the track of the narrator. However, this new methodology will not totally undo the traditional modes of interpretation although it might challenge it. Rather, the new interpretation enables the reader to have a broader and holistic perspective in reading biblical text as a whole, allowing one to "interact and cross-fertilize with one another."[32]

---

30 R.S. Sugirtharajah, "A Brief Memorandum on Postcolonialism and Biblical Studies," *JSNT* 73 (1999), 4.

31 Leela Gandhi, *Postcolonial Theory: A Critical Introduction* (Edinburgh: EUP, 1998), 8.

32 Todd Penner, "Madness in the Method? The Acts of the Apostles in Current Study," *CBR* 2/2 (2004), 261.

The proposed study is assigned into three parts comprising of six chapters. The first part of the study is delineating the postcolonial method to read the Acts of the Apostles. The second part elaborates the discursive world of Acts consists of two chapters with a brief history of Roman imperialism and colonialism in the eastern part of the empire as well as explain the Jewish world with its cultural nationalism. The third part of the study also divides into two chapters where the postcolonial reading is applied to the text. They explain the narrative world of the early Christian witness in and around Palestine (Ac. 1-12) and their witness outside Palestine (Ac. 13-28). The final chapter brings the implication of the postcolonial reading for the theological education and action in India.

Part 1

DELINEATING THE METHOD

Chapter 1

Mapping a Viable Postcolonial Theory in Reading the Acts of the Apostles

1.1 Introduction

Colonialism and its practices have not only been a historical fact but also a contemporary experience of the present day for one third of the world population. This population continues to experience the after-effects of colonialism not only in the economic-political realm but also in the socio-religio-cultural realm too. However, the study of colonial impact of the first century biblical world has been neglected by focusing on the modern and postmodern western colonial forms. There has been a radical shift in the world of biblical criticism during the last quarter of the millennium in the emerging understanding of the role of culture and experience of the text and the reader. There are three distinct paradigm shifts in biblical criticism from mid-seventies-: historical critical method, literary criticism, cultural/sociological criticism and postcolonial criticism.[1] Segovia analyzed the progress of this criticism by taking into account the fruitful era of a decade (1996-2007) with its methodological formation and its application.[2]

---

[1] F.F. Segovia, "And They Began to Speak in Other Tongues": Competing Modes of Discourse in Contemporary Biblical Criticism," in *Reading from this Place. Social Location and Biblical Interpretation in the United States*, vol.1, edited by F. F. Segovia and M. A. Tolbert (Minneapolis: Fortress Press, 1995), 1-32.

[2] F.F. Segovia, "Tracing Sugirtharajah's Voice from the Margin: From Liberation to Postclonialism," in *Postcolonial Interventions: Essays in Honor of R. S. Sugirtharajah*, edited by T.B. Liew (Sheffield: Phoenix Press, 2009), 219. The first experimental work in the biblical field was done by Laura E. Donaldson, ed., *Postcolonialism and Scriptural Reading*, *Semeia* 75 (1998); Sugirtharajah, ed., *The Postcolonial Bible* (Sheffield: Sheffield Academy Press, 1998); F. F. Segovia and R. S. Sugirtharajah, eds., *A Postcolonial Commentary on the New Testament Writing* (New York: T & T Clark, 2007).

The influence of liberation theology and hermeneutics from the Latin American context of resisting the socio-economic domination cannot be neglected in this new field of study.[3] In this regard mapping the origins and trajectories of the postcolonial biblical criticism has to be done by incorporating both the biblical and secular theoreticians. It is the secular theoreticians who stimulated the seriousness of colonialism and its effects on literature (Said, Bhabha and Spivak). Further, the postcolonial biblical critics like Sugiratharajah, Segovia, Samuel, Joy and others have taken the task of using postcolonial methodology in their hermeneutical studies.

1.2 Postcolonial Theory Delineated by Theorists: Edward Said, Gayatri C. Spivak and Homi K. Bhabha

Said, Spivak and Bhabha conjoin to theoretical basis and practical application of postcolonial perspective. While the first two give meaning as a reading strategy, the latter gives meaning to its condition of being.[4] All the three participate within a reactionary ethical mode against the dominating knowledge of imperialism. Over against Said's concept of exclusive domination of the colonized, Spivak explains the non-speakable resistance of the subalterns, and Bhabha reveals the complex-ambivalent nature of resistance in the colonial discourse.

1.2.1 Edward Said

The complex identities of Said, as a Palestinian Arab (national identity) and as an exile in New York (Diaspora intellectual) are constantly reflected in his work. His position as the exile empowers him for a double perspective. For him, the political realities of the world are very much true to each individual and it cannot be separated from literary works and theory. He appreciates his position of an exile because of its ambivalence and creative empowerment for enabling him to be a free-ranging critic of the old order.[5]

Said is considered to be the theoretical progenitor of the 'colonial discourse theory.'[6] He established himself as a postcolonial critic through his celebrated work *Orientalism.*[7] As a cultural critic he established his stamp on postcolonial studies in his constant interaction with the political realities of the world, especially in

---

[3] R.S. Sugirtharajah, *Voice from the Margins: Interpreting the Bible in the Third World* (London: SPCK, 1991, 1995, 2006).

[4] R.S. Sugirtharajah, *Postcolonial Reconfigurations: An Alternative Way of Reading the Bible and Doing Theology* (London: SCM Press, 2003), 15.

[5] Ashcroft and Ahluwalia, *Edward Said,* 42.

[6] Bill Ashcroft, G. Griffiths and H.Tiffin, eds., *Key Concepts in Post-Colonial Studies* (London and New York: Routledge, 2004), 186. The 'colonial discourse theory' explains the colonial relationships in hybridity, ambivalence and mimicry.

[7] Edward Said, *Orientalism* (New York: Vintage, 1978). Said innovatively articulates the colonial impact in fictional works and historical documents, evaluating the colonial constructions of European disciplines.

Palestine for the last four decades.[8] He establishes the link between the political and cultural setting of the literary works in the context of empire-building. He is a great literary and theoretical analyst of the closely knitted texts and the world. His analysis of European imperial activity in Palestine is very much reflected in other societies, making him a pioneering postcolonial theorist.

1.2.1.1 Said as a Literary Critic

Said as a literary critic, takes up issues, problems and values make him as a great literary critic to bring about a change in the society.[9] He positions himself above ideology, political party and beliefs. Through his critical literary work, he proves himself an intellectual who speaks and writes boldly against imperialism. He motivates other intellectuals to speak against injustice criticizing the US government for their stand in the Gulf war and the ongoing war in the West-Asian region. He is able to see how power operates through knowledge by critically seeing the way in which the West represents and dominates the East through their cultural productions-the discourses of arts, humanities and social sciences.[10] According to him, the text intrinsically connects the socio-economic cultural and political world of the time as well as with other text of the time, thus recreating the textual construction of a colonial world.[11] Thus, the colonizer colonizes the mind of the reader through the power of the language and the text.

1.2.1.2 Colonial Discourse and Postcolonial Theory

Colonial discourse is given much importance in postcolonial studies which is a primary contribution of Said for analyzing the Western Oriental texts. The colonial discourse is an important concept used by the colonists to colonize the 'other' by representing their culture as superior. Said's *Orientalism* shows how the West intellectually dominates and regulates colonialist relations socially, politically and ideologically.[12] Said's discourse analysis is widely displayed through his critical analysis of a wide variety of texts from various fields-the discourses of arts, humanities and social sciences, sharing a consistent colonial ideology both in

---

[8] Bill Ashcroft and P. Ahluwalia, *Edward Said* (London/New York: Routledge, 2007), 130-135.

[9] Edward Said, *The World, the Text and the Critic* (Cambridge: Harvard University Press, 1983), 28.

[10] Western imperial powers have dominated the East by the power of knowledge in representing the Orientals by making use of their culture. Said's works demonstrate this phenomena of representing the Arab world and Palestine in opposing positions.

[11] Ashcroft and Ahluwalia, *Edward Said*, 18, 27.

[12] Said, *Orientalism*, 3, 15, 39-40. The West constructs the other in a discursive manner. The colonial encounter of the West since the middle of the 18th century is a systematic expansion of knowledge through various fields of science ("sciences of ethnology, comparative anatomy, philology and history") and literature ("novelists, poets, translators" and travelers).

the language and subject.[13] Colonial discourses exercise power relations based on their selection, exclusion and domination.

Before the 19th century, the actual colonial domination by the West over the Orient was done by cultural expansion and domination by literary works.[14] Over against the Foucautlian conception of power in discourse, Said promotes the room for resistance to intervene critically. He gives the possibility of an alternative discourse within the dominant hegemonic formation.[15] In his later days, he gives more importance to postcolonial theory because of the political cause for the Palestinians. The colonial discourse theory explains the colonial relationships in hybridity, ambivalence and mimicry.

1.2.1.3 Culture and Imperialism

According to Said, culture is mainly related to imperialism which is dynamic and complex. It is "the practice, theory, and the attitudes of a dominating metropolitan centre ruling a distant territory."[16] The cultural productions, especially the novels of the West subtly portray the imperial nature. For him, even after the post-colonial era, imperialism works through other cultural formations of education, literature and arts-beyond the economic and political levels.[17] The power of the state is equated with the power of culture by which the imperial powers hegemonize 'the other.' The imperial culture of the West maintains imperialism by the way the colonizers operate the political and ideological system. However, over against the totalitarian nature of the imperial domination of the centre, there is an alternative cultural resistance of colonial discourse based on local narratives, nationalist resistance and "non-essentialist, indigenous, non-Western variant of nationalism,"[18] which are against the totalizing grand claims of the West.

1.2.1.4 Contrapuntal Reading

Contrapuntal reading is an innovative reading strategy of Said to analyze the imperial culture that works through the Western novels to continue the imperial process. According to him, written texts are similar to musical texts. The 'contrapuntal performance,' "elaborate[s] intricately a particular musical theme."[19] As a reading

---

[13] Robert Young, *Postcolonialism: An Introduction* (Oxford: Blackwell, 2001), 388.

[14] Said, *Orientalism*, 92-110.

[15] Said, *The World, the Text*, 153.

[16] Edward Said, *Culture and Imperialism* (London: Vintage, 1993), 15.

[17] Said, *Culture and Imperialism*, 12. He forcefully exposes the inextricable link between culture and imperialism in his celebrated book, *Culture and Imperialism*.

[18] Sobhanlal Datta Gupta, "Imperialism and Colonialism: Towards a Postcolonial Understanding," in *Science, Technology, Imperialism and War*, vol. xv Part. I, edited by Jyoti Bhusan Das Gupta (New Delhi: Pearson Longman, 2007), 439.

[19] Ashcroft and Ahluwalia, *Edward Said*, 93. "In the counterpoint of Western classical music, various themes play off one another ...in the resulting polyphony there is concert and order, an

analysis, this is a resistant strategy where the colonizers and the colonized work together for liberation. In this process, the contradictory dimensions of the text reveal the imperial as well as the anti-imperial resistive elements of the text.[20] This method provides space for the possibility of both the metropolitan centre and the margins to work together because in cultural resistance there is a "constant overlap and interchange, the continual counterpoint and contestation."[21] He is mapping here a theory of resistance by carving an in-between space suggested by the postcolonial theorists.[22] This reading strategy hopes for a human liberation from the parochial sentiments of separatist nationalist ideas that lead to nativism and conflict.[23] For him, identity is fluid and it is related to socio-historical and political mandates.[24] His contrapuntal position gives a significant way to write back and speak for the margin.

1.2.1.5 Critical Appraisal

Said's genuine concern about the proliferation of imperial activity makes him constantly interact with the political realities of the world. His critical stand on decisive positions with critical consciousness based on the issues, problems and values are a model to follow. His stand for multicultuaralism by critiquing the exclusive essentialist attitude of the West is significant. However, Bhabha criticizes the "self-confident and self-consistent, monolithic and monologic" colonial discourse portrayed by Said.[25] There are voices against Said for the existent counter-hegemonic voices in colonial discourses.[26] For example, the socio-religio-political history drawn by Deissmann (1910) shows that the New Testament

---

organized interplay that derives from the themes, not from a rigorous melodic or formal principle outside the work." Said, *Culture and Imperialism*, 59-60.

[20] Ashcroft and Ahluwalia, *Edward Said*, 93.

[21] Ashcroft and Ahluwalia, *Edward Said*, 106.

[22] The term Said uses is 'the voyage in' where the human community and liberation will be celebrated than a separatist nationalism. Said, *Culture and Imperialism*, 261; Ashcroft and Ahluwalia, *Edward Said*, 109.

[23] Said, *Culture and Imperialism*, 264, 276.

[24] Said, "Afterword", in *Orientalism*, 332.

[25] Stephen D. Moore, "Questions of Biblical Ambivalence and Authority under a Tree outside Delhi; or, The Postcolonial and Postmodern", in *Postcolonial Biblical Criticism. Interdisciplinary Intercessions*, edited by Stephen D. Moore and F.F. Segovia (London/New York: T & T Clark, 2005), 88; Homi K. Bhabha, *The Location of Culture* (London/New York: Routledge, 1994), 61-63.

[26] D. Porter, "Orientalism and its Problems', in *The Politics of Theory*, edited by Peter Hulme, Margaret Iversen and Dianne Loxley (Colchester: University of Essex, 1983), 160 cited by Ashcroft and Ahluwalia, *Edward Said*, 74. Young argues conflictual representation in his portrayal of Orientalism as hegemonic consistency. Robert Young, *White Mythologies: Writing History and the West* (London: Routledge, 1990), 130.

is a resistant discourse of the first century Christians from the East.[27] Moore-Gilbert criticizes Said for a totalitarian, uniform vision of Western Orientalism by neglecting the individual Orientalists who brought scholarly achievements.[28] There may be counter productions for Said's uncritical attitude in appreciating localism and eastern identities, resulting in fundamentalism.[29]

1.3 Gayatri Chakravorty Spivak

Gayatri C. Spivak was born in Calcutta in 1942 during the British colonial rule of their imposition of the artificial famine created by the British military in the context of the Second World War. Later she migrated to the center from the periphery of the third world to critique the western imperial ideology.[30] Her works have an unparalleled influence in the field of postcolonial criticism with special focus on the third world subaltern women and the underprivileged. Her critical theory along with a humanitarian vision makes her an intellectual with social commitment towards the exploited, oppressed and the disempowered. Her contribution to postcolonial theory and literature give a new pedagogical stand for ethical commitment to the subalterns. She brings the idea of the history of colonial women not only from the imperial dominated point of view but also from the point of view of colonial resistance. She is a well known feminist and literary critique of the Western as well as non-Western literary works. Her intellectual trajectory has been wide in its arena from 'Marxist-Feminist-deconstructionist' to a cultural critique (imperial colonial discourse-race-ethnicity-diaspora) and postcolonial.[31]

1.3.1 The Countering Element in Spivak's Postcolonial Criticism

Contrary to the negative impact of colonialism in the colonial literary texts, Spivak finds the challenging and subverting nature of postcolonial literary texts. The subaltern critical studies greatly helped the postcolonial criticism about the resistance voice in the colonial context. This is a major theoretical and methodological concept as the postcolonial criticism is concerned. She criticizes the writing out of the popular struggles and peasant rebellion from the literary texts of the dominant history. Moreover, she hopes for "a rhetorical space for

---

[27] Adolf Deissmann, *Light from the Ancient East: The New Testament Illustrated by Recently Discovered Texts of the Graeco-Roman World*, translated by L.R.M. Stoughton (London: Hodder and Stoughton, 1910), 269-70.

[28] B.J. Moore-Gilbert, *Post-Colonial Theory: Contexts, Practices and Politics* (London: Verso, 1997), 75.

[29] Gupta, "Imperialism and Colonialism," 440.

[30] Donna Landry and G. MacLean, eds., *The Spivak Reader: Selected Works of Gayatri Chakravorty Spivak* (London: Routledge, 1996), 1, 16.

[31] Landry and MacLean, *The Spivak Reader*, 3.

subaltern groups to re-articulate the suppressed histories of popular struggles."[32] She specifically takes initiative in bringing examples from the re-imagining history and the literary history of the subaltern women to question and challenge the authority of the master narratives.

1.3.2 Spivak's Contribution to Subaltern Studies

Spivak's philosophy of deconstruction makes an impact on the subaltern studies of rewriting history from below- "from the point of view of peasant insurgency" during the colonial period.[33] It is done by asking those who are in the 'center' to unlearn their racial-national-gender-privileges, to enter into the territory of the subaltern masses who cannot speak.[34] In her much debated question 'Can the subaltern speak?' where the speech of the subalterns cannot be heard by the privileged class and if it is heard their status is changed,[35] is her plea for the cause of the subalterns. She exposes the oppressive and the silencing features of colonialism and patriarchy.

The exploitation and oppression from the economic and political fields lead Spivak to stand with the subaltern in this postcolonial world for taking an ethical stand to interpret their challenges.[36] The intellectual and theoretical sources like the historic-political discourses of India (eg. fictions, short stories, and Subaltern Studies collective) have deliberatively forgotten to write the histories of women, peasants and the tribals etc.[37] The subaltern voice can be retrieved only through re-inscribing the history of the subalterns by critiquing the dominant historical representation.[38]

In the essay 'Can the Subaltern Speak?,'[39] Spivak voices for the disenfranchised and criticizes the colonial self-righteous nature of the acted saviours of the dominant elites. The political representation of these subaltern groups historically and structurally alienated them rather representing them. This saying has been understood passionately as representing one 'who tries to speak for them.' She radically criticizes for not taking serious steps in accounting for the active

---

[32] *Gayatri Chakravorty Spivak* (New York: Routledge, 2003), 124.

[33] Landry and MacLean, *The Spivak Reader*, 203. Spivak adopts the philosophical critique of deconstruction by following the path of Derrida.

[34] Landry and MacLean, *The Spivak Reader*, 4.

[35] Landry and MacLean, *The Spivak Reader*, 6.

[36] Subaltern is an inclusive term which accommodates all social group and struggles with no fixed 'strict class' analysis, especially the women and the colonized. Morton, *Gayatri Spivak*, 45-46.

[37] Stephen Morton, *Gayatri Chakravorty Spivak* (New York: Routledge, 2003), 47.

[38] Morton, *Gayatri Spivak*, 51; Gayatri C. Spivak, *A Critique of Postcolonial Reason: Towards a History of the Vanishing Present* (Cambridge, MA: Harvard University Press, 1999), 272-73, 281, 308-09.

[39] G.C. Spivak, "Can the Subaltern Speak?', in *Marxism and the Interpretation of Culture*, edited by Cary Nelson and Lawrence Grossberg (London: Macmillan,1988), 271-313.

involvement of the subaltern women in the anti-British colonial insurgency in India because of the male dominancy in the colonial archives and the historical records.[40] According to her, the act of self sacrifice is an exceptional signifier which signifies her own desire to take away her life by herself. Together within the religio-political system, the female becomes the passive victim of patriarchal violence. Thus, she argues from the perspective of Hindu patriarchal codes and the imperial discussions of the widow sacrifice to show that it makes no space to translate the speech-act by which the sexed subaltern tried to speak,[41] through the act of sati/widow sacrifice.

1.3.3 Re-writing and Re-imagining Postcolonial History

Spivak's literary writings always focus on the emancipation of the subaltern women for which she takes the initiative in re-imagining and re-writing the erased history.[42] The re-written stories and fictions clearly depict the resistance of the subaltern women against the postcolonial state that gives false claims- "in the name of decolonization and democracy."[43] Through the re-written stories of Mahasweta Devi, she has counteracted the dominant knowledge and the representation of the West. She thus highlights the counter voices of the tribal and subaltern women, who can speak only through their body language. Thus, "Literary texts can provide the alternative rhetorical site for articulating the histories of subaltern women."[44]

1.3.4 Strategic Essentialism

Essentialism and strategic essentialism have emerged in the context of Spivak's critical challenge to the Western feminist thought for an ethical paradigm shift among the third world subaltern women. The term 'essentialism' shows the true essence of things. This term has a negative connotation during the close of the twentieth century because of the specific categorization of gender, race

[40] Spivak, "Can the Subaltern Speak?, 281; Morton, *Gayatri Spivak*, 59. As a counter point of this saying, Spivak traces their material practices and cultural histories through the recovering of women's histories in the colonial archives (1757-1947).

[41] Morton, *Gayatri Spivak*, 62; Spivak, *A Critique of Postcolonial Reason,* 296-302; idem, "Can the Subaltern Speak?', 299. For Spivak, if the Gandhian notion of *Satyagraha* is considered as a resistance movement then what about the widow sacrifice which is considered to be the same act of resistance. Spivak, "Can the Subaltern Speak?', 307-308; Morton, *Gayatri Spivak*, 65-66.

[42] For eg. The Bengali-language writer Mahasweta Devi's English translation of the short story 'Breast Giver' "challenges the truth claims of elite historical discourse in India by narrating the story of national independence from the point of view of a subaltern woman." According to Devi, it is 'a parable of decolonization' because of the portrayal of the protagonist in the story Jashoda who is compared to Mother India, a term which is related to the anti-colonial resistance movement. Morton, *Gayatri Spivak,* 124-25; G.C. Spivak, *In Other Worlds: Essays in Cultural Politics* (New York: Methuen, 1987), 244.

[43] Morton, *Gayatri Spivak*, 131.

[44] Morton, *Gayatri Spivak,* 55. Spivak shows the active involvement of the third world subaltern women's resistance through Mahasweta Devi's 'Breast giver', and 'Draupadi'.

or sexuality "based on prior biological explanations."[45] This essentialism concept does not take the cultural differences (race, sexuality, religion, and ethnicity) into serious consideration and thus it has resulted in a shift to an anti-essentialist position.[46] The race and gender theorists strongly condemn the redefined theories not based on scientific claims rather socio-religious formulations for subjugating the inferior. This anti-essentialist thought leads to the flexible positions in socio-political field for a new concept called strategic essentialism. She criticizes the 'essentialist' feminism for their political interest in making a theory based on the privileged female of the white race, thus generalizing/universalizing sexuality.[47] She also criticizes the classic Marxist theory of labour through the story of Devi's 'Breast Giver' which is "based on an essentialist notion of sexual difference."[48] Thus Devi strategically gives her reproductive body to be employed to produce economic value.

Spivak realizes the subaltern consciousness of using '*Strategic* use of positive essentialism' with a political interest.[49] This could be an effective strategy of the subalterns "which mimes the negative representation of the minority groups."[50] Different minority groups have accepted this concept as a positive term of identification. For Spivak, this is a strategic situation,[51] because the essentialist, invariable and fixed properties may not go well with the experiences of the subaltern women and the colonial experiences.

1.3.5 Critical Appraisal

Spivak's much celebrated and controversial essay "Can the subaltern speak," has varied implications of whether she will allow the resistance to speak.[52] She answers that there is no transaction between the subaltern speaker and the listener. Her deconstruction seems to invoke a contradiction between the ideological commitment she has for the disenfranchised subalterns in the third world and her use of western theoretical concepts and language to do it. By the ethical dimensions of deconstruction and the goal of postcolonial reading practice, she counters the globalization plan of the first world. Her wider relationship with the socio-political and the cultural world make her to cross boundaries from the academic

---

[45] Morton, *Gayatri Spivak*, 73.

[46] Morton, *Gayatri Spivak*, 73.

[47] Spivak, *A Critique of Postcolonial Reason*, 147-48.

[48] Morton, *Gayatri Spivak*, 126. The essentialist notion of sexual difference makes women devalued because of their labour 'does not directly produce exchange value or money.'

[49] Morton, *Gayatri Spivak*, 75 (italics in the original); Spivak, *In Other Worlds*, 205.

[50] Morton, *Gayatri Spivak*, 74.

[51] G.C. Spivak, *Outside in the Teaching Machine* (New York: Routledge, 1993), 4. Thus it will be most suitable as a "context-specific strategy, but it cannot provide a long-term political solution to end oppression and exploitation." Morton, *Gayatri Spivak*, 75.

[52] Landry and MacLean, *The Spivak Reader*, 287.

realm to the global economic and political relations. She very well understands the complexities of the Indian social history and strives for the liberation of women, the peasants and the minorities.

Strategic essentialism is a flexible position for the marginalized subalterns in the rigid socio-political field for discursive resistance. This strategy can be effectively used by the minority groups because of the colonizing nature of the essentialist fixed properties. Moore-Gilbert poses objection to Spivak about the inability of the subaltern to speak from the historical accounts and the present day voices.[53] However, for Spivak, these subaltern resistant voices are filtered voices of male dominant political systems of representation/anti-imperialist liberation movements.[54] Her re-written work of the Bengali-language writer and activist Mahasweta Devi shows the counter and reactionary role of the subjected subaltern women. Her critique of Eurocentric humanism and the use of deconstruction to build up a viable discourse for the subaltern groups make her distinct from other postcolonial critics.

Gilbert criticizes the method of deconstruction as it becomes kind of 'negative science' by silencing again the subaltern by the 'dominant system of representation.'[55] Moreover, if the subaltern cannot speak, then the oppressor (particularly the West and the native elite) shall speak for the 'other'.[56] The radical criticisms of Spivak give the impression that the subaltern may not speak because s/he is constructed, but they can powerfully resist against the oppression and injustice done to them by their powerful non-verbal actions. However, she is still argumentative about the nonspeakable position of 'the new' subaltern in the context of globalization and neocolonialism where they are kept quiet by the World Bank and WTO-the agents of capitalism.[57]

1.4 Homi K. Bhabha

H.K. Bhabha is a Parsi who has a hybrid transnational identity. His diaspora identity of Mumbai-Oxford-Brighton-Chicago-Boston as well as his ethnic experience as a Parsi made him to think beyond national boundaries.[58] He is a great thinker of the 21st century who articulates the resistance of the colonized by analyzing the complex doublings in their discourses. In an age where different cultures clash with each other based on the "longstanding inequalities between

---

[53] Moore-Gilbert, *Post-Colonial Theory*, 107. He points out evidences of historical examples of resistant movements of subaltern women recorded (eg. " '.... the bazaar prostitutes' role in the 1857 Indian "Mutiny" .... To the "bandit queen" Phoolan Devi today").

[54] Morton, *Gayatri Spivak*, 66.

[55] Gilbert, *Post-Colonial Theory*, 102.

[56] Gilbert, *Post-Colonial Theory*, 104.

[57] Spivak, *A Critique of Postcolonial Reason*, 371-80.

[58] Huddart, *Homi Bhabha*, 78-79. Bhabha's forefathers migrated in the eighth century to India to avoid Muslim persecution.

nations and peoples," his search for "a traditional philosophical sense of the relationship between one's self and others, between subject and object" have serious consequences.[59] He makes use of psychoanalysis for the purpose of finding solutions in contemporary questions related to colonial complicated selves.[60]

Bhabha has been greatly influenced by two prominent French philosophers, Derrida and Foucault (deconstruction and discourse analysis). He is influenced by Said's *Orientalism* in critically looking at the colonial discourse. However, over against the totalitarian, monolithic, unitary, dichotomy (margin-center) and authoritative nature of colonial discourse narrated by Said, he brings out the complex, ambiguous, hybrid and mimetic portrayal of the relationship between the colonizer and the colonized. He provides a conceptual vocabulary "for the reading of colonial and post-colonial texts, beginning with those of British India in the nineteenth century" which explains the role of the colonial doublings as a protest that the colonizers need to explain their own identity and self-image.[61] Similar to the earlier discussed theoreticians, he also accepts the unavoidable presence of colonialism in the present day world and its influence in complex ways.[62] He transforms our understanding of colonialism in both the method and object of study by emphasizing on the postcolonial theoretical concepts like hybridity, diaspora, migrancy, border-crossing and nationalism.[63] He is eclectic in his selection of theoretical concepts mimicry, hybridity (Freud) and ambivalence (Bakhtin) and gives distinctive inflection.[64]

1.4.1 Colonial Discourse Analysis

Bhabha applies poststructuralist methodologies to colonial texts resulting in 'colonial discourse analysis' characterized by ambivalence.[65] Here, he gives emphasis to both the colonizer and the colonized. He tries to analyse the colonial power in colonial discourses which is potentially subversive in the liminal space-between the colonizer and the colonized. This discourse is characterized by mimicry and hybridity "that threatens to fracture the colonizer's identity and authority."[66] He argues against the concept of 'fixity' which is an important feature of colonial discourse to construct the ideology of otherness.[67] He stresses an equal position of

[59] David Huddart, *Homi K. Bhabha* (London/New York: Routledge, 2007), 6.

[60] Huddart, *Homi Bhabha*, 100.

[61] Huddart, *Homi Bhabha*, 2. "Bhabha's work demonstrates that the West is troubled by its 'doubles', in particular the East."

[62] Huddart, *Homi Bhabha,* 3-4. He identifies "the complexities of a world marked by colonial and neo-colonial wars, counter-globalization movements and widespread cultural confrontation."

[63] Huddart, *Homi Bhabha,* 121.

[64] Moore, "Questions of Biblical Ambivalence," 87.

[65] Huddart, *Homi K. Bhabha,* 4.

[66] Moore, "Questions of Biblical Ambivalence," 88.

[67] Bhabha, *The Location of Culture*, 66.

unexpected forms of resistance as well as anxieties from the side of the colonizer in spite of their apparent mastery.[68] His psychoanalytic approach to the colonial power tries to thwart the traditional understanding of the exclusive domination of the colonized and reveals the anxiety that "opens a gap in the colonial discourse."[69]

Bhabha's study tremendously transforms the outlook of how one observes colonialism. He reinterprets the discourses of colonialism by analyzing varied writings on art, photography and cinema. By examining the colonial history, he finds it hard to maintain the rigid distinctions between the colonizer and the colonized. Textual analysis brings "the hidden gaps and anxieties present in the colonial situation" as well as the colonial resistance of the colonized.[70] For him, colonial discourse is a narrative knowledge of stereotypical production of the colonizer and the colonized but evaluated antithetically.[71]

1.4.2 Colonial Ambivalence

Bhabha describes the colonial relationship as always ambivalent (simultaneous attraction and repulsion) that disrupts the simple definition of domination of the colonizer.[72] According to him, "the colonial presence is always ambivalent, split between its appearance as original and authoritative and its articulation as repetition and difference."[73] In colonial relationship, the colonized would like to mimic the colonizer but unfortunately the mimicry of the ambivalent subjects turns to become a mockery that disturbs the authority of the colonial discourse.[74] He strategically uses Freud for the idea of ambivalence in "colonial discourse structured according to the conflictual economy of the psyche."[75] Ambivalence functions in stereotypes to perform "the most significant discursive and psychical strategies of discriminatory power."[76] The ambivalence of mimicry "suggests that the fetishized colonial culture is potentially and strategically an insurgent counter-appeal."[77]

---

[68] Huddart, *Homi Bhabha*, 8.

[69] Huddart, *Homi Bhabha*, 6.

[70] Huddart, *Homi Bhabha*, 2. Bhabha targets the resistance of the colonized not necessarily in the form of violence and domination, but especially in the form of cultural confrontation and literature by the subalterns (3, 6).

[71] Bhabha, *The Location of Culture*, 70.

[72] Ashcroft, et al., *Key Concepts*, 12-13. Ambivalence is a psychoanalytical concept adopted in postcolonial discourse theory which shows a continual fluctuation between the relationship of the colonizer and the colonized subjects.

[73] Bhabha, *The Location of Culture*, 107.

[74] Ashcroft, et al., *Key Concepts*, 13.

[75] Young, *White Mythologies*, 185-86.

[76] Bhabha, *The Location of Culture*, 66.

[77] Bhabha, *The Location of Culture*, 91.

1.4.3 Colonial Mimicry

For Bhabha, mimicry as "transformed into a strategy of resistance" in colonial relationship is so central[78] that it works both explicitly and implicitly. This is a disruptive strategy of ambivalent relationships used by the colonized subjects to mimic their colonial masters. "[C]olonial mimicry is the desire for a reformed, recognizable Other, as a *subject of difference that is almost the same, but not quite*."[79] The anxiety reflected during the process of stereotypes in colonial discourse opens a space for the colonized to resist through approximating to the colonizer's culture.[80] "The *menace* of mimicry is its double vision which in disclosing the ambivalence of colonial discourse also disrupts its authority."[81] His postcolonial theory is "a comic approach to colonial discourse, because it mocks and undermines the ongoing pretensions of colonialism and empire."[82] The British education that started with a colonial intention of creating the go-between subjects has fortunately or unfortunately created 'mimic man/woman.'[83] In the process of mimicking, the colonizer wants the colonized to become civilized and reformed but does not want him/her to come to the position of the colonizer.

For Bhabha, mimicry "is an exaggerated copying of language, culture, manners, and ideas," however it brings a "repetition with difference."[84] To the colonizer, it is a matter of resemblance and a threat/menace.[85] The colonized as well as the colonizer make their attempts to be "authentic" through mimicry-through a process of writing and repetition-is the final irony of partial representation."[86] In the colonial situation, mimicry is used as a mask to mock the colonizer and thus anti-colonial in effect.

The characteristic feature of mimicry as a visual strategy is explained by the psychoanalytic concept of 'camouflage' to destroy colonial authority.[87] This concept clearly explains the performances of mimicry and how does it counter the colonial authority. In the process of mimicry, the original identity of the colonizer

---

78 Huddart, *Homi Bhabha*, 61. "[M]imicry emerges as one of the most elusive and effective strategies of colonial power and knowledge." Bhabha, *The Location of Culture*, 85.

79 Bhabha, *The Location of Culture*, 86 (italics in the original).

80 Huddart, *Homi Bhabha*, 58.

81 Bhabha, *The Location of Culture*, 88 (italics in the original).

82 Huddart, *Homi Bhabha*, 57. "By adopting the colonizer's cultural habits, assumptions, institutions and values, the result is never simple reproduction of those traits. Rather, the result is a 'blurred copy' of the colonizer that can be quite threatening." Ashcroft et al., *Key Concepts*, 139.

83 Bhabha, *The Location of Culture*, 87.

84 Huddart, *Homi Bhabha*, 57.

85 Bhabha, *The Location of Culture*, 90.

86 Bhabha, *The Location of Culture*, 88.

87 Huddart, *Homi Bhabha*, 68. "Camouflage, which refers to blending in with something in the background that none the less is not entirely there itself." This refers to "almost the same but not quite."

is undermined. There are no clear facts in the process of colonial mimicry and the colonizer's identity loses itself in slippery.[88]

1.4.4 Culture and Hybridity

For Bhabha, culture is not pure and it is hybrid in its nature in colonization.[89] "In a colonial situation, the production of cultures is an inevitable consequence of contested authority."[90] According to him, hybridity is produced in the 'third space' of colonial/postcolonial provenance ('Third space of enunciation') where the colonized feel not the exoticism of multiculturalism but the articulation of culture's hybridity.[91] This space serves as an alternative site to examine and critique and generate a new meaning. Similarly, border crossing challenges "existing social relations, power equations, cultural codes, and identities,"[92] finally resulting in a hybrid culture. He defines hybridity as a colonial representation of "strategic reversal of the process of domination…in strategies of subversion that turn the gaze of the discriminated back upon the eye of power."[93] He uses many terms in order to bring out the cultural interaction i.e., in-between cultures, borderlines of cultures and *liminality*[94] which includes both space and time. Hybridity brings "transformative, cultural, linguistic, and political impacts on both the colonized and the colonizer," thus motivated disruption of homogeneity.[95] This theoretical concept is used for political empowerment and the enlargement of multiculturalism by the question of solidarity, placing social difference for a vision/revision and construction/reconstruction of a new community.[96]

---

[88] Huddart, *Homi Bhabha*, 80.

[89] Ashcroft, et al., *Key Concepts,* 118.

[90] Huddart, *Homi Bhabha,* 125.

[91] Bhabha, *The Location of Culture,* 38. In this third space of cultural hybridity, they elaborate strategies of selfhood for a person or society; the envisioned people celebrate the difference without hierarchy. The 'third space of enunciation' is a strategic essentialist identity that emerges in the contradictory and ambivalent space of transculturality in the context of colonialism. Samuel, *A Postcolonial Reading,* 31.

[92] D.N. Premnath, "Introduction," in *Border Crossing: Cross-cultural Hermeneutics,* edited by D.N. Premnath (Maryknoll, New York: Orbis Books, 2007), 7.

[93] Bhabha, 'Signs Taken for Wonders: Questions of Ambivalence and Authority Under a Tree Outside Delhi, May 1817', 156, 154, cited by Young, *White Mythologies,* 189.

[94] The term 'liminality,' "stresses the idea that what is in-between [in] settled cultural forms or identities – identities like self and other- is central to the creation of new cultural meaning. To give privilege to liminality is to undermine solid, authentic culture in favour of unexpected, hybrid, and fortuitous cultures." Huddart, *Homi Bhabha,* 7.

[95] Ashcroft, et al., *Key Concepts,* 119-20.

[96] Bhabha, *The Location of Culture,* 3. The in-between hybrid space is important for postcolonial critics because in the hybrid space its construction takes place both in cultural statements and systems.

1.4.5 Critical Appraisal

Cultural critics generally agree that Bhabha's work is foundational for postcolonial criticism for criticizing the binary positions of colonial relationships. He becomes a cultural critic of the present due to his initiative for worldwide debates for the marginalized. The theoretical concepts like hybridity and mimicry are the innovative methods that challenge the fictitious notions of cultural purity. His impressive achievements are by taking greatest insight in analyzing colonial counter relationships where the colonized subjects enter into the third space of enunciation. Bhabha's concepts of mimicry and hybridity have subversive potentials in the colonial cultural context. His 'colonial' usage of psychoanalytic theory applies in 'Third World' cultures without acknowledging the distinctive cultural differences.[97] However, the use of psychoanalysis for Bhabha is the only way to possibly read "the ambivalence operating within the process of colonial authority."[98]

Benita Parry extols Bhabha for allowing the subaltern to speak "and his readings of the colonialist text to recover a native voice," and she accuses him of the "self-righteous rhetoric of resistance"[99] by "accommodating the longstanding insights of anti-colonial writers and activists."[100] Any theoretical concepts like hybridity, mimicry in its theory alone will remain inadequate without the emancipatory angle for the subaltern marginalized. Most times the theoretical concepts seem to engage in philosophical level only. Bhabha offers static concepts to the colonial conditions like 'mimicry and 'hybridity' which are 'curiously anthropomorphized'.[101]

1.5 An Overview of Mapping Postcolonial Biblical Criticism

The turn of the last millennium held several consultations (SBL annual meetings 1997-2002) for pursuing a postcolonial optic under the leadership of Stephen D. Moore, F.F. Segovia, Laura Donaldson, Kowk Pui-lan and R.S. Sugirtharajah.[102] Earlier, postcolonial biblical criticism took its stand with literary and cultural studies and it has pointed out the way in which the Bible is used as an agent

---

[97] Moore, "Questions of Biblical Ambivalence," 89.

[98] Young, *White Mythologies,* 196.

[99] B. Parry's 'Problems in Current Theories of Colonial Discourse', from *Oxford Literary Review* (1987) 9 (1-2), 40, cited by Huddart, *Homi Bhabha*, 154.

[100] Huddart, *Homi Bhabha*, 156.

[101] Young, *White Mythologies*, 186.

[102] Moore and Segovia, "Postcolonial Biblical Criticism," 1-10; Laura E. Davidson (ed), Postcolonialism and Sriptural Reading, *Semeia* 75 (1998). Sugirtharajah's role in bringing Postcolonial Biblical Criticism to the forefront of biblical studies is much appreciated. Some of the earlier works on postcolonial studies gave momentum to this field of study. They are- R.S. Sugirtharajah, "From Orientalist to Post-colonial: Notes on Reading Practices," *AJT* 10, 1 (1996), 20-27; *idem*, *The Postcolonial Bible.*

of colonialism.[103] However, the biblical discourse itself is the result of colonial experience and thus the biblical literature shows all the discursive traits of mimicry, hybridity and ambivalence. This literature has the potential to challenge the colonial dominance through the effect of 'mocking', 'travestying', 'irony' and 'affiliation as well as antagonism.'[104]

The reality of the empire, imperialism and colonialism[105] are the key concerns in postcolonial biblical studies, and the turn of millennium brought about a cluster of works preoccupied with the empire and colonialism.[106] The ideology of colonialism was very much at the root of the life of the two third of the world humanity. Moreover, colonialism could be in the area of territory, knowledge, culture, art, literature and power. Hence, this criticism aims for the liberation and decolonization, conscientization, construction, and to loosen the ideological concepts made through the years of colonization.[107] This reading has the potential to "challenge the traditional modes of understanding history and offer a new understanding of history from the point of view of the people of the margins such as women, Dalits, subalterns and the oppressed classes."[108]

Postcolonialism in its hyphenated form 'post-colonialism' refers to the historical period, the aftermath of colonialism; in its un-hyphenated form, it signifies "a reactive resistance discourse of the colonized."[109] In terms of chronology, the cultural, linguistic and political experiences of the European colonies are its

---

[103] Samuel, *A Postcolonial Reading of Mark's story*, 33. It is true that western theology and Bible commentaries have the discursive colonial practices.

[104] Samuel, *A Postcolonial Reading of Mark's Story*, 33.

[105] Samuel, *A Postcolonial Reading of Mark's Story*, 2-3. Imperialism: "the control exercised by one nation state over another and its inhabitants to exploit and develop the resources of the land, for the benefit of the imperial government.... Colonialism, on the other hand, implies settlement, but also necessitates controlling and 'civilizing' indigenous people," Sugirtharajh, *Postcolonial Criticism and Biblical Interpretation*, 24. In its Latin roots *'imperium'* describes the sovereignty over the Mediterranean world and on its modern sense 'the acquisition of an empire of overseas colonies' not only in military dominance but also the power of imperial discourse. Ashcroft, et al., *Key Concepts*, 123. To Segovia, the term 'imperial' refers to "all that pertains to the center" and 'colonial' "all that pertains to the periphery." Segovia, *Decolonizing Biblical Studies*, 134, 140.

[106] R.A. Horsley, *Jesus and Empire: The Kingdom of God and the New World Disorder* (Minneapolis: Fortress Press, 2003); *idem*, ed., *Paul and Empire: Religion and Power in Roman Imperial Society* (Harrisburg: Trinity Press International, 1997); Michael Prior, *The Bible and Colonialism: A Moral Critique* (Sheffield: Sheffield Academy, 1997); Warren Carter, *Matthew and Empire: Initial Explorations* (Harrisburg: Trinity Press International, 2001).

[107] Segovia, *Decolonizing Biblical Studies*, 156.

[108] Joy, "Mark 10:17-27 in the Light of the Issues of Poor," 159.

[109] Sugirtharajah, *Postcolonial Criticism and Biblical Interpretation*, 13. "The unhyphenated 'postcolonial 'would refer to colonial discourse theory, while hyphenated 'post-colonial' would stand for the field as a whole, of which colonial discourse theory would represent but one component." F.F. Segovia, "Mapping the postcolonial Optic in Biblical Criticism: Meaning and Scope," in

prime agenda[110] and in terms of the latter, a 'critical discursive strategy' formulated by the colonized are the main concern.[111] This criticism need not limit its ambit to the modern European colonialism alone, as it has a wider scope of inclusiveness for this criticism. Biblical texts, specifically the New Testament texts have originated in "diverse colonial and postcolonial religio-cultural locations and from among the colonized subject populations of biblical antiquity."[112] Postcolonial studies in biblical criticism seriously take into consideration the socio-political reality of the West-Asia and Mediterranean basin, where the influence of imperialism and colonialism must have shaped the biblical texts.[113] The recent postcolonial studies in the field of NT studies make clear the discursive nature of the texts. There are both resistances to the socio-political powers and at the same time accommodation of certain colonial values. This mixed nature of the literature gives new impetus to the reader about the colonial nature of the period. Hence, in postcolonial biblical studies, colonialism becomes the centre of its study.[114]

From the perspective of postcolonial studies, the imperial-colonial relationship is studied from "the literature of ancient Israel and the literature of early Christianity."[115] In this process, three dimensions of disciplines work together in order to understand the imperial-colonial framework-the world of biblical antiquity, the history of Western interpretation, and the present context in which the text is read.[116]

1.6 Postcolonial Application in Biblical Studies: (R.S. Sugirtharajah, F.F. Segovia, Simon Samuel and David Joy)

Colonial impacts in the biblical text and its socio-cultural biased western interpretation have been neglected for centuries. The study of humanities afresh however gave new impetus to critically read biblical text and its interpretations in the light of the ancient and modern day colonialism. Possibly the anti-colonial resistant writings of the above mentioned literary critics made way for postcolonial biblical practitioners to apply the theories of contrapuntal reading, deconstruction, re-imagining, re-writing, strategic essentialism, ambivalence, mimicry and hybridity in biblical texts for unraveling the colonial influence in literature. In

Postcolonial Biblical Criticism: Interdisciplinary Intersections, edited by Stephen D. Moore and F.F. Segovia (London: T & T Clark, 2005), 43.

[110] Ashcroft, et al., *Key Concepts*, 186.

[111] Samuel, *A Postcolonial Reading of Mark's Story*, 3. This 'critical discursive strategy' is an 'in between' spatial category where the colonizer through his/her discourse will 'accommodate and disrupt both the native and the alien colonial discourses of power'.

[112] Samuel, "Postcolonialism as a Critical Practice," I, 18.

[113] Segovia, *Decolonizing Biblical Studies,* 125.

[114] Sugirtharajah, *Postcolonial Criticism and Biblical Interpretation*, 74.

[115] Segovia, "Mapping the Postcolonial Optic," 24.

[116] Segovia, "Mapping the Postcolonial Optic," 24.

the second angle of inquiry, the study will analyse the four postcolonial critics both from the Western diaspora of the center and from the Indian context of the margins to demarcate a clear postcolonial methodology in analyzing the Acts of the Apostles.

1.6.1 **Sugirtharajah** (Resistance and Restorative Model)

Sugirtharajah has influenced postcolonial hermeneutics through his prolific writing as a critique of Eurocentric traditions and colonial practices. The Birmingham professor of biblical studies has proved himself in postcolonial biblical scholarship through his gigantic project in postcolonial criticism. He is a cultural hybrid from the margins (Sri Lanka) who yearns for the emancipation of the third world subaltern marginalized. Through his writings, he challenges and confronts many to perceive the imperial and colonial dynamics both in biblical texts and its western interpretations. He is the chief proponent of postcolonial studies as a critical reading strategist and acts as a critic of the Third World Literature studies for the purpose of liberation and decolonization from Western/non-western imperialism.[117]

1.6.1.1 Meaning and Definition

For Sugirtharajah, Postcolonial criticism is a resistant discourse that works against all imperialist forms of colonial ideologies of political, cultural representations and assumptions.[118] It is not about periodization but critiques the totalizing forms of Eurocentric theories.[119] This is a heterogeneous project using varied hermeneutical methods which deals with a variety of issues related to empire, diaspora, race, ethnicity and gender.[120] Further, the postcolonial interpretation criticizes both the Bible and its "totalizing forms of western interpretations."[121] It provides a platform for multi-ethnic, multi-religious and multicultural voices, to assert their denied rights and disrupt the centre.[122]

The model Sugirtharajah adopts in postcolonial criticism is resistant/ recuperative model because of "his emphasis on resistance, opposition and

---

[117] Sugirtharajah, *Postcolonial Reconfigurations*, 13-16.

[118] R.S. Sugirtharajah, *Asian Biblical Hermeneutics and Postcolonialism: Contesting the Interpretations* (England: Sheffield Academic Press, 1998), x. Resistance to imperialism does not consist only in reaction against the colonial practice but also in perception and restructuring society (17).

[119] Sugirtharajah, *Postcolonial Reconfigurations*, 15.

[120] Sugirtharajah, *Asian Biblical Hermeneutics*, 15-18.

[121] Sugirtharajah, *Asian Biblical Hermeneutics*, 18. The explicit and implicit colonial codes used in the text will be probed.

[122] R.S. Sugirtharajah, *Postcolonial Criticism and Biblical Interpretation* (Oxford: Oxford University Press, 2002), 13.

liberative praxis against colonialism, anti-Eurocentricism and 'pro-Otherness."[123] This model initiates a postcolonial contextual theology. For him, postcolonialism has replaced liberation hermeneutics, "perceives its task as critiquing, problematizing, and exposing contradictions and inadequacies in both the text and its interpretation."[124]

1.6.1.2 Postcolonial Application- 'Contrapuntal Reading'

Edward Said's 'Contrapuntal reading' is the strategy used by Sugirtharajah in reading two 'texts' ('cross-textual reading' one from the West and the other of a different location) as a hermeneutical agenda used for decolonizing.[125] This is a reading strategy by which both the experiences (exploited and the exploiter) studied together for confrontation as well as complementary. The contrapuntal reading brings out the "convergences, contradictions, discrepancies, oversights and omissions in them and to show that no one text has the finished and once-for-all meaning, and to challenge and to prevent claims of any text possessing the 'last' word."[126] This reading suggests intertextuality and finding eastern influences in the New Testament.[127] Moreover, it advocates for a multiplicity of perspectives by using intertextual continuum and looking for hermeneutical relations.[128]

1.6.1.3 Postcolonialism and Biblical Interpretation

The two main tasks of Postcolonial biblical criticism according to Sugirtharajah, are to interrogate the colonial ideology in both the biblical text and its interpretations and its emancipatory reading with postcolonial concerns.[129] He criticizes the diverse nature of the Bible in terms of colonialism and therefore "colonialism dominates and determines the interest of the biblical texts."[130] He articulates clearly the aim and the concern of postcolonial criticism i.e., for searching the colonial concerns in interpreting the biblical text and the twin task of 'writing back' and 'listening

[123] Simon Samuel, *"Postcolonial as a Critical Practice in Biblical Studies," DTJ* 2/2 (2005), 116.

[124] R.S. Sugirtharajah, *Troublesome Texts: The Bible in Colonial and Contemporary Culture* (Sheffield: Sheffield Phoenix Press, 2008), 123.

[125] Sugirtharajah, *Postcolonial Reconfigurations*, 16. Sugirtharajah, *Troublesome Texts*, 146; For example, reading Bultmann's *John* with Appasamy's *Christianinity as Bhakti Marga*.

[126] Sugirtharajah, *Troublesome Texts*, 146.

[127] Sugirtharajah, *Postcolonial Reconfigurations*, Ch. 3, 'Imperial Critical Commentaries, 54-85.

[128] Sugirtharajah, *Asian Biblical Hermeneutics*, 21-23. According to him, this study of sacred texts of Christian-Hindu-Buddhist-Confucian will provide multiplicity of perspectives and replace totalizing claims.

[129] Sugirtharajah, *Asian Biblical Hermeneutics*, 18-19.

[130] Sugirtharajah, *Asian Biblical Hermeneutics*, 19. He argues that the literary context reflects the victimizing nature of the colonizers (Egypt, Assyria, Persia and Rome) as well as the legitimizing colonial intentions. He argues the book of Esther for incorporation and assimilation.

again' from the perspective of 'the other.'[131] He accepts its Asiatic origin and its community location for biblical interpretation.[132] He criticizes the exegetical practice which colludes with colonialism and colonial mission.[133]

He accuses the historical-critical scholarship as an ally of imperialism because of its colonial nature.[134] It justifies the superiority of the Christian texts and makes division with our neighbors.[135] He is critical of using this method for the use of Dalit reading, or Korean minjung or Japanese burakus subaltern reading because of its colonial nature.[136] However Dalit interpreters argue that in this method ethics and hermeneutics go hand in hand.[137]

Sugirtharajah disagrees with the popular concept that the New Testament writings are the product exclusively of Hellenistic and Hebraic thinking.[138] He criticizes the biblical scholars for ignoring the contributions of the eastern religions and emphatically argues for "a cultural and literary milieu which was indeed influenced by Indian, Buddhist and Hindu thought patterns."[139] He suggests for widening the hermeneutical horizons by incorporating the rejected books on the basis of Gnostic teaching and widening the milieu of early Aramaic Christianity.[140] He also criticizes the survivalist agenda adopted by Jesus and Paul

[131] Sugirtharajah, *Troublesome Texts,* 144-46.

[132] Sugirtharajah, *Troublesome Texts,* 130. Its nascent faith is very well influenced by the eastern religious traditions (Buddhist and Eastern teachings).

[133] Sugirtharajah, *Postcolonial Reconfigurations,* 17-23. He gives examples from the New Testament for the way in which exegetical practiced have been used for colonial exploitation. For instance Matt. 28:19 and Acts 13-14; 15:40- 18:22; 18:22-21-16 are used for the missionary efforts during the colonial period. According to him, it is William Carey who used the Matthean commission as a proof text for evangelization.

[134] Sugirtharajah, *Troublesome Texts,* 140. Historical-critical methods are colonial because of its claim for universal validity and production of western culture. It aims for a teleological progress which results in an unfair advantage for the colonizers. They neglect the indigenous approaches like allegorical, symbolical, figurative and metaphorical reading practices. Sugirtharajah, *Asian Biblical Hermeneutics*, 127.

[135] Sugirtharajah, *Asian Biblical Hermeneutics*, 126. It undermines the sacred writings of other religions and the exclusive nature of the historical-critical method makes it colonial.

[136] Sugirtharajah, *Asian Biblical Hermeneutics*, 129. He accuses the antagonism of these subaltern leaders against the dominant culture.

[137] M. Gnanavaram, "'Dalit Theology' and the Parable of the Good Samaritan", *JSNT* 50 (1993), 61. For Gnanavaram, the historical-critical method will not dictate terms for interpretation rather these critical tools only serve to do theology better. He argues for a circular nature of interpretation where one goes to the text with their context and brings the text to their context, thus argues for an interconnection between the two.

[138] Sugirtharajah, *Postcolonial Reconfigurations*, 28.

[139] Sugirtharajah, *Postcolonial Reconfigurations*, 28. The possible trade links between India and Mediterranean Roman Empire have been well accepted.

[140] Sugirtharajah, *Troublesome Texts*, 53-54.

in the context of Roman imperialism.[141] Further he compares Jesus with his non-political ideals against the imperial system.[142] According to him, in the area of current biblical scholarship, postcolonial reading works as a corrective tool in the process of Europeanization,[143] racialization,[144] and the negation of 'the other.'[145]

1.6.1.4 Application of Postcolonial Methodology in Letters of John

The postcolonial reading of Johannine letters are done by locating the geographical position of the author as a Roman metropolitan city.[146] By analyzing some of the features of colonial discourse like 'focusing on exclusive truths and intolerance against divergent views', Sugirtharajah identifies some hermeneutical strategies which support colonial intentions.[147] He finds the imperial ideology of silencing the subalterns in the texts by the use of binaries.[148] He finds relationship between the Johannine epistles and Mahayana Buddhism.[149] The contrapuntal reading method finds the restricted notion of love in Johannine letters in comparison with

---

[141] Sugirtharajah, *Asian Biblical Hermeneutics*, 20. For him, Jesus does not critique the Roman Empire. By co-opting with the imperial system, Paul asserts the support of God and history for the empire (Rom. 13).

[142] Sugirtharajah, *Troublesome Texts,* 26. He joins with Micklem's claims of Jesus' indifferent attitude against the imperial revenue system. Sugirtharajah citing Nathaniel Michlem, *The Galilean: The Permanent Element in Religion* (London: James Clark & Co., 1920), 106.

[143] Sugirtharajah, *Postcolonial Reconfigurations*, 103-104. In biblical scholarship, placing Europe at the centre (theoretically, politically, racially, and theologically) is called Europeanization. In this regard they make Christianity as a European faith.

[144] Sugirtharajah comments that as long as biblical scholarship is rooted in the western intellectual and philosophical frameworks, racial tendencies will continue. Sugirtharajah, *Postcolonial Reconfigurations,* 105-106.

[145] Sugirtharajah comments that there is a negation of 'the other' like African and Asian presence in the biblical texts. The Buddhist and Hindu presence in the Mediterranean world is not adequately recognized. He presents a case from the 'Jesus Seminar' that persistently avoided the question related to the possibility of Eastern presence and its influence in the development of early Christianity. Sugirtharajah, *Postcolonial Reconfiguration*, 108, 106-07.

[146] R.S. Sugirtharajah, "The First, Second and Third Letters of John," in *A Postcolonial Commentary on the New Testament Writings*, edited by F.F. Segovia and R.S. Sugirtharajah (New York: T & T Clark, 2007), 413.

[147] The author's impatience against the theological ideology is branded as 'the sons of Satan' and 'antichrist.' The author's hermeneutical strategies in the midst of dissensions are: emphasizing his own credentials for authority, authenticity of the message, conferring an elected role for the supporters, 'project an imperial Christ' (1Jn.4:14; 2:22), by restricting hospitality (2Jn. 10) and using 'colonial rhetoric of flattery and threat to divide the community' (1Jn.4:4). Sugirtharajah, "The First, Second and Third Letters of John," 414-416.

[148] The binary distinction of darkness/light (1Jn.2:7-11), children of God/children of the devil (1Jn.2:28; 3:10), and the Spirit of God/the Spirit of antichrist (1Jn.4:1-6) etc., by which the author justifies his theological/imperial dominance. Sugirtharajah, "The First, Second and Third Letters of John," 416-418.

[149] Sugirtharajah, "The First, Second and Third Letters of John," 418-20.

other readings.[150] The postcolonial ambivalence exhibits its nature in the imperial intentions and praxiological impulses.[151]

1.6.1.5 Critical Appraisal

Sugirtharajah's ethical and ideological commitments are greatly significant in a context of post-colonial atmosphere of military interventions under the pretext of humanitarianism and liberation. He is a postcolonial ethicist who (in)directly involves the day-today activities of people's struggles more than as a hermeneutician. His struggle for the liberation of the marginalized and the subaltern makes him the messiah of the poor. The contrapuntal reading strategy that he adopts has its own danger in reading the colonial text for its silences and gaps.[152] In this process of reading with other religious traditions of Hinduism/Buddhism, one realizes that they too equally operate on certain colonizing premises.

Over against the accusation of Sugirtharajah that the history of biblical text and its interpretation for its colonial nature, one should perceive with caution about the proposal for an adoption of the Sanskrit text in doing postcolonial interpretation. Most Christians in the third world come from the depressed classes and thus adopt indigenous methods to read the biblical text, especially the Sanskrit texts or tradition of the elites, as they bring more imperial burden upon the subaltern masses. The contemporary Dalit theology challenges the religious and the philosophical perspectives that legitimize the oppression. They question the dominant traditions of Hindu philosophy and question the status quo.[153] Contextual interpreters, such as Dalit interpreters of the Bible (Gnanavaram, Carr, Devasahayam), have the same criticism on Sugirtharajah for his dependence on the use of Sanskritic tradition as they criticize the Sanskritization methods of interpretation by the early Indian Christian theologians.[154]

His multifaceted approaches (resistant, hybrid, multi, interfaith, intertextual) make him ubiquitous and make others difficult to follow his postcolonial method in biblical text. There may be 'fundamentalists' / 'colonialists' in Christianity who have the colonial attitude of the West to conquer the world through

---

[150] Sugirtharajah, "The First, Second and Third Letters of John," 420.

[151] Sugirtharajah sees the ambivalent nature of Johannine letters in the praxiological impulses where it sees the veiled presence of Buddhist concepts exhibit the coalition nature of Christian tradition. Sugirtharajah, "The First, Second and Third Letters of John", 421.

[152] According to Samuel, only with 'a double consciousness (with a forked tongue)' one can read a colonial text. Samuel, *A Postcolonial Reading of Mark's Story,* 18. Segovia cautioned Sugirtharajah against the non-western interpreters who too demonstrate the tendency of 'nativism and triumphalism.' Segovia, "Tracing Sugirtharajah's Voice from the Margin," 235.

[153] Gnanavaram, 'Dalit Theology', 68.

[154] Gnanavaram, "Dalit Theology", 59- 83; Dhayanchand Carr, "A Biblical Basis for Dalit Theology" in *Indigenous People: Dalits; Dalit Issues in Today's Theological Debate,* edited by James Massey (Delhi: ISPCK, 1994); V.V. Devasahayam, *Doing Theology in Biblical Key* (Madras: Gurukul, 1997).

deceptive means. However, this (mis)represented modern concept is the 'tool' of Hindu fundamentalism in the Indian subcontinent where Christians have been marginalized for centuries. Thus, the minority Christians locate themselves in the 'third space' for political empowerment similar to the first century colonized Christian minority. Christian faith originated in the West-Asian context and it also made its roots primarily in the West-Asian geographical locations. However, during the course of time Christian roots in West-Asia has narrowed down and the West took its place. This must have led to the process of colonization not only through military power but also by way of interpreting the biblical text.

Fiorenza is critical of the binary division that Sugirtharajah proposes in postcolonial biblical hermeneutics[155] and she advocates applying the existing biblical interpretive paradigms with other theoretical frameworks.[156] The 'Manichean' construction of the monolithic totalities of the West/Orient, colonizer/colonized has become a problem in Sugirtharajah's concept of the understanding of colonialism.[157] Fiorenza suggests a collaborative hermeneutics which include feminist biblical criticism and liberation theology who paved the path for postcolonial biblical studies rather than colonizing the 'voices from the margins'.[158]

1.6.2 **Fernando F. Segovia** (Liberation and Decolonization)

Segovia's Cuban national identity and the later part of his Hispanic American diaspora experiences of colonialism made him to be a postcolonial diaspora cultural critic (diasporic intercultural criticism) with multiple identities (Cuban-American) who lives in the in-between worlds.[159] At the watershed of biblical criticism, the role of Segovia is well appreciated as one of the emerging voices of the non-Western world. As an editor to a giant project *A Postcolonial Commentary on the New Testament Writings*, Segovia proves himself as a postcolonial critic of our time.[160] He brings postcolonial studies under the umbrella of cultural studies with plurality of interpretations. In postcolonial studies, the reality of the empire is considered to be a structural reality than a symbolic city where the ideologies

---

[155] Liberation hermeneutics, church, third world and 'ordinary' readers against postcolonialism, academy and diasporic expert readers, third world margin and first world center, religious community and academy. Fiorenza, "Transforming the Margin", 23- 24.

[156] Fiorenza, "Transforming the Margin," 25.

[157] Fiorenza, "Transforming the Margin," 34. It set aside the complexity of colonial politics.

[158] Fiorenza, "Transforming the Margin," 35-39.

[159] F.F. Segovia, *Decolonizing Biblical Studies: A View from the Margins* (Maryknoll, New York: Orbis Books, 2000), 125.

[160] According to the introductory comments made by Segovia, almost all of the NT books were the product of colonial context. Segovia and Sugirtharajah, *A Postcolonial Commentary*, 1-68.

are in binomial opposition.[161] This structural reality of the Roman Empire must have affected the literary productions of the early Christians.[162]

1.6.2.1 Segovia's Postcolonial Optic

Segovia emphasizes the overwhelming reality of the empire all through the stages of world of antiquity, modernity, postmodernity, postcolonialism and at present the world of neocolonialism.[163] For him, the Bible is ideologically constructed in the socio-religio-political space both in antiquity and at present by its readers.[164] Thus the postcolonial biblical scholarship has brought transformation into the Eurocentric authoritarian Christian theology through 'liberation' and 'decolonization.'[165] Segovia's 'liberation model of hermeneutics' is probably one of the trajectories that influenced the contemporary postcolonial biblical criticism.[166] Hence, this model aims for resistance aiming at uneven geopolitical, geoeconomic power relationships inextricably intertwined with liberation of socio-cultural and economic concerns.[167]

In diaspora theology, the idea of objectivity is criticized for 'flesh-and-blood' reader and his/her socio-political location.[168] This is a theology of diversity and pluralism, it gives value to all matrices and voices. As a theology of engagement and dialogue, it makes a "critical conversation with other theological voices from both margins and center alike."[169] Segovia proposes this theology as a cross-cultural approach based on the "simultaneous application across the various

[161] Segovia, *Decolonizing Biblical Studies*, 125-126. In the binomial opposition there is a political, economic and cultural center and subordinated periphery.

[162] Segovia, *Decolonizing Biblical Studies*, 126.

[163] F.F. Segovia, "Biblical Criticism and Postcolonial Studies: Towards a Postcolonial Optic," in *The Postcolonial Bible*, edited by R.S. Sugirtharajah (Sheffield: Sheffield Academic Press, 1998), 56.

[164] Segovia, *Decolonizing Biblical Studies*, 43; Segovia, "Biblical Criticism and Postcolonial Studies," 58.

[165] Segovia, *Decolonizing Biblical Studies*, 121. For Segovia, the modern Christian theology emanated from the Euro-American center for long and the 'theology of the diaspora' promotes pluralism, dialogue, and multiple voices. Segovia, "Biblical Criticism and Postcolonial Studies," 52, 64.

[166] Stephen D. Moore and F.F. Segovia, "Postcolonial Biblical Criticism: Beginnings, Trajectories, Intersections," in *Postcolonial Biblical Criticism. Interdisciplinary Intersections*, edited by S.D. Moore and F.F. Segovia (London/New York: T & T Clark, 2005), 6; Segovia, "Tracing Sugirtharajah's Voice from the Margin," 222.

[167] The Liberation hermeneutics intersects with the uneven power relationships of gender, class, ethnicity and sexual orientation. Moore and Segovia, "Postcolonial Biblical Criticism," 10.

[168] 'Flesh-and-blood' refers to the real reader with specific social configuration with politics of identity on the basis of the socio-cultural-political framework in which one's essential identity has been defined. F.F. Segivia, "Toward a Hermeneutics of the Diaspora: A Hermeneutics of Otherness and Engagement," in *Reading from this Place: Social Location and Biblical Interpretation in the United States*, vol. I, edited by F.F. Segovia and M.A. Tolbert (Minneapolis: Fortress Press, 1995), 59.

[169] Segovia, *Decolonizing Biblical Studies*, 123.

dimensions."[170] He advocates an explosion of different voices-the voices of the multicultural, geographical, ethnical communities who hope for liberation and decolonization by analyzing the social location of the flesh-and-blood reader. In his 'Notes toward refining the postcolonial optic,' he suggests the postcolonial critics to take into account the socio-economic factor together with the cultural reality.[171]

1.6.2.2 The Diasporic Model of Reading

Segovia's minoritarean diasporic identity is emphasized at the colonial center for the purpose of reading the Bible towards liberation and decolonization.[172] For him the social location is very important in interpreting the text. As a diasporic critic, he appreciates the heterogeneity and the multi-voices of the margins. In his leading diasporic hermeneutics, he analyses three levels of texts for an intercultural critical engagement-ancient biblical texts which were written in the context of colonialism, the Western influenced modern biblical texts and the postmodern biblical studies of the non-Westerners in and outside the West.[173] Decolonizing will take place through this contrapuntal reading by challenging the Eurocentric leanings of the text and it complements the multidimensional global discourses.[174] However, one should pay "close attention to issues of historical and cultural distance."[175] For Segovia, this model is an optic and not the optic in full engagement and dialogue with all other models and other optics.[176]

In postcolonial studies, he deals with ancient texts, modern readings of texts and the heterogeneous experiences of the readers of texts in the light of the socio-political reality of colonialism.[177] While criticizing the colonial elements in biblical texts, he respects the hermeneutics of otherness and their experiences with localized voices to speak. In postcolonial studies, culture, ideology and power are the crucial questions that deal within the literary productions of both the center

---

[170] Segovia, *Decolonizing Biblical Studies,* 123. The diaspora theology will take place by analyzing the texts of both the ancient Judaism and early Christianity. It also analyzes the readings and interpretations of texts from the Western tradition and the analysis of the real readers of the texts and producers of the texts both inside and outside the West.

[171] F.F. Segovia, "Notes toward refining the Postcolonial Optic," *JSNT* 75 (1999), 107.

[172] The reading strategy of Segovia is called 'a hermeneutics of the diaspora' or 'hermeneutics of otherness.' F.F. Segovia, ed., *Interpreting beyond Borders* (The Bible and Postcolonialism, 3; Sheffield: Sheffield Academic Press, 2000), 59-83, cited by Uriah Y. Kim, *Decolonizing Josiah: Toward a Postcolonial Reading of the Deuteronomic History* (Sheffield: Sheffield Phoenix Press, 2008), 29, F.N.47.

[173] Segovia, "Biblical Criticism and Postcolonial Studies," 54; Kim, *Decolonizing Josiah*, 30.

[174] Segovia, ed., *Interpreting beyond Borders*, 59, cited by Kim, *Decolonizing Josiah*, 30.

[175] Segovia, "Notes toward refining the Postcolonial Optic," 108.

[176] Segovia, *Decolonizing Biblical Studies,* 131.

[177] Segovia, *Decolonizing Biblical Studies,* 125, 154.

and the margins.[178] Here the subordinated margins have a crucial role to play in resisting the center by deconstructing the binomial global reality.[179]

1.6.2.3 Application of Postcolonial Methodology in Gospel of John

According to Segovia, the gospel is a religious text preoccupied with geopolitical overtones leading to postcolonial reading. He analyses the text as a cultural production in the imperial-colonial framework of colonial Rome and her allies in Palestine with its geopolitical dynamics with "a challenge of absolute power."[180] He applies the text into composition and not in interpretation levels. He prefers to apply the imperial-colonial formations transhistorically and cross-culturally, especially in the context of Roman colonialism which is foundational for Western empires.[181] He applies the above discussed principles of the hermeneutics of otherness and engagement for drawing out a multidimensional meaning of the text.[182] For him, the readers' location and perspectives are important in critical reading.

In the first part of the postcolonial analysis of the text, he proposes a method of conflict and resolution. The text is divided in bipolar terms-'world above'/ 'world below', light/darkness, life/death, truth/falsehood, God/Satan, Word/Spirit and grace/sin portray the conflicting reality where Satan opposes the work of Jesus (the enfleshed Word) by associating with the imperial authorities.[183] Here, the postcolonial resolution is narrated through the gospel to dispense the power below by establishing an alternative dominion over the established colonial reign.[184]

In the second part of his analysis, the gospel prologue proves to be a deconstructive and subversive alternative path which places the collaborated Judeo-Roman political powers under the supremacy of the power of Word/ God.[185] The journey motif of Jesus across the worlds of reality by his birth-life-death, and the cycle of geographical journeys (Galilee-Samaria-Jerusalem) reveal his 'other-worldly' identity through his deeds and words in the eastern part of the

---

[178] Segovia, *Decolonizing Biblical Studies,* 126.

[179] Segovia, *Decolonizing Biblical Studies,* 129. The binomial reality is structured by the West in terms of uncivilized, primitive, barbarian, backward, undeveloped over against civilized, advanced, and cultured, etc.

[180] F.F. Segovia, "The Gospel of John," in *A Postcolonial Commentary on the New Testament Writings*, edited by F.F. Segovia and R.S. Sugirtharajah (London: T & T Clark, 2007), 161, 65.

[181] Segovia, "The Gospel of John," 159.

[182] Hermeneutics of otherness includes contextualization by identifying the voice of otherness in biblical texts, readers and critics for liberation and empowerment of all readers through the reading strategy of intercultural criticism. Segovia, "Toward a Hermeneutics of the Diaspora," 67.

[183] Segovia, "The Gospel of John," 166-67.

[184] Segovia, "The Gospel of John," 174.

[185] Segovia, "The Gospel of John," 170. The God of Judaism is the deity of the colonial periphery. He can be known only through the Word and not through the empire channels.

Roman Empire.[186] This journey also discloses Jesus' alternative identity of God's reign by the speech and miraculous signs but finally leads to the religio-political confrontation with the colonial forces. The embodied word of God in Jerusalem has logically climaxed for the final dominion over the imperial world (geopolitical victory) through the execution-burial-resurrection and glorification of Jesus.[187] He finds this alternative world discourse as an anti-imperialistic discourse.

1.6.2.4 Critical Appraisal

The Biblical scholars have much gained from the 'Diasporic reading' strategy of colonial resistance through liberation and decolonization. Contrary to Sugirtharajah's understanding of biblical text itself as colonial, Segovia finds the text anti-imperialistic in nature. He tries to find resistant voices through the reading of the biblical text. Sugirtharajah criticizes the application of Segovia for the lack of the "hybridized form of textual interpretation as an interpretive strategy in biblical studies."[188] In the postcolonial optic, he emphasizes the heterogeneity and polyphony of the margins for liberation and decolonization, but how far the cacophony of voices resists the imperial voices is debatable. In the midst of the cacophony of voices, the colonialist voice naturally gets its space but how the carnival of voices resist the imperial voice is a question to be answered. In his task of refining the postcolonial optic, he admits that "there is no self-evident project of resistance and emancipation for all in the periphery," and he appreciates the incredible diversity of the marginalized to bring victory.[189] This optic is probably not satisfactory to the oppressed subalterns in their geographical locations of the third world because certain diverse elements are demonic for them. Samuel criticizes his intercultural criticism that leads to direct conflict with the 'sub-cultural carnival' forgetting consensual-conflictual stand of the postcolonial discourses.[190]

1.6.3 C. I. David Joy (Postcolonial Subaltern Reading)

Born and reared in the post-colonial context of India, he is a theoretician as well as a praxis oriented Christian priest. His genuine concern for the liberation of the subaltern masses reflects in his writings and interpretation. Joy is one of the budding pioneers among the Indian postcolonial biblical interpreters who has done a major introductory writing in the postcolonial field. His innovative postcolonial hermeneutical application through the book *Mark and its Subalterns* is

---

186 Segovia, "The Gospel of John," 175-77.

187 Segovia, "The Gospel of John," 186-87.

188 Sugirtharajah, *The Postcolonial Criticism and Biblical Interpretation,* 191.

189 Segovia, "Notes toward refining the Postcolonial Optic," 112.

190 Samuel, *A Postcolonial Reading of Mark,* 25. For Samuel, Segovia fails to a consensual-conflictual hybrid position of the "diasporic postcolonial interculturalism," and a hybrid culture of double articulation as a mode of resistance.

a great asset in the New Testament studies.[191] In the present context, where secular postcolonial writers re-read history from a postcolonial angle, he is attempting to re-read biblical texts through postcolonial subaltern hermeneutics.

1.6.3.1 Definition and the Nomenclature of the Term Postcolonial

Joining with R.C. Young, he also understands the focus of postcolonial criticism in critiquing the forces of oppression and domination in the neocolonialist context where the colonial situation continues even today.[192] Thus, he suggests in this new paradigm of postcolonial liberation, a proper understanding of the readers' context as well as the texts for the postcolonial reading of the Bible.[193] He defines the term from different angles and describes it as a loose term for the marginalized world or the use as a periodization and its relevant concerns of imperialism and neocolonialism.[194] The issue of colonialism is the major concern for postcolonial biblical reading and thus he finds out the imperial relationship between colonialism and mission, translation of the text, racial prejudice and national bias.[195] For him, the starting point of postcolonial interpretation is the voice of the exploited community.[196]

For Joy, 'postcolonial' means periodization as well as a methodology and therefore the issues of this period get prime importance.[197] Hence, postcolonial reading exposes an alternative resistant reading strategy where the native cultures get a proper recognition; it critically evaluates the colonial motifs both in the text and in interpretations; and addresses the issues of gender, race, class, caste and ethnicity.[198] For him, the context of first century Roman colonialism and the milieu of the researcher possibly reveal the true meaning of the text.[199] The people at the margins become the basis for the re-reading of the passages for a postcolonial interpretation.[200]

---

[191] C.I. David Joy, *Mark and Its Subalterns. A Hermeneutical Paradigm for a Postcolonial Context* (London: Equinox, 2008).

[192] Young, *Postcolonialism*, 15; C.I. David Joy, "Mark 10:17-27 in the Light of the Issues of Poor and their Representation: A Postcolonial Reading," *BTF* (June 2006), 159.

[193] Joy, "Mark 10:17-27 in the Light of the Issues of Poor," 159. The gravity of exploitation will be exposed by a proper analysis of the context.

[194] Joy, *Mark and Its Subalterns*, 55. The looseness of the marginalized world explains in terms of 'commonwealth', 'Orientals' and 'Third World.'

[195] Joy, "Mark 10:17-27 in the Light of the Issues of Poor," 159.

[196] Joy, "Mark 10:17-27 in the Light of the Issues of Poor," 160.

[197] Joy, "Mark 10:17-27 in the Light of the Issues of Poor," 160.

[198] C.I. David Joy, "Re-visioning God and Re-conceiving God's Mission in the Postcolonial Indian Context," paper presented at UTC Alumni Association, 6th Oct, 2009.

[199] Joy, *Mark and Its Subalterns,* 60.

[200] Joy, *Mark and Its Subalterns,* 57.

1.6.3.2 Application of Postcolonial Methodology in Gospel of Mark

Joy's attempt in exploring a hermeneutical path for the people of India is commendable.[201] The first thing for him to do is deconstructing a legitimate historiography in the light of the voiceless subalterns of India,[202] secondly, find out a relevant Markan (biblical) hermeneutics in a pluralistic Indian context by linking the text internally as well as linking with extra textual hermeneutics.[203] In addition, the text that deals with socio-economic, political and ideological class struggles must give sufficient attention in both the production as well as the reception of the biblical text.[204] Thirdly, the postcolonial reading of the text must take into account the immediate living situation of neocolonialism and counter any kind of imperialism.[205]

Joy's model work, *Mark and its Subalterns*, illustrates the identity and function of the marginalized in Mark in a colonial context for developing a hermeneutical paradigm for the postcolonial and neocolonial power dynamics of the Indian context.[206] He accepts the liberative potential of the Bible in the context of plurality of cultures and scriptures. In turn, he explains the multiple opinions of the contemporary New Testament scholars for re-examining the identity of the marginalized as he re-reads the text and the context to locate and identify the subalterns in Mark. He legitimizes the multi-dimensional interpretative operations mainly liberation, feminist, subaltern and postcolonial methods.[207]

The first part of his model deals with the various contextual readings from the postcolonial context, analyzing the previous interpretations on Mark with basic principles of liberation, and subaltern readings with an application from a postcolonial view point."[208] The second part deals with the exegesis of selected representative passages including interpretations by Indians with active subaltern role in the Roman colonial context for a postcolonial hermeneutical model. Other issues discussed in this section are economics, the poor, race, gender, subaltern purity and socio-political background of the text.

Joy explains a clear polarity of the Indian hermeneutics from missionary hermeneutics where the colonialist mocks the colonized other for their superstition,

---

[201] C.I. David Joy, "The Social and Religious Origins of the Gospel of Mark and its Hermeneutical Implications: A Post-Colonial Critique", *BTF* 33/1 (2001), 11.

[202] There is a paradigm shift of the historiography of the post-colonial India that was inherited from the powerful ruling class to a people centered historiography.

[203] Joy, "The Social and Religious Origins," 13-14.

[204] Joy, "The Social and Religious Origins," 15.

[205] Joy, "The Social and Religious Origins," 16-20.

[206] Joy, *Mark and Its Subalterns*, 1 The subalterns in the Mark's gospel are identified as the marginalized, the poor and women, etc.

[207] Joy, *Mark and Its Subalterns,* 4-5. He applies the historical-critical method, sociopolitical methods, re-constructing the traditional interpretations from the point of view of the margins.

[208] Joy, *Mark and Its Subalterns,* 6.

laziness and bribery for justifying their civilizing mission.[209] He challenges for the need of interpreting the Bible through indigenous socio-political reality and with a liberation view point.[210] Joy's postcolonial interpretation suggests Mark as an anti-colonial document.

For him, the implicit portrayal of the resistance of the Galilean community to colonialism is displayed by the author's critical attitude towards the Roman policies and domination.[211] The Galilean subalterns in Mark, the most crushed community become the launching pad for his study. The subaltern voices of conflict and resistance against imperial oppression in Mark can be clearly heard by placing the text in its real socio-political and religio-cultural context.[212] The apocalyptic Son of Man image and messianic expectation have been used as a revolutionary figure in terms of resistance and protest.[213]

Joy makes his study on the basis of Markan elements of subaltern resistance against Roman imperialism using three of the relevant texts (Mk.10:17-31, Mk.7:24-32 and Mk.5:1-20) in the light of the author's present day colonial/neocolonial oppressions.[214] The multi-faceted resistance to the religio-cultural as well as to the political-philosophical framework depicts the nuances of the oppression and exploitation.[215] According to him, the postcolonial study reveals the strategy of Jesus by using the available political and social terms for the purpose of dethroning the imperial evils. The discussion on the issue of the poor in Mark is interwoven with the exploited subjects from Galilee who became part of the Jesus' movement.[216] For him, placing the text in the postcolonial context means analyzing the text in the light of colonial exploitation.

The second postcolonial reading is in the light of race, gender and hybridity (Mk.7:24-30), in a complex matrix of Roman colonialism and Jewish patriarchalism that offer a clear direction for decolonizing Mark.[217] The woman is considered as hybrid by breaking the boundary of gender-race which is a

---

[209] Joy, *Mark and Its Subalterns,* 14-16. An overview of Indian hermeneutics describe the efforts of Indian Christian communities and their attempts to interpret the scriptures, though the efforts were limited to traditional teaching and doctrinal formulations. A.J. Appasamy's efforts in interpreting the Bible in the Indian context are specially identified.

[210] Joy, *Mark and Its Subalterns,* 21. One of the main emphasis is to re-read the Bible in the light of other scriptures.

[211] Joy, *Mark and Its Subalterns,* 63.

[212] Joy, *Mark and Its Subalterns,* 82.

[213] Joy, *Mark and Its Subalterns,* 98, 105.

[214] Joy, *Mark and Its Subalterns,* 117.

[215] Joy, *Mark and Its Subalterns,* 122-23.

[216] Joy, *Mark and Its Subalterns,* 125-27. The identity of Jesus' as a person belongs to the marginalized (Mk.6:3), the tem 'crowd', the healing ministry of Jesus' are considered as a protest against the center.

[217] Joy, *Mark and Its Subalterns,* 164. Jesus was liberating the woman from her Judaistic oppressions. Markan Jesus questioned the patriarchal marriage structures (Mk.10:2-9; 12:18-17).

paradigm for women's liberation. Applying it in postcolonial India, Joy mentions the cultural colonialism of race, sex, ethnicity and class by which they were badly subjugated. The postcolonial reading where Jesus addresses her as daughter which is a radical shift in Jesus' position.[218] By breaking the boundaries of gender, race, religion, she enters into a dialogical approach as a model for a bold and creative move in a postcolonial context.[219]

The third postcolonial biblical reading is done on Mk.5:1-20. He reads it in the light of issues such as class, nationalism and subalternity in Indian cultural context which is rooted in caste system. Joy criticizes the traditional hermeneutics in interpreting this story as a mere miracle story to reveal the power of Jesus.[220] To him, Gerasenes, a Roman colonized gentile territory, has a symbolic meaning[221] which along with the oppressive Roman colonial presence, the depressed social system and the confused personality of the demon possessed help him to unearth postcolonial subaltern insights.[222] The presence of the empire in the text reveals the split personality of the demon possessed and the people of the land.[223] Jesus' position in the text for challenging the religio-political establishments creates a new space for the oppressed subalterns who aspire for liberation in the postcolonial context.[224]

1.6.3.3 Critical Appraisal

Joy's attempts in developing a postcolonial subaltern hermeneutics in the Indian context show his heart for the liberation of the marginalized and the depressed classes who have been crushed by the imperial political and caste ideologies. He connects the basic principles of liberation-feminist, postcolonial feminist hermeneutics and subaltern readings with postcolonial hermeneutics. The socio-political and colonial backgrounds of the text explain the significance of Jesus' movement in Galilee. His postcolonial reading of the three model passages by emphasizing the issues of the poor, race, gender, hybridity, class, nationalism and subalternity explain the liberative model for the subalterns. Equal distribution of wealth to the masses is a clear message of the text by realizing the sin of colonial

---

Jesus broke the cultural silence of women and challenged the patriarchal power (Mk.5:21-43; 14:3-9) (148).

[218] Joy, *Mark and Its Subalterns,* 154-55. The religio-ethnic tension between the Hellenized Phoenician and the marginalized Jew are very important to interpret the text.

[219] Joy, *Mark and Its Subalterns,* 163-64.

[220] Joy, *Mark and Its Subalterns,* 173. Joy criticizes Myers along with other subaltern readers for not considering for postcolonial context.

[221] Joy, *Mark and Its Subalterns,* 171.

[222] Joy, *Mark and Its Subalterns,* 176.

[223] Joy, *Mark and Its Subalterns,* 176.

[224] Joy, *Mark and Its Subalterns,* 177.

exploitation. In the context of dominant political and caste ideologies that suppress the marginalized, the postcolonial subaltern reading is the suitable hermeneutics.

Joy's hermeneutical implications aim to counter all kind of imperialism by following Spivak's deconstruction model for a legitimate historiography of the Indian subalterns. For an inclusive nature, he adopts the historical-critical method under a common ideological umbrella for a postcolonial biblical interpretation. Even though his postcolonial interpretation of the Bible gives the starting point for the voice of the exploited people of India, in his experimental works, the economic and neocolonial issues of the readers are not given serious attention.

In the postcolonial reading of the text, he gives much attention to the production of the colonial Western interpretations for emphasizing the presence of the subalterns and colonial presence. Additionally, he understands the New Testament text as anti-colonial. However, he misses the in-between space taken by the first century colonized Christians to resist the Roman colonialism. The suffering *huios* imagery and Jesus' colonial execution seem to make the story more complicated than treating the story of Mark simply as an anti-colonial literature. The ambivalent position of *huios*-Jesus and the hybrid Markan characters prove not just an anti-or pro-colonial rather an ambivalent postcolonial posture. Giving equal importance to both the first century as well as the present day colonial context seems to be the right way of doing a postcolonial interpretation.

1.6.4 Simon Samuel (Strategic Essentialism and Transcultural Hybridity)

Simon Samuel is one of the Indian postcolonial biblical hermeneuticians who innovatively approximate theoretical concepts from different theories and field. He is an ordained minister of the Christian Evangelistic Assemblies. He is a revolutionary ideas challenge people for a praxis oriented Christian life. He authored number of articles and books having contemporary significance. His methodological model challenges other models in this field on the basis of his theoretical conviction and innovativeness. Through his successive articles on "Postcolonialism as a critical practice in Biblical Studies," he makes his creative methodological findings clear to the other biblical practitioners.[225] His doctoral dissertation published under the title *A Postcolonial Reading of Mark's Story of Jesus* is a popular reading among the postcolonial students.[226]

1.6.4.1 Definition and Meaning

For Samuel, postcolonial reading is a "literary and counter-cultural discursive strategy" of the colonized who engages creatively by cultural productions like

[225] Samuel, "Postcolonialism as a Critical Practice," 97-119; *idem*, "Postcolonialism as a Critical Practice in Biblical Studies," Part II, *DTJ* 3/1 (2006), 5-20.

[226] The researcher discussed this work earlier.

novels and discursive responses.[227] He makes the difference between the colonial-postcolonial discourse by describing the first as the discourse of the colonialist and the latter as the discourse of the colonized population "that critically scrutinizes and engages the colonial contacts and perceptions of power."[228] This complex and ambivalent discourse "originates in the interstitial space between the colonists and colonized which accommodates and disrupts both the native and the alien colonial discourses of power."[229] Thus, the common polarity concept and sequentiality of this discourse has been removed and brings new meaning of the interstitial 'spatial' category of Bhabha.[230]

1.6.4.2 Explicate Postcolonial Hermeneutics in Biblical Studies

According to Samuel's analysis, any ancient or modern literature of the colonial context that exhibits the accommodative and disruptive nature of colonial discourses of power within the interstitial cultural space will be considered for postcolonial application.[231] Therefore the discursive responses of the ancient people (Greeks, Jews and others) exhibit the similar discursive responses of the modern colonial history.[232] He takes the opinion of Segovia for the continuous overwhelming inescapable reality of the empire and colonialism in the world in which one lives.[233] His analysis takes into consideration the different postcolonial relationships, its issues, its motivations and native resistance against colonialism.[234]

Samuel is against the notion of considering the Bible as a colonialist discourse on the basis of its Asiatic origin and its proliferation under persecution in the Afrasian countries.[235] The assumption of the present study is that the New Testament discourses primarily originate from the colonial context by the subjected community in response to imperialism and colonialism in the first century CE. There are other contemporaneous discourses of the same period which exhibit

---

[227] Samuel, *A Postcolonial Reading of Mark's Story*, 1. This cultural discursive strategy seems to work both as a literary-cultural practice and as a critical practice of the colonized and dominated.

[228] Samuel, *A Postcolonial Reading of Mark's Story*, 3.

[229] Samuel, *A Postcolonial Reading of Mark's Story*, 3.

[230] Samuel, *A Postcolonial Reading of Mark's Story*, 3.

[231] Samuel, *A Postcolonial Reading of Mark's Story*, 3.

[232] Samuel, *A Postcolonial Reading of Mark's Story*, 4.

[233] Segovia, "Biblical Criticism and Postcolonial Studies," 56; Samuel, *A Postcolonial Reading of Mark's Story*, 4.

[234] Samuel, *A Postcolonial Reading of Mark's Story*, 13-14. The postcolonial criticism gives importance to the socio-political-economic-cultural-ideological relationships, and the related issues emanate from colonialism.

[235] Samuel, *A Postcolonial Reading of Mark's Story*, 13.

similar characteristics of complicity and resistance to both the Roman and their native cultures.[236]

Samuel tries to read the story of Mark as a postcolonial discourse of the subjugated subaltern community who tries to place them in the interstitial space between the Roman colonialism and the dominant Jewish native cultural nationalism.[237] In his findings, the Markan portrayal of Jesus is both affiliative and disruptive to both to the native Judaistic and alien Roman colonial discourse of power.[238] He criticizes the polarities in the Markan studies (pro-and anti-) by following the complexities of the colonial discourse of the nature of accommodation and disruption.[239] The simultaneous nature of complicity and resistance reveals the postcolonial discourse.

1.6.4.3 Methodology

The methodology Samuel specifically constructed to read postcolonial literature is Strategic Essentialism and Transcultural Hybridity. Spivak's anti-essentialist position leads the concept of 'strategic essentialism' over against the nativist motto of empowerment for cultural essentialism which is destructive. He suggests the native subaltern subjects to opt for an identity i.e., a strategic essentialist identity "with a potential to elaborate strategies of transculturality in the context of internal and external colonialism."[240] For him, the deconstruction of the 'in-between' space can only be possible through the postcolonial theoretical concepts proposed by Spivak, Bhabha and Boehmer because the colonial context is an ambivalent space[241] of constant negotiation and mutual dependence. He gives sufficient consideration to the theoretical concepts of Bhabha's hybridity, mimicry and ambivalence that are widely used in the postcolonial literature for the purpose of deconstruction. Bhabha adopts the insight of hybridity to explain the strategies of the colonized in making selfhood by which it bring out sites for collaboration and contestation for individuals and cultures.[242] The consensual and conflictual

[236] Samuel reads a postclassical Greek novel Chariton's *Chaereas and Callirhoe.*

[237] Samuel, *A Postcolonial Reading of Mark's Story*, 4.

[238] Samuel, *A Postcolonial Reading of Mark's Story*, 5.

[239] Samuel, *A Postcolonial Reading of Mark's Story*, 5. The nature of accommodation and disruption strategy functions both in the Roman colonial rule and native Jewish nationalism. This strategy is followed in Mark by presenting "John as a prophetic messenger and Jesus as a *huios*-human hybrid being."

[240] Samuel, *A Postcolonial Reading of Mark's Story*, 31.

[241] Samuel, "Postcolonialism as a Critical Practice," II, 12. Samuel cited E. Boehmer, *Colonial and Postcolonial Literature: Migrant Metaphors* (Oxford: Oxford University Press, 1995).

[242] Bhabha, *The Location of Culture*, 1-2; Samuel, "Postcolonialism as a Critical Practice," II, 13. M.M. Bakhtin, *The Dialogic Imagination: Four Essays*, Michael Holquist, ed., translated by Caryl Emerson and Michael Holquist (Austin: University of Texas Press, 1990), 304-305. Bhaktin finds this intentional hybridity in novelistic literature "to explain the consensual and conflictual nature of social and cultural transactions" in a postcolonial context. Bakhtin calls this phenomenon

engagements of cultural differences are the nature of the postcolonial methodology of strategic essentialism and transcultural hybridity.

1.6.4.4 Application of Postcolonial Methodology in Gospel of Mark

Samuel connects the European and the Roman colonial frameworks of the first century CE by assuming the transhistorical view of colonial histories,[243] finding similarity in the discursive strategies used in both the colonial context and "the perceptual and cultural spheres of the colonized."[244] Therefore Mark's story of Jesus is considered to be a postcolonial discourse of the subjected minoritarian community that accommodate and disrupt as well as create a strategic space between the native Jewish and alien Roman discourses of power.[245] He has taken the initiative of studying these dynamics of mimicry, ambivalence and hybridity lying underneath the Markan text.[246]

In his postcolonial reading of Mark, Samuel analyses the superscription –'beginning of the gospel of Jesus Christ, Son of God' (ἀρχη του εὐαγγελιου ̓Ιησου Χριστου [υἱου θεοῦ] 1:1) and the introduction (1: 2-11) for understanding the postcolonial response (mimetic and menacing) to the colonial masters of the time. He examines its 'intentional hybridity' (mimicry) under Roman dominion of cultural complexities.[247] This superscription is studied under the Roman imperial cult which has a political meaning of the beginning of a new order that is considered to be good news of Jesus the messiah, Son of God.[248] The same thing is studied in biblical and post-biblical perceptions that have more or less similar meaning of God as the beginning/foundation/dominion of a victorious reign.[249] He suggests the possibility for this element of slippage and fluidity as a great role played in the superscription of the story for strategic essentialism and transcultural hybridity. Therefore, in postcolonial discourse of Mark, the usage of mimicking the dominant Roman and Jewish discourses have potential for disruption.[250]

'intentional hybrid' or 'conscious hybrid' because of the nature of its deliberate doing by the colonized to challenge the colonizer. Samuel, "Postcolonialism as a Critical Practice," II, 14.

[243] Samuel, *A Postcolonial Reading of Mark's Story*, ix.

[244] Samuel, *A Postcolonial Reading of Mark's Story*, ix. The discursive response of the colonized and dominated subject (pro , anti and postcolonial) against European colonialism of the recent past and Roman colonialism in the first part of the CE seems to be the same.

[245] Samuel, *A Postcolonial Reading of Mark's Story*, x.

[246] Samuel, *A Postcolonial Reading of Mark's Story*, 84.

[247] Samuel, *A Postcolonial Reading of Mark's Story*, 89.

[248] Samuel, *A Postcolonial Reading of Mark's Story*, 92. The word 'beginning' (ἀρχη) of Rome refers "not only to the *imperium* of Rome but also to a certain significant theo-political 'beginning.'"

[249] Samuel, *A Postcolonial Reading of Mark's Story*, 93. The words Messiah and Son of God potentially invoke complex mixture of meaning according to the period and the sources.

[250] Samuel, *A Postcolonial Reading of Mark's Story*, 97.

The introduction of Mark (1:2-8) employs the midrashic interpretation of Isaiah for the coming of Jesus, the Son of God which has an affiliative and disruptive strategy.[251] John the baptizer became the connecting link as a strategic affiliation to the Isiahnic prophecy (Isa. 40:3) to prepare the way for Jesus, the stronger one. The second midrashic portrayal of 'beloved *huios*' has two potential nuances of a royal son figure as well as a suffering son figure.[252] This anomalous hybrid figure of Jesus the *huios* in Mark has both authority and suffering i.e, the affiliative-disruptive design.

The postcolonial analysis comes to its climax in the fifth chapter through the same postcolonial concepts of 'the strategic essentialism and transcultural hybridity.' He portrays the Markan *huios*-Jesus who accommodates and disrupts not only his own native Jewish space but also the space of the Roman colonial culture.[253]

The portrait of *huios*-Jesus in the discursive geographical landscape of Mark exhibits great potentiality because of his indeterminate fluid nature. The son of humanity (υἱος του ἀνθρωπου) has power to act as well as destined to suffer, die and rise again.[254] In order to fully understand the portrayal of the *huios*-Jesus in Mark, Samuel first studies the portrayals of biblical and postbiblical discourses where he "is an anomalous divine-human agent who appears in the contexts of colonialism whenever the elect of Israel are in serious trouble."[255] In all Jewish portrayals, the Son of humanity is used as a powerful political symbol.[256] Jesus' position in the first half of the gospel of Mark reflects the position of a hybrid figure (Son of Humanity) who is endowed with the authority (ἐξουσια) of God in the formation of a transcultural community from the Jewish and 'other' peripheral communities (1:12-8:30). He makes the kingdom proclaimed, teaches, disrupts

[251] Samuel, *A Postcolonial Reading of Mark's Story*, 101.

[252] Samuel, *A Postcolonial Reading of Mark's Story*, 106. Samuel coins the *huios* concept in Mark in order to portray the hybrid nature of Jesus, the hero in the story.

[253] Samuel, *A Postcolonial Reading of Mark's Story*, 110.

[254] Samuel, *A Postcolonial Reading of Mark's Story*, 110-11. Samuel explains the liberative role of the anomalous beings in the discourse of community who faces socio-political upheavals.

[255] Samuel, *A Postcolonial Reading of Mark's Story*, 154. The Son of Man acts in the heavenly realms for the task of liberating the suffering Israel. This "anti-colonial native essentialist figure" is a divine-human hybrid who camouflages his essentialist identity. The following examples portray the Jewish discourses which originated in colonial contexts (Hellenistic and Roman). Book of Daniel pictures one like the son of humanity who receives dominion in heaven (Dan.7:13ff.) in the context of suffering under colonial powers, (114); the *Similitudes of Enoch* (1*Enoch* 31-71) depicts the Son of Humanity who appears to have many identities ('Righteous one', the 'Elect One,' the 'Messiah' and the man Enoch) and corporate figure of authority (heavenly-earthly and individual-corporate) executes judgment on Israel's enemies, (115-16). 4 Ezra 13 portrays a vision in which something like the figure of a 'Man' comes out of the sea, envisaging suffering and eschatological vindication for the suffering Israel (117).

[256] Samuel, *A Postcolonial Reading of Mark's Story*, 118-19.

the authority of the religio-political leaders, pronouncing forgiveness of sins (Mk.2: 1-12) and confronts the religio-political authority. In certain confronting places, Jesus camouflages his authority by affirming the popular identity of the Son of Humanity.[257] However, the authority of the Son of Humanity can be an imitation with a difference.[258] Moreover, "ironically, the Markan Jesus seems equally disturbing to the Roman colonialists and suffers colonial execution at their hands, which make him a postcolonial figure rather than an anti-or pro-colonial figure."[259]

The suffering as well as the rising Son of Humanity with the community 'on the way' (Mk.8:31-10:52) makes an established strategic space for the transcultural community which is an inclusive community.[260] The postcolonial dynamic of the suffering motif is given through the model of the suffering Son of Humanity who comes to serve and give his life which is against the invoking imperial agenda.[261] The Markan concept of suffering Son of Humanity challenges and potentially disturbs the Judaistic anti-colonial nationalist essentialist agenda of Jewish apocalypticism.[262] In addition, this suffering motif in Mark challenges the transcultural community to participate in the suffering Son of Humanity.

The last scene of the *Huios*-Jesus in Jerusalem temple city (11:1-16:8) challenges both the religious and political leaders of the time. His entry marks many conflicting issues with the religious leaders of the time. The Passover meal is considered to be a mimicry and covenant hybridization (Mk.14:17-26).[263] The trial and crucifixion of Jesus in Mark seems to be ambivalent to place its blame on the corrupt Jewish leaders and the Jerusalem crowd (Mk.15:12-15) instead on the colonial Rome.[264] The tearing apart of the temple curtain (Mk.15:38), the

[257] Samuel, *A Postcolonial Reading of Mark's Story*, 124. In the context of the healing of the paralytic, he identifies himself with the Son of Humanity who has authority to heal and forgive. Here Markan Jesus appropriates the authority but this authority extends to have divine status to forgive sins. The Son of Humanity changes his forms from human at times and at other times exercises divine power and authority.

[258] Samuel, *A Postcolonial Reading of Mark's Story*, 155. Jesus' authority is exercised in his acts of ritual aggression, his authoritarian travel to the north-south, the temple city with authority and power. In a colonial context, Jesus' authoritarian actions seem to disturb the Jewish nativism that indirectly supports the Roman colonial allies.

[259] Samuel, *A Postcolonial Reading of Mark's Story*, 155.

[260] Samuel, *A Postcolonial Reading of Mark's Story*, 128.

[261] Samuel, *A Postcolonial Reading of Mark's Story*, 157.

[262] Samuel, *A Postcolonial Reading of Mark's Story*, 156.

[263] Samuel, *A Postcolonial Reading of Mark's Story*, 144-45. The celebration of the Passover in the context of Jewish festival depicts the affiliation with its native religio-cultural tradition that it mimics certain aspects to hybridize the covenant (Ex.24:8).

[264] Samuel, *A Postcolonial Reading of Mark's Story*, 151-52. The relatively sympathetic treatment of the Roman soldiers in the trial scene is shown by carrying the cross by a passerby, avoiding the horror scene, the conduct of pretty quick crucifixion (Mk.15:24a) versus the ridiculing part is taken

cry of the Roman centurion (Mk.15:39) and the darkness over the whole land (Mk. 15:33) symbolize the disruption in the religious Jewish side but ambivalent in its acceptance from the political side.[265] However, the later position of Joseph of Arimathea portrays "postcolonial ambivalence and boundary crossing strategy of Mark."[266]

The portrayal of Jesus in terms of strategic essentialism is narrated by Mark in Jesus' affiliating and disrupting the native Jewish institutions, traditions, systems of power and discourses.[267] The ambivalent portrait of the Roman colonial position is pictured by the execution of Jesus but ironically points out to the confession of the Roman centurion as the Son of God.[268]

1.6.4.5 Critical Appraisal

The postcolonial model of Samuel is creative as well as applicable to a colonial context both ancient as well as the present. The model is brought out of two postcolonial theoretical leaders of our time-Spivak and Bhabha. Samuel's postcolonial reading of Mark's story of Jesus is a well constructed thesis that portrays the ambivalent position of *huios*-Jesus who plays the position of strategic essentialism and cultural hybridity. This is a challenge to the popular existing debate of either anti-or pro-colonial writing of the biblical text. Reading the story of Mark in the first century Roman-Judeo context also challenges the modern postcolonial critics like Sugirtharajah.[269] His notion of considering the Bible as a postcolonial discourse on the basis of its Asiatic origin and its proliferation under persecution in the Afrasian countries over against the understanding of the colonial nature of the biblical literature is very much radical to the present day understanding the Bible as either pro-or anti-colonial.[270]

The strategic essentialism and transcultural hybridity model offers a right solution to the decentralizing power centers by applying the theoretical concepts of mimicry, ambivalence and hybridity. A praxis-oriented theoretical study is possible for the present day readers who face colonial threats both from the religio-cultural fundamentalism and neocolonialism.

Samuel leaves out the implication part of the text for the present day audience who faces neocolonialism in its every day walk of life. In fact, the Greco-Roman colonial context of the first century will definitely help to understand the present day colonial context. The Indian subalterns who face various neocolonial

---

by the common passers, the chief priests, the scribes and the two crucified nationalist rebels (Mk.1: 29-32).

265 Samuel, *A Postcolonial Reading of Mark's Story*, 152.

266 Samuel, *A Postcolonial Reading of Mark's Story*, 153.

267 Samuel, *A Postcolonial Reading of Mark's Story*, 157.

268 Samuel, *A Postcolonial Reading of Mark's Story*, 157.

269 Samuel, *A Postcolonial Reading of Mark's Story*, 161.

270 Samuel, *A Postcolonial Reading of Mark's Story*, 13.

and the imperial marginalization in society are totally left out because he does not attempt to bring the two colonial contexts together for analysis which is a serious flaw in the study.

1.7 A Viable Model for a Postcolonial Reading of the Acts of the Apostles

A detailed theoretical analysis of Said, Spivak and Bhabha show the diversity of colonial representation as well as the multifarious theoretical tools used by them. Said's early model presents an all-encompassing system of Western domination over the orient without referring at all of the political resistance. However, Spivak and Bhabha reveal the resistant elements in colonial discourses. Above all Spivak brings both the elements of imperial domination as well as the colonial resistant voices of the subaltern women by challenging the authority of the master narratives and re-imaging the history of the subaltern women. Spivak's ethical paradigm shift for the third world subaltern women to challenge the Western feminist thought in the context of fixed categorization of gender, race or sexuality is called 'the strategic essentialism.' This self-identified context-specific strategy seems to be useful in evaluating the colonial situation of the first century Christian minority.

Joining with Bhabha, the present study tries to analyze the resistant voice of the colonized community in Acts from the interstitial space ('the third space') where the colonizer-colonized relationship is complex bordering on negotiation and resistance. The analysis of the biblical narratives exhibits the characteristics of mimetic, ambivalent and hybrid activity, because of their unique origin in the interstitial space. At the same time the discourses are imaginative, faith-centered, ficto-historical writing and popular colonial writing.[271] These discourses probably have the potential to empower the colonial subjects to disturb and challenge the authority.

The contributions of the postcolonial biblical interpreters are mainly focused to give liberation to the colonially marginalized both in the present and in the past. Their reading challenges the monologist Western interpretation of the Bible by locating the resistant voices. It focuses on multiple issues of the empire like diaspora, race, ethnicity and gender. The resistance and restorative model through contrapuntal reading of Sugirtharajah, the liberation and decolonization model of Segovia, the postcolonial subaltern reading of Joy and the strategic essentialism and transcultural hybridity of Samuel are the fundamental foci of the above mentioned biblical hermeneuticians.

The ancient colonial and imperial practices by the Hellenists or the Romans of biblical times had not been considered seriously for the current postcolonial studies because of the main attention on the modern European colonialism. For this, biblical scholars need to stretch "the ambit of this approach to include the discourses of biblical and postbiblical antiquity."[272] By doing so, scholars who

[271] Samuel, *A Postcolonial Reading of Mark's Story*, 33.

[272] Samuel, "Postcolonialism as a critical Practice," Part. II, 105.

practice the postcolonial approach in biblical studies have compared the socio-cultural formations of the biblical discourse into the pro-, anti- or postcolonial category of the ancient world with the modern colonial context.[273] Above all, the context of the origin of the New Testament discourse is the first century Greco-Roman colonial context. The anti-colonial nature of the first century majoritarian Christian discourse is well portrayed by the publications of Richard Horsley and others.[274] Similarly, it is probable that the majoritarian Christian community who lived in the third space must have strategically used the postcolonial theoretical concepts of mimicry, hybridity, ambivalence to resist the colonizers. The colonial domination however has been continually challenged by the majoritarian transcultural Christian hybrids by locating them at 'the third space of enunciation.'

Samuel applies the theoretical framework of 'strategic essentialism and transcultural hybridity' to read the gospel of Mark.[275] Therefore, there is no reason to exclude any biblical discourses and specifically the study of Acts of the Apostles by following the model of strategic essentialism and transcultural hybridity.[276] The overwhelming inescapable reality of the empire and colonialism has been reiterated by postcolonial biblical practitioners.[277] So, finding out the way of how the New Testament community responded towards the Roman colonial regime and the Jewish cultural nationalism would be a probable position that a student of the New Testament can take.

In the light of the previous study of Segovia, Samuel and Joy, the Acts of the Apostles also could be placed as a resistant literature of the early Christians who lived in a dual colonial subjection of both the Roman colonist and the native elite Jewish nationalists. It is surmised that the socio-political-religious and cultural factors must have influenced the first century as well as the present day Christian subalterns in their theological formulations. The researcher will examine these influences in the Acts of the Apostles by using the postcolonial theoretical concepts like mimicry, ambivalence and hybridity ('Strategic Essentialism' and

---

[273] Samuel, "Postcolonialism as a critical Practice" Part. II, 105.

[274] Horsley, *Jesus and Empire*; *idem*, *Paul and Empire*; *idem*, *Paul and Politics: Ekklesia, Israel, Imperium, Interpretation: Essays in Honor of Krister Stendahl* (Harrisburg: Trinity Press International, 2000); *idem* and N.A. Silberman, *The Message and the Kingdom: How Jesus and Paul Ignited a Revolution and Transformed the Ancient World* (New York: Grossett/Putnam, 1997); cf. Warren Carter, *John and Empire Initial Explorations*. New York: T & T Clark, 2008. *idem*, *Matthew and Empire*.

[275] Samuel, *A Postcolonial Reading of Mark*, 12. He finds that the Markan community faces dual colonial subjection of the Roman colonist and the native breed of elite Jewish nationalists (x).

[276] Samuel, "Postcolonialism as a critical Practice," I, 106.

[277] According to Brett, "there is no need to exclude the study of the ancient colonial relationships within which the bulk of biblical materials was produced- whether the colonizer was Egyptian, Assyrian, Babylonian, Persian, Hellenistic or Roman." Mark G. Brett, "The Ethics of Postcolonial Criticism," *Semeia* 75 (1996), 219.

'Transcultural Hybridity' model). The researcher will apply the postcolonial reading of the text to the Indian context in bringing both the cultural context together for the purpose of liberation of the marginalized.

Part 2

THE DISCURSIVE WORLD OF ACTS

Chapter 2

A Brief History of Roman Imperialism & Colonialism in the East

2.1 Introduction

The Acts of the Apostles needs to be studied in the backdrop of the colonial rule of the first century Rome. Roman emperors, the imperial cult, the imperial authorities (Cornelius, Agrippa I, Felix, Festus, Agrippa II, Caesar), the imperial culture (patron-client system, benefaction), the administrative centers (Caesarea and Rome) and the trial narrations give the multifaceted descriptions of the first century Rome under which the Christian community grew in the Greco-Roman world.

This chapter is intended to give a bird's-eye view of the historical development of the Roman imperial state that had become the world superpower and how they colonized the east. Certain questions need to be discussed to understand the discursive world of Acts. How the Roman emperors ruled over the vast empire which had varied socio cultural and religious-political affiliations? How did the Roman Empire colonize the eastern part of the empire, especially the Judea-Galilean part of the Mediterranean world with a varied political-religio-cultural milieu? How was power relations worked out in such a way that the civilized areas of the eastern part of the empire became ambivalent in its political responses?

2.1.1 A Brief History of the Roman Empire Expansion

The city of Rome as a single political unit began her national story from a small settlement in ca. 600 BCE in central peninsular Italy.[1] The pervasive idea of the Roman operation to expand its power over cities and peoples for the purpose of

[1] According to Goodman, the city of Rome was originally founded by the middle of the 8th century (753 BCE) by Romulus and Remus in central peninsular Italy out of a mixture of

building an empire was in the perception for long.[2] Meanwhile the Roman Senate was formed by the patricians (during V and IV BCE), and the agricultural land owners by persistent struggle both internal and external.[3] There were constant fights in order to keep the state from the neighboring threats form Etruscans, Celts, Latin confederates and the Greek world.[4] After a series of wars on earth and sea, Rome became economically progressive and wealthy.[5] At the same time, the consecutive wars made Rome to subdue the "restless and rebellious Greece" by the Macedonian wars (214-205, 200-197 and 171-167) and the Achean War (146 BCE), Phoenician city of Carthage in North Africa by Punic wars (264-241, 218-201, 149-146), Asia Minor by the Mithridatic wars (89-85; 73-66 BCE) and Judea-Palestine by Pompey's victory over the Seleucid dynasty.[6] Soon the imperialistic policy of adding newly acquired eastern territory to the Roman province became a new pattern for the future.[7]

The Roman hegemony started from Italy (270BCE), spreading her wings to the four corners of the earth ("from Spain to Syria and from Britain to North Africa.") from the western Mediterranean (Carthage 264-241 BCE and 218-201 BCE), Macedonia (defeat of Philip V 197 BCE) and Syria (Antiochus III of the Seleucid's empire).[8] This imperial unification was done under the colonial emperors from Augustus and his successors bringing more than fifty million populations under one umbrella.[9]

The Roman colonial expansion came to a watershed by the victorious campaign of Roman Governor General Pompey not only in terms of territorial

---

predominant monarchy combined with senate and assembly. Martin Goodman, *Rome and Jerusalem. The Clash of Ancient Civilizations* (New York: Vintage Books, 2007), 34.

[2] R.A. Horsley, "Jesus and Empire," *USQR* 59, 3/4 (2005), 54. The Roman civilization had its connection with the past history of ancient Troy (Virgil's *Aeneid*).

[3] Helmut Koester, *History, Culture, and Religion of the Hellenistic Age* (Philadelphia: Fortress Press, 1982), 283.

[4] Koester, *History, Culture, and Religion*, 284-85.

[5] The production of Roman silver coins in 270BCE shows Rome's economic progress and wealth. From the First Punic war (264-241 BCE), Rome started to build its own navy and ships. Koester, *History, Culture, and Religion*, 285.

[6] Koester, *History, Culture, and Religion*, 291; G.L. Thompson, "Roman East," in *DNTB*, edited by C.A. Evans & S.E. Porter (Leicester, England: IVP, 2000), 963-64.

[7] Koester, *History, Culture, and Religion*, 286; e.g., Sicily (241 BCE), Sardinia and Corsica (238BCE), Dyrrhachium (299BCE), Gallia Cisalpina (222 BCE) Dalmatia (219) and Carthage (146 BCE).

[8] Richard P. Saller, "Roman Empire," in *The Oxford Companion to the Bible*, edited by B.M.Metzger & M.D. Coogan (New York: Oxford University Press, 1993), 657. The four corners show "from Spain to Syria and from Britain to North Africa." S.R. F. Price, "Rituals and Power," in *Paul and Empire. Religion and Power in Roman Imperial Society*, edited by R.A. Horsley (Pennsylvania: Trinity Press International, 1997), 48.

[9] Saller, "Roman Empire," 657.

expansion but also in terms of the economic growth exploiting wealth and goods of the nations.[10] Strategically, the position of the Mediterranean Sea (*mare nostrum*, "our sea") became so important for the Roman administration that the great centers of the ancient world (Athens, Cyrene, Rome, Alexandria, Antioch, Constantinople and Palestine) became connected to one another through the great sea route for exploiting, military interventions and the connectivity between colonial centers.[11]

The political atmosphere of Rome changed to a total reign over the whole of the Mediterranean world through the reign of Octavian Augustus since the battle of Actium in 31 BCE.[12] He had created a utopian universal rule in the history of the Mediterranean world of pluralistic nations and cultures by synchronizing different political moorings to anticipate for an empire of peace and prosperity.[13] For this utopian world, the emperor appropriated "cultural renewal" forms that were familiar to the east with visual communications of temple structure (Apollo, Jupiter, Quirinus, Minerva etc).[14] The new building imageries promoted the colonial culture. The imperial policy was to subjugate those powerful nations as a majestic sovereign power with their military might (*JW* 5.366ff; 3.71-108) and it was proved in subjugating the Jewish revolutionaries (*JW* 3.104). In the west, the Roman imperial system adopted a cultural unification for which they constructed similar Roman type temples, theaters, and city gates, golden mile stones (20 BCE) to symbolize her positions, engraved coins and water systems.[15] The images of the empire were reflected through cultural and recreational amenities like gladiator shows, participated by plebs, the princeps, knights and senators in their official order carrying their imperial emblems of rank.[16]

After a complex process of political unification in terms of development in military strategy, socio-religio-cultural and constitutional realms, Rome as a world empire made a lasting significance in the world history.[17] A new imperial

[10] Horsley, *Jesus and Empire*, 19. "The bulk of the grain (and other food) imported to Rome was extracted from subject peoples, disproportionately from North Africa and Egypt, in the form of tribute and taxes in kind."

[11] M.I. Finley, *The Ancient Economy* (London: The Hogarth Press, 1985), 30.

[12] Goodman, *Rome and Jerusalem*, 35. At the battle of Actium, Octavian, the adopted son of Julius Caesar won over the rival power of the east (Mark Antony) and inaugurated a new era of the Roman Empire. Colin M. Wells, "Roman Empire," in *ABD*, vol. 5, edited by David Noel Freedman (New York: Doubleday, 1992), 801-06.

[13] P. Zanker, "The Power of Images," in *Paul and Empire. Religion and Power in Roman Imperial Society*, edited by R.A. Horsley (Pennsylvania: Trinity Press International, 1997), 86

[14] Zanker, "The Power of Images" 86.

[15] Zanker, "The Power of Images," 86.

[16] M. Griffin, "Urbs Roma, Plebs and Princeps," in *Images of the Empire*, edited by L. Alexander (Sheffield: JSOT Press, 1991), 44.

[17] S. Angus & A.M. Renwick, "Roman Empire and Christianity," in *The International Standard Bible Encyclopedia*, vol. 4 Q-Z, edited by Geoffrey W. Bromiley (Michigan: Wm. B. Eerdmans

administration was formed with full sovereignty resting with the emperor, who had the hegemonic and globalizing powers. The imperialistic nature of jurisdiction, law and nomenclature were forcefully imposed on the imperial subjects. However, on occasions, the Caesars offered secular position to the individual province like Palestine, concessions on military demands based on religious demands, and special privileges to the diaspora Jews explain the discursive nature of Roman domination and expansion.[18]

2.1.2 *Pax Romana* under Roman Empire

The Augustinian age is the starting point of the political era of *Pax Romana* to designate and propagate the imperial policies of the Roman Empire with profound peace from wars and battles.[19] The Latin name (*Pax Romana*) itself signifies the imperial influence over her colonial subjects. *Res Gestae* claims Caesar Augustus to be the architect of the ideal *Pax Romana*, which gained 'peace with victory' over land (Gaul, Spain and Germany) and seas (free from pirates), all over the world.[20] This phrase became a Roman cult sanctioned by the support of Greco-Roman religion where the King became the commander, judge and priest.[21] However, there were continuous wars at the provincial peripheries in the following two and half centuries for national freedom and socio-economic liberation. The consecutive wars in the eastern part of Rome show how winning 'peace with victory' became a military propaganda of the empire to slowly conquer the world with less military power.

First Century poets like Virgil (*Aeneid*) and historian Livy (*History*) acclaim high about the popular ideal of *Pax Romana*. Contrary to these false praises, there were writers like Tacitus (56-120 CE) who challenges the false claims of

---

Publishing Company, 1988), 208. The history, biography (early third century history of Cassius Dio, Suetonius' biographies of the 10 emperors); literature of Virgil and Horace; Ovid's poems; Augustus own description of his achievements (*Res Gestae*); Latin historical works (Annals of Tacitus); archaeological excavations (aqueducts, army camps); dedications, inscriptions, decrees, emperor speeches, certain official documents and coinage includes official imperial portraiture explain the historical background of the Roman empire. Wells, "Roman Empire," 802. Virgil "to build civilization upon a foundation of peace, to spare the conquered and destroy proud aggressors," (*Aen* 6.852-853) cited by Wells, "Roman Empire," 803.

[18] Smallwood, *The Jews under Roman Rule*, 38-43.

[19] N. Lewis & M. Reinhold, eds., *Roman Civilization. Source Book II: The Empire* (New York: Harper & Row, 1966), 80; J.E. Bowley, "Pax Romana," in *DNTB*, edited by C.A. Evans & S.E. Porter (Leicester, England: IVP, 2000), 771.

[20] *Res Gestae Divi Augusti*, describes Augustus' administrative power (para. 1-14), his expenditure for public purposes (para. 15-24) and his great valour for winning the war with peace (para. 25-35) cited by Lewis & Reinhold, *Roman Civilization*, 9-19; Bowley, "Pax Romana," *DNTB*, 722. An altar to the Peace of Augustus was built for the combined political and religious celebration on the Campus Martius. Augustus claimed to conquer nations for bringing peace. It may be similar to the present day Western nations' mediatory role in fighting for other nations.

[21] Lewis & Reinhold, *Roman Civilization*, 103; Bowley, "Pax Romana," *DNTB*, 771.

the imperial propaganda and exposed the evil face of it by showing the reality of murder, ravaging the country in warfare and profit making business (*Ann.* 12.33; *Agric.* 30.7).[22]

When the imperial center enjoyed military-imposed peace and prosperity in terms of gymnasia, gateways, temples and festivity all through the year declaring the prosperity of the empire, the frontiers of the empire mainly the eastern part of Roman provinces including Judea bled with war and slavery. The abusive nature of the governors, proconsuls, procurator, and the client kings in the Roman provinces help the readers to know the negative experiences of the ideal of *Pax Romana* in despotic administration to safeguard their jurisdiction. Josephus records the provocations from the part of the Roman administrators (governors, clients and emperors) who led the Jewish nationalists to political resistance (*JW* 2.41, 84-92, 169-77, 184, 245-46, 272-77). Schuürer in writing the history of the Jewish people points out the ineffectiveness of the governors that led to the political failure resulting in the Jewish-Roman war.[23]

Under the guise of *Pax Romana,* Rome extracted tribute and land wealth from the imperial colonies for the purpose of military support.[24] The abundant economic resources in different parts of the empire through agriculture, mining (copper, gold and silver) and trade promoted the imperial peace irrespective of the working source of the slave trade in the empire.[25]

The Romans established and preserved *Pax Romana* by terror and forceful persuasion through military, socio-cultural means or by giving vivid lessons to the subject peoples of the consequences if they oppose Roman rule, i.e., in delaying payment of taxes or mild political resistances.[26] The violently conquered Roman colonies were ruled by force, imposing 'peace with bloodshed' (*Ann.*1.10.4), with continuous war with the dissents on the frontiers.[27] The resistant Jewish subjects were brought under the imperial jurisdiction of *Pax Romana* by creating terror in the hearts of the people by slaughter, enslavement and crucifixions.[28]

---

[22] Bowley, "Pax Romana," *DNTB,* 773. Tacitus explains the Roman military power (*Ann.* 3.60). Cicero reveals the bemoaning face of the colonial subjects and the incensed kings in the provinces (*Verr.* 2.3.207). 'O Roman, to rule the nations with your power… to crown peace with law, to spare the humbled and to tame in war the proud,' (Virgil, *Aen.* VI. 851-3).

[23] E. Schürer, *The History of Jewish People in the Age of Jesus Christ,* vol. 1, edited by G. Vermes, et.al (Peabody: Hendrickson, 1998), 356-57.

[24] Horsley, *Jesus and Empire,* 34.

[25] Lewis & Reinhold, *Roman Civilization,* 157.

[26] R.A. Horsley, *Jesus and the Spiral of Violence. Popular Jewish Resistance in Roman Palestine* (San Francisco: Harper and Row, 1987), 43-44. Cassius "extracted seven hundred talents of silver," some were sold as slaves and four towns were reduced to slavery (*Ant.* 14.272-275; *JW* 1.219-220).

[27] R. Bauckham, "The Economic Critique of Rome in Revelation 18," in *Images of the Empire,* edited by Loveday Alexander (Sheffield: Sheffield Academic Press, 1991), 57.

[28] Horsley, *Jesus and the Spiral of Violence,* 44; Klaus Wengst, *Pax Romana and the Peace of Jesus Christ,* translated by J. Bowden (Philadelphia: Fortress Press, 1987), 11.

Religion was used as a tool by Rome to propagate the imperial sovereignty as destined by gods. Imperial peace was maintained under the guise of *Pax Romana* and the same was legitimized on the pretext of divinity of the emperor, who was the saviour and bringer of abundant blessings.[29] It is probable that the successive Roman emperors used the same policies to exploit the divine concepts to propagate their imperial governance to maintain security and peace over the nations.[30]

The ideology of *Pax Romana* had been politically motivated for the peace in the pretext of taxes and tributes for security and freedom from the outside threat on the basis of military dominance.[31] Josephus says that 'the nobility of the east enslaves under the pretext of peace' (*JW* 2.379). The economic provincial exploitation made benefits in terms of infrastructure, temples, marble palaces for the nobles, aqueducts, streets and bridges (*Res Gestae,* 19-21). The urbanized civilization under *Pax Romana* brought through marble temples, colonnades, "better sanitation, medicine, education, irrigation, public health, roads, freshwater system, baths and public order."[32] The imperial legal system was formulated within the judiciary system as a part of imperial peace, where monopoly and money ruled the Roman upper classes.[33] There were vivid descriptions of the policy of victory and subjection by imprinting different portrayals of victory images on Roman coins which explain the motto 'War, victory and peace,' for the Romans and for non-Romans servitude.[34]

This probably is the context where Luke describes of the spread of the Christian community with a counter imperial culture (eg. salvation through Jesus; peace through Jesus Christ; Ac. 5:31; 10:36; 13:23) of discursively disrupting

---

[29] The imperial cult probably started in the time of Augustus, as he was associated with the goddess Pax and also as he constructed a temple in honour of the Roman Empire (*Ara Pacis Augustae*). The goddess was considered to be the embodiment of security and peace, Bowley, "Pax Romana," *DNTB,* 774; Wengst, *Pax Romana,* 9. The emperors (Flavian) were considered as the manifestations gods (eg.Jupiter) on the earth to receive their favours. Warren Carter, *Matthew and the Margins. A Sociopolitical and Religious Reading* (Bangalore: Theological Publications in India, 2007), 40.

[30] Bowley, "Pax Romana," *DNTB,* 774. The *Temple Pacis* ('Peace Temple') built by Emperor Vespasian in 75 CE probably to celebrate the 'peace with victory' of the great triumph over the Jewish resistive forces in Palestine (cf.Pliny *Nat.Hist.*36.102). Josephus called this as the 'temple of peace' (*JW* 7.158).

[31] Wengst, *Pax Romana,* 19-22, 30.

[32] K. Brannigen, "Images-or Mirages-of Empire," in *Images of Empire,* edited by L. Alexander (JSOT Sup.122; Sheffield: Sheffield Academic Press, 1991), 105; Wengst, *Pax Romana,* 28, 41.

[33] Wengst *Pax Romana,* 37-39. Wengst gives examples for the irregularity in the legal system (eg. Pliny's reports, *Epistles III,* 4,7).

[34] The inscription of the Roman coins like the war god *Mars Victor,* Victoria in different posture (standing on the globe, on the hand of goddess Roma), and emperor Octavian in military attire, Wengst, *Pax Romana,* 11-12, 24. The relationship between peace and military power, refer *Res Gestae,* 26.

the imperial *Pax Romana.*[35] The powerless early Christian community must have carved a space in-between the dominant Greco-Roman military, political and cultural context and the relatively dominant native Jewish religio-cultural nationalistic context.

2.1.3 The Roman Imperial Governing Class and the Elites

In the process of political expansion of the Roman Empire, the senators and equestrians were considered to be the nobility of Rome based on their wealth and property. They naturally become the legates and proconsuls, prefects and procurators. They simultaneously turned out to be the rich colonials by collecting taxes and by maintaining political relationship with the center.[36] When the Romans conquered the eastern part of the empire, the democratic form of the Hellenistic polis was transferred to the government, and over to the propertied class of local council (βουλη) as they were embodied with "legislative and executive power."[37]

In the newly conquered lands, the provincial representation of the Roman Empire was administered by a Governor appointee to look after the administrative and military affairs.[38] The Governorship had links with the Roman businessmen and lease holders, with the intention of exploitation and extortion. There was unrest among the Roman provinces due to the despotic and corrupt nature of the Roman governors. The peace of the state was threatened due to the exploitative motive of the Roman Empire over the provinces and the elative position of the equestrians.[39] Similarly, the imperialist leaders gained power over the senate by their organizing tactics, military valor and administrative skills. Thus, there were dictators and 'divine' leaders during the Roman imperialism. However, the intellectual Jewish as well the Greco-Roman literary elites responded to the Roman imperium and colonialism discursively.[40]

---

[35] Wengst maintains that Luke disrupts the *Pax Romana* while adopting the imperial language, *Pax Romana*, 89-105, 137.

[36] J.M. Arlandson, *Women, Class and Society in Early Christianity. Models from Luke Acts* (Massachusetts: Hendrickson Publishers, 1997), 24.

[37] Arlandson, *Women, Class and Society*, 25. The governmental body of the Greek council consists of the local council of boulh and bouleeutai of wealthy land owners and the popular assembly (ἐκκλησια) consists of public assembly (δημος). For eg., the Governor of Syria (57-55 BCE) "reconstituted the civil administration under an aristocracy" (*JW* 1.167; *Ant.* 14.89-93), (25; FN.45).

[38] Koester, *History, Culture, and Religion*, 286. The governor appointee has the power to administration of taxes and military and the office has the power to publish his administrative policies.

[39] koester, *History, Culture, and Religion*, 294.

[40] For example, Rome's supremacy and her territorial accomplishments were praised (Vergil's *Aeneid*; Horace, *Ovid and prose*, (*Livy* 1.16.7); Strabo, and Philo (Embassy). Gilbert, "List of Nations in Acts 2," 511.

2.1.4 Roman Imperial Domination in the East

The defeat of Carthage by the end of the third century BCE made Rome as one of the super powers in the western Mediterranean,[41] and then slowly it extended its power towards the east by attacking the Macedonian kingdom along with its Greek allies (Achaean City league) in 146 BCE.[42] By destroying the classical Greek cities like Corinth, Romans moved in the eastern direction of Asia Minor, which had weakened the economy of the Greek peoples due to the financial support given for periodic expeditions.[43] The Roman general Pompey made use of the squabbles of the rulers of the east to make his power supreme over the Seleucid dynasty and thus Syria became a Roman province.[44] By the middle of the first century BCE, "the Roman warlords finally took decisive military action, on an unprecedented scale, to expand and consolidate Rome's imperium in the east."[45]

Strategically, Pompey increased the military forces in the east keeping his eye on Pontus, Syria and Judea.[46] He was able to solve three serious problems that the Roman senate was unable to solve-the problem from the pirates in the eastern Mediterranean, the separate Iberian state and the war threat from the east (Mithridates).[47] The great victory over the Mithridates gave Pompey great honor both in the west and east. He had a triumphant victory over the eastern Mediterranean world (Syria and Palestine) and became the savior and benefactor of the east.[48] A universal dominion was achieved by his operation in the east that brought not only the geographical expansion but also the economic inflow to Rome.[49]

2.1.5 The Strategic Assimilation and Rejection of Cultures in the East

The eastward expansion of the Roman Empire was tactfully slow and steady (Macedonia-Achaia, Asia Minor, Syria, and Egypt). Moreover, the Greek culture

---

[41] Horsley, *Jesus and Empire*, 17.

[42] Horsley, *Jesus and Empire*, 18.

[43] Horsley, *Jesus and Empire*, 18.

[44] J. Stambaugh and D. Balch, *The Social World of the First Christians* (London: SPCK, 1986), 21. The aggressive Seleucids under Antiochus III (223-187 BCE) extended its empire to certain parts of India.

[45] Horsley, *Jesus and Empire*, 18.

[46] Horsley, *Jesus and Empire*, 18.

[47] Koester, *History, Culture, and Religion*, 296-97. Both the West and the Eastern Mediterranean sea piracy came under the control of Pompey with in hundred days.

[48] Koester, *History, Culture, and Religion*, 297-98. Pompey settled the conflicts between the two Hasmonian brothers by appointing Hyrcanus as high priest. He was able to impose certain negotiated agreements with client kingdoms in the surrounding areas of Syria- Judea-Antipator; east of Jordan-Nabataean Arabs; frontier of Euphrates with Commagene and Armenia. Stambaugh and Balch, *The Social World of the First Christians,* 15-16.

[49] Horsley, *Jesus and Empire*, 18.

that enveloped the whole Mediterranean kingdom also was strategically absorbed into the one political imperial regime.[50] As a matter of political strategy, the hegemony of Roman imperialism over the eastern part of the Hellenized culture was made by adoption, inculturation and wiping out some other superior civilizations (eg. Carthage and Etruria).[51] The economic value of the eastern empire was kept reserve in as a profitable strategic location for Rome which they looted through taxes, tithes and tribute.

In certain occasions, Rome terrorized the subjected people through the "practice of crucifixion, mass slaughter and enslavement, massacres of whole town and annihilation of whole peoples."[52]

The imperial power relations were reflected in multiple manifestations of patronage, priesthood and power in different Roman provinces of the first century world.[53] The imperial honors, temples, festivals and sacrifices became part of the traditional custom of honor given to gods.[54] "The visual expressions of the emperor were incorporated into the regular life of the communities through public celebrations."[55] Roman supremacy was displayed through the statue of Augustus, and goddess Roma who appeared astride a globe, also in inscriptions, statues and public maps.[56] In addition to these strategic tools, to promote the political ideology of universal rule, the listing of nations (cf.Ac.2:9-11) may have been used by the Roman emperors and monarchs.[57]

The Roman warlords conquered the eastern part of the empire and controlled the states by appointing client kings of local origin. They exploited their revenues

---

[50] Charles B. Puskas, *An Introduction to the New Testament* (Peabody: Hendrickson, 1989), 6. The eastward expansion of the Roman Empire goes like this-Macedonia-Achaia in 148 BCE, Asia in 133 BC, Syria in 64 BC, and Egypt in 30BC. 'The imperial temple (Ό σεβάστος ναός) constructed in the first century in different parts including many cities of Asia Minor extol Rome's universal rule (dedicatory inscriptions to the θεοὶ σεβαστοι). Gilbert, "List of Nations in Acts 2," 516.

[51] Goodman, *Rome and Jerusalem*, 35. Rome adopted the hybrid culture by adopting the superior Greek culture in terms of "art, architecture, literature and philosophy." The Roman imperialism has been done by destroying Greek cities (Corinth and Lucius Mummius in 146 BCE), looting, bringing the attractive Greek objects of art and ideas in the Roman center for display. Angus & Renwick, "Roman Empire and Christianity," 210.

[52] Horsley, *Jesus and Empire*, 28. In 4 BCE, the Roman general Varus crucified about two thousand men (*JW* 2.71-76; *Ant.* 17.295). Roman governors Felix (52-60) and Festus (60-62) crucified large number of brigands (*JW* 2.253, 271).

[53] Horsley, ed., *Paul and Empire*, 4.

[54] Price, "Rituals and Power," 49. Emperor statues were erected beside the traditional gods in the temples.

[55] Price, "Rituals and Power," 49. The rich culture of imperial cult in Asia Minor is discovered through temples and coins.

[56] Gilbert, "List of Nations in Acts 2," 513.

[57] Inscription of 46 names over the victory of Alpine nations by Augustus (Pliny, *Nat.Hist* 3.136-37; 7.98). Gilbert, "List of Nations in Acts 2," 513.

in long distant resistant jurisdiction by way of the tax system.[58] Similar to the earlier empires (Ptolemaic and Seleucid), the Romans continued to keep "the temple-state as an instrument of imperial rule," and made the peasantry specially to be in debt and impoverishment.[59] The eastern judicial political tower was located in Syria by a Roman governor general to administer the eastern provinces (Judea, Egypt and Africa).[60]

2.2 Roman Emperors and their Colonial Strategy

Emperor Augustus prepared the ground for the later emperors' autocratic reign from the republican order of rule. It seems Julius Caesar is the architect and Augustus Caesar is the founder of Roman colonialism. The emperor cult became popular and Augustus became a semi god whose words became the last word. In the hierarchical structure, the Senate of Rome became a supporting agent in terms of administration and judiciary.[61] The praetors, councils and the governor of a province held *imeprium* which gave authority to administer laws including command in war and death penalty.[62]

2.2.1 Gaius Julius Caesar (64-44 BCE)

The Roman Empire began to formulate itself in power in the context of civil wars, when Julius Caesar was appointed as *pontifex maximus*, a highly respected life-long office in the Roman state in 64 BCE.[63] This post included the supervision over the religious aspects of life in the state. In the beginning of his reign, along with Pompey and Crassus he formed a Triumvirate to strengthen the existent political institution. Later he disintegrated the triumvirate with the aim of a dictatorial ruling and he quieted all uprisings with his autonomous power. However, his rally for conquering new territories like Gaul (58-51 BCE) gave some setback at home.

Julius Caesar had the political vision of a universal empire of merging the heterogeneous cultures and populations with Roman citizenship.[64] He showed interest in planting provisional colonies with a military motif of building an

---

[58] Horsley, "Jesus and Empire," 55.

[59] Horsley, "Jesus and Empire," 55-56. The client kings collaborate with the priestly aristocracy which made the diplomatic function of the Roman imperialism over the temple state.

[60] Wells, "Roman Empire," 803. The provinces of Egypt and Africa were made the close supervision of the emperor because of its food resource.

[61] Wells, "Roman Empire," 803.

[62] Wells, "Roman Empire," 804.

[63] Koester, *History, Culture, and Religion*, 298. There were allegations against Julius Caesar's moral life and he was accused of a secret plot in the Catiline conspiracy (an attempt in usurping power, Catiline made a bloody suppression).

[64] Angus & Renwick, "Roman Empire and Christianity," 208. Cultural imperialism had started working in his reign by dedicating temples in his honor and recognizing him as a 'demigod'.

empire under his rule.[65] Greece and Asia Minor accepted the cultic veneration of the ruler as divine for the great victories of Caesar seemed to have been not well accepted by the Roman republic.[66] Building up an international commonwealth of nations around the Roman Empire and by uniting with the ancient cultural centers of Mesopotamia, Persia and India along with Slavic and Germanic peoples (Southern Russia and central Europe), Caesar led a military campaign in the east and planned a campaign in the west also.[67] By foreseeing the threat of the invisible king and god, the republican opponents assassinated Caesar in 44 BCE.[68]

2.2.2 Octavian Caesar Augustus (44 BCE-14 CE)

The political significance of Rome skyrocketed after Augustus' endeavour of developing it as the capital of the empire for administrative purposes.[69] He tactfully played a war of national patriotism that finally gave him victory by the defeat of Antony at Actium (31 BCE), and he incorporated Egypt as a Roman province.[70] Along with the elated divine status, he developed certain administrative changes to concentrate authority in him through military power. He also got the control over the senate.[71] He was clever enough to avoid his craving for autonomy by legitimizing his actions, by restoring and incorporating the *Republica* and Republican institutions.[72]

The new period of the 'principate' was inaugurated by Augustus who is considered to be the architect of the Roman Empire.[73] He broadened its base by strategically planting veteran colonies in the eastern part of the empire (Corinth, Alexandira, Troas) for economic gains of the center in exclusion or

[65] He adopted the vision of colonial expansion from the Roman generals who sent war veterans into the defeated provinces as a reward to inherit the land and citizenship. Samuel, *Postcolonial Reading of Mark's Story*, 56.

[66] Koester, *History, Culture, and Religion*, 300.

[67] Koester, *History, Culture, and Religion*, 300. By this universal hope in mind, Caesar gave certain concessions in certain period to Jews in the east.

[68] Koester, *History, Culture, and Religion*, 300.

[69] Andrew D. Clarke, "Rome and Italy," in *The Book of Acts in its Graeco-Roman Setting*, vol. 2, edited by David W.J. Gill and Cornad Gempf (Grand Rapids, Michigan: Wm. B. Eerdmans Publishing Company, 1994), 456.

[70] Octavian was conferred the title "Augustus" in 27 BCE for his foundation on "divine law as well as his *felicitas.*" From this time on "the victorious heir of Caesar was known by the name of *Imperator Caesar divi filius Augustus.*" Koester, *History, Culture, and Religion*, 304.

[71] Koester, *History, Culture, and Religion*, 304. The new development gave power over the financial administration, grain supply and imperial roads.

[72] Saller, "Roman Empire," 657.

[73] Stambaugh and Balch, *The Social World of the First Christians*, 16. Octavian's title *princeps* ('first man') gave him the new period from Republic to Principate and it was considered to be the first of the Roman emperor.

by integration of the native cultures.[74] The Roman senate conferred him with three large provinces (Gaul, Spain and Syria), including the power of the armed forces.[75] The link between the emperor and the Roman religion made Augustus the mediator between the imperial citizens and the traditionally venerated ancient Roman gods.[76]

During Augustus' reign, the border of the empire had widened to the north-east-south with secure borders.[77] He was considered to be the saviour and a benefactor of peace (*Pax Augusta*) to all. Prosperity reigned as the unrest built due to civil war over the years came to an end. The emperor's birthday became known as the beginning of the 'good news' (εὐαγγελιον) due to a famous calendar decree of 9 BCE.[78]

Augustus made use of the opportunity for the political downfall of the Republic, where the unrest, civil wars and domestic power struggles assumed the role of *princeps* for revamping the collapsed institutions and structures. He strategically charted the new emperor status with the plan of building up Rome as the 'first city' with magnificent building projects and temples (*Divus Julius and Arcus Augusti*).[79] These building projects were done by the enormous wealth collected through tax revenues.

2.2.3 Tiberius (14-37 CE)

The imperial policies and appointees (Pontius Pilate as Governor of Judea *Ant.*18.35) in the eastern provinces had shown Tiberius' political diplomacy. In contrast to the earlier emperor, Tiberius was least bothered of the divine honors and he tried to give higher position to the office of the *princeps*. However, the title *divus* appeared on a denarius of Tiberius and a papyrus from 37 CE called him

[74] Samuel, *Postcolonial Reading of Mark's Story*, 57-58. Augustinian integration of cultures was made by mutual adoption of Greco-Roman clothing, learning Greek rhetoric and grammar.

[75] Charlesworth, *The Roman Empire,* 11. Augustus instituted a professional army in line with the modern terms with set terms of service.

[76] Charlesworth, *The Roman Empire*, 13-14.

[77] Koester, *History, Culture, and Religion*, 306. The northern border extended as far as Danube, Asia Minor provinces and Palestine on the east, Egypt and Africa as the southern frontier.

[78] H. Josef Klauck, "The Roman Empire," in *The Cambridge History of Christianity: Origins to Constantine,* edited by Margaret M. Mitchel and Frances M. Young, vol. 1 (Cambridge: Cambridge University Press, 2006), 70.

[79] Clarke, "Rome and Italy," 458-59. *Divus Julius eastern* and *Arcus Augusti* were two commemorating marks for the achievement and reputation of the two emperors (Julius and Augustus Caesar). Augustinian census has been introduced (Lk.2:2; eg. Judea, Cappadocia and Dacia) for the purpose of getting the accurate information from the provincial subjects for imposing direct taxes *(tributum soli and the tributum capitus).* D.W.J. Gill, "Taxation, Greco-Roman," in *DNTB,* edited by C.A. Evans & S.E. Porter (Leicester, England: IVP, 2000), 1160.

"son of god." It showed the trickery in his political position as an emperor.[80] He was the emperor during the earthly ministry of Jesus (Lk. 3:1). During Tiberius' reign, the state power was in the hands of the power mongers, like in the case of praetorian prefect Sejanus who was anti-Jewish in his legal policy.

2.2.4 Gaius Caligula (37-41 CE)

Son of Claudius and the nicknamed Caligula came to power in Rome because of the unclaimed succession from the previous emperor. The catastrophic nature of the attributed divinity to the emperor gave way to think Caligula as an incarnation of Jupiter. He also ordered his statue to be erected all over the empire (eg. Militus and Rome) including the synagogues of Alexandria and in the temple of Jerusalem he attempted to convert the temple into a shrine of the imperial cult (*Ant.*18.261ff; *JW* 2.184ff).[81] There were wide protests against his over possessed divine insanity and it made the Alexandrian Jews to send delegates to Rome under the leadership of Philosopher Philo. Finally, the emperor was killed by an imperial guard (*JW* 2.204; *Ant.*19.110).[82]

According to Taylor, Christian eschatological discourse was formulated in the context of Caligula crisis (cf. Mk.13:14-18) and in the context of Jewish-Roman conflict.[83] However, a Jewish mass slaughter was avoided by the wise intervention of Petronius, the legate of Syria (*JW* 2.204, *Ant.*19.110).[84] Caligula's outrageous provocation probably precipitated in the escalation of the catastrophic Jewish-Roman war.

2.2.5 Claudius (41-54 CE)

Claudius, "a grandson of Augustus Livia," a learned historian, a legal expert, administrator, happened to be the next heir on the throne by chance (*Ant.*19.36).[85] However, he managed to receive many credits by restructuring the "imperial house," master-planning an administrative structure with different departments for petitions, treasury and archival; reforming financial administration, citizenship

---

[80] Donald L. Jones, "Roman Imperial Cult," in *ABD*, vol. 5, edited by David Noel Freedman (New York: Doubleday, 1992), 806.

[81] Koester, *History, Culture, and Religion*, 310. Stambaugh and Balch, *The Social World of the First Christians*, 27.

[82] Smallwood, *The Jews under Roman Rule*, 236-46.

[83] N.H. Taylor, "Palestine Christianity and the Caligula Crisis. Part II. The Markan Eschatological Discourse," *JSNT* 62 (1996), 18.

[84] Smallwood, *The Jews under Roman Rule*, 175-180. The Jewish religious and nationalistic feeling aroused outrageous response from the Galilean Jews even to the extend of giving their lives (*JW* 2.187, 192) and a peasant strike of neglecting the grain harvest made Caligula to drop the project (*JW* 2.202-03).

[85] Koester, *History, Culture, and Religion*, 310.

and religious matters.[86] In external politics, he brought back the direct Roman administration over the provinces which were given over to the vassal kings by the previous emperor.[87] His personal life however, made him to be a victim of his future, specially his marriage with Agrippina, a sister of Caligula.

During Claudius principate, the Roman diaspora Jews were exterminated (49CE?) from the capital of the Roman Empire (Dio Cassius *Hist.* 60.6.6; Ac.18:2). The reason behind the expulsion of the whole Jewish race is unclear; whether it was with a sense of justice or due to some local disturbances in the city or a disciplinary action of the Christian preaching and proselytism or the anti-Semitic feeling started by Sejanus (*JW* 2.463; 6.427; 7.45).[88] However, the Jewish expulsion exhibits the imperial attitude of Claudius of his annoyance over against his exclusive imperialistic feelings.[89] The Jews all over the empire were under surveillance irrespective of their position in the empire. He permitted "the erection of statues to himself and his family through out the city."[90] His imperialistic nature was exhibited through the promotion of the imperial cult and the stamped coin with his image.[91] He was not tolerant enough to accommodate other religious sects which do not heed to the cultural imposition of imperial cult and deification.

2.2.6 Nero (54-68 CE)

Tiberius Claudius Nero, son of Agrippina and the adopted son of Claudius became the next emperor who started his reign with great popularity in reforming the administration. He appointed able governors, easing the tax burden and provided food security to the subjects (Tacitus *Ann.* 13.50-52; Suetonius *Nero* 10-19). As a countering administrative strategy, he started his reign as a new era of happiness, tenderness and clemency of the sovereign.[92] The senate authority was acknowledged and re-established in the Republican tradition. Quite fascinated by the Greek civilization, he introduced athleticism, gymnasium and artistic exhibitions in Rome (57-61 CE).[93] He became despotic in later years due to his passion for greatness and popularity. Later he left the governance in the hands

---

[86] Koester, *History, Culture, and Religion*, 310-11. One of the departments is "a chancellory for military and political affairs."

[87] Koester, *History, Culture, and Religion*, 311. Claudius declared Judea and Samaria as imperial province after the death of Agrippa in 44 CE.

[88] Smallwood, *The Jews under Roman Rule*, 201-210.

[89] Smallwood, *The Jews under Roman Rule*, 210-216. Christianity was considered in the early days in the eyes of the Roman rulers as a heretical Jewish sect.

[90] Jones "Roman Imperial Cult," 806.

[91] Stambaugh and Balch, *The Social World of the First Christians*, 27.

[92] S.A. Cook, F.E. Adcock and M.P. Charlesworth, eds., *The Cambridge Ancient History, vol. X, The Augustan Empire 44 BC-AD.70* (Cambridge: Cambridge University Press, [1934], 1985), 704.

[93] Cook, et al., *The Cambridge Ancient History*, 717-18.

of his advisor Seneca, who was a Stoic philosopher and Barrus.[94] The moral corruption and perversion of his personality not only destroyed his close family members but also the kingdom itself.[95] The imperial tyranny had gone about by spending the wealth of the empire for recreational purposes in building theaters and clubs (*Ann.* 14.16; 15.2-5; Suetonius, *Nero* 52; *JW* 2.250-51).

Nero's despotic nature is engraved in history for purportedly burning the city of Rome (64 CE) for the selfish motive of rebuilding the city according to his plan.[96] In addition to the heavy budget for rebuilding the city, he also lavishly spent for a new imperial palace.[97] The Neronian persecution of the minority Christians in Rome (*Ann.*15.38-44; Suetonius, *Nero* 16, 38; *Nat.*17.1.5) had gone to the extent of redirecting the accusation of the public towards the marginalized.[98] They were accused of being incendiaries and were brutally punished by throwing to the beasts in the amphitheatres, fasten on crosses, lighted as lamps in the imperial gardens and circus (*Ann*, 15.44), which probably led to the Christian apocalyptic literature.[99] The way by which the Roman emperor brutally suppressed the Jewish war (66-70 CE) clearly portrays the imperial attitude of the center over against the margins.

The Neronian imperialism continued to reign by depicting him as a deified emperor (eg. coins in Asia Minor), recognized by different deities (Zeus, Hercules/Apollo, Helios) 'god' with radiate crown (65 CE).[100] The Jewish resistance against the looting of the temple treasury and market (*JW* 2.305f.) resulted in arrest and crucifixions. Simultaneously, cultural nationalism steadily grew to have power over the temple and the fortresses in Masada. The Jews stopped sacrifices for Rome and the *princeps* (*JW* 2.409), which seemed to have finally led to the Great War by the Romans (66-70 CE). The Jewish nation had to surrender over against Vespasian and his sixty thousand troops (*JW* 3.64-69). The final programme was

---

[94] Koester, *History, Culture, and Religion*, 312. Barrus was a financial expert who led the financial affairs of Nero during his first year.

[95] As a result of Nero's suspicion on the way to his future career made him to kill his step brother (Britannicus) and his own mother Agrippina, once she was recognized as *Augusta Mater Augusti*. He murdered all the members of the imperial family based on a threat of conspiracy for his life. Several close friends and advisors took their life by themselves (Seneca, Petronius-Nero's advisor and poet Lucan) because of the threat of life. Koester, *History, Culture, and Religion*, 312-13.

[96] On 18 July, 64 CE a furious fire raged in the city of Rome for nine days followed by robbery and crime while Nero was in his holyday trip to Antium. Cook et al., *The Cambridge Ancient History*, 722-23.

[97] Cook et al., *The Cambridge Ancient History*, 723.

[98] Cook et al., *The Cambridge Ancient History*, 725.

[99] Cook et al., *The Cambridge Ancient History*, 725-26. Tertullian reports about the persecution of Nero as the *institutum Neronianum* (190 CE; *To the Gentiles* 1.7.8-9) cited by Paul McKechnie, *The First Christian Centuries. Perspectives on the Early Church* (England: Apollos, IVP, 2001), 61.

[100] Jones "Roman Imperial Cult," 807. On coins Nero was inscribed as Herculi Augusto. Cook et al., *The Cambridge Ancient History*, 732.

entrusted to Titus, his elder son who burned down the Temple (*JW* 6.252) and its gates (*JW* 6.220-228).

The end of Nero was sad because he had to flee and commit suicide because of political crisis. Twenty-seven year old Galba, the governor of Spain took the place of Nero as his successor.

2.2.7 Galba, Otho, Vitellius and Vespasian (69-79 CE)

Witnessing successive three emperors in one year with bloodshed and open rebellion claiming the emperor's office explains the fight for political power among the Flavian dynasty. Finally, T. Flavian Vespasianus took the post of emperorship with his long plan to siege Jerusalem. Having given the responsibility of Jewish war to his son Titus in Egypt, with four legions, he left for Rome to confront Vitellius. He settled some household problems in Rome, but finances were ruined because of the subsequent wars for emperorship, civil war and insurrections in different parts of the empire (Gaul and Jerusalem).[101] As soon as he came to power, he concentrated on building the political infrastructure in Rome (Suetonius, *Vespasian* 9-10, 17-19; Dio Cassius, *Hist.*65.10), which strengthened the senate. He was serious in the administrative process. He also continued the imperial cult by dedicating a temple to Claudius and he was called 'Lord' (κυρίος).[102]

2.2.8 Titus (79-81 CE) and Domitian (81-96 CE)

Emperor Titus cannot be erased from the memory of Roman history as his imperial victory in destroying a great nation and her religious cultural heritage centered on the Jerusalem temple in 70 CE. By this time the Jewish-Roman war was settled by Titus by the conquest of Jerusalem (*JW* 4.486-502, 545-555; 4.588-663). His great victory over Jews was exhibited through the victory parade over the streets of Rome displaying the prisoners with the spoils from the Temple.[103] Titus' two years emperorship was known for various catastrophes including a major fire in Rome (80CE), and a serious plague in the capital wiped so many lives.[104]

Nero's brother Domitian continued the rebuilding programme of the ruined city of Rome, strengthened the administration by consolidating the civil service, when both upper and lower Germany came under Rome and completed the conquest of Britain.[105] He promoted the imperial cult by installing his image all over the province (Suetonius, *Domitian* 13; Dio Cassius, *Hist.*67.4; 8.1).

---

[101] Koester, *History, Culture, and Religion*, 315.

[102] Jones, "Roman Imperial Cult," 807.

[103] Puskas, *An Introduction to the New Testament*, 41. Smallwood, *The Jews Under the Roman Rule*, 329.

[104] Koester, *History, Culture, and Religion*, 315. Some of Titus' personal qualities (integrity, mercy and kindness) made him the title *Clementia Titi.*

[105] Koester, *History, Culture, and Religion*, 316. A major fire in Rome in 80 CE during the reign of Titus.

Further, the extensive persecution started against the Christians who resisted the imperial worship (cf.Rev.2:2-3, 10, 13; 6:9-11; 7:9-17; 11:7-10; 12:13-17; 13:7, 10, 16-18; 17:6; 18:24;20:4). He claimed himself as both 'lord' and 'god,' brought opposition from both inside and outside. He eliminated his own family members and expelled Stoic philosophers (his friends and enemies) because of his suspicion. There was a pessimistic mood among the historians over the financial burden created over his subjects by increasing the military pay, public banquets and games (Suetonius, *Domitian* 12.2; Doi Cassius, *Hist.*65.7.2; *JW* 7.218).[106] Pliny calls Domitian's period as 'that comfortless age' (*Epistles* X, 2.2ff) and his letter relates the Christians' isolation from the sacrificial meals at the temple (*Epistles* X, 96, 9ff).

Ignatius' *Letter to the Romans*, Polycarp's *Letter to the Philippians and the Martyrdom of Polycarp* give some proof of the imperial persecution against the minority Christians in the competitive fight for claiming the lordship of the emperor. The imperial cult in Asia Minor became very prominent during Domitian period and the Jews were forced to offer ritual sacrifice before the images of the gods and the emperor.[107] The apocalyptic mood got intensified among the Jews and his desire for divine adoration resulted in persecution of the newly formed Christian movement. They were forced to participate in emperor worship (Rev.13:4-8, 15-16; 14:9-11; 15:2; 16:2; 19:20; 20:4).[108] The persecuted minority Christians made use of the apocalyptic space of visions of glorious heavens, parabolic and pictorial language (eg.Rev.21) with code language connected with Jewish apocalypse (Ezekiel, Isa.25-27; 40-45, Zech.9-14) to counter the socio-cultural-religio-political oppression.[109] The annual cultic festivals became very much collaborated with the worship of the emperor especially on his birth day festivals.[110] The apocalyptic imagination became a resistive discourse as the resurrected Christ was portrayed as the counter force to fight the imperial force with 'the sword of his

---

[106] Johnson, "Roman Emperors," *DNTB*, 971.

[107] Wengst, Pax Romana, 120.

[108] Koester, *History, Culture, and Religion*, 316. Christians probably thought Domitian as the antichrist (Revelation of John). His huge marble statue in Ephesus became a focal point for imperial cult in Asia Minor. Probably John's reference to 'the beast and its image,' (Rev.13:12, 15) points to this statue. Jones "Roman Imperial Cult," 807; S.R.F. Price, *Rituals and Power: The Roman Imperial Cult in Asia Minor* (Cambridge: Cambridge University Press, 1984), 197-98.

[109] The book of Revelation is the best example to show the political resistance of a subjective community through the apocalyptic writing and the theology of suffering becomes significant. He portrays the apocalyptic vision of the risen Christ (Rev.1:9-20), the heavenly throne (Rev.4-5), the final Kingdom of God and the messianic judgements (Rev.6-19), the last judgement scene (Rev.20:11), the new heaven and the earth (Rev.21:1-8) and the new Jerusalem (Rev.21:9-22:5). G.R. Beasley-Murray, "Revelation, Book of," in *DLNTD*, edited by R.P. Martin & P.H. Davids (Leicester, England: IVP, 1997), 1030-35.

[110] Beasley-Murray, "Revelation," 1028.

mouth' (Rev.19:15).[111] The imagery of the beast who has 'power over all races, peoples, languages and nations' (Rev.13:3, 7; 17:15) probably mimicked with symbols of ambivalent contrast of Jesus' ascension (Ac.1:10-11), as the lion of Judah (the Messiah) and the lamb that was slain (Rev.17:14; 19:16). Moreover, he finally takes victory over the demonic forces.[112] The enthusiastic pursuit of the imperial cult probably led to think of the emperor as an anti-Christ.

Persecution of Christians continued for the remaining emperors of Nerva (96-98 BCE), Trajan (98-117 CE) and Hadrian (117-138 BCE). However, this period is not within the scope of our study.[113]

2.3 The Roman Imperialism under Procurators/Governors/Prefects

The eastern part of the Mediterranean slowly acquired the shadow of Roman colonialism, since the time of Pompey. By settling the quarrel between the Hasmonean brothers (Hyrcanus II and Aristobulus II) for the position to power, Pompey reinstated the pro-Roman Hyrcanus to the position of high priest. This political step helped the Romans to step over the religious administration in Palestine and Caesar honoured them as 'friends and allies' of the Roman empire (*Ant.*14.213-216).[114] However, the national feeling aroused by the anti-Roman Aristobulus loyalists (*Ant.*14.83-85, 93-96, 100) but Emperor Julius shifted them to Syria. The Jewish kingdom slowly subjected to direct Roman rule after a certain period of keeping them under their own religious overlords (Jewish high priesthood) and client kings (Herod and his sons).[115]

The changed political situation in Rome made Palestine and the religious center in Jerusalem to come directly under the rule of Rome.[116] By integrating Palestine into the larger imperial economy, the burden of the common people (mainly the Jewish community) was increased from paying one set of tribute to

---

[111] Beasley-Murray, "Revelation," 1035-36.

[112] Wengst, *Pax Romana*, 53, 129. The symbolic Roman eagle is probably mimicked by the lion of Judah, the expected Messiah (IV Ezra 4.11).

[113] Bishop of Antioch, Ignatius was put to death (106 CE; Ignatius, Romans 5.2-3) and Bishop Simon was executed in Jerusalem (Eusebius, *Eccl.Hist* 3.32.6) cited by McKechnie, *The First Christian Centuries,* 63.

[114] Smallwood, *The Jews Under the Roman Rule,* 30-37, 39. Hyrcanus took initiative for a treaty with Rome for an official protection and for the diaspora Jews (*Ant.*14.216, 242, 258).

[115] Smallwood, *The Jews Under the Roman Rule,* 21-30; E.P. Sanders, *Judaism: Practice and Belief 63 BCE-66 CE* (London: SCM Press, 1992), 30-43. For certain period the Jewish kingdom was a vassal state (*Ant.*14) under the supervision of the Roman governor of Syria and later by direct rule of governors as a direct Roman province.

[116] Koester, *History, Culture, and Religion*, 390-91. Hyrcanus persuaded the Alexandrian Jewish community to support Caesar. Idumean Antipator's loyalty for Rome rewarded him as the Judean administrator and Hyrcanus received the position of an ethnarch for his loyalty to the Roman politics.

three set of tributes (Rome, client king and temple-state).[117] It is through the client kings and the procurators that Rome maintained her '*Pax Romana*' by the commanded troops in the provincial borders.

2.3.1 Roman Imperialism under Herod the Great

Herod's total obeisance and loyalty to the Roman emperor (Octavian) made him to the position of the king of Judea (*Ant.*14.383-393) and later added Samaria, Jericho, north and east of Galilee.[118] Herod's building projects in Caesarea (sea port *Ant.*15.293, 331-341), Samaria (temple *Ant.*15.292-296) and Judea (temple *Ant.*15.380ff.) portray the Roman lordship throughout his realm. To please the emperor, he renamed the city of Samaria to Sebaste (*Ant.*15.292-296) and the port as Caesarea.[119] He made on the people the financial burden for the extraordinary building programme. He projected himself as a munificent benefactor caused the exchequer empty with his extended reign.[120] For deifying the emperor and for the promotion of the imperial cult, he constructed three temple complexes in Caesarea (*JW* 1.414; *Ant.*15.339), Sebaste (*JW* 1.403; *Ant.*15.298), and Banias (*JW* 1.404; *Ant.*15.363-64).[121] However, by using the mask of a client king of the Jews he tried to implement the cultural policies of Rome which triggered the sentiments of the religious Jewish population.[122] There were protests from the Jewish side against the imperial cult when there were religious offences.[123] In addition to the frivolous spending for the building projects, he also constructed massive fortifications to ensure his security (eg. Masada), exhibiting his political opportunism.[124] Herod's imperial and colonial nature of expecting a total loyalty from the subjects cost the life of so many who were resistant to his autocratic positions.[125]

---

[117] Horsley, *Jesus and Empire*, 32. The ordinary peasants in Galilee, Samaria and Judea who were under the Hasmonean reign had shifted to three layer political leadership.

[118] Koester, *History, Culture, and Religion*, 392.

[119] As soon as the title of Augustus (Σεβαστος) was assumed by Emperor Octavian, Herod tried to honor him with the political intention of benefaction.

[120] Horsley, *Jesus and Empire*, 33.

[121] McLaren, "Jews and the imperial Cult," 259.

[122] Affixing a golden eagle representing the imperial power of Rome over the Jerusalem temple gate made great uproar in the city of Jerusalem (*Ant.*15.281ff., 17.158, 167).

[123] Birds were sacrificed outside the synagogue in Caesarea Maritima that made a protest from the Jews in 65/66 BCE (*JW* 2.258-92).

[124] Horsley, *Jesus and the Spiral of Violence*, 44. "Herod maintained an army of foreign mercenaries, a secret police, and a spy network throughout the country."

[125] The subjects' movements were observed and many were taken to the fortress of Hyrcania and put to them to death (*Ant.*15.366-368).

2.3.2 Roman Imperialism under Archelaus, Pontius Pilate, Herod Antipas and Philip

The Jews were not happy to have the Herodian dynasty to continue in power, so they sent a delegation to persuade Augustus to take over. However, the emperor did not heed to the cry of the subjects, rather he continued his longstanding relationship by handing over the dynasty to Herod's sons: Archelaus to be the "ethnarch" (4BCE-6 CE-Judea and Samaria), Antipas to be the "tetrarch" (4 BCE-39 CE- Galilee and Perea) and Philip to be the "tetrarch" (4 BCE-34 CE- north and east of the Sea of Galilee).[126]

Archelaus' position as a brutal Roman client prince is well attested by the New Testament account (Mt. 2:22-23).[127] He could not fulfill the promises given to the clamorous subjects for appointing the "High Priest of great piety" (*Ant.*17.339, 341) during the crucial period of the political transfer.[128] In order to regain the political support as a pro-Roman, Archelaus tried to do all what he could with less result to justify his administration.[129] Finally, he was exiled to Vienne Gaul and as a result Judea came under the direct Roman administration.[130]

After the deportation of Archelaus, Pontius Pilate came as the next prefect (26-36/37 CE) of Roman administration. He became ill-reputed for the reports of incidents of unrest[131] due to his imperial nature of installing a new garrison with special identifying standards in the Antonia fortress of Jerusalem.[132] He installed shields with inscription of both his name and the emperor and kept them on the walls of Herod's palace.[133] Jewish nationalist feelings were raised up due to his pro-Roman activities of introducing the imperial cult in Jerusalem, coins depicting

---

[126] Koester, *History, Culture, and Religion*, 394-95.

[127] The story of Joseph and Mary changed their plan in returning back to Galilee in the light of Archelaus rule in Judea.

[128] Smallwood, *The Jews Under Roman Rule*, 114-115.

[129] Smallwood, *The Jews Under Roman Rule*, 114-117. Archelaus rebuilt a palace at Jericho which was destroyed by the rebels in 4 BCE (*Ant.*17.340).

[130] Koester, *History, Culture, and Religion*, 395. Judea, Samaria and Idumea came under the direct control of the Roman emperor through a Prefect and for military aid depend on the military legate of Syria (Quirinius-Lk.2:2).

[131] Koester, *History, Culture, and Religion*, 396. Pilate "brought the military ensigns into Jerusalem, but had to withdraw them because of widespread public protest." He quelled the uproar ruthlessly in Jerusalem for building a major water supply in Jerusalem. Smallwood, *The Jews Under Roman Rule*, 156.

[132] Stambaugh and Balch, *The Social World of the First Christians*, 26. The identifying standards carried by the soldiers bearing the image of the emperor irritated the Jews.

[133] Stambaugh and Balch, *The Social World of the First Christians*, 26.

the designs of cultic worship, looting the temple treasury for aqueduct and racial offences by annihilating the Jews in masses.[134]

Herod Antipas carried out the Roman imperial rule by following the footsteps of his father in the construction of Roman-style cities using the economy of the Galilean peasantry.[135] He was known for honoring the imperial house by renaming and rebuilding Sepphoris, the capital of Galilee in the emperor's honor (*Ant.*17.27).[136]

In the colonizing process, Philip the tetrarch was equivalently loyal enough to Rome by naming the new constructions and fortifications by the emperors and their families (*Ant.*17.106-107).[137]

2.3.3 Roman Imperialism under Agrippa I & II

Emperor Caligula appointed Herod's grandson Agrippa I as the tetrarch and later the king (*Ant.*18.228-37; *JW* 2.181) of Abilene, north-east of the Sea of Galilee, the vacant tetrarch of Philip.[138] His direct association with the Roman administration made Emperor Claudius to appoint him as king over the eastern part of the Mediterranean world, including Judea (*Ant.*19.274-75, 362; *JW* 2.215-16).[139] His Hasmonean decadency through his grandmother Mariamne made him goodwill of the Jewish leaders and he had close association with the Jerusalem leadership.[140] He was very diplomatic in his administration in the political capital of Caesarea. He was considered as a close friend of Caesar, and Rome gave him position and power more than what he could imagine.[141]

He conspicuously participated in the Jewish festivals and rites as a conciliatory mode; otherwise he was Roman in heart which is displayed on the inscription of his portrait on the coins and erecting statues at his political kingdom.[142] His grandiose schemes made him to borrow and put burden on his own subjects

---

134 Smallwood, *The Jews Under Roman Rule*, 160-169. Luke records the death of Jews from Galilee by Pilate (LK.13:1).

135 Horsley, *Jesus and Empire*, 86.

136 Smallwood, *The Jews Under Roman Rule*, 118-119.

137 Smallwood, *The Jews Under Roman Rule*, 118. Philip renamed the new capital Panion to Ceasarea Philippi and the fortified village of Bethsaida as Julias after the name of the daughter of Augustus.

138 Koester, *History, Culture, and Religion*, 397.

139 Smallwood, *The Jews Under Roman Rule*, 192.

140 Koester, *History, Culture, and Religion*, 397. Apostle James was executed by King Agrippa I (Ac.12:1ff).

141 Smallwood, *The Jews Under Roman Rule*, 192.

142 Smallwood, *The Jews Under Roman Rule*, 193. Emil Schürer, *The History of Jewish People in the Time of Jesus*, vol. 2 (Peabody: Hendrickson, 1998), 162. Statues of his family members were erected at Sabaste and Caesarea (*Ant.*19.357).

through an addition of house tax (*Ant.*14.209).[143] His death was reported in an unpleasant manner in the context of a dispute with the neighboring countries (Tyre and Sidon), with an economic blockade (Ac.12:20; *JW* 3.38-39).[144]

Agrippa II, son of King Agrippa was a loyal Roman administrator, educated at the imperial court in Rome. He received some minor provinces (Galilee, Perea, Judea, Samaritis and Idumea).[145] Agrippa II annoyed the religio-cultural feelings of the Jewish subjects through spying the sacred pursuits by building a dining room in view of the inner court of the temple and later the destruction of the western wall (inner court) of the temple.[146] The imperial nature of the King was known by renaming Caesarea Philippi to Neronias and striking the emperor's head on the coins (*Ant.* 20.158-59).[147] By taking a diplomatic position as being a loyal Roman imperial client King, he took all political measures to prevent a nationwide revolt in Jerusalem against the imperial rule.[148]

2.3.4 Roman Imperialism under Felix, Festus, Albinus and Gessius Florus

After Agrippa I, the Roman administration planned to gain firm control over Jerusalem and Judea by brutal means. The procurators Felix, Festus (52-62 CE), Albinus (62-64 CE), Gessius Florus (64-66 CE) were incredibly corrupt whose stupidity and brutality widened the hostilities between the Jews and the Romans.[149] They held military and administrative offices in their respective provinces directly appointed by the emperor (*JW* 2.169; 2.244-47; *Ant.*20.14; 20.162, 182).

The governors were designated differently during the first century context as proconsul (Ac.18:12), a legate (*Ant.*15.405; 18.88), prefects/procurator.[150] They had the power to try civilian cases to execute judgement and they were responsible for the financial affairs of the province (*Ant.*17.335), and had the right to imprint Roman coinage for that province.[151]

The major responsibility of the Judean procurators was to address the widespread unrest and tension due to the political task of subduing the colonial

---

143 Smallwood, *The Jews Under Roman Rule*, 196-97.

144 Smallwood, *The Jews Under Roman Rule*, 198.

145 Koester, *History, Culture, and Religion*, 397.

146 Smallwood, *The Jews Under Roman Rule*, 278. The western wall of the inner court of the temple stopped the view of the procurator's troops to watch their proceedings.

147 Smallwood, *The Jews Under Roman Rule*, 273.

148 Smallwood, *The Jews Under Roman Rule*, 274. The courtesy visit of Agrippa and his sister to the new procurator Festus prepared the way for his frequent diplomatic visit to Jerusalem (Ac.25:13ff; *JW* 2.598; 5.49), (180-81). Luke reports his involvement in Paul's trial in Caesarea (Ac.25-26), his courtesy visit to Felix, the new procurator.

149 Koester, *History, Culture, and Religion*, 401.

150 Rapske, "Roman Governors of Palestine," *DNTB*, 979-80.

151 B.M. Rapske, "Roman Governors of Palestine," in *DNTB*, edited by C.A. Evans & S. Porter (Leicester, England: IVP, 2000), 980-81.

states like Judea and Palestine. The political position of the Judean province alarmingly worsened by the time of Felix the procurator (*Ant.*20.160). Moreover, the Jewish revolts become delicate during his reign due to the imperial imposition of nationalism in Judea and Palestine. As a brutal imperial King, Felix (52-60 CE) tried to suppress the growing resistant movements by making stringent measures of crucifying both the brigands and the peasant sympathizers.[152] Felix's repressive measures resulted in more insidious tactics and created more insurgency movements like Sicarii movement (*JW* 2.254-55; *Ant.*20.186-87) and messianic movements.[153]

Following the footsteps of his earlier procurators, Festus (60-62 CE) also tried to stop the resistance movements of Palestine, through arrest and brutal killings (*Ant.*20.185, 188; *JW* 2.271, 273).[154] The political situation deteriorated under Albinus for his disgraceful form of bargaining and bribery from the political prisoners.[155]

The corrupt and oppressive administration of Florus (64-66 CE) heightened and forced the political situation for a climatic Jewish-Roman War in Palestine (*JW* 2.77-341).[156] The religious-cultural tolerance of the Jewish masses must have wrecked by seeing the looting the temple treasury, plundering of the city and capturing of the fortress of Masada by the Roman troops.[157] In all this, the Roman administration failed to address the major issue of Jewish cultural nationalism.

2.4 The Emperor/Imperial Cult and Greco-Roman Religions

Perceiving the power behind the imperial cult as a political phenomenon in the process of colonization, the Roman state exploited it.[158] The Hellenistic royal cult ("god revealed in the person of the emperor") of attributing divinity to rulers combined with the personality adoration of the Romans might probably be the reason behind the later popularized emperor cult.[159] In spite of various elements behind the development of the emperor cult, slowly Caesar's divinity was manipulated well by the Senate and the emperor.[160] There were different titles used by the rulers by which one would assume the divinity they posed during

---

[152] Smallwood, *The Jews Under Roman Rule*, 274.

[153] Smallwood, *The Jews Under Roman Rule*, 274-75.

[154] Smallwood, *The Jews Under Roman Rule*, 277

[155] Smallwood, *The Jews Under Roman Rule*, 282. He released some of the prison inmates for bribe while some others he executed before his recall.

[156] Smallwood, *The Jews Under Roman Rule*, 283. According to Josephus, "it was Florus who forced us to go to war with Rome because we preferred to perish at one fell swoop than piecemeal," (*Ant.*20.257).

[157] Puskas, *An Introduction to the New Testament*, 39.

[158] Prince, "Rituals and Power," 52.

[159] Koester, *History, Culture, and Religion*, 366, 369.

[160] Koester, *History, Culture, and Religion*, 367.

their rule.[161] Popularity for the imperial cult started since the time of the formal deification of Augustus in 14 CE.[162] By this time, not only the divinity of the emperors but also the cult of Rome got the predominant position.[163]

There is a significant relationship between the state promoted/owned religion and the imperial cult. The emperor cult created a strong affinity with the official religion of the Roman state and it was reciprocal in its relationship. The propaganda made by the emperor cult through erecting of their images along with other deities, emperor temples, coins and various inscriptions praising their rule become an ordinary matter. For example, the imperial cult in Asia Minor became so prominent that Augustus was worshipped along with goddess Roma (29CE; 1.*Eph*.2.232-245; 5.1498; 6.2048) and the emperor became 'the temple care taker' (νεοκόκορος).[164] Herod's temple for Roma and Augustus (22-10 BCE; *JW* 1.414-15; *Ant.*15.339) and Herod's temple dedicated to Tiberius at Caesarea Maritima (14-37 CE) display the relationship between the imperial cult and eastern religion.[165] In the later context, the political imposition of the imperial cult led to the persecution of the minority Christians who countered the move.

The imperial cult was added into the traditional religions of the Greco-Roman provincial and civic cults. Local deities were Hellenized or Romanized.[166] The assimilation of Greek deities into the Roman imperial culture (Artemis as Diana, Ares as Mars, Isis) seems to have had political intentions.[167] The consensual strategy of approximating the eastern Greek gods for their Roman gods shows the cultural and religious misuse during the process of colonization.[168] The Greco-

---

[161] *Imperator Caesar, Augustus* ("one who deserves reverence"). Koester, *History, Culture, and Religion*, 369.

[162] Bruce W. Winter, "The Imperial Cult," in *The Book of Acts in its Graeco-Roman Setting*, vol. 2, edited by David W.J. Gill and Cornad Gempf (Grand Rapids, Michigan: Wm. B. Eerdmans Publishing Company, 1994), 94. "[The] major Julio-Claudian imperial temple at the Roman colony of Pisidian Antioch dating from the middle to late Augustus period has been uncovered," (94).

[163] Koester, *History, Culture, and Religion*, 369. The divinity to rule over the nations is given to Rome. There were personal deities and powers (*pax* and *Victoria*) attributed to the emperors.

[164] S.J. Freissen, *Twice Neokoros: Ephesus, Asia and the cult of the Flavian Imperial Family* (Leiden: Brill, 1993), 29-49; D.E. Aune, *Revelation 6-16*, *WBC* 52B (Nashville: Thomas Nelson Publishers, 1998), 778.

[165] Aune, *Revelation 6-16*, 778.

[166] Wells, "Roman Empire," 803. The emperors were equated with regional deities of the Sun-god of Rhodes (Nero) and Zeus of Olympia (Hadrian). Charlesworth, *The Roman Empire*, 14. In Roman colony like Lystra (Ac.14:8-18), the gods Zeus and Hermas were Greek names.

[167] Angus & Renwick, "Roman Empire and Christianity," 213. These gods were part and parcel of their society life, like agriculture, reproduction, fertility, sun, moon, politics, war, industry, blacksmith, craftsman, merchant, messenger, etc. Stambaugh and Balch, *The New Testament in its Social Environment*, 127. For eg., Zeus for rain god, Aphrodite for reproduction and fertility, and Artemis-monthly for the cycle of moon.

[168] Roman Jupiter, Juno, Minerva, Vulcan with Greek Zeus, Hera, and Athena simultaneously used by the Romans. Stambaugh and Balch, *The New Testament in its Social Environment,* 128.

Roman gods and their festivals became part of the social life and they expressed solidarity with the emperor and the city life.[169]

2.4.1 The Imperial Cult, Festivals and Visual Images for Colonialism

The Roman emperor became a living embodiment of the traditional festivals, temple, rituals, images and sacrifices where the emperor adopted the image of the traditional gods through dedications, assimilations and identifications.[170] The Emperor cult, permeated into both the public life and space by new cultural phenomena of public festivals where feasts were hosted by rich benefactors focused on imperial events (eg.birth days of the emperor).[171] The new culture of celebrating the whole subjects on public festivals made the competitive spirit in terms of status, titles between states and provinces.[172]

The imperial feasts were usually connected with the festivals and ritual sacrifices for gods and the emperor, and this gave a sense of community feeling.[173] The imperial cult even transformed the year calendar in honor of the birthday of Augustus.[174] The imperial strategy of accommodating the rulers within the old framework was by erecting imperial temples and sanctuaries in the most prominent places of the city along with the ancient ones.[175] Honorary arches, city walls and towers were begun to develop in various parts of the empire in order to honor the imperial house.[176] The emperor cult was much interlinked with the religious rituals and so the first century Christian community came under suspicion of political loyalty.[177]

---

[169] Stambaugh and Balch, *The New Testament in its Social Environment*, 129.

[170] Price, "Rituals and Power," 57. The "traditional festivals often had an imperial title added to them; the Heraea of Samos became the Sabasta Heraea" (58). The names of the imperial festivals are in association with Sebasteia, Caesarea, Hadrianea, Antoninea and Severeia, etc.

[171] Horsley, *Paul and Empire,* 21. "The decree of the provincial council of Asia in 9 BCE that Augustus's birthday would be the beginning of the New Year serves as an example of how the emperor could become inscribed into the consciousness of the public through organization of the calendar."

[172] Prince, "Rituals and Power," 56.

[173] Zanker, "The Power of Images," 74.

[174] Price, "Rituals and Power," 59. The province of Asia made the change in the calendar system from the old luni-solar calendar (the autumnal equinox) to Julian system began on September 23 which is the birthday of Augustus. The emperor's names were given for the months (for e.g, "Kaisarios" or "Tiberios")

[175] Price, "Rituals and Power," 61-64. "At Miletus there was a temple of Augustus." In Ephesus, "the richest city of the province," the upper square was redesigned to incorporate a "royal portico" (*stoa basilica*) dedicates to Artemis, Augustus and Tiberius" (62). In later years, an imperial temple to Domitian at Ephesus was located at the strategic centers.

[176] Zanker, "The Power of Images," 85-86.

[177] Wengst, *Pax Romana*, 50. Governor Pliny's report to Emperor Trajan about the Christian's resistance to invoke the gods and offering incense to the statue of the emperor (*Epistles* X, 96,5).

The imperial cult proved how much the cultural images have power on the visual communication and how much the emperors used it for political purposes. The integration of religio-economic and political life of the east were adopted by placing the 'images of power' like the temple of Roma and Augustus at the central places of social life.[178] The imperial cult especially gave a new sense of belonging to the Roman Empire politically, economically and religiously and it was used as a medium of communication with the emperor.[179]

2.4.2 The Colonial Strategy of Unification under Imperial Cult

In the Roman eastern provinces, the imperial cult spread widely and rapidly due to its political backing. Since the days of Augustus, there was a radical change in the imperial cult of worshiping Augustus' *genius* (his spirit), Nero as 'lord' (κυριος), Vespasian as 'Saviour' (swthr), Domitian as *dominus et deus*.[180] The imperial society worked in a strategy of getting the support of the provincial elites who were the power players of the "social-economic networks of imperial society."[181]

This political-religious interlink operated better in position of molding the people culturally to work according to the terms of the emperor and thus "politics can work through religion."[182] Augustus reconstituted the "Roman civil religion" appropriating the Hellenistic socio-cultural setting of rites, institutions and deities for getting closer to the divine power.[183] A new power dynamics was thus constructed through the image of the emperor.[184] Through this imperial cult, a web of power relationships with imaginary unity of *oikoumene* was created between the subject and the ruler, the local elites and the populace, between different cultures.[185] The unifying effect of the imperial cult was very significant where the whole community participated mystically in the mis/represented restoration of the state.[186] "In its emphasis on the importance of repaying the debts of benefactions the imperial cult was at one with Hellenistic ruler cults."[187]

[178] Zanker, "The Power of Images," 73. For eg., Imperial images at Athenian Acropolis, Ephesus and Caesarea.

[179] Zanker, "The Power of Images," 73.

[180] Price, "Rituals and Power," 52. "In Rome and Italy, he decreed that worship should be directed not to himself, but to his *genius,* the divine spirit which presided over his life and from which his power emanated." Stambaugh and Balch, *The New Testament in its Social Environment*, 131.

[181] Horsley, *Paul and Empire,* 11.

[182] Horsley, *Paul and Empire,* 12. The imperial cult works better in position of military and administrative forms.

[183] Horsley, *Paul and Empire,* 14.

[184] Prince, "Rituals and Power," 68.

[185] Prince, "Rituals and Power," 71.

[186] Zanker, "The Power of Images," 86.

[187] Prince, "Rituals and Power", 53.

The emperor cult became popular and universal except for the Jewish resistance in Judea and Galilee.

2.4.3 The Jewish Resistance and Dissident Voices to the Imperial Cult

There were troubles in Caesarea, Alexandria, Jamnia and Dora over the issue of the imperial cult, especially the erecting of the emperor's statue in the Jewish synagogues (*Ant.*19.300-11). There were conflicts over the issue of the identity (legal status) of the Jewish population amidst the Greeks and the Romans.[188] Gaius and Domitian "pushed the limits of the unwritten ground rules the most."[189] For instance, Gaius issued an order to erect his statue in Jerusalem as a punitive measure (*JW* 2.184, 195; *Ant.*18.261; Philo, *Leg.Gai.*203; Tacitus, *Hist.*5-7) and as a result, there were violent protests from the Jewish community.[190] Josephus criticizes the Jews for their lack of loyalty, by their unwillingness to erect images of the emperor (*Apion* 2.73; *Ant.*18.257-58).[191] Even though the "Roman Empire was a pluralistic *oikoumene*,"[192] the majority imperial cult oppressed the minority Judean ethnic minority culture. In a colonial state, the deification of the emperor brings conflicting perspectives from the ruling as well as the colonized Jewish side. Philo accuses the Roman official (*Leg.Gai.*201, 199) and the Greek population for the act (*Leg.Gai.*200), because in the emperor's state one crime should not be countered by another.[193]

The Jewish exchange of Roman money for the Tyrian currency as the temple tax is a clear example of their resistance. However, both the implementation of the imperial edict and the Jewish response many a times were ambivalent and discursive.[194] Augustus himself gave an unspecified edict by exempting the Jews from participating in the imperial cult. It is possible that Luke's exhortation to the primitive Christian community with regard to the imperial worship and its close association with the imperial idolatry, he discursively disrupts the political move through his discourse (Ac.15:29; 17:16, 22-31; 19:21-41).

2.5 Mapping the Roman Imperial Administration

The Roman imperial reign adopted a hybrid culture by taking elements from the conquered Greco-Asian-Judean provinces and states, making Rome the

---

188 McLaren, "Jews and the imperial Cult," 262.

189 McLaren, "Jews and the imperial Cult," 275. Apion and his colleagues were criticized for not honouring the emperor by worshipping him as god (*Ant.* 18.257-58) and the resulting dismissal of the Jewish embassy by Gaius (*Leg.Gai.* 353, 357).

190 McLaren, "Jews and the imperial Cult," 266, 268.

191 McLaren, "Jews and the imperial Cult," 275.

192 Bruce J. Malina, *The Social Gospel of Jesus. The Kingdom of God in Mediterranean Perspective* (Minneapolis: Fortress Press, 2001), 46.

193 McLaren, "Jews and the imperial Cult," 265.

194 McLaren, "Jews and the imperial Cult," 258; Smallwood, *The Jews under Roman Rule*, 137.

administrative center of the Roman *oikoumene*. Roman law, nomenclature, architecture and style were adopted by the propertied classes in general.[195] The Roman colonial policies made her the largest and the wealthiest empire in the ancient world from the four corners of the world (North Britain, South Egypt, West Spain and East Euphrates River). The wealth of the empire flowed to the 'center' from the 'periphery' provinces and client kingdoms through different sources like agricultural produce, land and head taxes and the wealth of the land. Indoor and outdoor games, imperial festivals were conducted to appease the elite of the society at the cost of the poor masses.[196] Moreover, the government tried to pacify the troubled masses by expelling the diaspora community or by attributing the administrative blame on 'others.'[197]

Roman imperial administration projected her progress with massive building projects, urbanization and economic prosperity through different taxes and long-lasting peace under the supervision of the military surveillance. For easy administration, the entire Roman Empire was divided into different provinces and other direct governing states. The authority of the visible rulers from emperor to the local institutions was magnified.[198] In the process of expanding the Roman borders, a social change was demanded in the form of Rome deliberately becoming the patron and the provincial governments becoming the beneficiary client[199] so as to benefit the emperor by always keeping the Roman supremacy high. The political administration in the light of the demise of Republican elections changed the whole structure. The emperor administered the eastern provinces through the Governors, Procurators, client kings, and chosen elites.[200] The distant imperial administration was kept through the Roman rulers, by paying permanent tribute, and the imperial cult worship.

The Roman proconsuls were given charge of the public order and local administration which was supervised through the Roman legions settled in each

---

[195] Wells, "Roman Empire," 803.

[196] "[T]he gladiatorial fights and wild beasts hunts" were spectacles for laughter at the cost of 'others' pains. Some Jews and Christians were the spectacles for laughter during the time of Nero and Domitian. Saller, "Roman Empire," 658.

[197] The Emperor Claudius' expulsion of the Jewish community from Rome (49 CE) and Emperor Nero blamed the Christians for the great fire in Rome (64 CE). Saller, "Roman Empire," 658.

[198] The Roman emperors held religio-political-military titles (*pontifex maximux*- supreme authority over profane and sacred, *pater patriae*-father of his country; *imperator*-commander; *princeps*-first citizen) from Augustus which shows his administrative power. Malina, *The Social Gospel of Jesus*, 48.

[199] Arlandson, *Women, Class, and Society*, 20. The cultural transfer of the *decurion* councils in the major cities of Asia Minor have been surrendered to the patron Roman Empire.

[200] Saller, "Roman Empire," 658. In Rome the "administration was largely left to the municipalities, with important matters referred to imperial officials in Rome."

province.[201] They were given power to call on census for economic gain from provinces, look after the financial factors of the administration (Strabo, *Geog.* 3.4.20), and to conduct judicial cases.[202] Moreover, Romanization was launched through the colonies (eg. Philippi and Corinth) and through settling the Roman veterans and freedmen. The handful of Roman officials could administer the affairs of the state by the help of local leaders like local magistrates (cf.Ac.16.19-23).[203] In order to improve the quality of certain provincial administration, Augustus himself assigned "the legionary forces of the army."[204] Further the rebellious eastern Roman provinces were reorganized strategically (Strabo, *Geog.* 17.3.24-25).[205]

The Roman administration divided the empire mainly into three types - Roman colony, free city (*municipia*) and the old Greek constitutions (e.g., Ephesus Ac.19:24-40) where the traditional forms of administration continued.[206] In their imperial expansion, Rome absorbed many states and nations, appropriated many cultures[207] while keeping their hegemony over many cultures. Further, the use of Latin as the official political language while keeping Greek as the *lingua franca* of the east, showed the imperial strategy of accommodating the life of the colonial subjects.[208]

---

[201] Stambaugh and Balch, *The New Testament in its Social Environment,* 18. The Roman governors had absolute power to administer over the province and they were the senators who would cater to the politics of Rome very well and not to the welfare of the people of the provinces.

[202] Stambaugh and Balch, *The New Testament in its Social Environment,* 25. Quirinius, Governor of Syria ordered a general census in the new province of Judea (cf.Lk.2:2; Mt.22:15-22; Mk.12:14-17).

[203] Saller, "Roman Empire," 658.

[204] Stambaugh and Balch, *The New Testament in its Social Environment,* 18. "[Military] officers and soldiers acting as major figures of authority in provincial administration (as in Ac.22.23-30, 27:1)." Saller, "Roman Empire," 659.

[205] Some rebellious provinces were governed by proconsuls for one year term (eg. Sergius Paulus in Cyprus, Gallio of Achaia; Ac.13:4, 7; Ac.18:12-17). Puskas, *An Introduction to the New Testament*, 9.

[206] Stambaugh and Balch, *The New Testament in its Social Environment,* 19. The Greek cities which continued the traditional civic administration had the recognizable body of 'people' (δεμος), assembly (ἐκκλεσια) and the representative decision making body (βουλη). D.W.J. Gill, "Roman Political System," in *DNTB*, edited by C.A. Evans & S.E. Porter (Leicester, England: IVP, 2000), 999.

[207] Stambaugh and Balch, *The New Testament in its Social Environment,* 161. "161 BCE., Greek philosophers were banned from the city; in 58 BCE., the senate destroyed altars of the Egyptian gods."

[208] Thompson, "Roman East," *DNTD*, 966.

2.5.1 Roman Military Structure

The political supremacy of Rome was so much that Rome started constructing her provinces in the east through systematic exploitation by the military forces.[209] Emperor Augustus deployed his legions at the strategic locations (Rhine, Spain, Africa, Egypt, and Syria etc.) where each were made up of at least four thousand eight hundred soldiers.[210] Such an organization of military power was important as she has been built on war and military power.[211] The Roman military was so strong that the ordinary masses wondered it as "the beast, and who can fight against it" (*JW* 2.362; 5.366-67). The military tyrannies were numerous because they were the peace keeping force. The military unit carried legionary standards with emblems to identify the units with an eagle and along with they carried the image of the emperor.[212]

Roman Empire was ruled and stabilized by wealthy generals of the leading families who ruled the country with the military prowess.[213] The Roman imperial government was established on cohort, number of legions, the supplementary troops as Para-military forces to have Roman control over her provinces.[214] The military soldiers had a good pay in comparison with the poor agricultural laborers, with tax exemption, legal privileges, retirement benefits of either a colonial property or cash gratuity.[215]

The legions were "permanently based in the provinces," and they were recruited from the sons of the auxiliary groups or from the natives.[216] Centurions, who held both military and social status, were real professionals of greater ranks or direct appointments from Rome of the equestrian rank or from the elite units.[217] The troubled areas in the east like the province of Judea were garrisoned with the

---

209 David Kennedy, "Roman Army," in *ABD,* vol. 5, edited David Noel Freedman (New York: Doubleday, 1992), 793.

210 Augustus built a strong military institution and made it the world power. Kennedy, "Roman Army," 790. There were 25 legions to the close of Augstus reign.

211 G.L. Thompson, "Roman Military," in *DNTB*, edited C.A. Evans & S.E. Porter (Leicester, England: IVP, 2000), 992.

212 Thompson, "Roman Military," *DNTB,* 992. The Roman client kings in Palestine had military troops in Judea-Palestine. The soldiers of these military troops were from other parts of the empire with a Roman officer to supervise (*JW* 1.672; 2.52).

213 Klauck, "The Roman Empire," 73.

214 Kennedy, "Roman Army," 789. "The military success of the Roman Republic had been founded on the effectiveness of her citizen armies, equipped as heavy infantry and organized into legions." Kennedy, "Roman Army," 789. One *legion* (4,800 men) consisted of ten *cohorts* (480 men).

215 Thompson, "Roman Military," *DNTB,* 994.

216 Kennedy, "Roman Army," 790.

217 Kennedy, "Roman Army," 790. "The financial attraction of the centurionate, however, was that the pay was probably some 16 times than of the basic legionary salary," (791).

military forces to settle political troubles.[218] Moreover, roads were constructed for "quick movement of supplies and military troops."[219]

2.5.2 Roman Jurisdiction: Citizenship and Law

Roman citizenship for the colonized was a privilege granted by the authority both as a reward as well as a co-opted loyalty strategically given for the inmates either for their service in the army or mercifully granted to a province fully or individually.[220] Legal privileges were given to the Roman citizens for legal protection, voting rights in popular assemblies, certain tax exemptions, protection from severe punishments including the right of appeal against capital punishment.[221] However, the slaves under the law had no rights and the non-citizens got a different treatment.[222]

The multicultural and complex nature of Roman eastern provincial setup made the jurisdiction to be ambivalent and vague.[223] There were public declarations of the law quite often through the Roman government officials from emperor to governors, as reported from the Roman historians (Livy, Josephus, Tacitus) and rhetoricians (Cicero and Quintillion).[224] The Roman governors usually were given the absolute authority over their provinces and they were directly accountable to the emperor and the senate.[225] There was always a chance of favouritism for the rich and the powerful in the Roman legal system, because the social status was made a strict mandatory for judges and jury members.[226] There were fewer chances for the poor and the subaltern to get their voices heard favourably in the court due to the differences of treatment under the Roman legal system.

2.5.3 Roman Economy and the Imperial Patronage

Roman colonialism and the prolonged imperial domination led to the rise of indebtedness, land loss, unemployment, bribery, poverty and hunger. It created a huge disparity between the rich and the poor. This institutionalized socio-

[218] One military cohort was stationed in the Fortress Antonia to closely watch the Jerusalem temple activities (*Ant.*20.192; *JW*5.244-45; cf.Ac.21:31-37).

[219] Thompson, "Roman East," 966.

[220] Stambaugh and Balch, *The New Testament in its Social Environment,* 30.

[221] Stambaugh and Balch, *The New Testament in its Social Environment,* 31; C.S. Wansink, "Roman Law and Legal System," *DNTB*, edited by C.A. Evans & S. Porter (Leicester: IVP, 2000), 987. For eg., Paul appealed to governor Festus against his capital punishment to be heard by Caesar (Ac.25:11; cf.Ac.16:35-39).

[222] Wells, "Roman Empire", 804. "Citizens came under the provisions of Roman law in all matters concerning personal status, inheritance, property ownership, and business contracts."

[223] Stambaugh and Balch, *The New Testament in its Social Environment,* 33.

[224] Wansink, "Roman Law and Legal System," *DNTB*, 985. There are historical accounts of senate decrees and the pronouncements of the emperors that have come out as legal documents.

[225] Wansink, "Roman Law and Legal System," *DNTB*, 986.

[226] Wansink, "Roman Law and Legal System," *DNTB*, 986. There is no consistency for Roman legal system in the provinces.

economic and political symbolic world created a new mode of power relations of reciprocity between a patron and a client as legally indebted to the colonial center.[227]

In the first century Roman agrarian economy very few owned land. Ones' status was based on the amount of wealth owned through the acquisition of land.[228] The sources of income to the imperial government were property tax, customs duties, tax on manumissions of slaves, head tax for the adults (12/14 - 65), circulation of goods, use of public facilities and several other new taxes (harvests, poll tax, cattle gracing on government land, harbor and border excises) introduced by the Roman emperors.[229] There were direct (cultivation and poll tax), and indirect taxation (between the borders and sea ports) on individual cities and sales tax on slaves.[230] Tax collection developed into a big business in the imperial context due to the commission on levy and customs and it became an agonizing mark of conquest.

Roman tax system burdened heavily the poor in Judea-Galilee through the annexation of the province in 63 BCE (*Ant.*14.202) and later the procurators collected tax through the Sanhedrin (*JW* 2.405).[231] Emperor Vespasian levied tax on the defeated Jews (two drachmas) in order to culturally humiliate them in the time of their crisis (*JW* 7.218; *Ant.*18.312; cf.Mt.17:24-27).[232] Moreover, the punitive tax imposed upon the Jewish community was for the purpose of confiscating their land and occupying them with the Roman veterans (*JW* 2.216-17). Meantime, the city dwellers in Jerusalem were burdened with city sales tax and tax for houses (*Ant.*18.90; 19.299). Bad crops and famine caused severe harm in the poorer classes in the form of loss of land and slavery.

The majesty of Roman infrastructure, her military presence all over the empire, the wealth of the Roman nobles, the urbanizing process, building projects

[227] H. Moxnes, *The Economy of the Kingdom* (Philadelphia: Fortress Press, 1988), 41-42. The socio-economic and political power relations were based on the reciprocal solidarity and loyalty from the side of the client.

[228] Arlandson, *Women, Class, and Society*, 20; Stambaugh and Balch, *The New Testament in its Social Environment*, 65. Pliny the younger and the governor of Bithynia is an example of a political person "at the top of the financial pyramid" (66). Pliny holds vast acres of farm land in Italy, several "town houses and country villas and hundreds of slaves."

[229] Stambaugh and Balch, *The New Testament in its Social Environment*, 78. The head tax for one denarius per person a year is calculated through a periodic census (cf.LK.2:1-5; Ac.5:37). Augustus introduced a variety of taxes on sale of slaves and inheritance. Titus introduced a special tax of two denarii a year from all the Jews in the empire.

[230] Gill, "Taxation, Greco Roman," 1162.

[231] T.E. Schmidt, "Taxation, Jewish," in *DNTB*, edited by C.A. Evans & S. Porter (Leicester: IVP, 2000), 1164. Josephus calculated a heavy tax due of ca.eight hundred talents (*JW* 2.92-97; *Ant.*17.318-20) by the time of Herod's death.

[232] Carter, *Matthew and the Margins*, 38. Warren Carter, "Paying Tax to Rome as Subversive Praxis: Matthew 17:24-27," *JSNT* 76 (1999), 17.

and entertaining projects were all run by the provincial revenues.[233] Tax-tributary system was justified on the basis of Roman sovereignty and the custodians of peace. Not paying tax to Caesar amounted to a 'charge of insurrection' (*JW* 2.404).

In the first century imperial economy, the patron-client relationship was very much strong in provisional cities based on the complex commercial enterprises centered on luxury goods (Ac.16:14, 40) or temple cities (Ac.19:24-27).[234] The hierarchical structure of social relations of dependency increased as the colonial expansion towards the east and the imperial patronage had become the political administrative system.[235] Powerful politicians had "become patrons of whole cities and client kingdoms" through their success in overseas wars.[236] They spent huge amount as bribery in order to keep their political positions firm. In the newly transformed system of patronage, the emperor created a vast network where each one was made dependable to the center patron/emperor along with the other administration of the empire as a pyramid finally converging on the emperor at the center.

2.6 The Socio-Economic Condition of the Eastern Roman Empire

Social condition under the Roman Empire was based on a "clear separation of social classes" which was evident in the social stratification based on the worth of property.[237] In an agricultural social context, the workers and slaves stood between the rich land owners and the poor. The economic disparity went to the extent where it seemed to be the only two classes: the 'imperial rich' and the 'imperial poor' in the society of the eastern empire where the slaves consisted of a major chunk. In this scenario, those who were associated with the 'center' became the custodians of wealth, power and social status.[238] The social location of the eastern province was conditioned by one's occupation.[239]

During the course of development towards the Roman Empire, the senators, the equestrians and the provincial aristocracy got their socio-political

---

233 Carter, "Paying Tax to Rome," 16.

234 Stambaugh and Balch, *The New Testament in its Social Environment*, 64, 71.

235 John H. Elliot, "Patronage and Clientage," in *The Social Sciences and the New Testament Interpretation*, edited by Richard L. Rohrbaugh (Peabody: Hendrickson, 1996), 152-53.

236 Stambaugh and Balch, *The New Testament in its Social Environment*, 64.

237 Zanker, "The Power of Images," 83. In games and festivals class distinction was evident. "At the front were seats for city magistrates, priests, and *docuriones*... senators... reserved for *plebs*... at the bottom of the social ladder women, foreigners, and salves-sat at the very back."

238 Saller, "Roman Empire," 657. The imperial wars and Rome's unparalleled victories made some citizens to become wealthy and politically powerful.

239 Arlandson, *Women, Class, and Society*, 16, 82. In Luke-Acts, occupational descriptions are given for the sake of analyzing their social background. For eg., proconsul, centurion purple-seller, tent-maker, widow, carpenters, wool dyers, linen workers, potters, silversmiths, goldsmiths, fishermen, fullers and leather workers, etc., who come under the category of artisans, mostly free, some slaves.

representation (administration, military) based on their ownership of property.[240] However, the 'imperial poor' were the lower classes of people in the Roman Empire. They by birth remained in the category for they did not own land or wealth. For this reason, they were heavily dependent on the rich patrons. While the artisans and craftsmen in the society could climb the ladder in their society for a better life, the economically disadvantaged freeborn (one third of the Roman population), freedmen, and the slaves (by birth and by conquest) remained at the bottom of the social ladder. However, the latter formed the larger segment of the Roman social pyramid.

Public health caring system was only for the wealthy upper class, and the common people depended on the "wandering physicians, miracle workers, magicians, and astrologers."[241] For the health-care was concerned, the case of the aged, widows and the disabled were in a deplorable situation.

2.6.1 Roman Commercial Enterprise

Commerce and trade continued even more rapidly after Rome took control of the Mediterranean coastal regions. Rome became the commercial center due to the "demand for mass consumption goods and luxury articles."[242] The empire depended on Egypt and Northern Africa for grain and other agricultural products. There were luxury and exotic items (perfumes, ointments, precious stones, incense, spices, silk and animals), imported from Asian and African countries during the imperial period.[243]

Rome became the main trading center by the time of Roman imperialism and colonialism. By seeing the commercial and military purpose, the emperors gave much attention to construct sea ports and construction of roads towards the eastern part of the empire.[244] One of the great achievements of Augustus and his successors were the Roman road system which connected the whole empire for accessibility to both military posts and enhanced travel-tourism and commerce.[245]

---

240 D.F.Watson, "Roman Social Classes," in *DNTB*, edited by C.A. Evans & S. Porter (Leicester: IVP, 2000), 1000-01. There were three established social class orders on the basis of law and property ownership: the 'senators', 'equestrians,' and 'the provincial aristocracy' (*decurians*) (1000).

241 Koester, *History, Culture, and Religion*, 332.

242 Koester, *History, Culture, and Religion*, 326-27.

243 Koester, *History, Culture, and Religion*, 327. Emperor Nero imported luxury items for public games in the arena.

244 Koester, *History, Culture, and Religion*, 328. The construction of roads was for the purpose of speeding up the transportation and postal delivery. At regular intervals, there were inns, military posts and postal stations. Just like any modern cities, routes, maps and major points of interest probably for the imperialistic purposes, were available.

245 Puskas, *An Introduction to the New Testament*, 9. Corinth became an important sea trade route by the time of Caesar, as he took initiative for the Isthmus of Corinth. The common seafaring

2.6.2 Slavery and the Slave Trade in Roman Empire

Roman imperialism caused severe crisis on the conquered provinces by the growing masses of the poor because the society was divided along economic lines.[246] Incessant warfare brought millions of conquered people into the empire capital to be used as slaves in the agricultural and industrial sectors.[247] Military conquests of the period led to socio-cultural dislocation of the poor masses and they became socially dead.[248] In the first century, probably one third of the population of the city of Rome was working as slave machines for the economic production of the rich nobles.[249] Slavery has been institutionalized during the Augustan era and it became an integral part of the socio-economic-religious and political structure.[250] Racial marginalization seemed to have made a cause for enslavement (Syrians, Asiatics, Jews).[251] In the eyes of the Roman law, they were "chattels without personal rights."[252] Therefore, the people of the east, mainly the Syrians and Judeans, were considered as inferior and could be enslaved.[253] Slaves were treated like property or machine without personal rights. They could be bought or sold, tortured or even crucified at their master's command.[254] They seemed to have lived a dehumanizing situation under their colonial masters. The emperor's later attempts in solving their problems by settling them in state-owned properties and in providing free provision of grain created social unrest in the capital city.[255] Slave trade became a profitable business as part of the Roman economic system and their sweat and blood brought wealth to the elite patrons of the society.

There were resistance to slavery but they were repressed and the Roman Senate ordered to terrorize them through strict orders (Tacitus, *Ann.*14.44).[256]

---

services were between Alexandria and Rome. Paul and the other missionaries made use of these roads and sea routes.

246 Koester, *History, Culture, and Religion*, 329. The poverty in Rome increased among the masses based on "the expansion of the large landed estates in Italy."

247 R.A. Horsley, "The Slave Systems of Classical Antiquity and their Reluctant Recognition by Modern Scholars," *Semeia* 83/84 (1998), 33.

248 Horsley, "The Slave Systems," 29.

249 Saller, "Roman Empire," 658. The military captured slaves from Asia Minor and Syria. They were used to expand the estate of the nobles. Horsley, "The Slave Systems," 34. Rome was boomed with slaves (*JW* 6.420). John Riches, *The World of Jesus: First-Century Judaism in Crisis* (Cambridge: Cambridge University Press, 1990), 17.

250 Horsley, "The Slave Systems," 59.

251 R.A. Horsley, "Slave Resistance in Classical Antiquity," *Semeia* 83/84 (1998), 136.

252 Cook et al., *The Cambridge Ancient History*, 756.

253 Horsley, "The Slave Systems of Classical Antiquity," 36.

254 Cook et al., *The Cambridge Ancient History*, 756; Saller, "Roman Empire," 658.

255 Koester, *History, Culture, and Religion*, 330-31.

256 Cruel laws were implemented by executing them in mass numbers for preventing some murderous plots and to keep them in fear for their lives (eg. Tacitus, reports of the massacre of four

Slaves were whipped, tortured, sexually exploited (forced castration; Pliny, *Nat. Hist.*30.41; 21.170), chained and branded.[257] Slave resistance either by running away or by revolt was a ubiquitous problem leading to civil war.[258] Manumission was politically motivated to manipulate the slave-master relationship and to promote obeisance to their masters. This system tried to maintain the exploitation through imperial patron-client relationship.[259]

Slave system was at its peak during the Roman imperial culture due to the escalating wars, bringing millions into the center as slaves.[260] The slave system increased rapidly due to military conquests, economic debt, poverty, in certain cases condemned criminals and the offspring of the slaves continued to remain as slaves. They were used in mines, in the urbanization process as construction workers in building roads, aqueducts, temples, household slaves for domestic work, and in the agricultural sector.[261] In social life, the slave system made a great impact on the socio-economic life of the imperial world. The household slaves were part of the extended family and had impact on the religio-socio-political system.[262]

The Roman imperial taxation probably caused great socio-political and economic imbalance resulting in slavery. Romans acquired land in the eastern part of the empire as debt payments causing slave system to flourish.[263] Ordinary people became the victims due to the imperial taxation (*Ant* 14.275) and colonial conquest (*JW* 3:532-42; *Ant.*17.289). Henceforth, the poor masses lost their ancestral lands and became the possessions of the Roman colonizers

---

hundred slaves of a Roman city prefect for contemplating murder in 61 CE; Jo-Ann Shelton, *As the Romans Did. A Sourcebook in Roman Social History* (Oxford: University Press, 1998), 175.

[257] Horsley, "The Slave Systems of Classical Antiquity," 43-45.

[258] Horsley, "Slave Resistance in Classical Antiquity," 140. Augustus returned 30,000 slaves to their masters (*Res Gestae* 25). There were three massive revolts by the peasant slaves from Sicily and Italy between 140-70 BCE, (143, 145).

[259] Horsley, "The Slave Systems of Classical Antiquity," 48-51. The cost of manumission would return back to the salve master and it was comparatively higher than the slave price. They could only try for a second class Roman citizenship.

[260] Stambaugh and Balch, *The New Testament in its Social Environment*, 124. In the early and later part of the first century, slaves were brought into Spain from the conquering lands. Josephus reports the enslavement of the populace in the Galilee-Judean provinces for the anti-Roman revolutions (*JW* 1.180; 2.68, 222; 3.304-305, 337-38; *Ant.*14.275; 17.289).

[261] Shelton, *As the Romans Did*, 166-173; Koester, *History, Culture, and Religion*, 331. The slaves were employed in large numbers by the emperors.

[262] Stambaugh and Balch, *The New Testament in its Social Environment*, 124.

[263] There were tax collectors appointed from the equestrian order with an additional support of the money lenders arranged from the Roman administration for lending money with high interest rates in lieu of land as security. Paul Trebilco, "Asia," in *The Book of Acts in its Graeco-Roman Setting*, vol. 2, edited by D.W.J. Gill and Conrad Gempf (Grand Rapids: Wm. B. Eerdmans Publishing Company, 1994), 294.

as property to be transacted in slave markets (*Psalms of Solomon* 2:6; 8:21; 17:12).[264] Institutionalized slavery led to dehumanization through branded marks on their bodies, and sexual exploitation increased (*Nat.Hist.*30:41; 21:170).[265] Consequently, the eastern part of the empire, especially Judea-Galilee was affected badly as many Jews were enslaved by the Roman warlords.

Luke describes the hybrid nature of the Christian community from the upper class to the lower class like the slaves. The urbanized social mapping was portrayed by the occupational description-'synagogue ruler', 'centurion', 'silversmith', 'purple seller' etc., which located the social position of the characters.[266] However, there were rich patrons who could provide accommodation to the traveling Christian missionaries (Ac.18:2-3, 18; cf.1Cor.16:19) and provide space (identity) for the new born Christian community with their large houses (Ac.12:12; 16:15, 40; 17:5-9; 18:7).

2.7 A Critical Evaluation of Roman Imperialism and Colonialism in the East

The brief trajectory of the Roman Empire in its formation since the time of Julius Caesar explains the magnanimity of the political programme that worked behind in order to make Rome an imperial power center. The imperial wings spread to the four corners of the globe with the intention of both the territorial and economic expansion. Through colonization, Rome became the capital of the empire which held the supreme authority and power over the entire world. The varied socio-religious-cultural and political affiliations of east were erased and significantly transformed by the political strategy of the imperial cult. Romans adopted and implemented this cult for their selfish interest and colonial motif.

The imperial system of *Pax Romana* made a utopian peace, political unity and economic prosperity over the entire Roman world where the underprivileged masses went into slavery and experienced terror for not becoming submissive to the Roman imperial policies. Moreover, the political peace was achieved through military conquest and oppression. Through the policies, the center became rich through the tax system and other revenues, and the imperial colonies of the east became paupers. The ideology behind *Pax Romana* and tax systems were to use them as a political tool to impose their supremacy, to subjugate the colonized and penalize the resistant.

Roman colonialism made the imperial cult a tremendous political strategy for influencing the colonial subjects by deifying them as 'gods' in equal position to the Greco-Roman gods. The political uprisings in Caesarea, Alexandria, Jamnia, Judea and Galilee reveal the resistance behind the cultural imposition of Rome on the Jewish minority. The Roman Empire made use of the ruler cult, Oriental

264 Koester, *History, Culture, and Religion of the Hellenistic Age*, 59; Joy, Mark and its Subalterns, 79.

265 Horsley, "The Slave Systems of Classical Antiquity," 38-44.

266 Arlandson, *Women, Class and Society*, 3.

temples, festivals and images to falsely unite them for the dominant colonial center's benefit. The expulsion of Jews from the political center on many occasions could be seen as anti-Semitic in treatment by some of the imperial rulers.

In the administrative system, the client kings in the east had to keep their positions by giving huge amount as bribery emptying the finance exchequer of the east. The commercial enterprise in the east was also used for the sustenance of the Roman Empire in many ways. The roads that led to Rome were mainly for the purpose of military and commercial needs, because the capital depended much on the east for grain and agricultural products. The institutionalized slavery position was also connected to the Roman economic system because of the huge number of prisoners brought to the center through military conquests.

The eastern provinces of the Roman Empire were the most affected by enormous debt and impoverishment. During the colonial process, classical Greek cities were destroyed and the economy of the east was drained for the maintenance of military purposes and imperial strength. Colonialism in the east was sustained by multiple systems of patronage, imperial cult and bribery from the client-rulers. The magnificent building projects (temples, emperor images and fortresses) of the emperors made them powerful in their stature at the expense of the ordinary masses.

The Roman client kings and procurators who acted on behalf of the empire imposed the imperial culture on the minority Jews annoying their religious sentiments. As a result, the Jewish cultural nationalist movements spread around Palestine resulting in political reprisals on many occasions. The Jewish vulnerability over the legal status under the colonial reign was comprehensible over the incidents that happened in Alexandria, Jamnia and Jerusalem. However, the ambivalent attitudes of the Jews as well as the rulers give religious freedom to the Jews on several occasions both in Jerusalem and in the diaspora. The ambivalent attitude of the Jews could be seen in relation to the imperial rule through the daily offering at the Jerusalem temple for Rome and the emperor. This shows a parallel ambivalent discursive space for the worship of the Emperor and Yahweh among the Jews. Since the destruction of the Jerusalem temple, the distinct sacred space for countering the imperial cult had gone forever.

Chapter 3

The Jewish World and Its Cultural Nationalism

3.1 Introduction

Majority of the Jewish community had been longing for their socio-religious-cultural and political independence ever since they lost their national freedom in 596 BCE. The dream of an independent Jewish state led to resistance to the then colonial/dominant powers beginning from Assyrian empire to Roman empire.[1] The Assyrian-Babylonian-Persian-Greek and the Roman imperial attacks prompted the frustrated Jewish community to turn to their religio-cultural traditions for a deliverer who would probably give them hope and strength for resistance. The Hellenistic-Roman empires disturbed the cultural heritage of the Jewish people through the imposition of emperor worship and installing images in their religious centers of Palestine. It is possible to think of the Jewish resistance in line with the peasant-public resistance which was directed not only against the religio-political and economic oppressions but also towards their elite Jewish high-priestly aristocracy.

Certain questions, however, need to be addressed to find out the details of the Jewish world of the first century that fought for its political and religio-cultural national independence. What were the socio-economic-cultural and political situations of the first century world that revolutionized the Jews to call for a national independence? What was the role played by the rural peasants from the Judeo-Galilean countryside which was exploited by its Hellenistic-Roman rulers? How did the Jewish religious sects, the messianic and prophetic movements contribute in the process of socio-political and religious liberation? What were

[1] Norman K. Gottwald, "Early Israel as an Anti-Imperial Community," *In the Shadow of the Empire: Reclaiming the Bible as a History of Faithful Resistance*, edited by R.A. Horsely (Louisville/London: Westminster John Knox Press, 2008), 9. Some consider Israel itself as an ancient empire and some others consider them to be a tribal community who tried to live a life of their own.

the ideologies that promoted the revolutionary movements? By answering these questions the attempt is to analyze the ambivalent position of Luke and Josephus against Rome.[2] In this regard, Horsley's immense contribution to understand the Second Temple Jewish history is extensively used.

3.2 The General Mapping of the First Century Jewish World

The imperial domination over Palestine continued all through the centuries whether it was the Babylonian, Persian, Greek, or Roman regime for their economic and political benefits. The cultural-political imperialism of the Seleucids and later the Romans precipitated the Maccabean revolt (168-167 BCE) and the Jewish-Roman (66-70 CE) war in Palestine.[3] Moreover, the economic exploitation by the imperial regime impoverished the peasant farmers leading to socio-economic divisions in Palestine.[4] During the course of the Persian, Hellenistic, and the first century Roman administration, the ordinary peasant masses were burdened with political demands (tribute and taxes) and religious obligation (tithes and sacrifices).[5] The Jewish economy was further negatively affected by the double taxation of the Roman administration[6] leading to poverty, hunger and mental trauma (cf.Lk.2:1-7; Acts.5:36-37). In addition to these taxation policies, loss of land, slavery of the peasant life, cultural imposition, severe draught and famine of the late 40 CE shattered the economy of the Jewish Palestine that led to the

---

[2] The discursive nature is perhaps demonstrated by blaming the revolutionary resistant movements for the destruction of the Jerusalem temple (*JW* 2.10, 3.297, 4.397, 556-565, 5.28) as well as condemning the atrocities of Rome (*JW* 2.272-76, 282f; 5.372, 403-06). M. Hengel, (Appendix) "Zealots and Sicarii. The Question of the Unity and Diversity of the Jewish Freedom Movement in 6-74 A.D," in *The Zealots: Investigations into the Jewish Freedom Movement in the Period from Herod I until 70A.D* (Edinburgh: T & T Clark, 1989), 385.

[3] H. Jagersma, *A History of Israel from Alexander the Great to Bar Kochba* (Philadelphia: Fortress Press, 1985), 57-143; Horsley, *Jesus and the Spiral of Violence*, 3, 7.

[4] Hengel, *The Zealots*, 28; Horsley, *Jesus and the Spiral of Violence*, 13. The intensity of the economic pressure is perhaps displayed through Jesus' parables (Mt.18:23-33; 20:1-15; Lk.16.1-13; Mk.12:1-9).

[5] R.A. Horsley & John S. Hanson, *Bandits, Prophets and Messiahs: Popular Movements in the Time of Jesus* (New York: Harper & Row Publishers, 1988), 56. During the Hasmonian rule, Gaius Caesar ordered a tribute of one fourth of their produce in the second year in addition to the tithes paid to Hyrcanus and his sons (*Ant.*14.202-3). J. Jeremias, *Jerusalem in the Time of Jesus* (Philadelphia: Fortress Press, 1969), 105. M. Gnanavaram's analysis of Matthew's socio-economic, religio-cultural and political structural issues reveals the ground reality of the first century Galilean poor, *Treasure in Heaven and Treasure on Earth: Attitudes towards Poverty and Wealth in the New Testament Communities and in the Early Church* (Delhi: ISPCK, 2008), 76-119.

[6] Horsley & Hanson, *Bandits, Prophets and Messiahs*, 57. Special levy of taxes were raised during the Roman civil war; punitive measures were taken by the governors (Cassius) for raising taxes as well as bringing to slavery four district centers-Gophna, Emmaus, Lydda and Thamna (*JW* 1.219-22; *Ant.*14.271-75); and administering economic devastations due to the power struggle over the land of Palestine.

upsurge of banditry.[7] The armed rebellions were visible expressions of the fury of the Jewish masses against the imperial powers. However, it also created different responses in the Jewish society over against the structural violence of the imperial forces.

3.2.1 The Political World of Palestine

The Palestinian Jewish life was very much integrated with the political life of the first century. Their life situation was complex in nature due to their varied diaspora locations, diverse political interest and outlook. Some of the aristocrats sided with the ruling party to benefit out of their allegiance but the poor and the marginalized resisted the repressive rule. The people of the land were frustrated over the unstable politics of the land by different type of rulers (Kings, Procurators, and Governors) at different times.

67 BCE is an important year in the socio-political life of the Jews because of the Roman general Pompey's new assignment in the eastern Mediterranean region. It led to the emergence of Judea as a Roman province.[8] The purpose behind the conquest was, probably, not to heed the request of the warring Hasmonian brothers but the geopolitical expansionist plans of Rome, in order to protect their imperial frontiers and trade.[9] Meanwhile, the Romans were gaining from the troubled waters by restoring the Hellenistic cities and other Jewish territories (Galilee, Perea, Idumea, along with Judea) under their control, which were subjected to pay tribute.[10] Pompey, on the pretext of settling the issues, was collecting huge sums of money from the client kings.[11]

Herod achieved the position of a king over Jewish Palestine through a clever tactic that made him known as the 'friend of Rome and Caesar.'[12] Guerilla warfare resumed in Judea and Galilee when he came with the Roman troops in 40 BCE.[13] However, during his early reign, he received praise from the Jewish people including Hyrcanus II for quelling the disturbances in Judea (*Ant.*14.277-299; *JW* 1.220-240). Politically, he wooed the Jewish masses and the Hellenized

[7] Horsley & Hanson, *Bandits, Prophets and Messiahs*, 61-63. A severe famine during the late 40 CE made queen Helena of Adiabene to give relief for the Jerusalemites (*Ant.*20.51-53, 101); Jeremias, *Jerusalem in the Time of Jesus*, 140-145.

[8] Hayes and Mandell, *The Jewish People,* 101. Pompey received two major responsibilities: subduing the pirates from the grain trade and to bring stability by settling the war with Mithridates.

[9] Hayes and Mandell, *The Jewish People*, 104. Judea was the "land bridge" for Roman armies to pass through.

[10] Horsley & Hanson, *Bandits, Prophets and Messiahs*, 30-31.

[11] Hayes and Mandell, *The Jewish People*, 106-07.

[12] Smallwood, *The Jews Under Roman Rule*, 71.

[13] Horsley, *Jesus and Empire,* 36-37. The rebellious revolt continued by successful raids on the Roman army troops, and attacks on the pro-Herodian officers enabled some to escape from Herod's military eye by running away to the mountains and caves (*JW* 1.314-30; *Ant.*14.14.430-54).

citizens by his building constructions including the Jerusalem Temple (*Ant.*15.38-425), the fortified royal palace (*Ant.*15.292-341) and new military colonies in Maritima-Sebaste.[14]

As far as the Jews were concerned, Herod's regime was oppressive for the ordinary masses. The Pharisees were against him because of his non-Jewish origins and pro-Hellenist stand (*Ant.*15.368-71; 17.41-45).[15] However, Herod tactfully alienated the Jews (Pharisees) from any participation in the political process of the community and made them mere religious interpreters.[16] He imposed a tight scrutiny over all public activity and prescribed severe punishment for the guilty (*Ant.*15.365-69).[17] He was very cautious (*Ant.*15.366-368) about the violent revolt of the Jewish subjects for which he fortified the city of Jerusalem (Antonia Fortress in 30s and Hasmonian Masada) with military strongholds.[18] The masses were waiting for an opportunity to release their resentments through voicing their socio-political woes. As a result, soon after his death in 4 BCE, there were popular revolts all over his kingdom, led by the messianic pretenders in each of the principle districts (*JW* 2.55-65; *Ant.*17.271-85). A Jewish national resistance (Judas the Galilean and Theudas) is reported to be active in the context of the growth of the Christian movement in Jerusalem (cf.Ac.5:29).

There was a renewed protest from the side of the Pharisees and rabbis over against the joint demand of oath of loyalty to both the emperor Augustus and King Herod for which they were fined (*Ant.*17.42).[19] On another occasion the offended *sophistai* (who tried to destroy the golden eagle which was placed over the temple doorway), were burned alive by the furious Herod (*JW* 1.648-50; *Ant.*17.149-51, 167). Similarly, his ethnic hatred revealed his mind by the imprisonment of a large number of prominent Jews for execution before his death (*Ant.*17.174-9, 193; *JW* i.659-60, 666).[20] The pro-Roman sentiments continuously flared up over his Semitic feelings and his imperial attitude showed as he imposed Romanism over the subject Jewish masses.

---

[14] Hengel, *Zealots,* 320; Horsley & Hanson, *Bandits, Prophets and Messiahs*, 32.

[15] Horsley & Hanson, *Bandits, Prophets and Messiahs*, 32. Herod was a "half-Jew" because of his Idumean father and Arab mother. The Pharisees refused to take loyalty oath to the king.

[16] Horsley & Hanson, *Bandits, Prophets and Messiahs*, 32-33.

[17] There were government spies in public sphere and moreover the political accusers were executed at the fortress of Hyrcania (*Ant.*15.365-69).

[18] Smallwood, *The Jews Under Roman Rule,* 73-85; Horsley, *Jesus and the Spiral of Violence*, 44. Herod was suspicious of any private meetings, and he punished severely any attempt to topple his reign (*Ant.*15.366-368).

[19] Smallwood, *The Jews Under Roman Rule,* 98; Hengel, *Zealots,* 321.

[20] Smallwood, *The Jews Under Roman Rule,* 99-103. The gospel tradition adds further explanation of the cruelty of this tyrant of eliminating a possible rival by hearing the birth of Jesus (Mt.2:1-18).

The major widespread revolts against Rome between 40 BCE and 132-35 CE reveal the cumulative effects of the continuous oppression and repression by the Romans.[21] The Roman retaliation against the popular revolts was severe in its form and some took the form of crucifying the insurgents in Judea and Galilee (*JW* 5:449-51).[22] However, the political collaboration of the Jewish elites (Herodians and High priestly families) with the Roman client kings turned the social situation plunge into internal conflicts before the great Jewish-Roman War.[23] The Jewish resistant movements functioned from the level of non-participation in Roman imperial tax system to the violent reactions of the banditry, Zealots, Sicarii, Prophetic movements and Messianic movements.

3.2.2 The Socio-Economic World of Palestine

The economic burden that Herod created by raising extra tribute from Galilee (*Ant.* 14.273; *JW* 1.221) and by undertaking expensive building project seemed to have been the reasons behind the social unrest among the masses (*Ant.* 14.450).[24] The oppressed Jews voiced their grievances to Archelaus, soon after his father Herod's death, over against certain key religio-political and economic issues.[25] The escalated Jewish protest during the Passover celebration over the lukewarm response of Archelaus, was suppressed with the help of armed forces resulted in the sacrifice of thousand innocent Jews in the holy place.[26] As a repressive measure to resist the open rebellion, Archelaus and Varus, the legate of Syria sent the Roman garrison for a period of transition which was resented by the Jerusalem crowd.[27] In addition, an imperial procurator Sabinus, later harassed the Jews through provocation from the Roman legions and his own armed slaves (*Ant.* 17.252-255; *JW* 2.40-44).[28] The countless multitudes of Jews from far and wide of Jerusalem (Judea, Idumea and Perea) flocked in zeal on the day of Pentecost with a nationalistic feeling of the liberation for a hand-to-hand combat (*JW* 2.43;

---

[21] Horsley, *Jesus and Empire,* 36-37.

[22] Horsley, ed., *In the Shadow of the Empire,* 81. Two thousand leading insurgents were crucified (*JW* 2.66-75; *Ant.* 17.286-95). Simon bar Gibora, one of the great rebel leaders was taken to Rome as a victory over insurgency (*JW* 7.132-55).

[23] Horsley & Hanson, *Bandits, Prophets and Messiahs*, 42-43. The details of the Jewish-Roman war are put in the Appendix.

[24] Sean Freyne, *Galilee from Alexander the Great to Hadrian 323 BCE to 135 CE* (Edinburgh: T & T Clark, 1980), 190; Horsley & Hanson, *Bandits, Prophets and Messiahs*, 32.

[25] The key economic issue is of cutting back the yearly tribute, and the abolition of Herodian tax (*Ant.* 17.206-208; *JW* 2.5-7). Horsley, *Jesus and the Spiral of Violence*, 50; Smallwood, *The Jews Under Roman Rule,* 106; Hengel, *Zealots,* 320, 325.

[26] Hengel, *The Zealots*, 325; Smallwood, *The Jews Under Roman Rule,* 110. There was a mounting protest in Jerusalem from the people of the countryside who came for the Passover festival.

[27] Hengel, *The Zealots*, 326; Horsley, *Jesus and the Spiral of Violence*, 51. Varus' intervention created severe chaos in Jerusalem.

[28] Horsley, *Jesus and the Spiral of Violence,* 51; Freyne, *Galilee*, 214.

*Ant.*17.254).[29] Conversely, the Roman military took over the largely unarmed Jews and killed three thousands of them, burned the temple porticos, and plundered the temple treasury (*JW* 2.46-50; *Ant.*17.257-264).[30] As a reactionary measure, the agitated Jews violently attacked the fortress with a great vision of a national liberation (*JW* 2.51-54; *Ant.*17.265-267).[31]

There was widespread resentment in Judea and Galilee over the issue of census and tax-payment to the imperial center resulting in violent and non-violent resistant movements in 6 CE.[32] The delay in collecting special taxes imposed by the legate of Syria, Cassius reduced their populaces to slavery (*JW* 1.216-22; *Ant.*14.271-75).[33] Meanwhile, there were popular movements by messianic pretenders (*JW* 2.55, 61-62: *Ant.*17.273-274, 278) supported by brigand groups broke out in the major districts of Palestine (Galiee, Perea and Judea) which disturbed the political atmosphere of Palestine.[34]

The imposition of temple tax was another financial burden over the ordinary Jewish community in addition to the burden of the political taxes. The priestly aristocracy enjoyed the religious tax system because they lived a luxurious life based on the exploited money on religious basis.[35] The imperial socio-economic crisis due to the double taxation and the alien rule in an agrarian rural Palestine dramatically raised the revolutionary activity in parallel with the popular movements.[36] The severe famine during the middle of the first century CE added force to it. Just before the Jewish-Roman War, the banditry became an epidemic

[29] Horsley, *Jesus and the Spiral of Violence*, 51-52; Smallwood, *The Jews Under Roman Rule*, 110-111.

[30] Smallwood, *The Jews Under Roman Rule*, 111; Hengel, *Zealots*, 207-08, 326.

[31] Horsley, *Jesus and the Spiral of Violence*, 52; Hengel, *The Zealots*, 326. A certain Judas from Galilee publicly protested against the census and tax collection by seeing it as an act of slavery (*Ant.*17.3-6).

[32] Smallwood, *The Jews Under Roman Rule*, 151-53. Caligula's desire of erecting his statue in Jerusalem's temple caused similar non-violent protest as a whole nation ready for a sacrifice (*JW* 2.185-203; *Ant.*18.261-309). J.D. Crossan, "Paul and Rome: The Challenge of a Just World Order," *USQR* 59/ 3-4 (2005), 13-14.

[33] Smallwood, *The Jews Under Roman Rule*, 46. Four toparchy capitals which led into slavery are Gophna, Emmaus, Lydda and Thamma. Horsley & Hanson, *Bandits, Prophets and Messiahs*, 57. Cassius made slaves of thirty thousand men in Taricheae of Galilee and other important towns of Judea (Emmaus, Lydda, etc. *Ant.*14.120, 272-75). Varus sold the inhabitants as slaves and set the city of Sepphoris on fire (*Ant.*17.288-89). Horsley & Hanson, *Bandits, Prophets and Messiahs*, 31; Hengel, *Zealots*, 323.

[34] Smallwood, *The Jews Under Roman Rule*, 111; Horsley, *Jesus and the Spiral of Violence*, 52-54.

[35] The ordinary peasants had to pay a dual tax system that burdened the socio-economic life beyond imagination. Joy's study on the repressive temple tax system based on the work of Grant, *Mark and its Subalterns*, 108-09; F.C. Grant, *The Economic Background of the Gospel* (Oxford: Oxford University Press, 1961), 96; K.C. Hanson and D.E. Oakman, *Palestine in the Times of Jesus: Social Structures and Social Conflicts* (Minneapolis: Fortress Press, 1998), 144.

[36] Horsley & Hanson, *Bandits, Prophets and Messiahs*, 49-50, 66.

(*Ant.*20.255) that seemed to have made the outbreak of the great revolt against the Romans.[37] The majority peasants who lived in villages of Judea and Galilee were in abject poverty due to the tax system and famine.[38] The class disparity between rich and the poor in Palestine has been identified by classical historians (Josephus and Philo).[39]

3.2.3 The Religio-Cultural World of Palestine

The religious center at Jerusalem became another imperial web of power similar to the Roman colonial powers. In the process of Roman colonialism, the intention of installing the statue of Gaius in the temple sanctuary was to proclaim Caesar as god. The imperial cult and emperor worship seriously hurt the religious sentiments of the Jews.[40] Emperor Gaius Caligula demanded divine honors from the reluctant ordinary Jewish peasants which prompted retaliation against erecting the statue of Zeus in the temple at Jerusalem. This action led to a major confrontation and popular outcry for a long period.[41] The Jews confronted the legate of Syria, Petronius and his legions in different places (Ptolemais and Tiberias). As a reaction, they were given the order to erect Gaius' image in the temple (*JW* 2.184 203; *Ant.*18.256-309). Other lesser incursions into the Temple precincts happened during the time of Herod the Great (*JW* 1.647-55; *Ant.*17.149-67) and Pontius Pilate (*JW* 2.175-77; *Ant.* 18.60-62).

Extreme Jewish nationalist feelings and the outbreak of terrorist-brigandage in an immeasurable number in and around Judea-Galilee was developed as a response to the rule of Pilate.[42] He provoked the religio-cultural sentiments of the Jews by erecting the images of Caesar in Herod's palace. Moreover, he looted the treasury of the temple, resulted in a revolt which killed thousands in Judea (*JW* 2.224-27; 2.232-40; 2.169-74; 2.176-77; 2.280; *Ant.*18.60-62; 20.105-12; 20.118-24).[43] It might have been a conscious provocation by disrespecting the Jewish cultural traditions and demonstrating the military garrison in the Antonia

---

[37] Horsley & Hanson, *Bandits, Prophets and Messiahs*, 69.

[38] Since the reign of Herod, the land became the property of the tenant farmers or imperial masters. The economic conditions of the ordinary people of Galilee can be analyzed in similar line with the gospel accounts. Mk.12:1ff; Matt.18:23; Lk.16:1ff. Hengel, *The Zealots*, 335.

[39] R.A. Horsley, "Like One of the Prophets of Old": Two Types of Popular Prophets at the time of Jesus", *CBQ* 47/3 (1985), 444.

[40] Horsley, *Jesus and the Spiral of Violence*, 114.

[41] N.H. Taylor, "Palestinian Christianity and the Caligula Crisis. Part. I. Social and Historical Reconsideration," *JSNT* 61 (1996), 101; Horsley, *Jesus and the Spiral of Violence*, 111.

[42] Smallwood, *The Jews Under Roman Rule*, 164. Anti-Roman feelings became prevalent during Pilate's reign and he retaliated against this move with crucifixion of terrorist leaders (Jesus bar Abbas) and other brigands. Gospel narrations give evidence to the crucifixion as a punishment for anti-Roman instigative move (Mt.27:15-16; 26:55; Mk.14:48; Lk.22:52).

[43] Horsley & Hanson, *Bandits, Prophets and Messiahs*, 37-43. More than one occasion Pilate became a pawn in the hands of the emperors in Rome to erect the images of Caesar either in

to carry the military standards through the roads of Jerusalem. The Roman military was kept "in close proximity to the high priest's vestments."[44] There was serious and prolonged popular protest together with the people from the countryside which demanded the withdrawal of the army unit from Jerusalem (*JW* 2.169-174; *Ant.*18.55-59).[45] The Jewish crowd confronted the military force of the Roman governor by a nonviolent demonstrative protest by offering their necks to the drawn swords, resulted in calling back the army to Caesarea (*Ant.*28.55-59).[46] The second major provocation of Pilate against the Jewish religious sentiments was through financing a grand aqueduct project by using the temple treasury (*JW* 2.175-177).[47] The peaceful demonstration on popular protest ("tens of thousands" *Ant.*18.60) was attacked by a military force which killed the demonstrators with batons and physical attacks.[48]

During the reign of Cumanus, the Jerusalem Jews were deliberately provoked by a soldier's indecent gesture in public during a Passover festival which resulted in a public uproar and death of many in the ensuing stampede (20,000- *Ant.*20.105-12; 30,000- *JW* 2.223-27). Repeatedly, the Jewish religious sentiments were provoked when a soldier, who was sent on a punitive expedition to Bethhoron, burned the scroll of the law from a synagogue (*JW* 2.228-229; *Ant.*20.113-114).[49] The Jewish cultural nationalist feelings were continuously roused by the unprecedented violence of the arrogant Roman governor Florus in 66 CE by his anti-Semitic acts. He forcibly tried to extract the Temple treasury with the help of the Roman troops (*JW* 2.280-283). Moreover, he scourged and crucified a number of Jewish aristocratic individuals (*JW* 2.321-326).[50]

3.3 The Growth of Cultural Nationalism and the Varied Forms of Resistance

The cultural elements of the pious Jews have been challenged all through the Hellenistic period through the Maccabean revolt. Moreover, the advent of Roman colonialism has greatly challenged the nationalistic feelings of the religious Jews.

Jerusalem or in Herod's palace. By seeing the intensity of the Jewish religious fervor, Pilate had to remove the image of Caesar from Herod's palace (*JW* 2.169-74).

[44] Smallwood, *The Jews Under Roman Rule*, 161. The military standards were 'symbols of the imperial cult and objects of worship to the troops.' Luke probably refers to the desecration of the temple by Pilate (Lk.13:1f). Hengel, *Zealots,* 208.

[45] Smallwood, *The Jews Under Roman Rule*, 161; Horsley, *Jesus and the Spiral of Violence*, 100. Keeping images were a violation of the Jewish law (Ex.20:4; Deut.4:16, 5:8).

[46] Horsley, *Jesus and the Spiral of Violence*, 104.

[47] Smallwood, *The Jews Under Roman Rule*, 162.

[48] Smallwood, *The Jews Under Roman Rule,* 162. Luke's mentioning of the blood sacrifices of the Galileans probably coincided with some of the protest against Pilate's sacrilege by looting the temple treasury (Lk.7:1).

[49] Smallwood, *The Jews Under Roman Rule*, 263-66; Hengel, *The Zealots*, 347-48.

[50] Horsley, *Jesus and the Spiral of Violence*, 54-55. He plundered and killed the Jewish houses and residents after sacking the upper market area of Jerusalem. Hengel, *Zealots,* 208.

Since the time of Antiocus Epiphanus-the succeeding Roman emperors-the client kings like Herod the Great and the consecutive wars mapped the development of a strong nationalistic feeling in the heart of the Jewish colonial subjects. The rise of an independent nation was at the heart of the pious religious Jews. Theocentric feeling of the worship of Yahweh, zeal for the Torah and the Jerusalem Temple were the motivational factors behind the nationalistic thinking.[51] Moreover, the Jerusalem Temple was a crucial nationalistic concern for the pious Jews who fought against the Roman forces in order to safe guard its religio-cultural identity.

The intellectuals gave rationale (coherent ideology) for their resistance to the Roman rule on certain basic principles of continually keeping the tradition that God Yahweh as the King of Israel (*Ant.*18.23; 4.223; *JW* 2.118, 433; Psalm of Solomon 17) and submitting to foreign rule made them idolaters. The political and cultural imperialism of the Roman government prompted the Jews to think for a nation of their own. Roman colonization and their oppressive rules prompted to visualize an overthrow of the conquering nation and the restoration of a state of their own.

The Jewish cultural nationalism was aroused during the Roman period when their religio-cultural feelings were attacked by the Roman soldier burning the Torah, the imposition of the emperor cult, graven images on the trophies, erection of the graven images of the emperor in the temple.

3.3.1 Mapping the Development of Cultural Nationalism

The Hellenizing policies were re-emphasized as soon as the Seleucids came to power. Antiochus IV initiated many Hellenistic reforms with imperialistic ambitions[52] and converted Jerusalem into a Hellenistic *polis* (2Macc.4:9-10; cf.1Macc.1:13).[53] The cultural ethos of the ancestral traditions was changed into a new culture of entertainment and new customs which was contrary to the Jewish law.[54] More severely, the purchase of the high priesthood by increasing the tribute to the Hellenistic rulers (2Macc.4:8) caused popular resistance in the city of Jerusalem (2Macc.4:39-41).[55] Judea revolted against the misdeeds of Antiochus

---

[51] W.R. Farmer, *Maccabees, Zealots, and Josephus. An Inquiry into Jewish Nationalism in the Greco-Roman Period* (New York: Columbia University Press, 1956), 46-124.

[52] J.H. Hayes and S.R. Mandell, *The Jewish People in Classical Antiquity: From Alexander to Bar Kochba* (Louisville, Kentucky: Westminster John Knox Presss, 1998), 49-59. Farmer connects the Jewish nationalistic sentiments of the Seleucids period and the later Roman period based on the common character in the Jewish ideology and actions. Farmer, *Maccabees, Zealots, and Josephus*,125-151.

[53] Hayes and Mandell, *The Jewish People in Classical Antiquity*, 52. Certain priests took part in the wrestling arena by despising the religious duties at the temple (2Macc.4:12, 13-15); the Hellenized Jews including some of the priests removed their mark of circumcision (1Macc.1:15).

[54] The Jews were enforced to eat swine flesh which was contradictory to their law (2Macc.7:1; 2Macc.6:18) and Sabbath profanation (2Macc.6:6).

[55] Hayes and Mandell, *The Jewish People in Classical Antiquity*, 50-52. Jason purchased the high priestly post of Onias by offering Antiochus an addition of the usual tribute of 300 talents and

IV (2Macc.5:11) and made him to retaliate terribly through massacres, slavery and by confiscating the wealth of the temple (1Macc.1:21-2).[56] The mounting resistance of the Judean Jews was confronted by Antiochus in decreeing an end to the temple worship and the observance of the law with a death penalty to those who disobeyed the command of the king (1Macc.1:44, 49-50; cf.2Macc.6:1-2).[57]

The Maccabean revolt seemed to be a success in recapturing Jerusalem. The Seleucids accepted "Judea as a semi-independent temple state."[58] A deconstruction of Maccabean history showed undue popularity gained for the Hasmonian leadership by rejecting the role played by the Judean peasants and their aspirations for establishing the religio-political freedom.[59] During the rule that lasted a century, the Hasmonian dynasty not only re-conquered Judean states but also succeeded in expanding the territory similar to the earlier Davidic kingdom.[60]

The Jewish cultural nationalism emerged in the context of Jewish revolt against Rome in different periods. It is logical to analyze more than one single national liberation movement of the Zealots during the Jewish-Roman war. Most of the Jewish sects had an overt or invert policy of national liberation. However, the Jewish popular movements like the messianic movements and the prophetic movements were prominent among the peasantry.[61] In addition to that, the Jewish festivals were the occasions of uprisings and repressions.[62] However, the feeling of national liberation was periodically flared up by bandit-peasant movements in epidemic proportions. The years of the bandit-peasant revolt, the mid-century prophetic movements, the late mid-century violent Sicarii movement, the Zealot movement during the actual war period (*JW* 2.259-260, 264, 443; 4.95, 272, 348-349) expected national freedom on the basis of the Jewish tradition of their covenantal laws (1Macc. 2:27; 1Macc. 4:9-10).[63] Moreover, the popular charismatic leaders who promised apocalyptic deliverances from the eschatological

---

Menelaus did the same against Jason by sending him to exile in the Transjordan (2Macc.4:33). Finally, Menelaus robbed the temple treasures and vessels to pay off his promised tribute (2Macc.4:27-32).

[56] Hayes and Mandell, *The Jewish People in Classical Antiquity*, 58.

[57] Horsley & Hanson, *Bandits, Prophets and Messiahs*, 15-16. Antiochus burned the scrolls of the law. In the place of traditional sacrifices, swine was offered (1Macc.1:44-47; *Ant.*12:253).

[58] Horsley & Hanson, *Bandits, Prophets and Messiahs*, 21-22. The Jewish sacrificial cult was reinstituted in Dec.164 BCE (1Macc.4:42-58; 2Macc.10:1-7) and an annual festival of Hanukka (1Macc.4:36-59; 2Macc.10: 8) was celebrated in commemoration of the rededication of the sanctuary under the leadership of Judas Maccabees.

[59] Horsley & Hanson, *Bandits, Prophets and Messiahs*, 22.

[60] Horsley & Hanson, *Bandits, Prophets and Messiahs*, 22-23. Simon attained the supreme religio-political leadership in perpetuity both as a high priest and a military commander.

[61] Horsley & Hanson, *Bandits, Prophets and Messiahs*, xvi.

[62] *Ant.*20.106-107; cf. *JW* 2.223-224; Mk.14:2; Matt.26:5. Some of the Jewish festivals were set against in the context of liberation from the imperial nations (eg., Festival of Passover, Purim).

[63] Farmer, *Maccabees, Zealots, and Josephus*, 47; Horsley, *Jesus and the Spiral of Violence*, 83.

acts of God (*Ant.*20.97-98, 169-72; *JW* 2.261-63) finally led to the full-scale rebellion in the sixth decade of the first century CE.[64]

3.3.2 Varied Forms of Resistance

As a result of Jewish cultural nationalism against the active move of Roman colonialism, the first century witnessed several uprising against Rome. The Seleucids, Herodian and Roman political domination had created among the Jews varied responses on the basis of their expectations to Jewish nationalism. Some fervently participated in the political process forming resistant movements; some others withdrew to isolated wilderness in anticipation of an apocalyptic battle hoping for their national liberation through divine intervention; and some took a postcolonial position of simultaneously affiliating and distancing, consensual-conflicting political strategy towards colonial rule. Non-violent and violent popular unrest and resistance against the Roman imperial oppressive reign probably took "*several distinctive social forms.*"[65]

3.3.2.1 Jewish Religio-Political Sects

During the first century Roman imperial reign, there developed other religio-politically oriented groups. They exhibited their aspiration for the national freedom differently either with violence or with mild resistance. The Maccabean tradition reappeared to defend the faith of their fathers. The common cause of resisting the colonial Roman force made the socio-religious groups to pool their intellectual, physical resources to formulate their identity for the cause of their nation.

Diverse Jewish socio-religious movements arose within Judaism during the Hellenistic-Roman period. These schools of thought differentiated themselves based on their affiliation with the religio-political power relations. They responded differently to the first century socio-religious-cultural and political ideology of the time. These discursive responses could be explicated by dealing with at least five of such distinctive Jewish religious groups of the time.

3.3.2.1.1 Qumran Community/Essenes

As a matter of protest against the Hasmonian successors for adopting the antagonistic Hellenistic cultures made a considerable number of Hasidim to withdraw into the wilderness of Dead Sea and refrain from associating themselves with the corrupted socio-political regime.[66] This Hasidim were disillusioned by religious and cultural compromises and deviations for the sake of their own

---

[64] R.A. Horsley, "The Sicarii: Ancient Jewish 'Terrorists,'" *JR* 59 (1979), 446-47.

[65] Horsley, "Like One of the Prophets of Old," 463 (italics in the original).

[66] Horsley & Hanson, *Bandits, Prophets and Messiahs*, 24; G. Vermes, *The Dead Sea Scrolls: Qumran in Perspective* (Philadelphia: Fortress Press, 1981), 125-30.

religio-political domination.[67] The Qumran community shows great affinity to the Essenes. They made an exclusive community with strict organizational system following rules and regulations (*JW* 2.122-153). Some of them followed strict celibacy (*Ant.* 18.21; *JW* 2.120) while others did not (*JW* 2.160-161). They were a peasant community (*Ant.*1.19) who strictly follow a communitarian life of common meal and common property (*JW*1.128-132; 1QS 6.2-5). They resisted the temple sacrificial system (*Ant.*2.145, 149). They "organized an ideal priestly theocracy in exile, a "true Israel" headed by the only "legitimate" priesthood."[68] It was a utopian eschatological community with an apocalyptic expectation followed by a rigorous obedience to the law of God especially the Sabbath observance (1QS1.1-3; 5.8; 6.22).[69] They considered themselves the righteous remnant, and the new covenant community who would witness the ultimate fulfillment of God's perfect new creation.[70] They also followed certain religious rituals like bathing as a mark of purity, and messianic banquet in anticipation of the arrival of the final deliverance by the messiah.[71] They expected three different divinely authorized figures (prophetic, kingly and priestly) from their own community in anticipation of their national freedom.[72]

The complex and fluid messianic expectations of that time was evident as the Qumran/Essenes anticipated a national independence through varied eschatological agents.[73] The illegitimacy of the Hasmonian priest-king and Herodian pro-Roman kings gave the ambivalent expectations from a priestly figure to the royal figure.[74] Similarly, the priestly Qumran community gave more

---

[67] The Zadokite priestly tradition was broken by the high priestly position of the Hasmonians (Jonathan and Simon). The Hasidim were expecting the advent of the reign of Yahweh according to the apocalyptic visions. Horsley & Hanson, *Bandits, Prophets and Messiahs*, 24.

[68] Horsley & Hanson, *Bandits, Prophets and Messiahs*, 25.

[69] E. Ferguson, *Backgrounds of Early Christianity* (Michigan: Wm. B. Eerdmans Publishing Company, 1987), 415. The collective apocalyptic of visions consisted of a "star, resembling a sword, standing over the city," (*JW* 6.289), the chariots and armed battalions encompassing the cities (*JW* 6.297-299). Horsley & Hanson, *Bandits, Prophets and Messiahs*, 142.

[70] Horsley & Hanson, *Bandits, Prophets and Messiahs*, 25. The Essenes rigorously interpreted the covenantal laws.

[71] Horsley & Hanson, *Bandits, Prophets and Messiahs*, 26. The War scroll heightened a war between the sons of light against the sons of darkness where the legions of angels would come to the rescue of the righteous. Christopher Rowland, *Christian Origins. An Acoount of the Setting and Character of the most Important Messianic Sect of Judaism* (Cambridge: SPCK, 1985), 74-75.

[72] Koester, *History, Culture, and Religion*, 238

[73] Horsley & Hanson, *Bandits, Prophets and Messiahs*, 102-03. R.E. Brown, "The Messianism of Qumran," *CBQ* 19 (1957), 53-80. The Essenes expected a prophetical (Deut.18:15-18), priestly as well as a lay head who was anointed.

[74] The anointed priest presides the eschatological banquet (1QSa 2:11-22). The Essenes used the prophetic texts (2Sam.7:12-14; Jer.23:5; Amos 9:11) to interpret the eschatological fulfillment of the expectation of a messiah (4QFlor 1:10-13).

importance to the covenant law and eschatological mysteries than the anointed royal figure.[75] The hybridity concept of the messiah in Qumran scroll reveals multifaceted figures of the political messiah "the Branch of David" (4Q285), "the prince of the congregation", "righteous messiah" who would establish justice and righteousness (1QSb 5:20-29; cf. Psa.Sol 17-18), a priestly one (4QTestimonia (4Q175), an eschatological prophet type (1 QS 9:11-12), Melchizedek (11QMelch), and Son of God (4Q246).[76]

3.3.2.2 Pharisees

The Pharisees were a scholarly lay movement of a religious sect within Judaism (Hasidim) who had political influence among the middle class intellectuals.[77] The transition of varied political administration and the crisis of political war caused severe crisis to the Pharisaic sect due to its complex allegiances. During the early Hasmonean dynasty, the Pharisees were a highly influential sect who apparently participated directly in the socio-political affairs by taking the role of scribes, lawyers, and teachers.[78] By taking these roles, they regulated and retained the existing religio-cultural positions in passing on the unwritten traditions of the former generations (*Ant.*13.296-297; 408).[79]

The strained relationship between John Hyrcanus and the Pharisees over the problem of socio-religious and political authority over Judea made the latter to come out as a group with laws for the social life of the people (*JW* 1.107-14; *Ant.*13.288-98; 18.11-17; 13.399-418).[80] Later, the Pharisees suffered severe causalities during the reign of Alexander Janneus, son of John Hyrcanus (*Ant.* 13:402-403). He crucified eight hundred and eight thousands of his opponents who "fled beyond the pale of Judea" (*JW* 1.97-98; *Ant.*13:380-383).[81] Unlike the Qumranites, they held on to an eschatological orientation not with an imminent final realization of the reign of God but for an essential living for the Jewish society in Israel.[82] This resulted in forming a grass-root level hybrid community

[75] Horsley & Hanson, *Bandits, Prophets and Messiahs,* 105.

[76] Laato, *A Star is Rising*, 290-316.

[77] During the Hasmonian political period, the Pharisees probably emerged from the Hasidim group in direct opposition to the step taken by the Essenes and they fought with the Maccabees. Horsley & Hanson, *Bandits, Prophets and Messiahs,* 26; J. Neusner, *From Politics to Piety: The Emergence of Pharisaic Judaism* (Englewood Cliffs: Prentice Hall, 1973), 45-66.

[78] Ferguson, *Backgrounds of Early Christianity*, 406-07; Horsley, *Jesus and the Spiral of Violence*, 68.

[79] Horsley, *Jesus and the Spiral of Violence*, 68.

[80] The non-Zadokite priestly issue prompted the Pharisees to ask the Hyrcanus to relinquish the post of high priesthood and be content with the political rule. Horsley & Hanson, *Bandits, Prophets and Messiahs*, 28.

[81] Horsley, *Jesus and the Spiral of Violence*, 68.

[82] Horsley & Hanson, *Bandits, Prophets and Messiahs*, 26-27. The significant eschatological belief in resurrection made the Pharisees distinctive (*JW* 2.119ff; Ac.23:6; Mk.12:26f.). Rowland, *Christian Origins*, 70.

of protest which was a resistant movement against the religio-political situation at Jerusalem in the form of founding synagogues as centers for teaching the Torah as a rule for their socio-religious, and cultural life of the Jews.[83] Josephus' description of the Pharisaic belief in the immortality of souls, of reward and punishment according to the virtue and vice seem to have pointed to their understating of eschatology and resurrection (*Ant.*18.14; Ac.23:6-9) in the political context of repressive killing by the imperial forces.

During the Herodian period, the Pharisees received favour and respect, and they were freed from "an oath of loyalty" to Rome.[84] Further, during the Roman imperial rule, they were excluded "from any effective political role."[85] There were some revolutionary Pharisees who were active in the political atmosphere of the Jewish-Roman War (*JW* 2.409-17) and some dissuaded people from revolt.[86] However, at the threshold of the revolt, some took oath to be loyal to Caesar while quite a number of the Pharisees refused to do it (six thousand, *Ant.*17.42) because of the commitment to their political ideology.[87] Josephus' pro-Roman position during the time of war made Pharisaic delegates to ask Rome to remove him from his position in Galilee (Life 196-98). However, after the mass destruction of the temple at Jerusalem, the Pharisees who survived gathered at the coastal town of Jamnia in 90 CE (1Macc 4.15; 5:58; 2Macc.12.8-9; *JW* 2.335), which became the centre of Rabbinic Judaism.[88] Lukan portrayal of the Pharisees explains the affiliative nature of this group to the newly formed minority Christian community (Ac.5:34-41; 23:9; 26:4-8).

3.3.2.3 Sadducees

A religiously wealthy conservative aristocracy named Sadducees was formed in the context of the Maccabean political regime to align with the priestly aristocracy that aimed for national independence.[89] The fierce opposition between Pharisees and Sadducees during the Jannaeus' reign greatly influenced the history of the first century BCE.[90] Their socio-religious life was based on the Law of Moses

[83] Alan Storkey, *Jesus and Politics: Confronting the Powers* (Grand Rapids: Baker Academy, 2005), 45.

[84] Anthony J. Saldarini, "Pharisees", in *ABD*, vol. 5, edited by David Noel Freedman (New York: Doubleday, 1992), 293. The Pharisees expanded themselves under the reign of Herod and Antipas. Storkey, *Jesus and Politics*, 46.

[85] Horsley, *Jesus and the Spiral of Violence*, 82.

[86] Saldarini, "Pharisees", 293.

[87] Horsley, *Jesus and the Spiral of Violence*, 69.

[88] Puskas, *An Introduction to the New Testament*, 41.

[89] Smallwood, *The Jews Under Roman Rule,* 17; Horsley & Hanson, *Bandits, Prophets and Messiahs*, 27-28. The Pharisees raised criticism against the illegitimacy of the royal throne on the basis of Davidic tradition and the traditional priesthood based on the Zadokite family.

[90] Smallwood, *The Jews Under Roman Rule,* 18; Horsley & Hanson, *Bandits, Prophets and Messiahs*, 29. The despotian Jannaeus' regime (104-76 BCE) made popular outbursts resulting in

(*Ant.*13.297; 18.16) without much extensive interpretation like the Pharisees and the scribes did.[91] The Sadducees' denial of the afterlife and judgement (*JW*2.163-65; *Ant.*18.14, 16; Ac.23:6-80) must have prompted them to live a life in its fullness by joining hands with the political establishment.[92] Their socio-economic interest prompted them to maintain their *status quo* which made them hostile with the messianic and apocalyptic resistant movements.[93] In the history of the Jewish world, most of the Sadducees supported the ruling group (Hasmonians, Herodians and Romans) to maintain their social life among the elites. They joined with the Jerusalem authorities to keep the religio-political power and were antagonistic to the marginalized Jesus movement.[94] They joined hands with the Roman imperial reign during the political crisis where the Jewish nationalism had been running its course. Many of the account in Acts substantiate the position of the Sadducees' collaborating with the high-priests and the dominant temple authorities (Ac.4:1-4; 5:17; 15:17-18).

3.3.2.4 The Zealots

The Zealotic movement grew as the fugitive Jewish peasants joined hands with brigands (*JW* 4.134) in order to form a coalition against the Roman military advancement in the northwestern Judea.[95] The growing influence of the Zealot movement and the ambivalent position of the Jerusalemites caused serious concern for the high priestly leaders who sought help from the city people.[96] The ambivalent position of the Jerusalemites toward the revolt is given by the report of Josephus about the peace-longing citizen body as well as the revolutionary nature of the Jerusalemites including the priest and the temple captain Eleazar (*JW* 4.150). The negotiation process with the ruling high priest continued for over a year as the Zealots were preparing their strategy for resistance with the help of the elite citizens in Palestine.[97]

Josephus commented that the Zealots proper who had a zeal for virtue (*JW* 7.270) originated by the middle of the Jewish revolt (ca.67-68 CE).[98] The basic reason for the Zealots' resistance was the class struggle between the

---

the vengeance by crucifying and slaughtering the opponents (*Ant.*13.372-83; 399-404).

[91] Horsley & Hanson, *Bandits, Prophets and Messiahs*, 28.

[92] G.W.E. Nickelsburg, *Ancient Judaism and Christian Origins. Diversity, Continuity and Transformation* (Minneapolis: Fortress Press, 2003), 166-67.

[93] Jagersma, *A History of Israel*, 70.

[94] Joy, *Mark and its Subalterns*, 101.

[95] Horsley & Hanson, *Bandits, Prophets and Messiahs*, 217-18; Smith, "Zealots and Sicarii," 17.

[96] Horsley & Hanson, *Bandits, Prophets and Messiahs*, 237-38. Josephus' portrayal of 'δεμος' means 'citizens' or 'crowd' as a collective body.

[97] Horsley & Hanson, *Bandits, Prophets and Messiahs*, 239.

[98] Hengel opines a strong bond of relationship between the Fourth Philosophy and the Zealots. M. Hengel, *Was Jesus a Revolutionalist?* (Philadephia: Fortress Press, 1971), 10-13, 32.

Herodian nobles and Jewish peasants (*JW* 4.414).[99] Zealots had the conviction for peoples' participation in the process of national freedom and were centered in Jerusalem to fight against Rome. Based Josephus's views, Smith does not agree with Stegemann on the relationship of Zealots with the priestly party of Jerusalem based on the words of Josephus.[100] Later this group became strong enough to take control over the religious city by terrorizing through murder and imprisonment of some prominent citizens, and appointed a Zadokite high priestly office by lot (*JW* 4.147-56).

Horsley counters the Jerusalem centered activity of a 'peasant-brigand-Zealots' for their priestly leadership by presupposing the connectivity of a group led by Eleazar, the son of Simon as well as Ananias in 66 CE.[101] However, it is a circumstantial factor that rendered them to be ambivalent in their position during an outbreak of violence (*JW* 4.151) as they had taken shelter in the temple fortress (*JW* 4.173) or had become "imprisoned in the temple" (*JW* 4.229). The Zealots started purging the temple city by attacking the ruling aristocracy and the Herodian nobles (*JW* 4.233-53). They executed Ananias, and his brother Ezechias (*JW* 2.430-41) with the help of the Idumeans (*JW* 4.224-32); they killed the high priest Ananus and Jesus son of Gamala (*JW* 4.139-41, 254-365).[102] In the purging process of execution of the nobles, the Zealots gave the priests time to join the cause of their political resistance rather than acting in hasty revenge (*JW* 4.327).

3.3.2.5 Sicarii

Despite the possible ambiguity of the origin of Sicarii movements in the broader context of Jewish resistance to the structural violence of Roman imperialism (*JW* 7.254-55), there was a distinctive political strategy that started in the mid-

---

[99] Horsley & Hanson, *Bandits, Prophets and Messiahs,* 225-26. The class conflict between the peasant subjugated masses and the collaborated ruling aristocracy is evident in the Zealotic principles of purging process of executing the ruling elites of Herodian nobility. The socio-political nature of Jewish Palestine has an exploitative nature of the Herodian-high priestly aristocracy and their tie up with the Romans. The Zealots accused Zacharias (*JW* 4.336) and high priest Ananus (*JW* 4.218, 224) for political betrayal. Antipas, the Herodian caught by Zealots for trial revealed his betrayal of delegating a group asking for Romans' help in suppressing the nascent rebellion (*JW* 2.418-19).

[100] According to Stegemann, the Zealots were probably priests who radically positioned themselves for their priestly tradition as well as for the religio-political liberation. They aimed for substantial radical reforms in the temple purity by selecting the high priestly race from the legitimate origin (*JW* 4.155). Stegemann, *The Jesus Movement,* 181-82. For Josephus, the Zealots were a coalition of brigand groups (*JW* 4:135-161). According to Smith, the Zealot movement was centered in Jerusalem as group from Galilee who were formed as a resistant movement to Vespasian's conquers of Galilee (mid-winter 67-68 CE). Smith, "Zealots and Sicarii," 14.

[101] Horsley & Hanson, *Bandits, Prophets and Messiahs,* 229, 232, 236.

[102] Horsley & Hanson, *Bandits, Prophets and Messiahs,* 218, 225. The political murder (*Ant.* 18.7; *JW* 2.256ff., 269) and nonviolent revolutionary resistances caused disturbances in the city of Jerusalem (*JW* 2.225, 267, 286, 295). Hengel, *The Zealots,* 341.

50 CE (*JW* 2.254-57, 264-65; *Ant.*20.163-65, 187-88).[103] This anti-colonial urban movement, which was located in Jerusalem during the reign of Governor Felix, worked as aggressive nationalists used the dagger as a political weapon (*Ant.*20.186).[104] Josephus connects the fourth philosophy and the Sicarii movement on the basis of their zeal (*JW* 7.255). This was in continuity of leadership from the beginning of the Jewish revolt in 66 CE and the Sicarii revolt in Masada (*JW* 2.433, 447; 7.253).[105] However, the Sicarii's actions from the beginning of the rebellion made these two groups different in their operational strategy and in the location of their formation.[106] The Sicarii's murder in broad daylight located in the temple city of Jerusalem reflects their political strategy (*JW* 2.254-56).[107] As a pragmatic tactic of terrorizing, they adopted selective kidnapping and assassinations of the wealthy and the powerful, joining with plundering their wealth (*JW* 7.254), kidnapping for ransom of their own Sicarii prisoners (*Ant.*20.187, 208-10; cf. *JW* 2.264ff).[108]

The Sicarii's subversive role accelerated and provoked anxiety about the stability of the society (*JW* 2.256-57; *Ant.*20.165-66). It made the ruling families to get help from the gangs of ruffians and goon squads which resulted in the escalation of the spiral of violence (*JW* 20.206-07).[109] It also evoked violent repression from the imperial colonialists.[110] The colonized community resorted to violent resistance because the non-violent resistance had been denied by the colonial imperialists.[111] However, the political history of Sicarii after the summer

---

[103] Horsley, "The Sicarii: Ancient Jewish 'Terrorists," 445; Crossan, *The Historical Jesus*, 117-23. The modern terrorist organizations seem to have adopted the strategies of Sicarii' in selective assassinations and kidnapping for political reasons of ransom to release prisoners.

[104] Freyne, *Galilee*, 231-32; Horsley, *Jesus and the Spiral of Violence*, 40. The ordinary brigands functioned in public with the support of the peasants (*JW* 2.253).

[105] Horsley, "The Sicarii: Ancient Jewish 'Terrorists," 442. Judas of Galilee to Menahem, the descendant of Judas (son/grandson) became the leader for the Sicarii in late 60's. Another leader Eleazar Ben Jair led the Sicarii at Masada.

[106] Horsley & Hanson, *Bandits, Prophets and Messiahs*, 212; Horsley, *Jesus and Empire*, 42. According to Josephus, Menahem was a 'teacher' (*JW* 2.445). The tactics of secret assassination and kidnappings of Sicarii groups probably differed in the strategy of the Jewish "intelligentia leadership of the 'The fourth philosophy.'

[107] Hengel, *Zealots*, 47; Horsley, "The Sicarii: Ancient Jewish 'Terrorists," 438.

[108] Horsley, *Jesus and the Spiral of Violence*, 41. During the reign of Governor Albinus (62-64 CE), certain Sicarii kidnapped Captain Eleazar, secretary of the high priest Ananias in exchange for ten of their prisoners as a pragmatic tactic to induce the governor. The High priest Jonathan was assassinated during the reign of Felix (*Ant.*20.163ff). Josephus accounts never mention any direct action against the Romans.

[109] Horsley & Hanson, *Bandits, Prophets and Messiahs*, 209.

[110] Horsley, *Jesus and the Spiral of Violence*, 43.

[111] Horsley & Hanson, *Bandits, Prophets and Messiahs*, 203. Organized political resistance is not possible in a colonial society dominated by a foreign empire.

of 66 CE was passive resistance (*JW* 7.309-14) by confining them atop of the Masada until the Romans' final besieging of Masada in 73 CE resulted in the suicide of all the occupants (*JW* 7.320-401).[112]

3.3.2.6 The Popular Resistant Movements

Generally, the socio-economic and political-cultural repressive conditions of the first half of the first century CE created popular resistant movements like popular social movements, social banditry, messianic and prophetic movements, and other general peasant uprising in the agrarian milieu of Palestine.[113] Most of the movements' main agenda was to have a political liberation from the imperialistic coalition government of Roman-Jewish aristocracy and to have a more egalitarian social setup.[114] Moreover, most of the resistant movements during the crucial period of 70 years (4 BCE-70 CE) were negotiating (opposition and defensive) with their imperial masters but became violent at the repressive contexts. The political resistance by the Jewish banditry motivated other peasants to take up massive popular revolt against the oppressive imperial Rome for national liberation.[115] The politically conscious Jewish crowd under the imperial reign of the Herodians as well as the Roman procurators initially communicated their resentment to their political authorities except on occasions when they resorted to violent revolt.

3.3.2.7 Messianic Movements in Palestine

Popular movements with messianic traditions sprouted in the socio-cultural and political context of Palestine (I Macc.2:57; 3:4 Sir 47:11, 22; 1Enoch 90.9, 37-38). However, the historical events of Jewish revolts provided fresh impulse for the formation of messianic expectations in the popular tradition of kingship.[116] In addition, two distinctive strands of Prophetic movements (Oracular and Action type) became active among the common people for the common goal of national freedom and socio-economic egalitarianism.[117] There were specific socio-historical

---

[112] Freyne, *Galilee,* 232. Horsley & Hanson, *Bandits, Prophets and Messiahs,* 214. "After holding out as long as possible, the Sicarii finally committed mass suicide (960 men, women, and children)." (*JW* 7.320-401).

[113] Horsley, "Popular Messianic Movements," 474.

[114] Horsley, "Popular Messianic Movements," 494.

[115] Horsley, *Jesus and the Spiral of Violence,* 37, 39. The involvement of the peasant banditry into the main stream of the Palestinian Jewish society in 66 CE made the Jewish revolt a Peasant Revolt.

[116] Antti Laato, *A Star is Rising: The Historical Development of the Old Testament Royal Ideology and the Rise of the Jewish Messianic Expectations* (Atlanta, Georgia: Scholars Press, 1997), 12-13. There were ancient civilizations (Mesopotamian and Egyptian) which provided important insights for the "coming ideal king". The Jewish socio-political circumstances revived the popular tradition of kingship. Horsley, "Popular Messianic Movements," 480.

[117] Horsley, "Like One of the Prophets of Old", 463. The oracular prophetic movements modeled the classical biblical prophets.

contexts for the popular messianic movements and specific occasions for the popular uprisings in 4 CE and 66-70 CE.[118] After the death of Herod, national and religious consciousness made social banditry to enter the political contour of messianic royal pretension.[119] Horsley refines the suggestions of Mayer's study of the prophets of the first century: prophets among the literate groups ("seers among the literate groups, especially Essenes and perhaps the Pharisees") and prophets among the peasantry ("oracular prophets-Jesus ben Hanania and John the Baptist and prophets who led movements").[120]

The messianic movements (*JW*.2.56-65; *Ant*.17.271-85) were formed for national liberation by "desperate men" (*Ant*.17. 271) in the context of resentment by Roman domination and economic exploitation.[121] There developed a great cultural national tradition for the formation of popular messianic movements and different eschatological figures with divergent expectations to liberate the fortunes of Israel.[122] The royal ideology of kingship tradition originated during the regime of David and Solomon and continued through Persian and Hellenistic periods (Sir.47:11, 22; 1Macc.2:57).[123] The paradigm shift of priestly rule during

---

[118] Horsley, "Popular Messianic Movements," 480.

[119] Stegemann, *The Jesus Movement,* 177. Josephus mentioned three royal pretenders-Judas the Galilean, Simon in Peraea, and Athronges in Judea (*JW* 2.55ff.; *Ant*.17.269ff) who attacked royal arsenal and palaces, and aspired for royal position. They were not from a reputed royal background.

[120] Horsley, "Like One of the Prophets of Old," 446; R. Meayer, "προφητης," in *TDNT,* vol. vi, edited by Gerhard Friedrich (Grand Rapids, Michigan: Wm. B. Eerdmans Publishing Company, 1969), 812-28.

[121] Horsley, *Jesus and Empire,* 50; Stambaugh and Balch, *The Social World of the First Christians,* 28. "The term messiah/messianic has come to be used rather broadly by some- in the sense of "eschatological" or even "political"... agents of redemption who are anointed and/ or recognized as kings." Horsley, "Popular Messianic Movements," 473. Some of the Jewish resistant movement leaders acclaimed as "kings" (Simon of the 4th BCE and 68 CE; Athronges, Judas son of Ezekias (4 BCE) and Menahem (66 CE), (*JW* 2.4, 1-3; *Ant*.17.10, 5-7).

[122] Horsley & Hanson, *Bandits, Prophets and Messiahs,* 88-91. Different eschatological figures are used during the second temple period: "a prophet like Moses", "Elijah returned", "suffering servant of the Lord," "one like son of man coming with the clouds of heaven" and "the son of David." J. Neusner, *Messiah in Context: Israel's History and Destiny in Formative Judaism* (Philadelphia: Fortress, 1984); D.C. Duling, "The Promises to David and their Entrance Into Christianity-Nailing Down a Likely Hypothesis," *NTS* 20 (1973-74), 68. The expectation of a Davidic king is in juxtaposition with the Davidic covenant (2Sam.7:16).

[123] Horsley & Hanson, *Bandits, Prophets and Messiahs,* 96 97. The concept of Davidic kinship (Ps.2:18; 45; 132) is slowly identified with "the anointed of Yahweh." The Son of God concept is influenced by ancient West Asia's idea of kingship. "[the] Israelite popular tradition of the people themselves "messiahing" (acclaiming, electing) their king on a conditional basis." Horsley, *Jesus and Empire,* 49. The died down great tradition of David royal ideology of the Persian-Hellenistic periods became revived during the second temple period into popular tradition of kingship. However, "there were groups of Hasidim and then the Pharisees who attempted to make the "great tradition" relevant and applicable among the people as a whole." Horsley, "Popular Messianic Movements," 479.

the second temple period and a direct rule from the Hasmonian dynasty turned their attention to the hope of an anointed royal figure.[124]

The messianic movements emerged by the time of Herod's demise and the reign of Roman governors.[125] These popular prophetic and messianic movements of hidden resistance emerged from the Galilean-Judean crowd of the countryside.[126] The mass movements from the Jewish peasants gathered under the charismatic figures in and around the town of Judea and Galilee (Bethlehem, Emmaus, and Sepphoris) for overthrowing the Herodian-Roman imperial domination.[127]

According to Josephus' account, Galilee, Perea and Judea were the principal areas of Jewish settlements where these messianic movements occurred (*JW* 2.56; *Ant.*17.271-73, 278-85).[128] There were many popular messianic pretenders and uprisings from people of humble origin centered on charismatic leaders like Judas, son of Ezekias (*Ant.*17.271-72; *JW* 2.56), Athronges (*Ant.*17.278-85), David ben Jesse, Simon (66-70CE) (*JW* 2.521), and Simon bar Kokhba (Jerusalem Talmud Ta 'anit 4.68; 132-35CE) who were called King of the Jews.[129]

3.3.2.8 The Prophetic Movements (Action and Oracular Type)

The popular prophetic movements developed during the Roman imperial reign of mid-first century Palestine on account of the deep-rooted popular memory of resistance and liberation from foreign domination in anticipation of God's eschatological reign.[130] By taking the deliverance models of Moses and Joshua, the action type prophetic movements became the typological delivering agents of God in the way of new eschatological actions.[131] The oracular prophets were distinctively messengers of both deliverance and judgments, and were accompanied

[124] Aristobulus, son of John Hyrcanus put a diadem on his head (*Ant.*13.301) and in a later stage the title of king and high priest (Judah Aristobulus I/ his son, Judah Aristobulis II). Laato, *A Star is Rising*, 256-59.

[125] Horsley & Hanson, *Bandits, Prophets and Messiahs*, 109. The fourteen and fifteen Benedictions explain the popular messianic expectations.

[126] Horsley, *Jesus and Empire*, 45-54.

[127] Horsley, "Popular Messianic Movements," 487. There were three main branches of messianism-Qumran, the NT and Rabbinical Judaism, based on pluralistic messianic expectations rooted in OT. The charismatic leaders were recognized as kings of the Jews.

[128] Horsley & Hanson, *Bandits, Prophets and Messiahs*, 117.

[129] Horsley & Hanson, *Bandits, Prophets and Messiahs*, 111-117. Judas, son of Ezekias a brigand leader organized at Sepphoris in Galilee a sizable force (*Ant.*17.271-72; *JW* 2.56); Simon, servant of king Herod organized people and they called him as king (*Ant.*17.273-76); Athronges, a shepherd also hold power over the people, designated as king, slaughtered Romans and the Herodians (*Ant.*17.278-85).

[130] Horsley, *Jesus and Empire*, 51-52.

[131] Horsley, "Like One of the Prophets of Old", 454. "It is evident that the action-oriented prophets and their movements should be understood as apocalyptically inspired movements convinced that eschatological fulfillment was at hand." Horsley, "Like One of the Prophets of Old," 456.

by a few disciples. However, the action type prophets gathered a great number of disciples from the peasantry.[132]

In the midst of the political conflict of the mid-first century CE, the Prophetic social movements involved and promoted thousands of people to expect a messianic kingdom.[133] Jewish expectations led to three different forms of eschatological prophets (1Macc 4.46; 14:41) as they were longing to have the triple quality of the Hasmonian high priest-king and prophet.[134]

In the middle of the first century CE (Agrippa I and Fadus), there were different incidents about the prophetic wide-spread movements symbolically activated by the prophet Theudas (Ac.5:36). He led a peasant crowd through river Jordan and later an Egyptian prophet led the people to Mount Olives in anticipation of an eschatological act of liberation in the pattern of the traditional political liberation like Moses and Joshua in signs and wonders for a new conquest (*Ant.*20.97-98, 169-71; *JW* 2.261-63; Ac.21:38).[135] The Jewish cultural tradition gave new meaning to the eschatological acts of deliverance since the time of the Babylonian captivity (eg., Isa.40:1-11; 51:9-11).[136] They provoked revolutionary actions of going out into the wilderness to see the display of signs and wonders of God's imminent liberation in an eschatological dimension (*JW* 2.259; *Ant.*20.168).[137] The action-oriented 'historical-eschatological typology' is

---

[132] Horsley, "Like One of the Prophets of Old," 460-61. Matthew gives certain evidences of the pseudo-prophets in Mt.24:26. It is probable that by associating and distancing from the oracular prophets, Jesus inaugurates Israel's renewal (Ac.3:22; cf. 7:37), predicts the destruction of the Jerusalem temple (Lk.13:35), does mighty acts of God (Lk.7:22; cf.Lk.24:19) and pronounces judgement against the temple. N.T. Wright, *Jesus and the Victory of God,* vol. 2 (London: SPCK, 1996), 163-71. John the Baptist used the prophetic tradition to pronounce the judgement and called people for repentance. He became as the one who prepares the way for Jesus (Lk.3:1-20; 7:18-35).

[133] Hengel, *Zealots,* 245.

[134] Horsley, "Like on of the Prophets of Old,'" 438. The eschatological return of Elijah (Mal.3; Sir 48:10) and prophet like Moses (Deut. 18:15-18) were probably the contextual expectations for the purpose of the tribes of Jacob (Sir 48:10), (439-40).

[135] Horsley & Hanson, *Bandits, Prophets and Messiahs,* 161-69, 186-87. The movement of Theudas was destroyed by Fadus (44-46CE), the governor of Judea (*Ant.* 20.97-98; cf. Ac.5:36) and an Egyptian prophet rallied thousands of Jewish peasantry into the wilderness for a symbolic re-entry into the temple and that was destroyed by Felix in 56 CE. Theudas was enacting a new conquest by commanding the river to be parted in reentering into the land of promise (*Ant.*20.97). Horsley, *Jesus and Empire,* 51-52; P.W. Barnett, "The Jewish Sign Prophets-A.D. 40-70-Their Intentions and Origins," *NTS* 27 (1980-81), 679-97; Meyer, "προφητης", *TDNT,* vol. vi, 812-28; Friedrich, "The Prophets and Prophecies in the NT," in *TDNT*, vol. vi, edited by Gerhard Friedrich (Grand Rapids, Michigan: Wm. B. Eerdmans Publishing Company, 1969), 828-61.

[136] Horsley & Hanson, *Bandits, Prophets and Messiahs*, 171. The eschatological typology is followed as the pattern of interpretation in apocalyptic literature in 4 Ezra 13:44-47 as well as the early Christian movement (1Cor.10:1-4; 5:7; 1Pet.3:20).

[137] "Large number of people, inspired and convinced of the imminence of God's action, abandoned their work, homes, and villages to follow their charismatic leaders out into the

an interpretive pattern for the popular prophetic movements enacted as God's deliverance acts.[138]

The popular oracular-prophets during the first century (John the Baptist and Jesus son of Hananiah) have had characteristics similar to the biblical prophets (Jeremiah, Ezekiel and Amos). They prophesied eschatological judgment against the temple and their collaborators (*JW* 6.300-9), that challenged their authority and power.[139] The tumultuous political situation gave space to the announcement of divine deliverance that gave morale and hope to the defenders as well as the apocalyptic visions interpreted by the prophets as God's imminent intervention (*JW* 6.283-85).[140]

3.3.2.9 The Peasant Involvement and Resistance

Contrary to the traditional understanding of the Maccabean revolt as a priestly revolt under the leadership of Judas Maccabees against the Hellenistic imperial reign, Horsley understands it as a peasant revolt because of its socio-economic and cultural character.[141] The ideology behind the newly formed peasant banditry was resistance to the imperial reign of the alien rule over the agrarian Palestine.[142] Judas Maccabees came to the position of a charismatic leader and recruited many from the villages. Some of the significant grass-root issues of the peasant masses were the confiscation of the peasant lands, replacing the Jews with Greeks (1Macc.3:35-36, 41) and selling the Jews as slaves for the overdue tribute to Rome.[143]

The social banditry in Galilee (*JW* 1.248-66; 1.302-26; *Ant.* 14.411-33, 450) influenced greatly the peasant masses and made alliances with other resistant groups.[144] The growth of the Jewish brigandage in epidemic proportions (*Ant.*20.124) prior to the Jewish-Roman War was due to the repressive measures taken by the Roman procurators like Cumanus, Felix and Albinus (*JW* 2.272-

wilderness." Horsley & Hanson, *Bandits, Prophets and Messiahs*, 162; Hengel, *Zealots*, 231.

[138] Horsley & Hanson, *Bandits, Prophets and Messiahs*, 172. Comparing with the early church and Jesus' movement in the light of action oriented prophetic tradition can interpret certain passages in the NT (Mk.13:22; Mt.24:26) in line with God's liberative acts. The eschatological significance for wilderness is explained in the passages- Isa.40:3; Lk.1:80; Mk.1:2ff. Hengel, *Zealots*, 250.

[139] John the Baptist was a popular prophet of judgment (Lk.3:16-17; cf.Mt.3:7-10;) and he used the peasant imagery of agricultural life.

[140] Horsley & Hanson, *Bandits, Prophets and Messiahs*, 182-85.

[141] Horsley & Hanson, *Bandits, Prophets and Messiahs*, 20.

[142] According to Hobsbawm, only in an exploited and oppressed agricultural society one finds the social banditry. E.J. Hobsbawm, *Bandits* (New York: Pantheon, 1981) cited by Horsley & Hanson, *Bandits, Prophets and Messiahs*, 49.

[143] Horsley & Hanson, *Bandits, Prophets and Messiahs*, 21.

[144] Horsley & Hanson, *Bandits, Prophets and Messiahs*, 79. In Gischala (Galilean town), the peasant farmers were influenced by the brigands (*JW* 4.84) and they made alliances with "the proletarian party in Tiberius, led by Jesus, son of Sapphias, and with groups of insurgent Galilean peasants (*Life*, 35, 66, 132-48).

73; *Ant.*20.215).[145] There was a close relationship of the brigand and peasants in giving shelter to the brigands from the imperial search. According to Josephus, the banditry created other revolutionary movements which climaxed in the war.[146] Horsley, along with Zeitlin and Smith, rejects the role of the Zealots' organized attack against Rome, rather the brigand-peasant revolt that joined with some intellectual and violent movements.[147]

There were large scale peasant uprisings and popular movements during the Herodian reign which resorted to terrorizing by raids across the Syrian boarders and Decapolis.[148] Moreover, the Jews were ready to fight against the Roman army strategically by 'a massive *peasant strike*' by consciously objecting the grain harvest.[149] This strike was considered to be deliberate and intentional on the part of the marginal peasantry by neglecting their fields during 'the time to sow the seed' (*Ant.*18.272). The administrators yielded to their demand (*Ant.*18.282-284) due to the economic factor of the expected Roman tribute. The massive peasant revolt (*Ant.*18.272, 274,287; *JW.*2.200) against the religio-cultural imposition of deification of the emperor by erecting statues of the emperor Gauis was stopped due to the emperor's death.[150]

3.3.2.10 Apocalyptic Worldview as a mode of Resistance

The attempt to Hellenize the Jewish country was resisted by the '*maskilim*,' an intellectual 'Hasidean' group, among them were many scribes (1 Macc.2:42; 2 Macc. 14:6).[151] Along with the motivation of the scribal-intellectuals, the Maccabean revolt was apparently led by guerrilla warfare.[152] Here in this section,

---

[145] Horsley & Hanson, *Bandits, Prophets and Messiahs*, 77-78.

[146] Horsley, "Ancient Jewish Banditry," 427.

[147] Hengel's traditional understanding of the six decade role of Zealots of an organized resistant movement finally climaxed in the Jewish-Roman war. M. Hengel, *Zealots. Investigations into the Jewish Freedom Movement in the Period from Herod I until 70 AD*, translated by D. Smith (Edinburgh: T & T Clark, 1989); Horsley, "Ancient Jewish Banditry," 409. S. Zeitlin, "Zealots and Sicarii," *JBL* 81 (1962), 395-98; M. Smith, "Zealots and Sicarii: Their Origins and relations," *HTR* 64 (1971), 1-19.

[148] Smallwood, *The Jews Under Roman Rule*, 44. Certain Ezechias was the brigand leader who led the raids.

[149] Horsley, *Jesus and the Spiral of Violence*, 116 (emphasis added). "Slay us first…We shall patiently endure…whatever the risks," say the Jews (*Ant.*18.264, 267, 269).

[150] Horsley & Hanson, *Bandits, Prophets and Messiahs*, 40-41. It was a massive non-violent peasant strike which would directly affect the economy of the country (*Ant.*18.287). The client ruler, Petronius was wise enough to delay the order of the Emperor Gaius to punish the objectors' slavery (*JW.*2.185) and suicidal death (*JW.*2.201-3; *Ant.*18.303-9). Smallwood, *The Jews Under Roman Rule*, 174-180.

[151] Horsley, *Jesus and the Spiral of Violence*, 63-64. "Then there united with them a company of Hasideans, mighty warriors of Israel, everyone who offered himself willingly for the law" (1Macc.2:42).

[152] Horsley, *Jesus and the Spiral of Violence*, 68.

the importance is given to the intellectual community who offered motivation for resistance through the apocalyptic literature. In addition, the economically and culturally exploited rural peasants during the successive Hellenistic rulers resisted and revolted against the cultural-political impositions of the coalition priestly-Hellenistic regime.[153] In the meantime, a group of scribal teachers opposed the cultural imposition of the Hellenist rulers. This resulted in a new resistant movement with a new vision of God's deliverance and vindication even if they die as martyrs for safeguarding the traditional Mosaic laws (4Macc 16:14-16; 17:8-11).[154] Certain divinely inspired resistant movements who belonged to the ordinary Jewish peasants were motivated through the apocalyptic literature produced by the intellectuals.[155] The Jewish brigands and their association with the peasants led to revolts probably based on apocalyptic and messianic motivation for God's reign with equality and justice.[156]

Apocalypticism can be considered as a protest movement, an ideological resistance by some faithful Jews who anticipated an imminent divine deliverance (4Macc 10:18-21).[157] In a colonial stage of repression, the scribes and sages crossed over to a position of hybrid space to articulate visions and dreams as representatives of the margins.[158] These apocalyptic visions and dreams (Dan.2; 12:1-3; Rev.4:1-11; 5:1-14; 13:1-18; 17:1-18; 20:1-22:5) must have given meaning to their suffering for their faith during the colonial persecution.[159] Restoring the reign of God as an instrument of salvation gave inspiration to the colonized Jewish community (2Macc. 2:21; 1Macc.2:50; 3:16-22, 54-57, 60).[160] Thus, in the case of overwhelming subjugation, the faith in the transcendent power or divine inspiration would have motivated dreaming for liberation.[161]

---

[153] Horsley & Hanson, *Bandits, Prophets and Messiahs*, 10. The Palestinian Jews were badly affected by this coalition both economically and culturally (11).

[154] Horsley, *Jesus and Empire*, 39. The apocalyptic literature of Dan.7-12 probably developed during this period.

[155] Horsley, *Jesus and the Spiral of Violence*, 129.

[156] Horsley, "Ancient Jewish Banditry," 425; R.A. Horsley, "Josephus and the Bandits," *JSJ* 10 (1979), 37-63.

[157] Horsley & Hanson, *Bandits, Prophets and Messiahs*, 16.

[158] Apocalyptic visions are unusual dreams with ecstatic experiences. "The contents of the dreams or visions were fantastic dramas played out on a cosmic screen." Horsley & Hanson, *Bandits, Prophets and Messiahs*, 18. The apocalyptic hope gave wings of freedom to the Jewish peasantry to fight against the oppressive forces but the subaltern peasants could not retain their political position for long because they (subaltern) 'cannot rule.' Horsley & Hanson, *Bandits, Prophets and Messiahs*, 44.

[159] Horsley & Hanson, *Bandits, Prophets and Messiahs*, 19. The resurrection of the dead and entering the Kingdom of God seem to be creative apocalyptic responses (Dan.12:1-3; cf. 2Macc.7).

[160] Horsley & Hanson, *Bandits, Prophets and Messiahs*, 19.

[161] Horsley, *Jesus and the Spiral of Violence*, 129.

The apocalyptic literature, produced during the second temple period, seemed to have shaped a new symbolic world which gave future hope through the concept of resurrection (Daniel 12:1-3).[162] The wise ones probably produced the literature at the time of persecution which gave a glorious hope of the future life to their fellow martyred sages.[163] This new apocalyptic visions of symbolic elements must have helped them to maintain their traditional faith in the midst of the unprecedented imperial persecution and martyrdom.[164] In line with the Israelite prophetic traditions, the apocalyptic literature was produced with revelations and visions which inspired them to fight for their freedom and liberty with help from a transcendent power.[165] Jewish apocalyptic literature seems to have renewed the "traditional symbolic universe" with God's redemptive/judgmental action in history.[166]

3.3.2.11 The Discursive Nature of Resistance

Fiensy defines 'mass movement' in the ancient time as a peasant movement of an integrated larger body, both political and religious, for over an extended period of time and ambivalent in its mode of function.[167] The banditry attracted large number of peasants especially the Galilean band which was competent enough to resist the Roman forces and Josephus strategically used them as mercenaries.[168] The ostensible leaders of the revolt, the religio-political aristocracy "secretly attempted to implement a moderating and mediating strategy" by which they negotiated with the Romans to avoid a great war.[169] In this respect, an ambivalent negotiating stand was taken by the prominent Jewish leader like Josephus the historian and some chief priests. However, some of the self-proclaimed messiahs who attracted many (Judas of Galilee-Ac.5:37, Simon bar Giora, John of Gishala,

[162] Horsley, *Jesus and the Spiral of Violence*, 135.

[163] Horsley, *Jesus and the Spiral of Violence*, 136. "Assumption of Moses 10 and Jubilees 23:27-31 appear to be part of an apocalyptic tradition building on the archaic song of Moses (Deut.32)."

[164] Horsley, *Jesus and the Spiral of Violence*, 137.

[165] Horsley & Hanson, *Bandits, Prophets and Messiahs*, 151. The apocalypticism expected the imminent redemption from God.

[166] Horsley, *Jesus and the Spiral of Violence*, 133-145. The Apocalyptic visions helped during the imperial subjugation to be loyal to their religious traditions and resist the imperial forces (eg., the Son of Man figure in Daniel). There is a misunderstanding created by the modern scholarly circles about the apocalyptic texts and their motivating effect of the "distinctive apocalyptic mode of revelation and symbolization.... failed to investigate the social context comprehensively so as to appreciate the actual structure of concrete historical conflicts." Horsley, *Jesus and the Spiral of Violence*, 132.

[167] This body may not be well organized like a present day political party. David Fiensy, "Leaders of Mass Movements and the Leader of the Jesus Movement," *JSNT* 74 (1999), 4.

[168] Horsley & Hanson, *Bandits, Prophets and Messiahs*, 78. The brigand Chief Jesus with his 800 brigands had sold their services to the pro-Roman town of Sephporis (79).

[169] Horsley & Hanson, *Bandits, Prophets and Messiahs*, 43.

Bar Kokhba etc.) for dramatic speedy delivery from their Roman oppression went through severe persecution from the political side. The apocalyptic eschatology was ambivalent in giving new emphasis to human history with symbolic language and heavenly figures. The first century Jewish uprising against the Roman rule for their national liberation probably made some to be postcolonial in their approach to accommodate and resist. As the different mass movements in the process of countering imperialism prevailed, one cannot see any dichotomy between the revolutionary and apocalyptic movements.

3.4 Jesus Movement and Jewish Cultural Nationalism

In the first century Jewish cultural world, probably, the eschatological expectation was very high which resulted in Jesus' movement. Here, Jesus and his proclamation of God's kingdom became a solace to the subjugated community.[170] The concept of the kingdom exhibited the already or imminent effect of God's deliverance act to the persecuted righteous sufferers and provided the verdict against the wicked by which God renews his people.[171] The conviction of God's sovereign activity in the socio-political and historical affairs helped to explain the mission of Jesus and his followers in the cultural world of Judaism.[172] The effectiveness of the term 'kingdom' as a symbol/ myth for challenging and disrupting the socio-political life gave hope for the Jews and the colonial universe.[173] In certain extreme circumstances, this apocalyptic imagery gave them hope for God's direct intervention, irrespective of the fatal defeat as a nation in actual history.[174] The kingdom concept was very significant in its socio-political-religious context and

---

[170] Horsley, *Jesus and Empire*, 77. "In the Lord's prayer the kingdom of God means sufficient food for hungry people and cancellation of debts….single-minded pursuit of the kingdom… Kingdom is associated with the overcoming of despair, despondency and disease."

[171] Horsley, *Jesus and the Spiral of Violence*, 168-170; Norman Perrin, *Rediscovering the Teaching of Jesus* (London: SCM Press, 1967), 173-85. According to Malina, the concept of the father figure in the teaching of Jesus makes the context of the designation of Jesus as the patron in a patronage system. Bruce J.Malina, *The Social Gospel of Jesus. The Kingdom of God in Mediterranean Perspective* (Minneapolis: Fortress Press, 2001), 31. "…in Galilee, Judea and Perea, it would have to be presented to a population ready to see theocracy as a solution to local problems" (34).

[172] Horsley, *Jesus and the Spiral of Violence*, 177. The prayer ("May he establish his kingdom") will have expressed the hope for the kind of dramatic irruption of God into human history that is the central theme of ancient Jewish (and Christian) apocalyptic thought. Norman Perrin, "Jesus and the Language of the Kingdom" in *The Kingdom of God in the Teaching of Jesus*, edited by Bruce Chilton (London: SPCK, 1984), 96; Bruce Chilton, ed., *The Kingdom of God in the Teaching of Jesus* (London: SPCK, 1984), 26.

[173] In the West Asian language, Kingdom and Kingship of God are closely associated with the ancient kingdoms of the world (Since the ancient Sumerian times, Cannanites) where God had acted as the King in creation and its sustenance. Chilton, *The Kingdom of God,* 92.

[174] The same apocalyptic imagery and hope were kept by the Qumran community (*War Scroll* 1 QM), Perrin, "Jesus and the Language of the Kingdom," 95.

in relation to people's response to the liberating activities of John the Baptist and Jesus (Lk.3:3-18; 4:16-44; 7:18-35).[175]

Kim critiques Horsley's evaluation of the Jesus movement in line with the similar revolutionary political movement of the first century.[176] The political position of Jesus and the first century Christians were different from the 'Zealotic' nationalistic position of insurrection and murder.[177] Jesus' movement was against the triumphant Zionistic ideology of the revolutionaries and their resistance to the religious imperial ideology which was located around the Jerusalem temple.[178] However, they were not escapist like the Essenes rather they were, probably, discursively resistant and ambivalent in their political approach. The biblical tradition of God's kingdom is in parallel with the Jewish belief in God's integral involvement in the liberating activity with the history of human life and the whole cosmos.[179] The kingdom of God was in affiliation with the Jewish eschatology adopted by Jesus in terms of liberation for the entire universe from the oppressive forces and not just in futuristic exclusive terms.[180] The eschatological hope further strengthened the Jewish Christians to look forward in anticipation for the restoration of Israel's fortune even in the bleakest days since the fall of the second temple at Jerusalem.[181]

In the broad spectrum of his presentation of Jesus' movement in the gospel account, Luke appears to be simultaneously accommodative and resistant to the Jewish dominant power center which is in collaboration with Roman colonial

---

[175] Horsley, *Jesus and the Spiral of Violence*, 169. Through centuries, the Kingdom of God concept was interpreted differently. For some it is about the eschaton/ the end of the world (Albert Schweitzer), the cosmic end (R. Bultman), an inner individualistic/ personal reality (Critical liberal interpreters). R.A. Horsley, "Jesus and Empire," in *The Shadow of the Empire: Reclaiming the Bible as a History of Faithful Resistance*, edited by R.A. Horsley (London: Westminster John Knox Press, 2008), 87.

[176] Sebastian Kim, *Christ and Caesar: The Gospel and the Roman Empire in the Writings of Paul and Luke* (UK/Michigan: Wm. B. Eerdmans Publishing Company, 2008), 108-111; R.A. Horsley, *Jesus and Empire: The Kingdom of God and the New World Order* (Minneapolis: Fortress Press, 2003), 105, 126.

[177] Storkey, *Jesus and Politics*, 54. Jesus was against "the triumphant Zion ideology," S. Freyne, *Jesus, A Jewish Galilean: A New Reading of the Jesus-story* (London/New York: T & T Clark International, 2004), 135-36.

[178] According to Taylor, the non-participation of Christians in the Caligula crisis "would have been constructed as a betrayal of nation and Temple," and they were persecuted for their disloyalty to the nation and the temple, Taylor, "Palestinian Christianity and the Caligula Crisis," Part II, 34-35.

[179] Horsley, *Jesus and the Spiral of Violence*, 168.

[180] Horsley, *Jesus and the Spiral of Violence*, 157-58. The socio-political context of Jesus reveals the imminent application of God's intervention in bringing his kingdom.

[181] Roland, *Christian Origins*, 105. The Jerusalem Christians must have fled to Pella. Eusebius, *Hist. Ecc* 3,5.3 cited by Hengel, *Zealots*, 301, FN.386.

rulers.[182] The birth of Jesus is introduced in the complex Judean politics connected to the Herodian rulers of Palestine (Herod the Great and Herod Antipas; Lk.1:5; 2:1-2; 3:1-2, 19-20), to the imperial rulers (Caesar Augustus and Tiberius Caesar Lk.2:1; 3:1a), and to the leading Jewish priests in the temple (Ananias and Caiaphas Lk.3:2).[183] Moreover, Luke presents the conflictual attitude of the marginalized movement to the Roman client king, Herod Antipas (Lk.3:19-20; 13:31-33; cf.Lk.9:7).[184] The Lukan story of Jesus is also closely associated with Jewish traditions (circumcision, ritual cleansing, worship at the Lk.2:1-40), Synagogue (Lk.4:16-30; 13:13:10-17), and the fulfillment prophecy of the redemption of Israel through the long-awaited Messiah (Lk.1:32-33, 68-80; 2:25, 29-32). The national restoration of Israel is in affiliation with the prophetic traditions[185] but it is not limited to the national-cultural bounds of Judaism. Luke's vision for universal salvation (Lk.2:29-35; 3:6; 4:16-30) often disrupts the exclusive claims of the first century dominant Jewish native centers.

For Luke, the ministry of Jesus starts in Galilee (Synagogue at Nazareth) and affiliates his ministry with the prophetic fulfillment of the jubilee ideology (Isa.61:1-2; Lk.4:16-30).[186] This revolutionary call of the jubilee year mimics and disrupts the first century dominant Jewish centers by offering the blessings to both Jews and Gentiles (Lk.4:24-29; 7:1-10).[187] Further, Jesus in his mission crosses regional, nationalistic, racial and gender boundaries (the Roman centurion's slave Lk.7:1-10; Jairus' daughter and the woman with an issue of blood Lk.8:40-56; Martha-Mary Lk.10:38-42; the Samaritan leper Lk.17:18) in order to extend the good news of God's kingdom to everyone. He also disrupts the religious traditions by disobeying the strict observance of ritual cleansing (Lk.11:38) and by healing the sick on Sabbath (Lk.6:7; 13:10-17). Jesus sends the twelve and the seventy/

---

[182] The Lukan pro-Roman (H. Conzelmann) and anti-Roman (Richard J. Cassidy) views of continuity and distancing to/from Judaism discussed by William M. Swartley, "Politics or Peace (Eirene) in Luke's Gospel," in *Political Issues in Luke-Acts,* edited b Richard J. Cassidy and Philip J. Scharper (Maryknoll, New York: Orbis Books, 1983), 18-25.

[183] Barrus, *Luke-Acts*, 134.

[184] Herod Antipas feared Jewish rebellion against his rule and thus he silenced the opponent voices by eliminating the deviants (*Ant.*18.118).

[185] Robert C. Tannehill, *The Narrative Unity of Luke-Acts: A Literary Interpretation*, vol. I: The Gospel according to Luke (Philadelphia: Fortress Press, 1986), 19, 286.

[186] Similar to the peasant movement, a large crowd from the Galilean village followed John the Baptist and Jesus (Mt.4:25; Mk.5:21; 6:34; 7:17; 9:15; 10:46; 11:32; 12:12; Lk.6:17; 9:37; Jn.7:31; 8:2; 12:9; *Ant.* 18.118; Tacitus, *Ann.*15.44; *Ant.*18.63). Fiensy, "Leaders of Mass Movements," 15. Antipas feared an insurrection by seeing the followers of John (*Ant.*18.118). As far as Jesus is concerned, he was both a religious leader as well as an artisan (τεκτων), who could be well accepted as a postcolonial hybrid leader. Fiensy, "Leaders of Mass Movements," 16-17.

[187] J. Massyngbaerde Ford, "Reconciliation and Forgiveness in Luke's Gospel," in *Political Issues in Luke-Acts,* edited by Richard J. Cassidy and Philip J. Scharper (Maryknoll, New York: Orbis Books, 1983), 82. The vengeance for the Gentiles is omitted

seventy two with authority 'to proclaim the kingdom of God and heal the sick' (Lk.9:1-6; 10:1-24) as a part of reconstituting a new community in affiliation and distancing with the native Jewish traditions. In this process, the disciples left everything for the sake of the kingdom (Lk.5:11; 9:3; 10:4) and Jesus challenged the wealthy elites to sell off their possessions for the sake of the poor (Lk.18:18-30; cf.Ac.2:42-47; 4:32-37).[188] The chief tax collector Zacchaeus' repentance (Lk.19:1-10) and his association with the pro-Roman tax collectors (Lk.5:27-30; cf.Lk.18:9-14) also probably teach the affiliative posturing of Jesus movement. Moreover, the proclamation of Jesus as the Lord (kuri/oj) and saviour (swthr) Son of God and the bearer of peace are disruptive propaganda to the imperial claims of the first century.

Jesus' mission was directed towards Jerusalem (Lk.9:51-19:27), but he was arrested, interrogated by the Jewish priestly aristocracy (Lk.22:47-53,66-71; cf.24:20) and was finally handed over to Pilate (Lk.23:1). His accommodative-disruptive posturing with the temple is repeated by Luke in teaching and preaching the good news (εὐαγγελιζομένου Lk.19:47-20:1) at the temple but the Jewish religious elites try to arrest him in the light of the disruptive teaching (Lk.20:19). In Jerusalem, Jesus mimics the royal and military conquering model of a Jewish messiah for challenging the abuse of the temple and the temple aristocracy (Lk.19:43-46). The story line demonstrates that Jesus is the Davidic Messiah (Lk.18:38-39; cf. Lk.1:32-33) who prophesies the forthcoming judgement on the temple (Lk.19:42-44; 21:5-36). This would naturally disrupt the dominant religious center.[189] Moreover, the frequent dialogic confrontation with the Jewish leadership (Lk.6:1-11; 11:37-54; 13:10-17) is climaxed by the false accusation against Jesus perverting the (our) nation and forbidding taxes to be paid to Caesar and calling himself as Christ/King (Lk.23:2; cf.20:25).[190] The Jewish authorities (chief priests and the scribes) vehemently demanded the crucifixion of 'the king of the Jews' over against the clear verdict of Jesus' innocence by Pilate (Lk.23:4, 14, 22). This makes the Lukan positive portrayal of a Roman governor who would like to release Jesus (Lk.23:1-4, 16, 20, 22). And this does not leave him from the accusation of heeding the popular cry in crucifying Jesus on the imperial cross (Lk.23:23-24). Luke also demonstrates the cruelty of Herod the tetrarch, his contemptuous treatment (mockery) of Jesus clothing him with an elegant robe

[188] Tannehill, *The Narrative Unity of Luke-Acts*, 246-248. Jesus taught and practiced forgiveness and love in the context of political animosity and hatred (Lk.6:27-36, 17.1-4, 23:34).

[189] Wright, *Jesus and the Victory of God*, 413-28, 569-70. The Roman imperial devastation of the temple is perhaps portrayed as God's judgement against the unrepentant Israel (Lk.6:27-36; 21:5-36).

[190] The political accusations of subverting 'our nation/ our people' (Lk.23:2, 14) and 'stirs up the people' (Lk.23:5) against Jesus are serious in the first century context. The religious opponents take the ambivalent answer of Jesus to the question of payment of taxes to Caesar' (Lk.20:20-26). The affiliation-distancing (to Rome) nature of Jesus is demonstrated in the section 'Living in-between Caesar and God.' Refer Samuel, *The Postcolonial Reading of Mark*, 140-142.

of a king (Lk.23:10-11).[191] The response of the Roman centurion ('this man was innocent' Lk.23:47), one of the criminals crucified with Jesus ('remember me... in your kingdom' Lk.23:42-43), and the Jerusalem crowd ('wailing' Lk.23:27; 'beating the chests' Lk.23:48) possibly demonstrate the further positive Lukan portrayal of Roman-Jewish opponents. Finally, Joseph of Arimathea, a member of the Jewish Sanhedrin demanded that a proper burial be given to the body of Jesus (Lk.23:54-56). This royal action from the native Jewish leader demonstrates the ambivalence of the dominant religious center.

The false expectation of the first century militant Jewish nationalism (Lk.17:22-24; 21:8-9; 24:21; cf.Ac.1:6) received condemnation by Jesus' repeated announcement of his death and suffering (Lk.9:22, 44; 17:25; 18:31-34).[192] For Luke, Jerusalem is the place where he would be rejected and killed by the Jewish-Roman authorities as well as resurrected back to life on the third day to appear to his disciples in Jerusalem (Lk.9:22; 18:31-33; 24:1-53). Moreover, Jerusalem is the Jewish religious center where the forthcoming mission will start (Lk.24:46-52; cf.Ac.1:1-11).

3.5. Josephus: The Jewish Historian and Jewish Nationalism

The religio-socio-political writings of Josephus (37-100 CE), about the Jewish nation are significant in the light of Luke's narration of the newly formed Christian community which was formally inaugurated in Jerusalem. It seems that both Josephus and Luke were contemporaries and there are parallelisms in their historic documents regarding the revolt of Judas the Galilean over the census done by Quirinius, revolt of Theudas and the Egyptian prophet. Further, the discursive literary style, the interpretive methods of the colonial period due to the postcolonial resistive discourse seems to have influenced each other. Josephus' literature becomes a great source of information to fill the gaps about the religious figures (Jewish high priest, Pharisees and Sadducees), political figures (Herod Agripa II, Berrnice), Jerusalem temple and its destruction, and the geographical sketch of Palestine as Luke is very selective in his information.

The political suffering of the Jewish nation under the colonial Rome is well depicted in *Jewish War* from the creation story, through the history of the Jewish nation ultimately climaxing in the destruction of the temple (17 BCE-74 CE) and sympathizing for the country's misfortune (*JW* 1.9). As a person from the Jewish aristocracy, Josephus responds to the Roman web of power from the position of Roman aristocracy as the Jewish tragic war was still fresh in his mind.

Josephus began his anti-Roman political life as a General in Galilee who revolted against Rome as described in his autobiography *The Life*. He proved

[191] Barrus, *Luke-Acts*, 136. Lukan disruptive attitude to the Roman client king is portrayed in the earlier part of Jesus' ministry that Herod wants to kill him and his response of calling him as the fox (Lk.13:31-33; cf. Lk.9:7).

[192] Tannehill, *The Narrative Unity of Luke-Acts,* vol. I, 257-258.

his political diplomacy as a patriotic Jew in his early days by releasing some priests from Roman imprisonment (*Life* 3.13). He shifted his political stand by becoming a personal friend of the Jewish client King Agrippa II, later favoured by Roman generals and emperors (Vespasian and Titus). He moved his headquarters to Rome with his Roman citizenship and stayed in Rome during his last thirty years (*Life* 76.423). He was probably cryptic in awaiting the fall of the final kingdom similar to the vision of Daniel (*Ant.*10.210).[193] He shifted his loyalty often and ambivalently spoke for his people after the fall of the temple. Scholars debate on the issue of his Jewish patriotism and few consider him an absolute traitor.[194] However, he speaks discursively through the speech of the revolutionary leader Eleazar about the "preference of liberty and death to slavery and life" (*JW* 7.323-36).[195] His political career seems to have shifted in the context of the tragic Jewish-Roman War, from a Roman prisoner to an ambivalent pro-Roman writer in Greek language while staying in Rome with the stipend provided by the Vespasian rulers.

He was critical of the Hasmonian dynasty and the successive native rulers for their lack of consistency in governance (*JW* 1.38). His Jewish religious affinity was reiterated by his faith in the power of God and its move across the universe similar to the Lukan portrayal of the spread of the Christian community.[196] According to Edwards, Josephus "ironically turns the tables," by placing the blame upon the disobedience of the Jewish nation in not giving heed to the voice of God, and by shifting his stand for the success of the Romans.[197]

The prologue of the *Antiquities* is constructed in a disruptive manner by upholding the philosophical moorings of the Judean constitution of high standing virtues in the context of imperial Rome where the educated masses doubted the deceptive model of imperial monarchy.[198] The abstract of the Jewish laws on social life also add to the apologetic purpose (*Ant.* 4.196; 20.268). Moreover, the prologue of *Antiquities* is similar in line with the Acts' prologue addressing

---

[193] P. R. Davies, "Daniel in the Lions' Den," in *Images of Empire*, edited by L. Alexander (Sheffield: JSOT Press, 1991), 174.

[194] Foe a scholarly discussion for on the question of his Jewish patriotism, refer Louis H. Feldmann, *Josephus und Modern Scholarship (1937-1980)* (Berlin/New York: Walter de Gruyter, 1984), 89-98. *Contra Apionem* was written by Josephus as an apologetic defense of Judaism in the context of anti-Semitism that sprang up in Alexandria.

[195] Davies, "Daniel in the Lions' Den," 174.

[196] D.R. Edwards, "Surviving the Web of the Roman Power: Religion and Politics in the Acts of the Apostles, Josephus, and Chariton's *Chaereas and Callirhoe*," in *Images of Empire*, edited by L. Alexander (Sheffield: JSOT Press, 1991), 190.

[197] Edwards, "Surviving the Web of the Roman Power," 191.

[198] S. Mason, "Josephus: Value for New Testament Study," in *DNTB*, edited by C.A. Evans & S.E. Porter (Leicester: IVP, 2000), 597-98.

the 'most excellent Epaphroditus' (*Ant.*1.pref. 5-17).[199] His interpretive skills have been applied to the biblical narrations to the extent in which he elevates the Jewish leaders both men and women (Abraham- *Ant.*1.148; Rebekha- *Ant.*1.247; Gedaliah- *Ant.*10.155; Esther- *Ant.*11.185; Moses- *Ant.*2.233) to their wisdom (Saul, David and Solomon- *Ant.*6.45; 7.158; 8.34); their courage to fight against their enemies (Abraham- *Ant.*1.172; Moses- *Ant.*2.238-51, 320-44) and cryptically refers to the fall of the Roman empire by interpreting Balaam's prophecy and Nebuchadnezzar's dream (*Ant.*4.125; 10.210).[200]

Mason is against the opinion of the work of Josephus, especially the *Jewish War* as a pro-Roman propaganda.[201] He clarifies it through the discursive writing of Jewish history countering the anti-Judean propaganda as a hostile nation, who serves a less powerful God and the isolation created by "a small handful of power-seeking tyrants" (*JW* 1.7-9).[202] The sovereignty of God over human history is very high in the ideology of Josephus (*JW* 2.140, 365-387) and he was against the revolutionary militancy (*JW* 5.362-419; 6.371) created by the rebel leaders.[203] Moreover, he was highly critical of the revolutionary native cultural nationalists and the reprisals against the Romans in and around Palestine (*JW* 2.457-493) who led the nation to a catastrophic end. He was also critical of the fraudulent and incompetent Roman governors and client kings who very much tested the Judeans' loyalty to be good citizens of the empire.[204] However, he possibly avoided the socio-economic (taxation), cultural (anti-Semitic feeling) and political reasons behind the uprising of the Jewish revolt as well as tried to protect the emperor Titus from the wrong information of the heinous act of burning the Jewish temple (*JW* 6.241; *JW* 7.1; *Ant.*250).[205]

Wright provides an analogue between the framework of Acts and the work of Josephus where he says that the fulfillment of the Jewish prophecy was considered mandatory (Ac.28:23-28; *JW* 6.312-15), the radical nationalism was challenged

[199] Josephus highly praises the Judean constitution which is elaborated in 3rd and 4th volumes of the *Antiquties of the Jews and Life.* Josephus cited the example of Hezekiah for not realistically accommodative to Assyria (*Ant.*10.5), but praises Jehoachin (*Ant.*10.100) and Gadalia (*Ant.*10.164-66) who became subservient to Babylonians.

[200] Feldman, "Josephus: Interpretive Methods and Tendencies," 592-93.

[201] Mason, "Josephus: Value for New Testament Study," 597. According to the analysis of Feldman, the title of Josephus' work *Jewish War* explains the side with which history is written. Louis H. Feldman, "Josephus (Person)," in *ABD* vol. 3 H-J, edited by D.N. Freedman (New York: Doubleday, 1992), 983.

[202] Mason, "Josephus: Value for New Testament Study," 596-97.

[203] Josephus analyses that the Romans would become the instruments for cleansing the temple; Mason, "Josephus: Value for New Testament Study," 597-58. Josephus equated "himself as a latter-day Jeremiah" (*JW* 5.392-93).

[204] Mason, "Josephus: Value for New Testament Study," 597.

[205] Feldman, "Josephus (Person)," 984. Josephus' gives a wrong historical account of Titus' request of sparing the Temple from the Roman attack (*JW* 6.241).

(Lk.21:24; Ac.1:7; *Ant.*10.206-09, 263), the sovereignty of God was understood to be behind the progress of the kingdom (Vespasian and Jesus), the true Israel is reconstructed (Josephus based on Jamnia rabbis and Luke on the followers of Jesus) and the kingdom finally shifted to Rome.[206]

Gnuse finds literary relationship between the narrations of Luke and Josephus in their prologue (Theophilus and Epaphroditus), historical memories, interpreting the socio-religio-political events (eg.Judas, the Galilean, Theudas, and Egyptian the prophet; Ac.5:36-37; 21:38; *JW* 2.117; 2.253-71; *Ant.*18.1-5; 20.97-99; 20.167-72) with some chronological differences.[207] There are specific events like the worldwide famine during the time of Claudius (44CE; Ac.11:28-29, *Ant.*3.320; 20.51-53, 110) and political personalities and their female partners (Felix-Drucilla; Ac.24:24, *Ant.*20.143-44; Herod Agrippa II-Berenice; Ac.25:13, 23, *Ant.*20.145).[208] There are similar uses of the form-critical format in the visionary experiences of Paul. This is probably another example for literary dependency.[209] Also, there is a similarity in the auto/biographical experiences of the education of Josephus and Paul which are stereotypically expressed to emphasize the credibility of the spokespersons to meet the expectation of the first century Greco-Roman audience.[210]

Rajak finds the postcolonial literary motif in the accounts of the 'long and discursive' speech delivered by Agrippa II with Queen Bernice from the roof of his palace to persuade the resistive Jews from revolting against Rome (*JW* 2.345-

[206] N.T. Wright, *The New Testament and the People of God* (UK: SPCK, 1992), 375. According to Wright, both "Luke and Josephus are literary cousins" (378). Josephus seems to be ambivalent "to show the Jewish race in a favourable light in the eyes of the Flavian dynasty, and to explain the great catastrophe as the work of foolish rebels rather than as the effect of large-scale long held national aspirations" (376). Wright's argument in placing Luke as an apologist may not reconcile with reality, rather ambivalent and discursive in keeping both associating and distancing.

[207] Robert Gnuse, '*Vita Apologetica*': The Lives of Josephus and Paul in Apologetic Historiography," in *JSP* 13.2 (2002), 151-52. Gnuse finds literary relationship between Lukan literature and Josephus's writings based on the similarities in speeches of renowned personnel, challenge the contemporary socio-political culture appealing for appropriate punishment for their wickedness (eg.Herod Agrippa I's retributary death; Ac.12:19-24; *Ant.*19.343-50), common ship-wreck narratives on their journey to Rome for religio-political cause (*Life* 13-16; cf. Ac.27:1-44), sinks in the same Adriatic Sea (*Life* 15; cf.Ac.27:27), and both landed at Puteoli (Life 16; cf. Ac.28:13). For him, Luke redactionally used Josephan material for theological purpose, (158). S. Mason believes for Lukan dependency on Josephus's literature, *Josephus and the New Testament* (Peabody, MA: Hendrickson, 1992), 96-100.

[208] Gnuse, '*Vita Apologetica*,' 157.

[209] Similar form-critical format can be seen between the dream experience of Jaddus, Hyrcanus and Josephus at Jotapata (*Ant.*11.326-28; 13.282-83; *JW* 3.351-54) and the dream experience of Lukan Acts (Ac.9:1-9; 16:9-10; 18:9-10). Gnuse, '*Vita Apologetica*,' 158-59.

[210] Josephus' educational qualifications are Sadducean by birth, origin in an aristocratic priestly family and trained under the Pharisees (*JW* 2.119-66; *Ant.*13.171-73, 297-98; 18.11-22; cf.Ac.21:39; 22:3; 26:5). Gnuse, '*Vita Apologetica*,' 159.

401) in the context of the tragic outcome of the Jewish revolt.[211] He analyses the speech as 'rhetorical ingenuity, a piece of tight rope walking' of the antipathy of the elite community in an ambivalent stance.[212] Josephus probably tries to show the incompetence of the Jewish king in handling the political situation (*JW* 2.332) that caused the rupture in Jewish-Roman political relations.[213] The irony of the episode portrayed by Josephus is that the rebellious crowd further screams irrespective of the plea of the royal couples with tears (*JW* 2.402) in the foregoing consecutive attack from the side of the Romans.[214] Josephus takes the diplomatic position of the disposition of the Roman legions in Palestine and the merciless penalties on the native authorities (*JW* 2.332). It is in this context that he invents a speech for Agrippa II who becomes the notorious hero in the history of the Jewish nation.[215] He analyzes the political 'fate' of the Jewish nation find them too weak to encounter the great empire as God is on the side of the imperial Rome (*JW* 2.360; 390-91).[216]

Josephus blames the left wing anti-colonial groups like Zealots as brigands for the tragedy of the nation (*JW* 2.1-10; 4.1-5; 7.1). He criticizes severely the Romans of their sins by comparing them with the Assyrians and hopes for the deliverance of the Jews in God's time (*JW* 5.403-406).

Josephus through his discursive writing of the Jewish national history teaches Jews of their historic mistakes in their relationship with the neighboring nations.[217] The accusations against him as an opportunist and a pro-Roman

---

[211] T. Rajak, "Friends, Romans, Subjects: Agrippa II's Speech in Josephus' Jewish War," in *Images of Empire*, edited by L. Alexander (Sheffield: JSOT Press, 1991), 122-23. Josephus gives great prominence to this episode because Agrippa's speech becomes a turning point in the great Jewish-Roman war. Luke presents the same pair in the trial scene of Paul at Caesarea with splendid attire (Ac.25:23) which may contradict the scene portrayed by Josephus.

[212] Rajak, "Friends, Romans, Subjects," 123.

[213] Rajak, "Friends, Romans, Subjects," 126-27. Josephus in his *Antiquities* reveals the inadequacy of the incompetent young Agrippa II to administer the troubled Judean kingdom, and by knowing the situation the emperor appointed Caspius Fadus as the procurator of Judea (*Ant.* 19.362). Agrippa's anti-Jewish phase and lack of diplomacy are evident by his order in collecting tributes soon after the conclusion of his speech (*JW* 2.407).

[214] Rajak, "Friends, Romans, Subjects," 123. It included the desecrating of the temple treasury by Florus, the attack on the unarmed Jews, the burning up of the Agrippa's palace by revolutionary nationalists (Sicarii) and especially the deliberate refusal of the Jewish aristocracy to send a delegate to complain against Florus. According to Josephus, this central event becomes the turning point in Agrippa's ejection from the city, attack on the Roman garrison in Massada and declaring a war against the Romans by stopping the sacrifices on behalf of the emperor (*JW* 2.409).

[215] Rajak, "Friends, Romans, Subjects," 123. There were crucifixions in Jerusalem under Florus reign (*JW* 2.308). There were other narrations that portray the degrading position of both Agrippa in relation to the high priests in mid sixties (*Ant.*20) and the notorious affair of Queen Bernice with Emperor Titus (125, 129).

[216] Rajak, "Friends, Romans, Subjects," 124. "[For] the Jews it is now too late to fight."

[217] Feldman, "Josephus: Interpretive Methods and Tendencies," 595.

propagandist probably stays as he analysed the situation in the political context of Palestine where there was a development of revolutionary zealotic uproar against a mighty empire that could be politically challenged by strategic terms.

3.6 Summary and Concluding Remarks

Jewish resistance and revolutionary movements from the time of Maccabean revolt (167-164BCE) to the spiral of violence against the imperial Rome in different periods climaxed in the Jewish-Roman War in 66-70 CE, and the later rebellion under Simon bar Kokhba (132-35CE). In the history of Israel, the impacts of peasant involvement and rural mass resistant movements have been greatly overshadowed by the elitist resistant movements. The Jewish religio-cultural sentiments have been provoked repeatedly by the colonial rulers like Nebuchadnezzar (587BCE), Antiochus IV (167BCE), Pompey (63BCE), Herod the Great (4BCE), Pontius Pilate and emperor Caligula (39-41CE). Distinguishing the main ideology of the resistant movements is probably difficult because it is integrally connected to the socio-economic-religio-cultural and political freedom of the Jews. The messianic overtones and eschatological hopes have been the reflections of the aspirations for this freedom.

The political-economic context of the eastern part of the Roman Empire, especially Galilee-Judea, where privatization of property, unemployment, debt-imprisonment on the marginalized led to the rise of popular movements of revolutionary peasant bandits was a natural outcome. This resistance started from the intellectuals who followed the martyrdom theology of the Maccabean revolt and then the spiral of revolutionary resistance in different periods of political crisis, especially during the religio-cultural provocations in different periods from the Roman judicial authorities etc. The brutal repressions of the Roman political authorities of Galilee-Judea raised many insurgents under the category of Zealots, Sicarii and bandits (λῃσταί), who generally advocated armed rebellions. However, there were popular resistant movements like peasant strikes on occasions when the Jews were looted and offended economically and culturally by the Roman authorities. Some followed apocalyptic traditions of divine intervention at the time of crisis through visions and prophesy.

The ideological foundation of these movements suggests the liberation of their national state which is equivalent to their religious and political freedom. Subsequently, there were a number of religio-political movements under the leadership of non/intellectual pretending messiahs which led the rural masses in revolutionary movements by following the prophetic tradition of their fathers.

There is a difference between the Palestinian Jewish peasant involvement against the Roman imperial oppression and the Jesus' movement with the rural Galilean peasants. Jesus' movement probably transcended the revolutionary open revolt and adopted a postcolonial method of accommodation and resistance, antagonism and affiliation towards the Roman imperial governance. However, the Lukan portrayal of the Jesus Movement (Gospel according to Luke) and its presentations are considered to be a movement with the ideology of neither eschatological distancing from the socio-political situation of the period nor confronting the evil system with revolutionary armed resistance. Further study on the Acts of the Apostles shows that they were ambivalent in approach, discursively challenging the Roman forces with strategic essentialism, and mimicking them as a cultural hybrid.

Similarly, there is a possibility of seeing a postcolonial stance of the first century Jesus' movement in negotiating the revolutionary Jewish nationalistic ideology with eschatological/apocalyptic elements of symbolic resistance as their stand in proclaiming Jesus as the Lord (κυρίος) and saviour (σωτηρ), Son of God and the bearer of peace. Subverting the dominant religio-political centers with the military power was the agenda of neither Jesus' movement nor the first century Christian community. However, the first century Christian community might have responded to the militaristic Roman Empire and the dominant native Jewish center in their writings by mimicking their imperial propaganda in a different strategic mode of mimicry, hybridity and ambivalence.

Both Luke and Josephus perhaps address the Jewish response to the Roman imperial order of the first century in ambivalence. Their diverse geographical locations, dissimilar social backgrounds must have influenced their political world view over against Rome. However, there are certain ideological similarities between them. For both of them, God of the universe is a powerful encountering force in the world history before whom no one can stand. One cannot categorically find them as pro-Roman or anti-Roman, rather they were probably postcolonial in their dialectical perception of evaluating the Roman imperial agendas. The presumable historical account of two different religious groups yet related through the Jewish tradition, are narrated in the context of Greco-Roman world. The New Testament literature especially the Acts of the Apostles possibly describes the socio-economic-cultural and political response of the colonial subjects over against the murderous situation of the Roman colonial constituency and the native dominant Jewish constituency. The following exegetical chapters will explore the Lukan contribution to this analysis.

Part 3

READING OF ACTS FROM A POSTCOLONIAL PERSPECTIVE

Chapter 4

The Narrative that Centers on the Early Christian Witness in the Roman World in and Around Palestine (Acts 1-12)

4.1 Introduction

Luke appears to carve a space discursively for the newly formed Jesus community between the Roman colonialism and the dominant Jewish cultural nationalism. As a result, one may notice Luke having special interest in narrating the inception of the Christian movement spreading across the Roman colonial world starting from the Jewish center, Jerusalem. Luke maintains that the socio-cultural and political identity of a minoritarian Jesus movement is formed by their witness to the resurrected Lord in the power of the Holy Spirit. He programmatically develops the narrative by stating that the Jesus community proclaimed the risen Lord in Jerusalem, Judea (Ac. 1:1-8:3), and later through the Hellenist Christians to Samaria and to the Eastern part of the Roman Empire (Ac. 8:4-12:25).

The study focuses on the formation of the followers of Jesus as a transcultural Christian community and their witness to the ends of the earth (Ac.1:8). In this process, Luke narrates the Pentecost event, the cataloguing of the Nations, Peter's speeches, Stephen's speech, the story of the Ethiopian eunuch, description of the Christian *politeia*, Paul's call to the nations, the story of the death of Apostle James and the deliverance of Peter etc., in the light of other imperial discourses to rupture colonialism and native dominant discourses.

4.2 The Formation of the Transcultural Christian Community in Jerusalem and Judea (Ac.1:1-5:42)

Apparently, Luke writes the story of the Acts of the Apostles to one named Theophilus in continuation to his earlier narrative (Lk.1:1). In the first book

(Gospel of Luke), he narrates the story of Jesus' birth, mission, death, resurrection and ascension. In the second book (The Acts of the Apostles), he begins with the story of the formation and the spread of a community under the leadership of Peter and the other empowered ministers from Jerusalem to Antioch (Ac.1-12) and from Antioch to Rome (Ac.13-28).

From the beginning of Acts, one discerns a transition of the rural Galilean followers of Jesus who comes to Jerusalem to be empowered by the Holy Spirit to call into question the claims of the imperial authority.[1] In Ac.1:1-8, Jesus brings them together in Jerusalem and commands them to tarry for the power (du/namij) from above before they start witnessing the Lord to the entire world. This imparts a new vision to the community to fulfill the eschatological mission in the context of socio-political and religio-cultural imperialism.

4.2.1 The Patronage of Theophilus and Literary Genre as a Political Discursive Strategy (Ac.1:1)

In the Roman colonial urban context, Theophilus (Θεόφιλε) could be either a Greco-Roman God-fearer or a representative of a community that loves God, who for Luke is an eminent friendly patron of the Roman nobility.[2] To him, Luke introduces the people of 'the way'- a discursive Christian movement in the Greco-Roman world (Ac. 9:2; 19:9, 23; 24:14) who survived under the policies of colonial Rome.[3] They, for Kelber, adopt the power of the scribal medium to construct their socio-political and religio-cultural identity which is used by the imperial powers to dominate the public discourses.[4] Hence, it is possible that

[1] G. Gilbert, "Luke-Acts and Negotiation of Authority and Identity in the Roman World," in *The Multivalence of Biblical Texts and Theological Meanings*, edited by C. Helmer (Boston: Brill Leiden, 2006), 87.

[2] The honorific appellation 'most excellent' (cf.Lk.1:3) is used for Theophilus in Luke's first volume (Lk.1:3). He uses similar titles in Acts to address Roman governors in formal setting (Ac.23:26; 24:2, 24; 26:2,7,19; cf.*Life* 430; *AgApion* 1.1) that reflects the social status of Theophilus in the political world of Rome. However, strategically masking the identity of a Roman personal with a well-attested Greek name with the meaning 'friend of God' or 'loved by God,' may be a subtle portrayal for Luke because of the political reasons. V.K. Robbins, "The Social Location of the Implied Author of Luke-Acts," in *The Social World of Luke-Acts. Models of Interpretation*, edited by J.H. Neyrey (Peabody: Hendrickson Publishers, 1991), 321-22.

[3] C. K. Barrett, *A Critical and Exegetical Commentary on the Acts of the Apostles*, vol. I (Edinburgh: T & T Clark, 1994), 66. Moxnes points out to the radical sabotage of the patronage system within the first century Christian community due to the economic position. Moxnes, 'Patron-Client Relations," 241-68. The words, Jesus community and Christian community are used interchangeably in this study.

[4] W.H. Kelber, "Roman Imperialism and Early Christian Scribality," in *The Postcolnial Biblical Reader*, edited by R.S. Sugirtharajah (Oxford: Blackwell Publishing, 2006), 96. For eg. The Qumran community probably created a geographical as well as a socio-cultural hybrid space of socio-religious identity by affiliating and being antagonistic to the then religio-political powers through the medium of scribality.

by perceiving the need of the hour, Luke uses the scribal medium to affirm the Christian identity against the politically dominant literary media with the help of Theophilus. Obviously, Luke wants him to know the truth of the Gospel of Christ and in all probability, to rope him into the early Christian wing for patronage and support.[5] Moreover, he is most likely narrating the story of Jesus and his community who happened to be the target of an overriding religio-political power.[6] Here, he affiliates with the patronage system in order to gain the socio-economic and political support for the persecuted community of Jesus.[7]

It is probable that Luke's patron, Theophilus, sympathetically hears the 'Christian symposia' on the development and growth of the Christian movement presented discursively through a historical[8]/ biographical[9]/ scientific /novelistic

---

[5] For a detailed treatment on the role of patron, refer W.Meeks, *The First Urban Christians* (London: Yale University Press, 1983); cf.Stambaugh & Balch, *The Social World of the First Christians*, 55, 140.

[6] The prologue starts with the story of the resurrected Jesus who was apparently killed by the Romans on a political cross charged with a political crime. Kelber, "Roman Imperialism," 98. In the earlier account of Luke, the earthly life of Jesus was very much associated with the political leaders of the time like Augustus, Tiberius, Quirinius, King Herod, Philip the Tetrarch and Lysanias the ruler of Abilene (102).

[7] Barrus, "The Gospel of Luke and the Acts," 142-43. In the urban setting of the Lukan and Pauline community, the rich were challenged by the act of distribution of goods. R.J. Karris, "Poor and Rich: The Lukean *Sitz im Leben*,' in *Perspectives on Luke-Acts*, edited by C.H. Talbert (Danville: Association of Baptist Professors of Religion, 1978), 112-25. Paul makes use of the patron-client relationship as he enters the Greco-Roman cities for the advancement of the gospel (Ac.13:12, 50; 17:4, 12; 19:31; cf.Lk.8:2-3). Kelber, "Roman Imperialism and Early Christian Scribality," 102.

[8] N.T scholars have understood Luke-Acts in different forms of history: 'general history,' (David.E. Aune, *The New Testament in its Literary Environment* (Cambridge: James Clarke & Co., 1998), 138-39; General historiography, H.J. Cadbury, *The Making of Luke-Acts* (London: SPCK, 1958); historical monograph, (H. Conzelmann, *Acts of the Apostles*, edited by E.J. Epp and C.R. Matthews; translated by J. Limburg et al., (Philadelphia: Fortress Press, 1987), M. Hengel, *Acts and the History of Earliest Christianity*, translated by J.Bowden (Philadelphia: Fortress Press, 1979), 36; apologetic historiography, (G.E. Sterling, *Historiography and Self Definition: Josephus, Luke-Acts and Apologetic Historiography* (Nov.TSup 64. Leiden: Brill, 1992), Hubert Cancik, "The History of Culture, Religion, and Institutions in Ancient Historiography: Philological Observations concerning Luke's History," *JBL* 116 (1997), 673-95); Hellenistic historiography (Herodotus, Polybius, Lucian and Josephus), (M.A. Powell, *What are they Saying about Acts?* (New York: Paulist Press, 1991), 10, 80-81); Hellenistic Jewish writing interpreting the events from a religious point of view, (B.S. Rosner, "Acts and Biblical History," in *The Book of Acts in its Ancient Literary Setting*, vol. 1, edited by B.W. Winter and A.D. Clarke (Grand Rapids: Wm. B. Eerdmans Publishing Company, 1993), 65-82). Here onwards *The Book of Acts in its Ancient Literary Setting* will be abbreviated as *BAALS*.

[9] Talbert considers the genre of Acts as a specific type of Greco-Roman biography known as "succession narrative" like that of Diogenes' Life. C.H. Talbert, *Literary Patterns, Theological Themes, and Genre of Luke-Acts* (GB:SBL & Scholars Press, 1974), 132. He finds common similarities between Diogenes' Lives and Luke-Acts through the life of the founder of a religious community, successor and teaching.

genre.[10] According to Palmer, Alexander and Downing, this flexibile, overlapping and fluid genre in the context of multiple hegemonic Greco-Roman discourses appropriately gives space for an ideological persuasion of the Jesus community.[11] For Barrus, the marginalized subjects 'write back'/ 'talk back' through the discursive writing style questioning the constructed religio-political myth of domination by the Roman Empire.[12] In addition, the Bakhtnian understanding of the novelistic features representing a field of reality, allusions, freedom of authorial interference, polemic freedom and open-endness for continuing the discourse[13] can be seen in the reading of the Acts of the Apostles. Hence, the potential of the Lukan narration employing a flexible genre exhibits the significance of the scribal medium to portray the complex and variegated responses of Luke against the Roman *imperium.*

4.2.2 Jesus' Commission and Ascension in Jerusalem: A Mimetic Political Strategy (Ac.1:2-11)

Luke begins the story of the resurrected Jesus empowering the marginalized Galilean from the Jewish center at Jerusalem (Ac.1:1-11).[14] He chooses Jerusalem

[10] Discussion on the overlapping from historical treatise-biographical-novelistic literature, refer F.G. Downing, "Theophilus's First Reading of Luke-Acts" in *Luke's Literary Achievement. Collected Essays*, edited by C.M. Tucket (Sheffield: Sheffield Academic Press, 1995), 93. For the technical treatises, biography and the ambivalence in the hybrid literary convention, refer L. Alexander, *The Preface to Luke's Gospel. Literary Convention and Social Context in Luke 1.1-4 and Acts 1.1* (Cambridge: Cambridge University Press, 1993). For the genre of entertaining and edifying, refer R.I. Pervo, *Profit and Delight: The Literary Genre of the Acts of the Apostles* (Philadelphia: Fortress Press, 1987), 11-13; L. Alexander, "Fact, Fiction and the Genre of Acts," *NTS* 44/3 (1998), 380-99. Even in the sub-genre in its narration- theological, apologetic, polemical, evangelistic, pastoral, and political.

[11] Cf.D.W. Palmer, "Acts and the Historical Monograph," in *BAALS*, vol. 1, edited by B.W. Winter and A.D. Clarke (Grand Rapids: Wm. B. Eerdmans Publishing Company, 1993), 1-29. Alexander compares the delighting part of the travel narrative of Acts and the Greek Romantic novels. L.Alexander, " 'In Journeying Often': Voyaging in the Acts of the Apostles and in Greek Romance," in *Luke's Literary Achievement: Collected Essays*, edited by C.M. Tucket (Sheffield: Sheffield Academic Press, 1995), 17-79. According to Downing, the journeying section of Paul gives a novelistic delight to the hearers in terms of imprisonment, lynching and shipwreck with the Christian mission in mind not the "reunion of fraught lovers." Downing, "Theophilus's First Reading of Luke-Acts," 103.

[12] Barrus, "The Gospel of Luke and the Acts," 144-147.

[13] Bakhtin, *The Dialogic Imagination*, 27. Bowersock explains the use of the novelistic writing in the complex period of socio-political and cultural dislocation of the first century for the blurred boundary between history and fiction. Barrus cited G.W. Bowersock, *Fiction as History: Nero to Julian* (Berkeley: University of California Press, 1994) in "The Gospel of Luke and the Acts," 145; Pervo, *Profit and Delight.*

[14] Moreland explains the significance of Jerusalem as the narrative and ideological setting of the Christian origin of the Lukan mythmaking in the context of socio-religious dislocation and the socio-political control. M. Moreland, "The Jerusaelm Community in Acts: Mythmaking and the

as the preparatory ground for the setting of the Christian community and projects this location as the starting point for the apostolic leadership. It has strategic importance in the first century as a Jewish religious center and the locus of eschatological deliverance with the fulfillment of the "expectation of the gathering and renewal of Israel."[15] The significance of Jerusalem is illustrated by the apocalyptic consummation anticipated at the native Jewish center. Further, the consummation is fulfilled in Jesus community by the coming of the eschatological spirit symbolized by ecstatic utterances. Luke's portrayal of the activity of the resurrected Jesus issuing orders to the Apostles (Ac.1:2 ἐντειλάμος τοῖς ἀποστό λοις) for a period of forty days in and around Jerusalem, probably, mimics the imperial order of the native dominant Jewish center and the Roman colonial center.[16]

The kerygma of the 'Kingdom of God' which begins at the starting of the narration (Ac.1:3) continues through the Apostles till, it finally, reaches Rome through Paul (Ac. 8:12; 14:22; 19:8; 20:25; 28:23, 31).[17] At the ascension, Jesus promises, 'you will receive power, when the Holy Spirit comes upon you and you will be my witness....until (the) end of the earth' (Ac.1:8) most likely alludes to the strategic veto power given to the apostles in the context of persecution from the religio-political power centers.[18] In gospel of Luke, the authority (ἐξουσία) of the kingdom is mainly exercised by Jesus and his disciples in terms of proclamation and miraculous deeds (Lk.4:31-44; 10:1-17). But now, the same authority is given to all the disciples to be his witnesses (μαρτυρες).[19]

Further, the Jewish nationalistic expectation of establishing an immediately political kingdom is perhaps, disrupted by the discourse between Jesus and his

---

Sociorhetorical functions of a Lukan Setting," in *Contextualizing Acts. Lukan Narrative and Greco-Roman Discourse*, edited by Todd Penner and C.V. Stichele (Atlanta: SBL, 2003), 299.

[15] Stegemann and Stegemann, *The Jesus Movement*, 189.

[16] The forty days mimic the religio-political leaders like Moses and Elijah (Ex.34:28; Deut.8:2; 1Kgs.19:8). Timothy Johnson, *The Acts of the Apostles* (SP 5; Minneapolis: Liturgical Press, 1992), 25; Spencer, *Acts*, 25.

[17] Jesus' death and successive events of resurrection and the coming of the Holy Spirit are considered as the end of the old era and the beginning of the new era. Wright, *Jesus and the Victory of God*, 322. Karl L. Schmidt notes, "The name and the message of Jesus Christ/Jesus himself are equated with the Kingdom of God." "βασιλεια," *TDNT*, vol. 1, translated and edited by Geoffrey W. Bromiley (Wm. B. Eerdmans Publishing Company, 1993), 589.

[18] The eschatological Spirit gives the disciples, the power to heal (Ac.6:8), caste out demons (Ac.4:7; cf.Lk.9:1) and most significantly the power to witness the good news of the kingdom in the face of persecution. Menzies analyses the Lukan collocation of Spirit and power (πνευμα and δυναμις) R.P. Menzies, "Spirit and Power in Luke-Acts: A Response to Max Turner," *JSNT* 49 (1993), 19.

[19] By analyzing the literary works of the first century (Tacitus, *Hist.*1.10;2:78;4:81; Suetonius, *Vesp.*5.2-6;7.2-3; Dio. 64.9.1; *JW* 1.23;4.623;3.401-404), Samuel finds the propaganda tactics of the emperor Vespasian by combining the miracles of healing in terms of propaganda and political power, *A Postcolonial Reading of Mark's Story*, 122, FN.52.

disciples. Luke makes use of the disciples' 'when' (v.6) question regarding the restoration plan of the Davidic kingdom for Jews to state the nature ('how' and 'what') of the kingdom which will be fulfilled through the life and witness of the new eschatological community (vv. 7-8).[20] The present reality of God's kingdom enables the disciples to participate in the proclamation of God's Kingdom yet distancing them from the political expectation of the dominant native Jewish center.

Contrary to the conventional expectations, Jesus commands his disciples to be his witness (μάρτυρες) to the ends of the earth by which they will fulfill God's universal plan of salvation. Luke presents the realized presence of God's kingdom through the arrival of Jesus the messiah who is crucified and by the coming of the promised Spirit.[21] The Palestinian Jewish disciples seem to have understood this as a sign of the fulfillment of the consummation of the Kingdom of God on the earth.[22] Moreover, there is a shift from the kingdom language to the Spirit language and the Kingdom focus to the Lordship of Christ. This is probably due to the early Christian community's understanding of the realized eschatology in the context of the Roman imperial claims of a political kingdom where Caesar is the Lord of the universe.[23] Here, Luke is probably mimicking the political imagery with a difference in order to disrupt the expectation of a political king and his kingdom with "nationalistic warfare and conquest."[24]

The first century imperial context underlines the significance of the heavenly ascent of the Roman emperors soon after their death through the official declaration

[20] Barrett, *Acts*, vol. 1, 71, 76. The restoration (ἀποκαθιστάνεις) of the kingdom for Israel was the heart cry of a patriotic Jew. The pious Galileans expected the restoration of Israel and the influx of the nations to Jerusalem to worship the God of Israel (Tob.13:1-14:7; Sir.36.1-17; Psa.Sol.11:1-9; 17:21-46). Spencer, *Acts*, 26. The Jewish religious center at Jerusalem provides the probability of a divine necessity as an eschatological fulfillment motive (Isa.2). Downing, "Theophilus's First Reading of Luke-Acts," 100-01; Cf. J.T. Squires, *The Plan of God in Luke-Acts* (Cambridge: Cambridge University Press, 1993), 188-89.

[21] In the Jewish cultural context, linking between the coming of the Spirit and the restoration of the Kingdom are significant. Ezekiel foresees the renewal/restoration of the Kingdom by the prophecy of placing a new Spirit in their hearts (Eze.36:27-7; cf.11:19f.; 18:31.). Youngmo Cho, "Spirit and the Kingdom of God in Luke-Acts: Proclamation as the primary role of the Spirit in relation to the Kingdom of God in Luke-Acts," *AJPS* 6.2 (2003), 187.

[22] Haenchen, *Acts*, 143. "there is no single clearly defined 'messianic expectation' in second-temple Judaism." Wright, *Jesus and the Victory of God*, 206.

[23] Carsten Timothy Lotz, "A Critical Evaluation of Youngmo Cho: Spirit and Kingdom in the Writings of Luke and Paul: An Attempt to Reconcile these Concepts," *EQ* 82.2 (2010), 138. Both for Paul and Luke, the realized Kingdom is only through the means of the Spirit. J.D.G. Dunn, "Spirit and Kingdom," *The Christ and the Spirit. Collected Essays of J.D.G. Dunn, vol. 2 Pneumatology* (Grand Rapids/Cambridge: Wm. B. Eerdmans Publishing Company, 1998), 131-141.

[24] Spencer, *Acts*, 26.

of reports, monuments and coins.[25] The Roman writers politically legitimize the emperor's imperial power to rule the inhabited world by mentioning the heavenly ascension of the emperor.[26] There are other parallel biblical assumptions for prophetic empowerment similar to Elijah's example and the Danielic vision of the Son of Man which is corresponding to the oppressed Israelite community. They are exalted to the cloud to receive the kingdom with authority and power to rule the universe (Dan.7:13, 14).[27] Thus, one may assume that Luke possibly uses his concept of ascension by collocating the religio-political traditions in a way of mimicking the *apotheosis*[28] of the Roman emperors with the Jewish prophetic traditions. This empowering concept of the Son of Man makes the earthly Jesus the perfect 'saviour' (σωτήρ) of the universe while it ruptures the deification of the earthly emperors. Besides it, Jesus' exaltation to the clouds after his suffering and death by the Romans[29] explain the vindication of the true Israel. It also implies to his cosmic rule (Ac.2:24-36) contrary to the imperial affixing of power to the imperial centers. However, Jesus transfers his authority to his disciples subverting the religio-political dominant centers located in Jerusalem.

4.2.2.1 Μάρτυρες ἐν τε Ἰερουσαλὴμ καὶ ....ἕως ἐσχάτου τῆς γῆς (Ac.1:8) Ruptures the Imperial Design of Colonialism

The concept of witness has great significance in the Roman political world of the first century. The Lukan usage of different derivatives of 'witness' (Μάρτυς) in Acts explains the great significance he has given to this courtroom language,

[25] G. Gilbert, "Roman Propaganda and Christian Identity in the Worldview of Luke-Acts," in *Contextualizing Acts: Lukan Narrative and Greco-Roman Discourse*, edited by T. Penner and C.V. Stichele (SBL, 20. Atlanta: SBL, 2003), 242-43. There are traditions of celestial occurrence indicating Caesar's ascension (Horace, *Carm.*1.12.47; Virgil, *Ecl.*9.47-49; Pliny, *Nat.Hist.* 2.93-94; Suetonius, *Jul.*88; Dio Chrysostom 45.7.1), and Augustus promoted it through the visual image of depicting the star of Caesar on coins.

[26] Gilbert, "Roman Propaganda and Christian Identity," 243, 245; *Aen.* 1.286-294. According to Suetonius, the ancient biographer of five of the emperors (Julius Caesar, Octavian, Claudius, Vespasian and Titus) conferred divinity after their death. L.J. Kreitzer, *Striking New Images: Roman Imperial Coinage and the New Testament World* (JSNT Sup 134, Sheffield: Sheffield Academic Press, 1996), 70.

[27] Elijah's departure to heaven and the subsequent empowerment to Elisha (2Kgs.2:9-14). A.W. Zwiep, *The Ascension of the Messiah in Lukan Christology* (NovTSup 87; Leiden: Brill, 1997), 41-75; Paul Palatty, "The Ascension of Christ in Luke-Acts. An Exegetical Critical Study of Luke 24, 50-53 and Acts 1, 2-3, 9-11," *Bible Bhashyam* 12/2 (Feb, 1986), 100-17; Wright, *Jesus and the Victory of God*, 374. Similar ascension in a cloud is narrated in the apocalyptic literature (Rev.11:22; Mk.14:62; 1Enoch).

[28] The religious practice of the Roman emperor's deification (Augustus, Caligula, Nero, Domitian etc.) may have strategically used in the process of NT Christological pattern of thought. Kreitzer, *Striking New Images*, 69.

[29] Wright, *The New Testament and the People of God*, 462.

probably, in the context of political hostility and conflict.[30] The legality of this term is discussed in the following chapter where the law court scenes are dealt in detail. The object of this witness is the human Jesus of Nazareth who is 'a man accredited by God to you by miracles, wonders and signs' (Ac.3:22) and is now resurrected. This resistant posture would vigorously contest the socio-religio-political dominant centers of the Roman inhabited world. The following reading of the text demonstrates the Spirit inspired witness to the resurrected messiah (Ac.3:15; 4:33) in the face of intense opposition and persecution.

Since the time of Pentecost, the first century apostles, deacons and the ordinary followers become witnesses to the resurrected messiah (Ac.2:32; 3:15; 4:8; 5:29-32; cf.10:39,41) before the synagogues, rulers and authorities.[31] The purpose of witnessing is for repentance (Ac.2:38; 3:19; 5:31; 17:30; 20:21) receiving the one sent by God. The witnessing is limited not only at the personal level but also extends to the community level. Also, this causes imprisonment and persecution to the Jerusalem Apostles from the Jewish-Roman dominant centers (Ac. 4:5ff, 17-21; 5:17-42; 6:9-14; 12:2-6). Moreover, the first century audience cannot ignore the forensic overtones of the 'witness' (μαρτυρέω) metaphor in Acts.[32] As the witness and mission are integrally connected, the query is: what is the political implication for the minority Jesus' community in witnessing and doing mission in the Roman context?

In all probability there is a political dynamics in witnessing to different geographical locations with people of varied socio-religio-cultural and political positions.[33] The early Christians face oppositions both from the Jewish religious center which is located at Jerusalem as well as from the Roman political centers outside Palestine.[34] Since the beginning of Pentecost, the Apostles' boldness

[30] There are thirty-nine occurrences of the word μάρτυς under six of its derivations (μαρτυρεῖν, διαμαρτύρεσθαι, μαρτύρεσθαι, μαρτύριον, μαρτυρία and ἀμάρτυρος) in Acts that explain the significance of this concept of witnessing (Ac.1:8, 22; 2:32; 3:15; 4:33; 5:32; 8:25; 10:39,41-43; 13:31; 18:5; 26:16,22; 28:23 etc). A.A. Trites, *The New Testament Concept of Witness* (Cambridge: Cambridge University Press, 1977), 128.

[31] In the Jewish, Roman settings as well as in the present Indian context, false witnessing is condemnable and true witnessing is necessary for the sake of a just society. False witnessing is despised in Acts' narration (Ac.6:13-14; 7:58; cf.22:19-20; 26:9-11). Peter G.Bolt, "Mission and Witness," in *Witness to the Gospel: Theology of Acts*, edited by I.H. Marshall and D. Peterson, (Grand Rapids: Eerdmans, 1998), 213, F.N, 74.

[32] Bolt, "Mission and Witness," 193. Luke's long narration on the forensic speeches in Acts 24-26 show the legal vocabularies and procedures where the term witness has a strong political implication. B.W. Winter, "Official Proceedings and the Forensic Speeches in Acts 24-26," *The Book of Acts in its Ancient Literary Setting*, vol.1, edited by B.W. Winter and A.D. Clarke (Grand Rapids: Eerdmans, 1993), 305-336. In the latter part of Acts, Paul who is the great persecutor of this movement becomes a great witness to both the Jews and to the nations (Ac.22:17-21; 23:11; 26:15-23). Cassidy, *Society and Politics*, 162.

[33] Cassidy, *Society and Politics*, 158-59.

[34] D.G. Horrell, "Introduction," *JSNT* 27/3 (2005), 225.

in witnessing both in word and deed create amazement to the religio-political authorities (Ac.4:13). This boldness (παρρησια) in speech-witnessing of the Apostles typifies the "outspokenness or forthrightness" of "the political right of the citizen to speak freely, even when opposed," that probably ruptures the political centers for silencing the voices of the colonial subjects.[35]

The mob violence in Acts shows the socio-political context in which the first century Christians are situated. The boldness of the Apostles to speak with authority and shamelessness is manifested in witnessing in the midst of persecution and suffering that would interrupt the imperial *Pax Romana*.[36] The Apostles' speech before the religio-political authorities as well as Paul's speech later before the Roman Governors (Felix, Festus) and King Agrippa II, reveal the same boldness to disrupt the Jewish-Roman power-centered civic life (Ac.24-26) as witnessing before the authorities thus may cause persecution, suffering and death in a similar way like their master.

The disciples' mandate to witness (διαμαρτυρόμενος) Jesus and his Kingdom till the ends of the earth (Ac.8:12; 14:22; 19:8; 20:25; 28:3, 31) probably mimic with a difference the imperial ideology of conquering the entire universe (οἰκουμένη) by the Roman military forces.[37] On the religious side of the native dominant Jewish discourse, Jesus redirects the disciples from the narrow nationalistic limited restoration of a small geographical territory to witness the Kingdom of God to the entire Roman world. The exclusive ethnic Jewish nationalistic kingdom ideology promoted by the Jewish religious center is most likely disrupted by the proclamation of the universal gospel.[38] This disruption is probably done by the Apostles' witness through affiliating and distancing from the Jewish religious traditions and at the center in Jerusalem.

Scholars often consider the geographical sketch as the programmatic outline for Acts (Jerusalem-Judea-Samaria- and the end of the earth (Rome?) in witnessing.[39] As a Greco-Roman theologian-historian, Luke is very much

[35] B.R. Gaventa, "You will be my Witness": Aspects of Mission in the Acts of the Apostles," *Missiology: An International Review* X/4 (1982), 418. Cassidy, *Society and Politics*, 45. The Apostles' bold witnessing before the religio-political leaders (Ac.2:29;4:13,29,31; 9:27,28; 13:46; 14.3; 18:26; 19:8,28, 26:26;28:31).

[36] Plato, *Republic,* 557b; Heinrich Schlier, "Παρρησια," *TDNT*, vol. v, translated and edited by Geoffrey W. Bromiley (Grand Rapids: Wm. B. Eerdmans Publishing Company, 1967), 871-75.

[37] Cho analyzes Agua and explains the fulfillment of Ac.1:8 by connecting the two verses with the verb 'witness' in Ac.1:8 'You shall be my witness' (ἔσεσθε μου μάρτυρες) and Ac.28:23 'witnessing the kingdom of God' (μαρτυρομενος τὴν βασιλείαν τοὺ θεοῦ cf.Ac.28:31). Agua, "The Lukan Narrative of Evanglization," 657; Cho, "Spirit and the Kingdom," 188.

[38] Christopher Roland and M. Corner, *Liberating Exegesis: The Challenge of Liberation Theology to Biblical Studies* (Cambridge: SPCK, 1990), 123-24.

[39] Witherington III, *Acts*, 110; Hengel, "The Geography of Palestine in Acts," 35. According to Conzelmann, programmatic in the semse of worldwide mission, *Acts*, 7. Psa.Sol 8:16 considers Rome as the end of the earth. A few NT scholars consider that in Luke's programmatic plan of

interested in the geographical space for the legitimacy of considering Jesus as the Davidic king in the process of negotiations with the native dominant Jewish discourse. Moreover, this universality of the gospel of Jesus needs to reach to 'the ends of the earth'[40] from the Jerusalem-centered Jewish world to the political-centered Rome. This is probably a political countering with the new vision of a transcultural Jesus community.[41] Luke is perhaps ambivalent in his treatment of the programmatic sketch of the commission of considering Rome as the 'ends of the earth' (ἐσχάτου τῆς γῆς) which would disrupt the Roman political schema of the first century.[42] Witnessing God's kingdom to the contours of the empire by the marginal and despised Galilean disciples is a political mimicry which possibly ruptures the powerful imperial regime based on the political influence of *Pax Romana*.[43] For Luke, the transcultural Jesus community with eschatological power (δύναμις) will witness God's kingdom not with the revolutionary Zionism of the first century which will be exclusive and destructive. Moreover, by mimicking the Roman imperial expansion of first century, the minority Christians reject the illusory claims of the imperial Rome with an alternative position which would be disruptive to the Roman political center.[44] In this process, witnessing God's

---

Ac.1:8, Rome was the final point which would be reached through the gospel. F.F. Bruce, *The Acts of the apostles: The Greek text with Introduction and Commentary* (England: IVP, 1976), 71. Barrett identifies the end of the earth in a representative manner and not connecting with the empire. Barrett *Acts*, vol. 1, 79-80.

[40] 'Until the ends of the earth' could mean in classical Greek, "a person or thing that was furthest outside," and thus Luke probably means the remotest parts of the inhabited world. H.G. Link, "ἔσχατος," in *NIDNTT*, vol. 2, edited by Collin Brown (Exeter: The Paternoster Press, 1971/1976), 55. Fitzmayer proposes and defends the idea of Rome as the end of the earth. However, for Shauf the partial fulfillment of Acts.1:8 for the Ethiopian episode because it is Ethiopia and not Rome which was considered as the end of the earth. Fitzmayer, *Acts*, 206-07; S. Shauf, "Locating the Eunuch: Characterization and Narration Context in Acts 8:26-40," *CBQ* 71 (2009), 773; Bauckham points to the four corners of the earth (India, Scythia, Spain and Ethiopia) centering on Jerusalem but the geographical catalogue in Ac.2 deprive the conventional ends of the earth. R. Bauckham, "James and the Jerusalem Church," in *The Book of Acts in its Palestinian Setting*, vol. 4, edited by R. Bouckham (Grand Rapids: Wm. B. Eerdman Publishing Company, 1995), 422.

[41] Barrus, "The Gospel of Luke and the Acts," 133.

[42] B.R. Gaventa, *The Acts of the Apostles* (Nashville: Abingdon Press, 2003), 65-66. Lukan audience could think of the extreme directions of Jerusalem as 'the end': Spain in the West (Strabo 1.1.5, 8; 3.2; Pliny Ep.2.3.8), India (Strabo 1.1.8) and China (Pliny, *Nat.Hist.* 12.1.2; 12.41.84), "Scythians, Germans, Britons, and a place called Thule possibly Iceland" (Pliny, *Nat.Hist.* 4.16.104) and 'Ehtiopia' (Africa) to the South (*Ant.*11.33, 186, 216, 272). C.S. Keener, "Power of Pentecost: Luke's Missiology in Acts 1-2," *AJPS* 12.1 (2009), 52-53.

[43] Gnanavaram, *Treasure in Heaven*, 124. Luke is reversing the order in the proclamation of the gospel by the despised Galileans to the urbanized rich, starting in Jerusalem. The same pattern continues in bringing the gospel to the Samaritans by the despised Hellenist Philip.

[44] Gilbert, "Luke-Acts and Negotiation of Authority," 104. The eschatological Spirit is not for the exclusive community but for universal (Ac.2:17-21; 10:44; 19:4-7). Dunn argues the Spirit for salvation (Ac.8:4-25), J.D.G. Dunn, *Baptism in the Spirit* (London: SCM Press, 1970); Steve

kingdom is not exclusive for the twelve but for all (Ac.2:38-39) who realized the eschatological salvation of God.

The temporal dislocations are a major concern for the postcolonial literature. Similarly for Luke the dislocation of the ministry is from Jerusalem-Judea-Samaria and 'until [the] end of the earth' (ἕως ἐσχάτου τῆς γῆς).[45] By mimicking the imperial expansion with its resemblance and menace, the counter-discourse of the expansion of Jesus movement is carried on by the assistance of ordinary Galileans, the Hellenists, certain men (τινες ἄνδρες) of Cyprus and Cyrene, and finally by Paul a Roman citizen.[46] In the Lukan imagery, the witness of the minority Christians reaches the center of the empire successfully not by replacing the emperor's throne but by preaching the gospel of the resurrected Jesus.[47] Likewise, the Holy Spirit is poured out on the disciples not for accumulation of power rather for distributing it to the repented community from Jerusalem to the entire universe.

In addition to the Roman imperial expansion concept, Luke may also have had the eschatological plan of the saving act of God that Isaiah foresees (Isa.2:2; 49:6), i.e, the gospel will go out into the entire world from Jerusalem.[48] The generally well-accepted concept of the universe (οἰκουμενεη) for the meaning of 'ends of the earth' (ἐσχάτου τῆς γῆς) is further substantiated by the cataloging of the fifteen different nations that gather on the day of Pentecost to witness the inauguration of the first century transcultural Christian community (Ac.2:9-11).

4.2.3 God's Kingdom Mimics the Imperial Kingdom

By introducing "the new Christian *politeia* and *oikoumene*," Luke de-eschatologizes the concept of the kingdom of God not only by envisioning the ancient "virtues dreamed of in the philosophical and political texts," but also by actualizing it through the first century Christian community.[49] Through the discursive message

Walton, "Acts. Many Questions, Many Answers," in *The Face of NT Studies. A Survey of Recent Research*, edited by S. McKnight and G.R. Osborne (Grand Rapids: Backer Academic, 2004), 246-47.

[45] B. Ashcroft, G. Griffiths and H. Tiffin, *The Empire Writes Back: Theory and Practice in Postcolonial Literatures* (London: Routledge, 2002), 8. Luke seems to refer this usage to mean the entire universe, more than the capital of the *Imperium Romanum*. By reaching the capital of the Roman Empire with the gospel does not end its mission. Barrett, *Acts*, vol. 1, 80.

[46] Barrus, "The Gospel of Luke and the Acts," 147. The theoretical concept of mimicry is for the purpose of disrupting the imperial authority by 'resemblance and menace.' Bhabha, *The Location of Culture*, 86.

[47] Luke constructs an image of the emperor whose name is not known, to give the final verdict for the countering movement but not able to appear before the audience.

[48] Michael W. Pahl, "The 'Gospel' and The 'Word': Exploring Some Early Christian Patterns," *JSNT* 29.2 (2006), 219.

[49] Todd Penner, "Civilizing Discourse: Acts, Declamation, and the Rhetoric of the *Polis,*" in *Contextualizing Acts. Lukan Narrative and Greco-Roman Discourse*, edited by T. Penner and

of challenging the totalizing claims of the Roman Empire for the sake of God's kingdom, Luke probably wedges into the in-between space for the persecuted subjects to maneuver a strategy of resistance that radically revalues the policies of the Roman Empire.[50] He also visualizes a transformative kingdom which transcends the exclusive Jewish ethnicity and geographical boundaries in the formation of the transcultural Christian community. Here, God and human beings work-together in partnership for transcending the dominant native Jewish center as well as the Roman imperial kingdom. Wengst explains the nature of the kingdom community for those who are liberated for their own identity, "those who are capable of speaking and thus put in a position to communicate.... giving those who cannot speak a voice, helping those who have made dumb to articulate themselves."[51]

Luke challenges the first century hegemonic religio-political centers of Jerusalem and Rome by mimicking the dominant power centers with an alternative vision of a new world order. The power of the gospel is spoken in the face of the Roman power centers with postcolonial theoretical concepts of mimicry and ambivalence. There is a paradigm shift in the proclamation of the kingdom where the disciples of Jesus preach Jesus as the Lord (Ac.1:21; 2:36; 10:36; 28:31) within the context of the imperial cult where the Caesar is called as 'Lord' and 'god.'[52] According to Luke, the central focus of the Kingdom has been changed in the new age by God's decisive act in history through the person of Jesus as the Lord of the universe.[53]

Luke assumes a paradigm shift in the political metaphor of the human 'kingdom' by locating it in the eschatological middle space. Here, the transcultural community is placed in the in-between space through affiliation and distancing to the dominant discourse of religio-political center. Jesus deconstructs the imperialistic ruler-centered politics to God-centered politics, from Jerusalem's ethnic-centered policies of imposing burdens on humanity to service-centered community where people are given importance.[54] In witnessing to God's kingdom, there is no national favoritism and ethnic priority. The politics of the first century Christian movement touches the life of the public assembly (δῆμος) for justice in socio-cultural-political issues.[55]

C.V. Stichele (SBL, 20; Atlanta: SBL, 2003), 103.

[50] Barrus, "The Gospel of Luke and the Acts," 139. In the colonial period, the subalterns criticized the hegemony of the center as well as seriously taking the "values of the ruling elites." Scott, *Domination and the Arts of Resistance*, 106; Bhabha, *The Location and Culture*, 37.

[51] Wengst, *Pax Romana*, 67-68.

[52] Kreitzer, *Striking New Images*, 71. Emperor Domitian insists that people address him as 'our lord and god' (Suetonius, *Domitian* 13.2).

[53] Lotz, "A Critical Evaluation of Youngmo Cho," 137.

[54] Storkey, *Jesus and Politics*, 125-26.

[55] Storkey, *Jesus and Politics*, 58.

4.3 The Pentecost Event Mimics and Ruptures the Imperial Ideology of Unification (Ac.2:1-12)

Before the Pentecost event as part of the empowerment mechanism, Luke's narrative reestablishes the leadership structure (Ac.1:12-26; Matthias is selected to the place of Judas Iscariot) of the twelve affiliate with Israel's restoration (1QS 8.1-2; 4Q259.2.9; cf.Lk.6:12-16; 10:1-17).[56] On the other hand, in the political setting of Rome, one may assume the reshuffling of the Roman senate by the time of the new era of Augustus Caesar. Moreover, the replacement of Judas' position and his desolation demonstrates the impending doom of those who oppose the plan of God and God's eschatological reign.

The diverse and interconnected verbal and visual communication strategy of the Roman imperial propaganda is used in the beginning of Acts probably to mimic through the birth of a great eschatological era.[57] In this process, has Luke visualized the minoritarian community for negotiation and bargaining for a political mileage by recollecting the colonized nationals who gathered during the pilgrim festivals in Jerusalem? Does the formation of the gathering 'from every nation' (ἀπο παντος ἔθνους) on the day of Pentecost negotiate with the old Jewish festival yet contest the idea of exclusive nationalism?[58]

The promised eschatological Spirit (πνεῦμα) comes upon the 120 disciples including the twelve apostles as 'they were all together on the same [place]... house they were sitting' (ἦσαν πάντες ὁμοῦ ἐπὶ τὸ αὐτο ... οἰκον οὗ ἦσαν καθή μενοι' Ac.2:1-2; cf.1:12-14). This event probably explains the communitarian concept of the first century Christian ecclesia which assembles in a marginal space of a house.[59] It may be quite possible that Luke sees the eschatological era as it breaks out into a visible phenomenon on the day of Pentecost. The eschatological Spirit enables the multilingual nationalities of 'devout men from all nations' (ἄνδρες εὐλαβεῖς ἀπὸ παντὸς ἔθνους) to experience the speech in 'other tongues' (ἑτέραις γλώσσαις) (Ac.2:1-5) and the multiethnic-multilingual pluralistic

[56] J.H. Charlesworth, *Jesus within Judaism: New Light from Exciting Archaeological Discoveries* (New York: Doubleday, 1988), 138; E.P. Sanders, *Jesus and Judaism* (Philadelphia: Fortress, 1985), 104; Keener, "Power of Pentecost," 55-56.

[57] Gilbert, "Roman Propaganda and Christian Identity," 236. Roman political propaganda uses both the verbal and visual aids all through the empire like imperial icons (statues, coins, and sanctuaries) as well as in public festivities. Luke uses the communication strategy of visual aids of split tongues as well as the audio aid of the sound of violent wind probably for the sake of mimicking.

[58] Penner, "Civilizing Discourse," 97. Josephus refers to "an immense crowd running together" for the Pentecost feast (*JW* 2.43; 6.299). This is also called as Feast of Weeks (Ex.23:16; 34:22; Num.28:26; Lev.23:15-21; Deut.16:9-12), which is celebrated as a Harvest festival.

[59] Luke is discursive in the portrayal of the place where the 120 disciples were gathered. It must have been in a liminal space near the temple so that the multinational pilgrims could easily witness the mighty acts of God.

community comprehend the message (Ac.2:5-6).[60] The universal representatives do not hear the false propaganda of Roman *imperium,* rather they hear the hybrid voices declaring the mighty acts of God (Ac.2:9-11) which may rupture the mighty acts of military propaganda of Caesars greatness. Luke possibly displays the hybridizing dialogue of direct speech from 'above' as a metonym to hear 'the mighty acts of God' through the angels, and the inspired disciples of Jesus who wait for the eschatological spirit.[61] This 'mighty acts of God' probably signify the reign of God which may unite the multinationals to crossover the postcolonial concerns of Jewish nativism, racial essentialism and linguistic individualism. The multinationals are the diasporic Jews from Parthia, Mesopotamia, Egypt, Lybia, Cretans and Arabs (Ac.2:10, 11). These hybrid Jews cross their socio-cultural-political and linguistic borders to find the 'third space of enunciation.'[62] There is a possibility that this new unity may mockingly mimic the imperial unification of the multinationals.

Similar to the propaganda of the emperor's glory, the multicultural audience recognizes the great activity of God which is later explained through the speech of Peter (Ac.2:14-36). This inspired and intentional speech in a religio-political context is given not to divide but to unite the multiple nationalities.[63] Thus, an *international* culture is formed on the day of Pentecost with multiple "'tongues' 'spaces' and temporalities" yet they comprehend the message in the 'eschatological space.'[64] This international culture of multiple tongue, universal space, and

[60] Barrus, "The Gospel of Luke and the Acts," 147. Bakhtin argues for 'polyglossia', 'heteroglossia' or 'hybridization' in novelistic literature having its goal for "the illumination of one language by means of another' in the context of historical colonization and multiple intersections of cultures. Bakhtin, *The Dialogic Imagination,* 361. Hanchen describes it as a miracle of language, *Acts,* 168. Wedderburn compares between the law and the Spirit by connecting the Sinai episode and the festival of Pentecost. A.J.M. Wedderburn, Tradition and Redaction in Acts 2:1-13," *JSNT* 55 (1994), 29-39; and Ludemann compares between the ecstatic speech and Paul's explanation in 1Cor 14:18, G. Ludemann, *Early Christianity according to Traditions in Acts,* translated by J. Bowden (Minneapolis: Fortress Press, 1987), 40-42.

[61] Barrus, "The Gospel of Luke and the Acts," 148. In the gospel account the hybrid speech gives birth to the distinctive characters like John and Jesus (Lk.1:20, 26- 55, 63; 2:29-38). The word metonym is from the Greek word μετωνυμία meaning a change of name to interpret a typical concept in a colonial cultural context.

[62] Kwok Pui-lan prefers to use 'border passage' than 'border crossing' because the journey is continuing. According to her, the cultural borders might be religio-cultural, "A Thelogy of Border Passage," in *Border Crossings,* edited by D.N. Premnath (New York: Orbis Books, 2007), 104.

[63] "An intentional hybrid is a semantic hybrid; not semantic and logical in the abstract but rather a *semantic that is concrete and social.*" Samuel, *A Postcolonial Reading of Mark's Story,* 27, (Italics in the original); Bakhtin, *The Dialogic Imagination,* 360.

[64] Bhabha, *The Location of Culture,* 38. The postcolonial significance of split-tongue, spaces and temporalities are given importance by Luke. Barrus, "The Gospel of Luke and the Acts," 148.

different temporalities create its unique space for new avenues for the first century Christian movement to grow in the liminal space with a heart for one another.[65]

This miracle of other tongues (ἑτέραις γλώσσαις) may pose a threat to the propaganda of colonial dominance for 'one culture and one language' over against the socio-ethnic-linguistic and religious minorities.[66] This phenomenon helps to celebrate the diverse language of the multiethnic culture by miraculously understanding one another irrespective of some funny comments from the public (v.13). This new phenomenon destabilizes the imperial dominance and disrupts the authority of imperial discourse by celebrating the plurality of the universal culture of immigrant diaspora Jews which excludes the totalitarianism and homogenization.

The dawn of a new age is inaugurated by the advent of the eschatological Spirit and it thus forms a new covenant community from the entire universe (οἰκουμένη). By making use of the available discourses (Jewish and Greco-Roman), Luke probably carves a space for the new born unidentifiable people 'of the way' (ἡ ὁδος) in the wider scope of the Roman Empire with negotiation and contestation.[67]

4.3.1 Lukan Cataloguing of the Nations Mimics Roman Empire Building

Luke probably is the first writer who pays much attention to the geographical locations by providing the number of nations from the four corners of the world. The purpose and source behind the catalogue are significant to analyze in order to understand the Lukan discourse.[68] The confluence of the Jewish-Greco-Roman

---

[65] Over against the understanding of the text in a postcolonial angle, there is a Zionist model of early Christian gathering on Mt.Zion. Witherington, *Acts*, 131.

[66] The imperial concept of 'one people' and 'one lip' is disruptive according to biblical tradition (Gen.11:4-5) and during the Hellenistic reign by Antiochus Epiphanus who tried to unify people under one religion and culture (1Macc.1.41). James M. Scott, "Luke's Geographical Horizon," in *The Book of Acts in its Greaco-Roman Setting*, vol. 2, edited by D.W.J. Gill and C. Gempf (Grand Rapids: Wm. B. Eerdmans Publishing Company, 1994), 530, FN.183. The Hindutva forces follow a similar imperial ideology of one tongue, one religion and one culture. Jyotirmaya Sharma critically analyses the Hindu cultural nationalism in India through the historical developments, *Hindutva. Exploring the Idea of Hindu Nationalism* (Viking: Penguin Books, 2011), 17-175.

[67] Nasrallah, "The Acts of the Apostles," 566. Border-crossing, hybridity, migration are the present day postcolonial concerns.

[68] NT scholars explain Pentecost and the catalogue of nations differently: theological purpose behind the geographical elements. H. Conzelmann, *Theology of St. Luke*, translated by Geoffrey Buswell (London: Faber and Faber, 1960), 27-73; for universal mission, Barrett, *Acts,* vol. 1, 119. for the worldwide mission perspective. Scott, "Luke's Geographical Horizon," 483-544; B.M. Rapske, "Acts, Travel, and Shipwreck," in *The Book of Acts in its Greaco-Roman Setting*, vol. 2, edited by D.W.J. Gill and C. Gempf (Grand Rapids: Wm. B. Eerdmans Publishing Company, 1994), 3-47. There are quite a number of arguments over the sources for Lukan catalogue (the ancient astrological list, the Jewish diaspora, Gen.10 and the table of nations (Scott, "Luke's Geographical Horizon," 483-544; and the Jewish eschatological gathering (Isa.11:11), (J.A.Brinkman, "The

world is very much significant for Luke, as he is most likely mimicking through the contemporary convergence of geographical locale in Jerusalem. In this process, he follows the ethnography of the imperial historians as well as the monarch himself for the sake of empire building.[69]

Since the time of the Augustan era, there was a slight shift from the military conquest to literal and cultural conquest of the inhabited world through political clients like Virgil, Dionysius, etc.[70] The Roman aspiration for universal domination was displayed visually on the statue of Augustus, on the coinage of goddess Roma and in public maps.[71] Besides the listing of nations and the geographic locations, these were the effective ways of promoting "the ideology of universal rule" for Rome by the emperors. Moreover, this promotion was done by the Greco-Roman writers.[72] According to Gilbert, Luke mimics the Roman propaganda of sovereignty over the universe by creating a contested terrain by proclaiming "the dominion not of Caesar but of God and his son Jesus... [which] speaks of the true *oikoumene* created through the Spirit, ruled over by Jesus, and mapped out by the list of nations in Acts 2."[73]

The second century Church Father Tertullian "could recognize the rhetorical similarities between the list in Acts and the expressions of Roman political propaganda... as proof for the universal rule of Christ."[74] Thus, one would assume that Luke appropriates the Roman political propaganda in listing the nations as the way of the expansion of Jesus movement in the imperial Roman world

---

Literary Background of the 'Catalogue of the Nations' (Acts 2:9-11)," *CBQ* 25 (1963), 418-27); G. Gilbert, "List of Nations in Acts 2: Roman Propaganda and the Lukan Response," *JBL* 121 (2002), 497-529.

[69] Scott, "Luke's Geographical Horizon," 483-544. Conception of geography is used for Roman imperial propaganda and administration (Julius Caesar, Agrippa's World map, *Res Gestae Divi Augusti*) that includes fifty five geographical names. The Jewish geographical world was influenced by the Greco-Roman traditions (*JW* 2.345-401) as well as her own ancestral traditions with Old Testament background (Gen.10, 1Ch.1:1-2:2; Ezek 38-39; Dan.11; Isa.66:18-20). Explaining the table of nations and the structure of Acts according to the ethnic division of Shem (Ac.2:1-8:25), Ham (Ac.8:26-40) and Japheth (Ac.9:1-28:31) by Scott is objectionable to the biblical interpretation (531-541). For Luke illustrates the genealogy of humanity from Adam (Ac.17:26-'From one man....," Ac.17:28-'We are his offspring.'

[70] Gilbert, "Roman Propaganda and Christian Identity," 247-48. Political writings like official records as well as literary works were made by the propagators of the imperial reign since the time of Augustus.

[71] Gilbert, "Roman Propaganda and Christian Identity," 248.

[72] Gilbert, "Roman Propaganda and Christian Identity," 249. Writers such as Virgil (*Aen*.6.780-782); Horace (*Carm*.4.14); Pliny the Elder (*Nat.Hist.* 5.132-133); and Josephus (*JW* 2.358-87) have their own list of nations to praise the power of the Roman Empire. Augustus' *Res Gestae* lists "fifty five geographical places conquered, pacified, added, or otherwise dominated by Rome" (249).

[73] Gilbert, "List of Nations in Acts 2," 529.

[74] Gilbert, "List of Nations in Acts 2," 518.

(Ac.1:8) which would possibly disrupt the Roman imperial strategy.[75] Soon after describing the imperial ideology of merging the universe through the cataloguing of the nations, the following speech of Peter makes a universal appeal by calling them as 'brothers' and 'all flesh' (Ac.2:29, 37, 14).[76] Through this discourse, Luke probably exploits the "Roman political ideology as a way to foster among its readers a clearer sense of their Christian identity and of the legitimacy of the Church."[77] By analyzing the implication of the list of nations in parallel to the Greco-Roman world, Luke prepares the readers to ask the question, who is their 'Lord/ Saviour' in the context of the dominant religio-political center at Jerusalem? The answer Luke emphatically gives is that there is 'no other name but Jesus' in Ac.4:12 which significantly would disrupt the imperial center in the context of the political milieu of the Roman emperor's worship and colonialism.

The Lukan account of the Pentecost event is a public display of not only the cataloging of fifteen different nations but also the linguistic feats which focus on Jesus as the ruler of the inhabited world in contestation to the imperial agenda.[78] By crossing the borders of ethnic and cultural exclusivism, Luke possibly adopts the concept of the whole inhabited world to communicate the gospel of God.

Similarly, Luke also envisions the entire universe (οἰκουμένη) from the Parthians to the Romans, perhaps mimicking the kingdoms of the world at different historical periods, teaching and correcting the language disorders (Babel tradition) and national unity on the arrival of the eschatological spirit.[79] The purview of the geographical horizon mentioned in Ac.2:9-11 encompasses the four directions where Jerusalem as the Jewish center and Rome as the political center of the then world are pushed to the periphery.[80] The centrifugal concept of Jerusalem as the center of Lukan geographical mapping is probably in line with the Jewish fulfillment prophecies (Isa.2:2-4; Mic.4:1-8; Zech.8:20-23). However, they are not to converge rather to dispel the gospel (εὐαγγελιον) of God's love, justice and peace to the entire universe. By placing the most stubborn and obstinate Parthia to become the forefront of the catalogue shows Luke's strategic challenge to Roman colonialism. Likewise, the political force behind the display

---

[75] Gilbert, "List of Nations In Acts 2," 524. In the overall purpose of Luke-Acts, Acts 2 can be seen as a political rhetoric to explain the identity of the minority followers in Jesus in relation to the Roman Empire.

[76] Men, brothers ("Ανδρες ἄδελφοι Ac.2:29, 37) and upon all flesh (ἐπι πασαν σάρκα Ac.2:14) express the universal calling of the nations.

[77] Gilbert, "List of Nations In Acts 2," 527.

[78] Gilbert, "Roman Propaganda and Christian Identity," 250; Wedderburn, "Traditions and Redaction in Acts," 44, 53. Luke has a role in the redaction of the final composition of the nations, Haenchen, *Acts*, 170.

[79] L. Nasrallah, "The Acts of the Apostles, Greek Cities, and Hadrian's Panhellion," *JBL* 127/3 (2008), 557.

[80] Scott, "Luke's Geographical Horizon," 527, F.N.169.

of the nations most likely is to disrupt the Roman imperial world by calling the representative nations of God's universe.[81] The new Christian identity is explained by mimicking the political image of Rome by making them as the subjects of the universal kingdom of Jesus who is the 'Saviour' (σωτηρ) and bringer of peace.[82] This accommodative-disruptive posturing to the dominant religio-political images is demonstrated to show how the first century marginalized Jesus community writes back to the empire.

4.3.2 The Spirit-Tongue Cross-Cultural Witness in the Context of Imperialism

Peter illustrates the Spirit empowered witnessing by the eschatological people of God through prophecy and visions to cross the national (all people), gender (sons/daughters), sequential (young and old) and class (slaves) barriers (Ac.2:16-21).[83] The proclamation of the good news of the kingdom through the activity of the Spirit is significant in the context of Roman colonial world in and around Palestine. This witnessing has a distinctive use in Luke-Acts for socio-political reasons.[84] In the Palestinian socio-religious-cultural and political Jewish milieu the minority Christian's proclamation-witnessing of the 'kingdom of God (βασιλεια τοῦ θεοῦ) may be dangerously disruptive.[85] However, the disciples receive the power (δυναμις) to witness through the empowerment of

[81] Gilbert, "Luke-Acts and Negotiation of Authority," 102, 528 (Strabo, *Geo.* 6.4.2; 11.1.2.1; 11.6.4; 11.9.2-3; 11.13.2; 16.1.28; 17.3.2). Luke places Judea as one among the other nations.

[82] Gilbert, "Roman Propaganda and Christian Identity," 254.

[83] For Luke, the Spirit-inspired vision has great significance to witness the salvation plan of God. Eleven out of twelve occurrences of the noun form vision (ὅραμα) comes in Acts (Ac.7:31; 9:10, 12; 10:3,17,19: 11:5; 12:9; 16:9,10; 18:9 (cf.Mt.17:9). The eschatological vision that breaks the ethnic barriers of prejudice and hatred in Cornelius' episode (Ac.10:17, 19; 11:5) envisions to cross national boundaries (Paul to crossover to Macedonia (Ac.16:9, 10). Keener, "Power of Pentecost," 205.

[84] Cho makes no connection with the imperial context of the narration. Cho, "Spirit and the Kingdom in Luke-Acts," 182. Luke uses the word proclamation fifteen times in place of ten in the gospel; εὐαγγελιζεσθαι (Ac.8:12; cf.Lk.4:43; 8:1; 16:16), κηρυσσειν (Ac.20:25; 28:31; cf. Lk.8:1), διαγγελλειν (Lk.9:6) and λεγειν (Ac.1:3). From the beginning of the earthly ministry of Jesus, the kingdom of God is centered in Luke's emphasis on the proclamation to convey a present reality. For the Gospel of Luke, preaching the Kingdom of God means bringing good news to the poor (εὐαγγελισασθαι πτωχοις), proclaiming liberation to the captives (κηρύζαι αἰχμαλώ τοις Lk.4:18), and proclaiming the jubilee year of the Lord (κηρύξαι ἐνιαυτὸν v.19) within the socio-political context of the first century Greco-Roman world (Lk.4:16-30). A.D. Agua, "The Lukan Narrative of the Evangelization of the Kingdom of God: A Contribution to the Unity of Luke-Acts," in *The Unity of Luke-Acts*, edited by J. Verheyden (Louvain: Louvain University Press, 1999), 650.

[85] Wright, *Jesus and the Victory of God*, 369.

the Spirit, to meet the challenges in and around them.[86] Also, the proclamation of the gospel of the kingdom is in the midst of the varied political discourses of power (the native dominant Jewish discourse, Greek cultural discourse and Roman colonial discourse) which try to supersede the marginalized groups who struggle for a holistic liberation.

Luke elaborates the significance of the relationship between the Spirit-tongue cross-cultural witnesses through the narration of the Pentecost event. The use of 'other tongues' (ἑτέραις γλώσσαις) is probably to point out the witnessing act in the cross-cultural Greco-Roman world. The following study explains the early Christians reinterpretation of the kingdom probably with a double vision and a forked tongue to the Jewish nationalistic agents of power as well as the Roman center. Here in this process, Jesus is proclaimed as both Lord and Christ (κυρί ος-χριστος Ac.2:36) to be in fulfillment with the aspirations of the dominant collaborative Jewish-Roman discourse. However, they distance themselves from the militaristic nationalism of the Palestinian Judaism and reconstruct the strategy of the kingdom in a reversal order.[87]

The Lukan use of other tongues also signifies the importance of the proclamation in the narrative world of Acts where the newly formed eschatological community addresses different linguistic nationalities ('cross-cultural' Ac. 2:7-11). For him repentance is the motif for proclaiming the gospel of benevolence, love, justice and peace. The repented ones receive the promised gift of God (Ac.2:38; 3:19; 5:31; 8:22; 11:18; cf. Ac.13:24; 17:30; 19:4; 20:21; 26:20) to live as the new 'community of equals' in the eschatological space.[88] The proclamation of the Kingdom calls for socio-economic-political and cultural changes which would rupture the dominant colonial centers.

The Pentecost narrative explains the manifestation of the exalted Jesus as Lord of the universe who comes to inaugurate a new universal covenant community. This event probably affiliates to the Jewish tradition of theophanies and the fearful reaction of the audience which leads to the glorification of God (Ac.2:1-12).[89] Luke further affiliates his discourse with the prophetic fulfillment of Isaiah (Isa.59:21)

---

[86] The Lukan gospel emphasizes the convincing proofs of Jesus' real identity through seeing (ἴδετε), feel (ψηλαφήσατε) and closely observing (θεωρεῖτε) for witnessing before a legal court (Lk.24:13-43). Bolt, "Mission and Witness," 196.

[87] Wright, *Jesus and the Victory of God*, 450.

[88] Crossan suggests 'companionship of empowerment' because there is subordination in the discipleship-master relationship, *The Birth of Christianity*, 337.

[89] J. Ruthven, "'This is my Covenant with them': Isaiah 59:19-21 as the Programmatic Prophecy of the New Covenant In the Acts of the Apostles (Part I)," *JPT* 17 (2008), 36-44, 47. Ruthen argues for a better parallelism to the literary structure of Isaiah 59:19-21 for the driving mighty wind, the tongues of fire as the covenant Spirit than reflecting the Sinai theophany (Ex.3:2; 19:16-20; Deut.4:11-24). The wind of God (*ruha,* Isa.59:19) generates wonder and amazement due to the theophanic sound. Ruthven suggests the fear due to the continuing messianic reign through the Apostles by wonders and signs.

in connecting between the Spirit and the "words in the mouth" (Ac.2:33; cf. Ac.8:35; 10:34; 8:14).[90] The eschatological Spirit places God's words in the mouth of the disciples for the growth of the covenant community (Ac.6:7; 8:4; 8:27-31; 12:24; 16:5-6; 19:20) that conceivably counters the imperial ideology of the first century.[91] In the successive narration of the Pentecost experience, similar to the day at Pentecost (Ac.2:1-11), the proclamation of God's word results in the outpouring of the Spirit forms the eschatological community in the Roman world in and outside Palestine (Ac.10:46; 19:6).

4.4 Peter's Speeches Disrupt the Jewish Religio-Political Center (Ac.2:14-41; 3:11-46; 5:29-32)

The narrative context of the Pentecost event, the Jerusalem temple (Ac.2:46; 3:1-3, 11f; 5:12, 25, 42), and the Jewish Sanhedrin (Ac.4:1-7; 5:17-28) are very significant in interpreting the speech for its discursive strategy of affiliation and disruption of the dominant religious traditions.[92] Peter becomes the spokesperson of the apostolic band in all these speeches proclaiming the resurrected 'Lord' (Κύ ριος) who is crucified. This proclamation probably disrupts the Jewish religio-political power center. In this process, he preaches repentance, in a corporate as well as at a personal level both to the Jews and the Gentiles (Ac.2:22-38; 3:17-26; 4:8-12; 5:28-32; cf. 10:42-43; 13:38; 14:15; 17:30; 26:18), by affiliating-distancing from the dominant power centers.[93] Moreover, the gospel proclamation brings healing to the whole being (Ac.3:1-10; 5:16; 8:7; 9:32-35, 36-43; 14:8-10; 19:11-16; 20:7-12) at the backdrop of the eschatological era. The further analysis of the speeches of Peter is shown as a split tongue, used most likely against both the kingdom of Caesar and the kingdom of Israel.

Peter' speech on the day of Pentecost (Ac.2:14-41) emphasizes two things: the outpouring of the Spirit is a sign of the eschatological time of salvation (Ac.2:20-22; 'last days' Ac.2:17), and the risen Jesus is the universal 'saviour' (σωτηρ). In his speech, Peter addresses the general Jewish crowd who rejected and killed their messiah by supporting their religious leaders. This Jesus of Nazareth, a marginal Galilean who was a man accredited by God in doing miracles and wonders, establishes the messianic reign on earth (Ac.2:22). Peter accuses the Jewish audience (Ἰσραηλῖται) for their heinous collaboration with the Roman

[90] J. Ruthven, "'This is my Covenant with them,'" 41-42.

[91] Ruthven, " 'This is my Covenant with them,'" 42.

[92] R.C. Tannehill, "The Functions of Peter's Mission Speeches in the Narrative of Acts," *NTS* 37 (1991), 400. Till Acts 12 the narrative world explains the Jewish leadership which was leading the nation on behalf of the imperial Rome. Recent scholarship considers that the speech is a Lukan composition.

[93] Jesus intends Jewish restoration by the proclamation of repentance not simply as a personal transformation but of the national welfare ("violent rebel activity"). Wright, *Jesus and the Victory of God*, 253, 256.

colonialist in crucifying Jesus of Nazareth (Ac.2:23).[94] However, the resurrection and exaltation make Jesus both 'Lord and Christ' (κυρίος and χριστος Ac.2:36; cf.4:10) that would conceivably disrupt both the Jewish-Roman imperial centers.[95] The saving purpose repeatedly portrays through the split tongue in the speech by challenging the Jewish messiahs and the imperial 'Lords' of the first century (Ac.2:21, 38).[96] Moreover, Luke narrates the effectiveness of the speech through the three thousand Jewish nationalists who move from the imperial center ('corrupt generation' Ac.2:40) to join with the liminal space of the first century eschatological community.

Peter preaches from the Jewish prophetic traditions that the exalted Jesus is the 'Christ' (χριστος Ac. 2:31, 36), the anticipated royal king of the Jewish nation. This probably is an ambivalent speech which affiliates and distances from the dominant Jewish discourse (cf.Joel.3:28-32; Psa.16:8-11; 110:1).[97] He prophetically utters the fulfillment of the eschatological era (Lk.4:16-20) in seeing, liberating, and announcing the salvation of God (Ac.2:14-41). In this new eschatological era, the spirit will give special gifting (visions and dreams), divine power (display of wonders and signs), and prophetic utterance to all flesh (πᾶσαν σάρκα Ac.2:16-21).[98] The new minoritarian Jesus community with reorganized status of power relationship where both men and women come together in anticipation of a commonwealth becomes a possible disruption to the religio-political centers.[99]

In the second speech, Luke probably mocks the exploitative structure of the Jewish religion through mentioning the lame man begging at the temple gate (Ac.3:11-36). The healing narrative emphasizes the spectacular evidence of the eschatological era of salvation brought by Jesus. Peter's speech from Solomon's colonnade blames the Jewish leaders for killing the 'author of life' (ἄρχηγος) and collaborating with Pilate the Roman prefect who condemns Jesus to death (Ac.3:13-15; cf.Lk.23:13-25). This might be a direct encounter to disrupt the

---

[94] By calling the Romans soldiers as the lawless men (ἀνόμον) who nailed him, Luke probably expressing his antagonism to the imperial administration. However, for Barrett, the main verb 'you killed' (ἀνείλατε v. 23) placing the responsibility of 'nailing'/ crucifixion on Jews, *Acts*, vol. 1, 143.

[95] Mimicking the religio-cultural codes from the Roman-Jewish discourses is for the purpose of affiliation and disruption.

[96] Traditional commentators interpret the salvation in exclusive spiritual terms of "forgiveness of sins, acceptability to God, (and) peace with God." Bayer, "The Preaching of Peter in Acts," 274.

[97] Penner, "Civilizing Discourse," 97-98. The intertextual reading of Peter from Psalm 110:1 and Ps.16 are for the purpose of messianic interpretation. According to Penner, the narration and Peter's speech give powerful political reasoning for the infant Christian movement.

[98] The eschatological mission of prophecy (Ac.2:18), visions and dreams (Ac.2:17) fall on every one irrespective of gender (male and female cf.Ac.21:9-11; Lk.1:41-45, 67-79; 2:26-28), class (all slaves). Keener, "Power of Pentecost," 57-62.

[99] Bradstock and Roland, *Radical Christian Writings*, xxiv-xxv.

religio-political collaborated institutions.[100] However, the attribution of Jesus' identity by using the messianic titles, 'Servant, Holy and Righteous One, Author of life and Prophet like Moses' (Ac.3:14-15), probably for affiliating with the native Jewish religio-cultural traditions.[101] Further, there is an ambivalence in his preaching for the threat of exclusion (Ac.3:23), a restoration based on repentance (Ac.3:19-22) and also promises concerning his audience (Ac.3:24-26). The repeated calls for repentance (μετανοέω) and turning (ἐπιστρέθω Ac.9:19, 35; 11:21; 15:19) towards God in the Apostolic preaching indicate a radical shift from their allegiance to the dominant center and a call for an alternate reign of the Jewish messiah.[102] The theme *metanoia* is probably significant in view of the addressees who are located at the dominant religio-political power center at Jerusalem.[103]

Peter in his third speech, appropriately connects the healing of the crippled (Ac.4:9, 12; 'has been healed', 'to be saved' σὲσωται, σωθῆναι) in 'the name of Jesus Christ of Nazareth' as an act of benevolence.[104] Similarly, the miracles done by the apostles in Jerusalem (Ac.5:15, 16) echo the activities of Jesus in Galilee (cf.Lk.4:38-41) that illustrate the eschatological reign of God.[105] In addition, they not only defy the order of the Sanhedrin but also return back to the temple courts to preach 'all the words of this life' /salvation (πάντα τὰ ῥήματα τῆς ζωῆς ταύτης). It explains the collapse of the Jewish dominant center through implementing the order of the risen Christ (Ac.5:20-21; 4:18-20).[106] Luke also portrays the erosion of the religious authority in exercising the imperial force on the Apostles because of the public support (Ac.5:25, 26). Moreover, the religious leaders are probably terrified by accepting the guilt of the man's blood over their

[100] The ὑμεῖς (second person plural) used in these verses (Ac.3:13-15) explain both the accusation and emphasized on the promises upon the audience. Tannehill, "The Functions of Peter's Mission Speeches," 405. Solomon's colonnade is situated across the Gentile court probably a liminal space where the early Christians gathered (cf.Ac.5:12). Polhill, *Acts*, 129.

[101] The messianic titles are used in the prophetic-apocalyptic traditions (1Enoch 38:2; 46:3; 53:6; Psa.Sol.17:35; Zech.9:9). Polhill, *Acts*, 132.

[102] Repentance and turning towards God's messianic reign are probably the challenge that Peter place before the Jewish community. According Beverly Roberts Gaventa, repent of ones sins and turning towards God are conversion languages of Luke, *From Darkness to Light. Aspects of Conversion in the New Testament* (Philadelphia: Fortress Press, 1986), 86-87.

[103] According to Tannehill, the promise of national restoration is a powerful stimulus for repentance.Tannehill, "The Functions of Peter's Mission Speeches," 406.

[104] Peter's accusation against the Jewish leadership is about their role in crucifying the benevolent Jesus.

[105] Emperor Vespasian's propaganda tactics of doing miracles in the colonial world is for the purpose of gaining power and authority (*JW.*1.23; 3.401-404; 4.623).

[106] In Acts, the concepts of salvation and life are synonymously used (Ac.3:15; 11:18; 13:46-Life; Ac.4:12; 11:14; 15:11; 16:17, 30ff). Polhill, *Acts,* F.N, 118, 166. The bold witness of the marginalized apostles (ἀγραμματοί Ac.4:13; cf.Ac.5:29-32) before the religio-political authorities portray a direct disruption of the imperial center.

heads (Ac.5:28) which explains the slippery position of the native Jewish center.[107] All these events demonstrate the total helplessness of the religious administration to control the marginalized subjects.

The Apostles' explanation of a higher authority under which they function ('it is necessary to obey God rather than men'), probably mimics the religio-political administrative leaders (Ac.5:29; cf.4:19).[108] In addition, Peter in his defensive speech, reemphasize the exalted Christ as the 'God, Prince and Saviour' (ὁ Θεὸς ἀρχηγὸν καὶ σωτῆρα) and accuse them of their guilt for crucifying Jesus.[109] Hence, the Roman execution is attributed to the Jewish leaders by stating that 'you killed (him) by hanging on a tree' (Ac.5:30; 10:39; 13:29).[110] The exaltation of the crucified Jewish messiah to the right hand of God (Ac.5:30-32; Ac.2:33) who bring salvation to humanity naturally disrupts the dominant Jewish power centers.[111] The climax of the speech is apologetic through reemphasizing the offer of forgiveness and repentance to Israel in spite of their consistent resistance to the offer of salvation.[112] However, the response to the speech on one side is fierce opposition to the Apostles (Ac.7:33) but on the other side is the sympathetic counsel of the Pharisee named Gamaliel. This affiliation brings to the scene the positive posture of the Jewish religious center (Ac.5:33-40; cf.23:6-9).[113] This scene is portrayed by Luke to show the boundary crossing strategy of the Jewish

[107] A total disruption of the Sanhedrin authority could be seen by scrupulously avoiding the name of Jesus in this second interrogation. Polhill suspects the post-70 era of using the name of Jesus as blasphemous in the context of the division between Judaism and Christianity. Polhill, *Acts*, 168.

[108] The statement mimics the imperial masters who exercise their authority over their subjects and the disruption occurs due to the Apostles understanding of the eschatological era.

[109] The word 'the saviour' (ἡ σωτηρία) must be analyzed in the light of the eschatological era where the salvation is for the entire person. This speech resembles the Christian *kerygma* of the crucifixion, the resurrection, exaltation of Jesus including repentance and forgiveness. Polhill, *Acts,* 169.

[110] The cross is considered to be curse according to the Mosaic Law (Deut.21:23; cf.Ac.10:39; 13:29; Gal.3:13).

[111] It is the religio-political imperial leaders who work in collaboration to crucify Jesus. The affiliation to Judaism is reflected through the OT passages used in Peter's preaching (Ac.4:11; cf.Lk.20.17).

[112] According to Tannehill, the physical healing in the narrative is symbolic to the wholistic salvation that offers in Jesus' name (Ac.4:12; cf.Ac.2:40). Tannehill, "The Functions of Peter's Mission Speeches," 407. The Salvation motif in Acts, please refer Robert C. Tannehill, *The Narrative Unity of Luke-Acts: A Literary Interpretation, vol. II: The Acts of the Apostles* (Minneapolis: Fortress Press, 1994), 39-40.

[113] An explicit death threat came against the Apostles probably from the Sadducean side. However, Gamaliel, a Pharisees intervention in the court must have changed the decision of executing death on the Apostles by two examples from Jewish history (Theudas and Judas the Galilean; *JW*.2.433; 7.253; *Ant*.18.4-10; 18.23; 20,102) of dying off the messianic movements. Refer for further explanation in the background study. During the burial scene of Jesus, one probably sees the same postcolonial ambivalent role from Joseph of Arimathea, a member of the council (Lk.23: 53) by moving from the colonial center to help the marginalized.

official establishment and postcolonial ambivalence of these religious leaders towards the marginal Apostles.

The imperial nature of the temple city is portrayed through the repetitive arrests and interrogations of the Apostles by the native Jewish administration (συνέ δριον) which is in collaboration with the Romans (Ac.4-5).[114] The Sadducean elites are annoyed by the messianic overtones of the Apostles' preaching about the resurrection of the dead (Ac.4:2, 3; cf.Ac.17:31, 32). Further, the escape of the Apostles from the prison to fill Jerusalem with their teaching (Ac.5:17-26; cf.12:6-11) will in all probability disrupts the dominant Jewish center at Jerusalem.[115] The Apostles repetitive 'sign and wonders' among the Jewish populace as the benevolence of the eschatological era make a sudden inflow of 'more and more men and women believe in the Lord and are added to their number' (Ac.4:4; 5:14).[116] Contrary to the strict order (παρήγγειλαν) of not to speak in Jesus' name, the Apostles continue teaching and proclaiming the gospel of Jesus Christ (Ac.5:42; cf.Ac.28:31) in the temple courts and houses which would challenge the Jewish power center at Jerusalem. The conflict between the eschatological community and the Sanhedrin finally leads to the flogging of the Apostles (Ac.5:40), the death of Stephen (Ac.6:8-8:1) and James (Ac.12:1). However, in the midst of persecution and suffering, Luke emphasizes the rapid growth of the Christian ecclesia in and around Palestine with specificity (3000 and 5000; Ac.2:41; 4:4; cf.Ac.6:7) and with great credentials. Hence this marginalized community discourse would be writing back to the Jewish collaborative and nationalistic agents of power with affiliative-alterity dynamism.

In most cases, the call for repentance (Ac.2:38; 3:19; 5:31) affiliates with the established Jewish 'prophetic traditions' for renewal and restoration (Jer.3:12-16; 7:3-25; 14:6f; Ezek.18:30; Zech.1:3; 7:8-10; Mal.3:7).[117]

---

[114] The religio-political leadership comprised of the priests and high priest (Annas, Caiaphas, John, Alexander), the captain of the temple guard and the Sadducees (Ac.4:1, 6). The same collaboration (High Priest-Herod-Pontius Pilate) can be seen in the execution of Jesus (Ac.4:27; cf.Lk.18:28-19:16). The Judean politics has been controlled by the Sanhedrin which is a replica of the imperial Rome. Cassidy, *Society and Politics,* 40.

[115] The revolutionary idea of messianic reign was disruptive to the Sadducean Jewish aristocracy because it was a threat to their imperial collaborated reign.

[116] The successive results of the conversion who have crossed the borders to join to the eschatological community (Ac.4:4) must have challenged the imperial center.

[117] Hans F. Bayer, "The Preaching of Peter in Acts," in Witness to the Gospel. The Theology of Acts, edited by I.H. Marshall and David Peterson (Wm. B. Eerdmans Publishing Company: Grand Rapids, Michigan, 1998), 263. Bayer explains the traditions of John the Baptist and Jesus as repentance preachers in affiliating to the prophetic traditions (Lk.3:3, 7-9, 17; 11:37-54; 12:32; 13:34f; 15:3ff; 19:42-44; 21:8-36) (265). As a response to the call for repentance, the crowd (Lk.3:3), the tax collectors (Lk.3:14) and the soldiers (Lk.3:14) asked John the Baptist 'what should we do'?

4.5 The Summary Description of the Christian *politeia* Strategically Mimics the Greco-Roman Ideal of Friendship (Ac.2:43-47; 4:32-37)

Luke gives a brief description of the Christian community ('the believers and the ones being saved' (οἱ πιστεύσαντες and τοὺς σῳζομένους) by collocating two passages (Ac.2:43-47; 4:32-37) describing the early Christian societal life of the first century. The socio-cultural and economic life of the community probably mimics the Greco-Roman *politeia.*[118] Moreover, the Christian community is identified with their witnessing life of 'fellowship' (κοινωνίᾳ Ac.2:42) and unity ('one soul, and everything in common, (ψυχὴ μία, ἅπαντα κοινά Ac.4:32).[119]

The early Christian community is formed in the context of social dislocation, economic poverty, and political anarchy.[120] A radically different vision of a transcultural cosmopolitan empire is formed in the first century context of Paul by the slogan, 'there is neither Jew nor Greek, neither slave nor free, neither male nor female,' (Gal.3:28).[121] This new beginning of the Christian community may be a discursive dissent to the *imperium* of Rome probably mimics and subvert the colonial system.[122] It may also be a move away from the violent opposition of the Jewish rebellious nationalism (*Ant.*18.6; *Life* 17, 262, 370f).

---

[118] *Politeia* (Πολιτεία) is derived from the word πόλις. It does not have an equivalent English translation. In the Greco-Roman context, this word means civic constitutions and leadership under which the city runs. In the summary description of the Christian *politeia,* Luke gives the core values of the new found faith. Penner, "Civilizing Discourse," 90. *Politeia,* Further, Luke emphasizes the increasing number of the Christian community by stating 'to the ones being saved (Ac.2:47) but still a minority. The Lukan phrase 'in the same [place]' (ἐπὶ τὸ αὐτο Ac.1:15; 2:1, 44, 47; 4:26) depicts the community's unity. Polhill, *Acts,* 120.

[119] Luke retains the combined Christian tradition of fellowship meal and Last Supper. The minority Christians are identified in their liminality by these terms 'the believers, from house' (οἱ πιστεύοντες, κατ' οἶκον Ac.2:46, 44, 4:32;10:43; 11:21;18:27;19:18) 'in the church and Christians' (ἐκκλεσια and Χριστιανοι Ac.11:26).

[120] Different types of communities have been formed in the political context of social dislocation of the Roman *imperium,* and the Christian group is one among them. Wendy Cotter, "The Collegia and Roman Law: State Restrictions on Voluntary Associations, 64BCE-200CE," in *Voluntary Associations in the Greco-Roman World* (New York: Routledge, 1996), 88. The detailed study of the first century Palestine socio-economic world, refer 3rd chapter. Esler points out the socio-economic depravity of the urban population of Syrian Antioch which was considered to be the Lukan community in terms of poverty, debt bondage and economic inequality, ***Community and Gospel,*** 171ff.

[121] A.Bradstock and C. Roland, eds., *A Radical Christian Writings: A Reader* (Oxford: Blackwell Publishers, 2002), 122......y and action should be about.

[122] Penner, "Civilizing Discourse," 70. An idealistic community could be seen in the community of friendship or philosophical schools. D.L. Mealand, "Community of goods and Utopian Allusions in Acts II-IV," *JTS* 28 (1977), 96-99; Alan C. Mitchell, "The Social Function of Friendship in Acts 2:44-47 and 4:32-37," *JBL* 111 (1992), 255-72; L.T. Johnson, *The Literary Function of Possessions in Luke-Acts* (SBLDS 39; Missoula, Mont.: Scholars Press, 1979), 1-5; *idem, Acts,* 62.

In the beginning of the narration of Acts, the Lukan discourse about the Christian *politeia* is formed with cardinal virtues of *koinonia* (fellowship) and *philanthropia* (the fellow-feeling) in the socio-economic-religious and political setting of the hegemonic imperial reign in the east.[123] The nascent Christian community in Jerusalem which participates in community meals and prayer, ironically, mimics the religiosity of the Jerusalem-centered Jewish worship.[124] The Apostles criticize 'the corrupt generation' of their days (Ac.2:41) because the value systems of the religio-political centers are not life-affirming to the majority colonial subjects.[125] Similarly, first century ecclesia counters the oppressive religious cum political structures of the temple centered dominant Jewish constituency (Ac.6:2-53).

According to Crossan, the act of communal sharing in the covenant community is an act of resistance against the imperial patronal sharing where it demands the personal power with a commercializing motive.[126] Moreover, the Christian community, the communal meal at the cultic center may portray as a resistant act in the poverty stricken Roman Palestine. By contextually affiliating with the Greco-Roman friendship tradition, the Deuteronomic tradition of sharing with the needy (Deut.15:4-5) and the Essenes practice of common sharing of goods (*JW* 2.122), Luke probably formulates a hybrid 'higher social order' with the socio-political system of the day.[127] Here in this process, the reciprocity ethics of friendship between the equals challenge the rich to cross the socio-economic structural borders by not expecting anything in return (Lk.6:34-35b; 20:35; cf.Lk.14:12-14, Gosp.Thomas.95).[128]

---

[123] Penner, "Civilizing Discourse," 89-90. In Luke's demonstration of the Christian *politeia,* it surpasses the mythic virtues of political Rome. "Jesus and early church as paradigms of what Christian polity and action should be about." Bradstock and Roland, *A Radical Christian Writings*, xvii.

[124] The first century Christian community combines the agape meal with Eucharist. Polhill, *Acts*, 119, F.N.143.

[125] Penner, "Civilizing Discourse," 90, 92.

[126] Crossan, *The Birth of Christianity*, 472.

[127] Mitchell, "The Social Function of Friendship," 272; Conzelmann, *Acts*, 23-24; Johnson, *Literary Function of Possession*, 1-5. Meelan proposes for the possible Lukan dependence upon the Greek utopian tradition, see Meeland, "Community of Goods and Utopian Allusions," 97; Barrett, *Acts*, vol. 1, 168. Capper argues for Lukan adoption of the social ideals of the Essenes. B. Capper, The Palestinian Cultural Context of Earliest Christian Community of Goods," in *The Book of Acts in its Palestinian Setting*, vol. 4, edited by R.Baucham (Grand Rapids: Wm. B. Eerdman Publishing Company, 1995), 323-355.

[128] Mitchell, "The Social Function of Friendship," 267. By seeing the complex meaning for the Greco-Roman friendship tradition given by the ancient authors like Plato, Aristotle (transcendental), Pythagorean (democratic), and Epicurean (exclusive and self-serving), Luke gives a unique way of expression. The Deuteronomic tradition (Deut.15:4) shows sharing the property with the poor among the Jewish circles only. In the first century socio-political *milieu*, friendship was normally sought by the equals with socio-economic and political gain in focus (256-57, 264-65).

Luke radically redefines the friendship system of his day to equalize the socio-economic relationship among the believers and achieve the social objective to challenge the rich to give away the riches. For instance, '...for as many as owners of lands or houses ... being sold ...were placing at the feet of the Apostles ... were distributing to each as anyone was having need' (Ac.4:34, 35; cf.Lk.16.9).[129] The episode of Barnabas (Ac.4:36-37) exhibits the ritualized friendship of a benefactor who bring 'the money and put it the apostles feet' (Ac.4:36).[130] Selling their possessions lead the socio-political elite to renounce their probable political power which is attached to the wealth and be in solidarity with the poor disciples of Jesus.[131] Luke does not limit the early Christians with the friendship ideal of 'togetherness' and generosity. He rather shows the contrasting picture of 'tragic deaths' (Judas, Ananias and Sapphira) to those who oppose the principle of fellowship due to their avarice and greed.[132]

Irrespective of the Jewish antagonism against the Christian movement, Luke also portrays the rapid growth of the Christian movement not only among the Jews (Ac.2:41, 47; 6:7; 21:20), but also among the Samaritans (Ac.8:4-25). "He (Luke) deliberately presents Christianity as the model *politeia* with an exemplary constitution and leadership" and qualities of communal sharing 'of having favour with all the people' (ἔχοντες χάριν πρὸς ὅλον τὸν λαόν), resulting in the rapid growth of the saving community (Ac.2:47).[133]

This hybridized community appropriates the political expressions of the Roman colonial ethos of *Pax Romana* as well as revives the "native religio-cultural and political expressions" in order to write back to the colonial centers.[134] In this context, Kwock Pui-lan, Segovia and Sugirtharajah explain the positive prospect of hybridity in the postcolonial discourse.[135] The Christian community

[129] Mitchell, "The Social Function of Friendship," 272. 'For as many as owners of lands or houses' (Ac.4:34) show Luke's analytical view of the rich owners in the light of economic disparity. The use of imperfect verbs (were bringing, placing, distributing ἔφερον, ἐτίθουν, διεδίδετο) describe a regular practice of selling their possessions in general and real estate. Barrett, *Acts*, vol. I, 255; Pollhill, *Acts*, 121. Esler points out the social stratification of the Hellenist cities of the Roman East where the few rich hold the major resources in the world. Esler, *Community and Gospel*, 171-79. Thus if the rich sells their possessions (lands and houses) and bring them for distribution to the needy, then the world would not have any poor.

[130] The ritualized gesture of Barnabas reverses the order of the first century tradition of a benefactor "to wield social power" through donations. Mitchell, "The Social Function of Friendship," 270.

[131] Gnanavaram, *Treasure in Heaven*, 146.

[132] Johnson sees Ananias and Sapphira episode as a negative contrast of making use of the possessions. Johnson, *Literary Function of Possessions*, 205.

[133] Penner, "Civilizing Discourse," 90.

[134] Samuel, *A Postcolonial Reading of Mark's Story*, 32.

[135] Pui-lan, "A Theology of Border Passage," 104; Segovia, "And they Began to Speak in Other Tongues," 1-32; R.S.Sugirtharajah, "Cultures, Texts, Margins: A Hermeneutical Odyssey," in *Asian Biblical Hermeneutics and Postcolonialism* (Maryknoll, New York: Orbis Books, 1998), 123-39.

thus enters into the transcultural space by crossing the gender national-ethnic-cultural-linguistic boundaries.[136] The eschatological community of believers starts experiencing the realized presence of God through their oneness and hospitality in the context of political isolation and *religio illicita*. The commonality and the common meal of table fellowship break the socio-religious-ethnic-racial and gender barriers. Within this eschatological community who live in covenant with God, the communal sharing affiliate with the patronal sharing of the Roman political system.

4.5.1 διεδίδετο...τις χρείαν εἶχεν Interrupts Greco-Roman Patronage System (Ac.4:35)

The early Christians 'were distributing their possessions as anyone having need' (διεδίδετο...τις χρείαν εἶχεν) as the manifestation of the Kingdom experience. It signifies their disowning the right of private property.[137] By doing 'righteous redistributing,' Luke challenges the socio-economic and political foundations of the Roman imperial economic structure where the rich accumulate wealth through the collaboration with the dominant culture of exploiting the poor through tax system and other means.[138] Luke probably disrupts the political system of the day through a radical renouncing of possessions for the sake of the eschatological kingdom values and this act empowers the people of the margins.[139] Luke's concern for the poor is described by stating that 'there was no needy person among them' (Ac.4:34), and the "πτωχεία (poverty) is abolished."[140] Luke finds a new space for the Christian community by reconfiguring the values of the Jewish-Greco-Roman civic life by affiliating and distancing simultaneously from the socio-political ideals of the time.[141] Luke probably visualizes the messianic era of the reconstituted Israel through this Christian ecclesia.[142] In the community of

---

[136] From Antioch, the followers of Jesus (of the way) are given an identity as 'Christians' (χριστιανοί Ac.11:26) which probably has religio-political connotation (Ac.11:26; 26:26; cf.1Pet.4:16; *Ant.*18.3.3.64; Pliny, *Ep.*10.96-97; Tacitus, *Annales* 15.44). The disciples of Jesus lived at the liminal space, i.e., 'on the way' 'along the way' (Mk.8:27, 31; 9:31, 33, 34; 10:17, 32, 52). Samuel, A Postcolonial Reading of Mark's Story, 131.

[137] Gnanavaram, *Treasure in Heaven*, 140-41. 152-55. Luke has a strong emphasis on 'alms giving' (ἐλεημοσυνη Ac.3:2-3, 10; 9:36; 10:2-4, 31; 24:17; cf.Ac.16:9; 18:22; Lk.11:41; 12:33) by relief work (Ac.11:27-30; 12:25; 24:17), and good works (Ac.9:36).

[138] Gnanavaram challenges the modern use of the phrase 'alms giving' for the radical Lukan concept of 'righteous redistribution.' Gnanavaram, *Treasure in Heaven*, Ch. 4, FN. 239.

[139] Gnanavaram, *Treasure in Heaven*, 153.

[140] Esler, *Community and Gospel*, 186.

[141] Penner, "Civilizing Discourse," 102. The early Christianity appears to be both radical and conventional in simultaneously affiliating and distancing from the dominant Jewish-Greco-Roman socio-religious and cultural values.

[142] S. Walton, "Primitive Community in Acts? Does Acts Present the Community of goods (2:44-45; 4:32-35) as Mistaken?," *EQ* 80/2 (2008), 104. The unity of heart and soul is seen among

sharing, Luke seems to have adopted the Greco-Roman, the Jewish (Essenes) ideals as well as Jesus' teachings on sharing of wealth with the needy as the fulfillment of the perfect *Pax Romana*.[143]

This socialistic ideology is brought home by Luke in selling the real estate of the wealthy and distributing the same according to the need (Ac.4:34-37). Here he shows not only the affiliation to the political system of the day but also contests for a higher ideal space of generous value system instead of the "competitive pursuit of social honor."[144] In this process, the wealthy Christians are challenged to empty their wealth for the sake of the poor, which would result in the economic equality among the first century minority Christians.

The subsequent chapters of Acts display differing statuses of sharing in the community (e.g., Simon Magus, Cornelius, Sergius Paulus, mother of John Mark, Lydia) for defending the system of 'giving alms to the needy' (ἐλεημοσυνη) when the gospel spreads to the wider Greco-Roman context.[145] Luke also gives examples of the socio-economic and political exploitation in the following narrations (Ac.16:19; 19:23-25; 24:24-26) and reflect upon the reversal of kingdom values through the newly formed community. He disrupts the economic pattern of life through the distribution of wealth and almsgiving for the sake of the poor (Ac.9:31; 11:28-30; 12:25) because it is wealth that controls the religio-political power structure of the first century CE.[146]

As a cultural hybrid, Luke discursively takes the radical position in bringing the poor and the rich in the in-between ecclesial space for fellowship where the former get a new identity as the people of God. The Hellenistic urban setting of Luke makes him to adopt a new strategy in bringing the gospel to challenge the rich to lose their economic-political power through giving up their wealth.[147] By bringing a social model of equality in fellowship and by renouncing the possession of the rich, Luke is redefining the socio-economic and political traditions for

---

them in the light of Jubilee legislation.

[143] Walton, "Primitive Community in Acts?," 105. The Essene community's practice of a voluntary sharing of possessions (Philo, *Every Good Man is Free* 76-79, 85-87; *Ant.*18.20-22; *JW* 2.122-27); Capper, "The Palestinian Cultural Context," 341-50.

[144] Barrus, "The Gospel of Luke and the Acts," 144.

[145] Karris, "Poor and Rich," 125. The voluntary practice (Ac.4:36-37; 5:1-11) probably abandons later in the context of the increasing widows, the Claudian famine (Ac.11:27-30; cf.24:17), the different arrangement by the inflow of the Hellenists (Ac.6:1-6) and the delay of parousia. Walton, "Primitive Community in Acts?," 100-01; Barrett, *Acts,* vol. 1, 168.

[146] Walton, "Primitive Community in Acts?," 102-03.

[147] Esler, *Community and Gospel,* 30. The community setting is well placed in Acts with a combination of the rich and the poor of an urban feudal setting (Ac.2:43-47; 4:36-37; 9:36; cf.Lk.16:19-31). Luke narrates a number of upper class members of the first century Church (Theophilus, Manaen Ac.13:1; Cornelius Ac.10; Dionysius, a member of Areopagus and Damaris Ac.17:34; cf.Joanna Lk.8:3).

the sake of Kingdom justice (Lk.6:1-5; 13:10-17).[148] The Lukan concept of 'fellowship' (κοινονια) is placed to cross the boundaries of benefactor role of return or the imperial nature of patron-client relationship that probably ruptures the political dominance. In their socio-economic relations, societal love becomes a tool that seeks to dismantle the socio-political and cultural oppressions. By being an alternative responsible society in a stratified Roman political system, the early Christian community starts to witness through love in action.[149]

A 'transnational' community is formed on the day of Pentecost celebrating the feasting of God's Kingdom around the table with great emphasis on universal salvation through the inclusion of the Gentiles in the successive narrations (Ac.2:16ff; cf. Ac.10:2; 4:34-35; 11:12; 14:8-20; 15:9; 17:16-34).[150] The Jerusalem Jesus community enters into a third space of 'basileia-ecclesia' of enunciation and emancipation.[151] This in-between space gives the margins a new identity in the midst of social dislocation, economic poverty and political anarchy. Soon new eschatological congregations are formed all over Judea (through the witnessing of the apostles and the disciples), Samarea (Philip), Caesarea (Peter), Antioch (centerain men of Cyprus and Cyrene) and further to the ends of the earth through the ministry of Jerusalem Apostles, the Hellenist disciples, Apostle Paul and his associates. Luke refer the congregation with a secular term 'ecclesia' for the popular assembly.[152] He seems to have adopted a hybrid culture by approximating (accommodation and rejection) the Hellenistic and Hebraic political wisdom as they enter into this space of new identity and citizenship.[153] Moreover, he challenges the eschatological community to dream, visualize and prophecy to the world (Ac.2:16-21) of the imperial culture of the first century.

---

[148] Gnanavaram, *Treasure in Heaven*, 143.

[149] Cassidy and Scharper, *Political Issues in Luke-Acts*, 109.

[150] Wright, *Jesus and the Victory of God*, 662.

[151] S. Samuel, "Remapping Mission Discourse: Mission Amidst Affluence and Affliction," *Remapping Mission Discourse: A Festschrift in Honor of the Rev.George Kuruvila Chavanikamannil*, edited by S. Samuel and P.V. Joseph (NTC-ISPCK, 2008), 166-67. 'Basileia-ecclesia' is a term coined by Samuel to identify the middle space created by the first century minoritaren Church at Jerusalem. Samuel criticizes the missionary work in India that deliberately avoids the margins in the formation of the renewed community of God.

[152] The first half of Acts refers ἐκκλησια to mean the Jerusalem assembly (Ac.5:11); people of Israel led by Moses (Ac.7:38); secular assembly in Ephesus in the context of the empire collaborated cult (Ac.19:32, 39, 41) and the last reference occurs in relation to the Ephesian Congregation (Ac.20:17, 29); cf.Mt.16:18; 17:18). Wozniuk Vladmir, "In Pursuit of a Politics of Holiness. Reconciling Hellenic and Hebraic Political Wisdom in the Acts of the Apostles," *Journal of Church and State* 45/2 (Sept, 2003), 286.

[153] Wozniuk, "In Pursuit of a Politics of Holiness," 284.

4.6 The Transitory Role of the Hellenists in Witnessing the Gospel from Jerusalem to Samaria and to the Nations/Gentiles (Ac.6:1-11:30)

The newly formed ecclesial community of equals has become a heterogeneous community of the native Aramaic speaking Jewish community and the Greek speaking diaspora community.[154] The conflict between the early Jewish-Christian cultural nationalists and the Hellenist Jewish Christians (Ac.6:1-8; 7:54-8:1) have been resolved through negotiating with the Jewish *politeia* and with the Greco-Roman virtues of *koinonia-philanthropia.*[155] Luke portrays that the leadership is not for power centeredness but to witness the resurrected Jesus and the Kingdom values. In the later context, the Apostles adopt a democratic procedure in the selection of the seven overseers (Ac.6:5; Aristotle, *Politica.* 3.11.11; 3.12.1) and display the Lukan antagonism to the dominant structures in political systems of governance.[156] Here, in the backdrop of 'the ideal communitarian paradise,' the Christian community expresses their resistance to the issues of impropriety in the daily distribution of food for which the resolution comes from the community by selecting the seven deacons (Ac.6:2-6). Luke disrupts the leadership power structure of the imperial government by the servanthood leadership style of the disciples.[157] The eschatological power (δύναμις) is for 'all the disciples' who come under the Lordship of Jesus in contrast to the accumulated powers of the religio-political dominant centers.

The role of Hellenists is portrayed through the narrative characters and the speech of Stephen. Stephen's Speech has probably been placed here to explain the theology of the diaspora Christians and their role in taking the gospel beyond the borders of Jerusalem. By keeping Jerusalem as the central locale for the gospel proclamation, Luke discursively criticizes the human construction of the exclusive ethnic religious center at Jerusalem because God needs not to be circumscribed into the four walls of the temple (Ac.7:47-50).[158] It is through the Hellenist Christian leaders, that Luke challenges the parochial sectarianism and the Jewish

---

[154] Penner, *In Praise of Christian Origins*, 327. The Hellenist Jewish identity may not be limited to the language only but to the other influences of the socio-cultural-religious-political Diaspora locale.

[155] Penner, *In Praise of Christian Origins*, 275. Penner compares the Aristotelian concept of *philanthropia* (fellow-feeling) which the nascent ecclesia mimics (cf.Ac.28:2). Deuteronomic history emphasizes community welfare by caring the widows (Deut.10:18-22; 24:17-22) (264-265).

[156] Penner, "Civilizing Discourse ," 96. The tyranny of Roman client kings and procurators are displayed by Luke in Acts. Luke constitutes a highly communitarian model of resolution in the context of disunity and discord (Ac.1:15-23; 6:1-6; 15:4-30; 21:18-26), (96, F.N.97).

[157] Cassidy, *Society and Politics*, 32. The structural power centers are mocked by Simon the magos who calls him as somebody who is 'great' (Ac.8:9) with the concept of service and humility by the actions of the apostle Peter (Ac.10:25-26).

[158] Stephen uses Jewish scripture (Isa.66:1) to attack the temple cult. Nasrallah, "The Acts of the Apostles," 558.

ethnic-cultural particularism by stating that God reveals to people at any time, anywhere.[159]

4.6.1 Stephen's Speech Disrupts the Jewish Dominant Center (Ac.7:2-53)

Similar to the earlier speeches of the Apostles, the narrative context of Stephen's speech is significant in developing the counter discourse of the eschatological community. The context explains the growth of the eschatological community and his potential of a Hellenist Christian 'performing great wonders and signs' in parallel to the Apostles and Moses (Ac.6:8; Cf.2:43; 4:30; 5:12; 14:3; 15:12).[160] It is significant to interpret the speech for its discursive strategy of accommodation-disruption of the native Jewish cultural nationalistic traditions. The rhetoric strategy of epideictic composition is brought in the speech to raise the position of the protagonist as a righteous man in the story.[161] The lengthy speech of Stephen probably is a witness speech (μάρτυρες) to the dominant native Jewish leadership than a defense.[162] The climax of the story explains how religio-political collaboration works together in breaking the 'Law of God' by officially trying Stephen before the Sanhedrin and cruelly stoning him to death (Ac.7:60). This demonstrates the disruption caused in the Jewish dominant center and proves the accused for their guilt. Contrary to the earlier disruption to the dominant Jewish center, the collaborative component of the Hellenists-zealous nationalists bring severe charges against Stephen for speaking against the Mosaic law, and against God and the temple (Ac.6: 11,13; 7:7). The charges are further amplified by 'false witnesses' unjustly accusing him of stating that Jesus of Nazareth would destroy the foundations of Judaism by destroying the temple and alter the Mosaic customs (Ac.6:13, 14; cf.Mk.14:57).[163]

By narrating the episode of Stephen's trial and martyrdom, Luke unravels the total disruption of the constitutional order and civic virtues follow by

---

[159] Samuel, "Remapping Discourse," 66. Stephen's speech criticizes the ethnic superiority and cultural national identity (Ac.7:2-53). Samuel used the term 'Jewish ethnic and cultural particularism' in the context of the early Christian mission practice, *idem*, "Mission Practice," 13.

[160] Stephen mimicking Moses, the national leader of the Jewish, 'full of Sprit and wisdom' (Ac.6:3, 10; cf.Ex.28:3; Numb.11:17, 25), 'performing wonders and signs' (Ac.7:36; cf.Ex.10:1; 11;9, 10; Deut.6:22; 7:19; 11:3;28:46). In this narrative characterization Stephen affiliates with Moses but contrasts with his opponents. Penner, *In Praise of Christian Origins*, 288-289.

[161] Penner, *In Praise of Christian Origins*, 292. Penner explains the epideictic as a form of rhetoric that focuses on the cardinal virtues of the Hero (piety, courage, gentleness, prudence, wisdom etc.) to praise and blame (229-230). Stephen's speech follows the epideictic nature of rhetoric which has the elements of praising the ancestral Jewish history as well as blaming.

[162] Polhill, *Acts,* 184.

[163] The Gospel account of Luke carefully avoids the accusations regarding the destruction of the temple probably to concentrate on the political accusation of payment of taxes to Caesar (Lk.23:2).

the dominant Jewish center.[164] Luke widely portrays the treacherous Jewish councils who take unlawful decisions against the Christian missionaries and the transcultural community with the support of the Roman imperial order. There is connectivity between the earlier speeches and Stephen's speech in its core message, however, the present speech further openly challenges the abuse of the temple run by the religio-political collaborators. Through Stephen's speech, Luke critically accommodates the Jewish history starting from the patriarchs Abraham-Jacob-Joseph (Ac.7:2-8; 9-16) of "[the] promise of deliverance and worship."[165] The presence of God with Moses (Ac.7:9), and wisdom of Joseph (Ac.7:10) demonstrate the affiliation Luke draws between the patriarchs and the accused. The word 'Temple' is avoided for the phrase 'in this place' (Ac.7:7) probably to cryptically disrupt the religious power structure.[166] Further, the portrayal of God's presence and his promises of deliverance-worship reflect the Jerusalem community of believers.[167] The speech is a historical survey of the Jewish nation by accommodating their discourse yet simultaneously disrupting the native Jewish nationalists for the misuse of the agenda set by God. He affiliates himself with the religious members of the Sanhedrin by calling them as 'brothers and fathers' (ἀδελφοὶ καὶ πατέρες Ac.7:2) in the familial sense of 'our fathers' (οἱ πατέρες ἡμῶν Ac.7:2, 11, 12, 19 etc).[168] Similarly by citating from the Hebrew scripture (Amos 5:25-27; Isa.66:1, 2), Luke may be negotiating with the tradition of their fathers. God's presence outside Palestine during the formative period of the people of Israel (Mesopotamia, Haran, Egypt) challenges and prepares the speech for its climax.[169]

The second major section of the speech revolves around Moses' role in liberation and the subsequent punishment in rejecting him probably reveals a judgmental tone. Similar to the patriarchs, Stephen presents Moses, the law giver, in exemplary features of his early life (Ac.7:20-22).[170] However, even in the affiliation process, he is critical in reading the Israelite national history for

---

[164] Penner, "Civilizing Discourse," 93. The corrupt society kills a righteous man by showing disrespect to the law and the tradition.

[165] Penner, *In Praise of Christian Origins*, 94, 289. The Jewish opponents may be characterized with the jealous brothers of Joseph who tried to kill him.

[166] Penner gives details for the change from temple to the phrase 'in this place' means 'the land,' (probably for a discursive purpose of affiliation and distancing), *In Praise of Christian Origins*, 308-309.

[167] Tannehill, *Narrative Unity, Acts of the Apostles*, 2:88-90.

[168] The fraternal bond has changed to disruptive remarks at the end of the speech by stating 'your ancestors' (Ac.7:51, 52).

[169] Heinz-Werner Neudorfer, "The Speech of Stephen," in *Witness to the Gospel: The Theology of Acts*, edited by I.H. Marshall and David Peterson, Grand Rapids, Michigan: Wm. B. Eerdmans Publishing Company, 1998, 281-286.

[170] Penner, *In Praise of Christian Origins*, 320.

their disobedience to the Jewish *politeia* established through Moses.[171] The second unit of the speech critically analyses the historical details of the liberation of people of Israel as a nation through Moses and God's presence revealed to the patriarchs outside Palestine (Ac.7:23-38; cf.Ex.2:11-14; 3:1-10).[172] The result of their disobedience brings punishment upon them to worship the heavenly bodies (Ac.7:39-43; cf.Ex.32:1, 4-6). Here, Luke subtly interpret both idolatry and the tabernacle of Moses with a citation from the Jewish scripture (Amos 5:25-27). Moreover, he exposes the rebelliousness of their forefathers by the making of a golden calf and the building of a temple by the same phrase 'in the works of their hands' or 'made with hands' (Ac.7:41, 48- ἐν τοῖς ἔργοις τῶν χειρῶν αὐτῶν; χειροποιήτοις). It most likely ruptures the Jewish religious center at Jerusalem.[173] By bringing prophetic order against the rejection to an exile, Luke makes allegiance to the tradition of their fathers (Ac.7:42-43; 49-50) for the disruptive purpose. However, the promise of deliverance/liberation is given as a thread of affiliation in the narrative (Ac.7:33, 39-50).

The tabernacle-temple discussion (Ac.7:44-50) is developed through the argument directly confronting the Jewish-political institution climaxed by making use of an Isaiahnic passage in midrashic interpretation (Ac.7:49; cf.Isa.66:1-2).[174] Here throughout the speech, "the major actor is God" (vv.44-45).[175] The probable accusation would be for misplacing the presence of God that goes along with them. Hence, the tabernacle has been transferred to a religio-political center of the first century by the building of the temple.[176] Moreover, he may be critical to

---

[171] Penner, *In Praise of Christian Origins*, 325.

[172] Penner, *In Praise of Christian Origins*, 320-321. Luke reports the injustice mainly done by the Israelite brothers (Ac.7:27-29) and the call narrative of Moses in a positive posture (Ac.7:30-34). However, Stephen argues God's presence outside Jerusalem by realizing it in the desert of Mount Sinai as holy earth/ land (γῆ ἁγία) and calls the Mosaic laws as the 'living words' received from angels (Ac.7:33, 38, 53).

[173] Penner, *In Praise of Christian Origins*, 312-313. The phrase 'in the works of their hands' is used for idol worship in the Jewish scripture (Deut. 4:28; Isa.2:8,18; 17:8; Jer.1:16; Lev.26:1,30; Dan.5:4). Luke uses the similar expressions in the Athenian speech to condemn the idolatry (Ac.17:24). Lukan use of Amos 5:25-27 in this place probably work in affiliation to the prophetic tradition and disrupting the dominant center simultaneously. He brings comparison between the tent of Moses in obedience and the tent of Moloch as 'works of their hands' for the tragedy happened to the people of Israel.

[174] Penner, *In Praise of Christian Origins*, 98, 312-313. The significance of the tabernacle in Ac.7:44 has been misplaced by the installation of the temple by Solomon. For a detail explanation of the affiliative-disruptive dynamism of midrashim, refer, Samuel, *A Postcolonial Reading of Mark's Story*, 97-98.

[175] Witherington, *Acts*, 272.

[176] Luke brings the parallelism and contrast between the tabernacle and the temple. One is with the heavenly pattern and the other is 'made by men' (Ac.7:46). The temple identity of realizing God's presence has been degraded through business motif and exclusive ethnicity (Lk.19:46; Mk.11:17). Josephus' speech also has similar affiliative-disruptive posturing in his accusations

the exclusive zealotic Jewish cultural nationalism which distorts this consecrated sanctuary. The ambivalent dynamism works in the progression of the speech from allowing God to make a place by Solomon (Ac.7:46) and later by challenging the temple system (Ac.7:47-49).[177] The speech concludes by disrupting the Jewish leadership. Here he criticizes the dominant leaders by using the language of the prophets, 'you stiff-necked people, with uncircumcised hearts and ears,' 'resist to the Holy Spirit,' 'betrayers and murderers' of 'the righteous one' (Ac.7:51-53; 3:14-15).[178] According to Polhill, the rhetoric style Stephen uses in the conclusion is not to condemn the listeners for their total destruction but for their repentance.[179] In addition, Stephen clarifies the opponents' accusation by stating his affiliation with the God of the patriarchs, the tangential faith in Judaism, yet distances himself with the ethnic exclusivity.

The stoning of Stephen to death portrays the fierce opposition that the infant ecclesia faces from the Jewish cultural nationalists. He is demonstrated as the righteous sufferer who suffers humiliation and death but whose vindication by the acts of resurrection (Ac.7:55-56; Lk.24:1-52; 4Macc.17:17; 7:2-3; Wis.Sol. 2:10-21; 3:1-11),[180] probably disrupts the Jewish nationalistic agents of power for eliminating the Hellenist-Christian movement. Moreover, the Son of Man who is also 'Lord Jesus (κυρίος' Ἰησοῦς Ac.7:59) revealed in his vision perhaps mimics the imperial judge who comes to the aid of the oppressed subject (cf.Dan.7:13-14). However, Luke envisions Stephen pleading for mercy for the murderers ('Lord, do not hold this sin against them' Ac.7:60; cf.Lk.23:34) instead for judgment on the persecutors (Wis.Sol.3:10). Further, Luke portrays the profound effect of Stephen's martyrdom in the life of Paul (Ac.22:20) as a witness for the same cause.[181]

---

against the wickedness of the contemporary Judaism and the defilement of the temple, hoping for their repentance (*JW* 5:395-397, 411-415).

[177] According the Neudorfer, the οἶκος motif (house of David, tabernacle, the temple) is important to explain the contention between Stephen and the opponents, but the adversative use of δέ (Ac.7:47) explains the logic of argument for tabernacle (σκήνωμα) than the temple, "The Speech of Stephen," 289-290.

[178] Stephen is in/directly accusing them not only for the death of prophets who predicted the coming 'of the righteous' (τοῦ δικαίου) but also murdering him. He makes use of the Jewish national history in condemning the native Jewish leaders from the prophetic tradition for their rebellion (Jer.4:4, 6:10; 9:26; Eze.44:7, 9; Isa.63:10) and murdering their prophets (Jer.26:20-24; 2Chr.24:20-21; cf.Lk.13:34). Fitzmyer, *Acts*, 385.

[179] Polhill, *Acts*, 205.

[180] Penner, *In Praise of Christian Origins*, 298-299. The righteous suffering is a significant topic in the context of the history of Jewish nationalism over against the imperial forces. A comparative Hebrew parallelism is seen in T.L. Brodie, "The Accusing and Stoning of Naboth [1Kgs.21:8-13] as One Component of Stephen Text [Acts 6:9-14; 7:58a]," *CBQ* 45, 1983, 417-432.

[181] Polhill, *Acts*, 210.

The conflicting situation in the center at Jerusalem comes to a climax through the martyrdom of Stephen and the scattering of the transcultural messianic community that produced "an unexpected development" (Ac.6:7; 8:1).[182] Hence, multiple cultural locations depict the discursive nature of Jesus movement from the religio-political center (Jerusalem) to other marginal locations (Samaria). There is transition from the Jerusalem apostles to the Hellenist Philip including the ambivalent proclamation strategy of 'certain men' (τινες ἀνδρες) of Cyprus and Cyrene both to the Jews and to the Greeks/Gentiles/Nations (Ac.7:58-8:1; 11:19, 20).[183] The hybrid culture of the Christian Hellenists in terms of their nationalism, ethnicity and the theological view of inclusivism leads them to take the gospel outside Jerusalem.[184] Thus, the Hellenists become the expedition force in preaching 'the good news of the kingdom of God and the name of Jesus Christ' (Ac.8:12; cf.8:25, 40; 11:20) to Samaria, the gentile Ethiopian and to the Gentiles in Antioch.

4.6.2 The Hellenist Philip and the Ethiopian Eunuch at the Crossroads for Identity (Ac.8:4-40)

Contrary to the traditional reading of Philip's mission to Samaria and to the Ethiopian eunuch, Luke probably has more things to speak through this story.[185] In the original setting of the story, Philip who himself is from the marginalized Hellenist group (racially inferior) and is chosen to serve in the tables come to another marginalized locale to proclaim Christ with miraculous signs (Ac.8:1, 4-5). The narration explains the negotiation between the multiple cultures and identities "along the shifting borderlines of competition and attraction, emulation and repudiation."[186] Moreover, in the colonial context of identity crisis, Luke

---

[182] Tannehill, *Narrative Unity of Luke-Acts,* vol. II, 102.

[183] S. Samuel, "The Acts of Philip and the Τινες Ανδρες (Certain Men) of Cyprus and Cyrene: A Remapping of Early Christian Mission Frontiers," *Remapping Mission Discourse: A Festschrift in Honor of the Rev.George Kuruvila Chavanikamannil,* edited by S. Samuel and P.V. Joseph (NTC-ISPCK, 2008), 41-71. The researcher uses interchangeably the terms gentiles and nations for the Lukan term ἔθνος/ ἔθνη. For Luke, ἔθνος means 'nations' including the Jewish nation (Ac.2:5; 10:22; 24:2, 10, 17; 26:4) and also Gentiles in opposition to the Jewish community (Ac.9:15; 22:21; 26:17). For further study refer, J.G. Muthuraj, "The Meaning of ἔθνος and ἔθνη and its Significance to the study of the NT," *BTF,* vol. 29, 1997, 25.

[184] Samuel, "The Acts of Philip," 63-68.

[185] Barrus, "The Gospel of Luke and the Acts," 148. The postcolonial possibility of ambivalence in using the novelistic genre may be seen clearly in this pericope. While continuing its impact in the multicultural societies, the powerful at the center creates social boundaries on the basis of race and ethnicity based on socio-economic and political environments for the sake of political power. T.B. Liew, 'Margins and (Cutting)-Edges', in *Postcolonial Biblical Criticism: Interdisciplinary Intersections,* edited by S.D. Moore and F.F. Segovia (London: T & T Clark International, 2005), 118-19.

[186] Barrus, "The Gospel of Luke and the Acts," 145.

introduces two characters-an Ethiopian[187] and a Hellenist, who cross their geographical borders in search of religio-cultural identity. In this process, Luke probably makes an allusion to a marginalized representation from another empire (Nubian) i.e., from the ends of the earth to cross the borders to an in-between space for a holistic identity.[188]

The African's ethnicity (Gentile), gender (eunuch/transcultural/ transgender), location (South-East) and the desert where both of them meet each other give evidence for translating the boundaries of borderlands/margins to become part of an eschatological community.[189] Moreover, in Luke's narration, the eunuch is portrayed as a hybrid of both 'eunuch and a court official (εὐνοῦχος and δυνάστης Ac.8:27).[190] He is considered to be a God-fearing gentile who is placed in the in-between space because of the split gender identity and his socio-geographical position. Both of them meet each other in the 'liminal zone' or the transcultural space of 'the desert road' on the way to the desert of Gaza where the marginalized subject probably enters into a self-hood of 'non-colonial identity,' through an undisturbed discourse.[191] The unnamed Ethiopian is complex in his personality who stays at another colonial world, returns from the Jewish religio-political center at Jerusalem.[192] His ethnicity (gentile), race (Ethiopian), and

[187] C.J. Martin, "A Chamberlain's Journey and the Challenge of Interpretation for Liberation," in *The Bible and Liberation. Political and Social Hermeneutics*, edited by N.K. Gottwald & R.A. Horsley (Maryknoll: Orbis Books, 1993), 485. According to the ancient Hellenistic-Roman world view, Ethiopia in all probability refers to the ancient civilized kingdom of Meroe (Sudan's capital) in the Nubian empire (8 BCE - 4 CE; cf.Ps.68:31; Zeph.3:10; Isa.18:7) as well as Ethiopian means a black skinned African. Pollhill, *Acts,* 223.

[188] The mention of Ethiopian eunuch introduces equally strong Ethiopian empire parallel to the Roman empire who undertook military expedition in 23 BCE and 61-62 CE. Nubian (Ethiopia) kings also are deified (incarnations of the sun god) in similar line with the Roman emperors. Homer (*Odyssey* 1.23) refers Ethiopia as the ends of the earth. Pollhill, *Acts*, 223, F.N.132. The eunuch becomes the part of the new found way (τὴν ὁδὸν αὐτοῦ χαίρων).

[189] Barrus, "The Gospel of Luke and the Acts," 148-50. His religious status is analysed for being an Ethiopian (Αἰθιοψ), an African gentile even though his religious piety is mentioned by his visit to the center of Jewish religiosity and holding the scripture of Isaiah in his hand. In the ancient social world, eunuchs used to be the officials to the female rulers. Shauf, "Locating the Eunuch," 764; F.S. Spenser, *The Portrait of Philip in Acts: A Study of Roles and Relations* (JSNT Sup 67; Sheffield: Sheffield Academy Press, 1992), 129. A eunuch cannot be a full Jew due to the physical infirmity.

[190] At the cross roads of identity, Luke seems to have brought the hybrid nature of the eunuch. In the ancient world context, the position of the eunuch (probably a castrated slave) makes them to be keepers of treasury and the princess/queens. Polhill, *Acts*, 223. The phrase 'who was over all the treasury of her' makes him a court official (δυνάστης v.27).

[191] In postcolonial view the in-between space is used by the colonized subject for cultural change and for 'non-colonial identity.' Ashcroft, et.al. eds., *Key Concepts*, 130.

[192] The Greco-Romans were curious of the wisdom from the east (eg. Ethiopia) as well as its location to the 'end of the earth' (Pliny, *Nat.Hist*.6.186; Strabo 17.1.54). Polhill, *Acts,* 223; Barrett, *Acts*, vol. 1, 425; Gaventa, *Acts*, 141-42.

gender (transgender) would determine his place in society and they do not allow him to fully participate in the Jewish worship 'center' at the Jerusalem Temple even though he would like to be one.

The episode is directed by the order 'getup and go' (ἀνάστηθη και πορεύ ου) of the angel of the Lord to go to the desert of Gaza, similar to the imperial orders of a military commander (Ac.8:26). God's mission to the southern part of Jerusalem is explained by the word south (μεσημβρίαν) which has a discursive meaning of both 'noon' and 'south'.[193] Philip acts like a Roman soldier who 'having run' (προσδραμων) to obey the command of his master in order to catch up with the chariot.[194] Strelan compares the running speed of Philip to the suprazonic speed of the prophet Elijah who runs ahead of King Ahab's chariot to reach ahead of the King (1Kg.18:46).[195] By mockingly mimicking the Jewish and Roman imperial tradition of subjugation and oppression, Philip, the model character runs to obey the voice of God in order to bring the 'saviour' (σωτηρ) in the life of a marginal.

In the colonial context of Rome, ethnic identity has been a major issue to tackle with. The interpretation based on the ethnic identity of the Hamite is condemnable in the light of Luke's holistic vision of witnessing from the beginning of the narration of Acts. In addition, Luke projects the holistic mission since the beginning of the Pentecost event (Ac.2:1-12) before the programmatic fulfillment of the mission to the Gentile Cornelius (Ac.10, 11). This mission strategy must be seen in the light of Lukan priority of the entire universe (οἰκουμενη) as the inclusive plan of God which would be disruptive to the dominant Jewish center.[196] In the narrative world of the early Christian community, Luke probably brings this transgender before the inclusion of Cornelius and Gentiles.

Philip, the deacon also starts to work from the marginal space between the position to serve at the tables as a Hellenist and from the position of an Apostle to proclaim the gospel. He crosses the borders of the margins in competing with the Galilean Jerusalem Apostles to preach the gospel to the Samaritans and later to the Ethiopian who are marginalized to the Jerusalem Jewish community. He is portrayed as the one who is on par with the position of the Jerusalem Apostles and the eschatological Spirit instructs him to meet the Ethiopian. By obeying the instructions of 'the Spirit,' the obedient Hellenist approaches and joins the chariot to bring him to the eschatological community.

---

[193] Etymologically μεσημβρίαν means noon; thus the departure time of Philip is mentioned. However, the position of the sun (the South) also refers to the same word in the first century context, thus the context of the text means the direction of the travel. Barrett, *Acts*, vol. 1, 422-23.

[194] Barrett, *Acts*, vol. I, 427.

[195] R. Strelan, "The Running Prophet (Acts 8:30)," *Nov T* 43/1 (2001): 34. Strelan compares the running mode of Philip to the prophets of Jewish tradition (1Kgs.18-21; Jer.23:21; Zech.2:4).

[196] The continental divisions of Asia, Africa and Europe are a later divisional concept by the Euro-centered imperial mind set up. Scott, "Luke's Geographical Horizon," 538, FN. 209.

By obeying the call of the Lord, Philip the Hellenist, 'a man full of Spirit and wisdom' (Ac.6:3), leads by the Spirit (Ac.8:29; cf.8:26) starts 'preaching them the Christ/concerning the kingdom of God and the name of Jesus Christ' (ἐκήρυσσεν αὐτοῖς τὸν Χριστόν /περὶ τῆς βασιλίας τôυ θεοῦ καὶ τοῦ ὀνόματος Ἰησοῦ χριστοῦ (Ac.8: 5, 12, 35, 40).[197] The preaching of Philip is compared to the proclamation of the first century preaching of the 'good news' (εὐαγγελιον) in the context of Caesar. The 'great signs' (Ac.8:13; cf.8:7) and wonders (Ac.8:7, 9-13) of the eschatological Spirit is manifested through the ministry of Philip in comparison to the Jerusalem Apostles.

In the narrative world of Acts, it is no mere coincidence that the eunuch reads from the scrolls of Isaiah because it gives him the greatest hope in the eschatological future and it is presently fulfilled through the gospel of Jesus Christ. These 'salvation' promises (Isa.56:3-8) are not revealed to the margins (eunuch) because the liberation for the margins as well as its 'interpretation'/ guide (ὁδηγήσει v.31) have been kept under the custody of the dominant Jewish center in Jerusalem.[198] From his hybrid position of the Hellenist Jew in Jerusalem and with the Spirit's guidance, Philip starts to exegete the Isaiah's servant passage (Isa.53:7-8) in the light of 'the good news about Jesus' (Ac.8:33-35), and finally Philip baptizes the Ethiopian.[199] The Isaiahnic passage evokes the suffering and the discursive silence of the resurrected Jesus before the Roman authorities where 'his justice was taken away' (ἡ κρίσις αὐτοῦ ἤρθη v.33a).[200] Similarly, Luke may have equated the suffering of their resurrected messiah with the suffering community of the first century CE who probably undergoes unjust suffering based on class, colour, gender, and ethnicity. Here, Luke seems to have used the *pesher* interpretation of Qumran which applies "the ancient text to contemporary persons and events (1 *QpPs*37 4:1-25; 1 *QpHab* 2:1-15)."[201] This probably is for the purpose of affiliation, yet distancing almost simultaneously to the native Jewish traditions. The Ethiopian may have enjoyed being with the humiliated messiah receives liberation, joy and happiness in this new eschatological era. However, it is surprising why Luke stops the narration of the southward witness with this

---

[197] Spencer, *Portrait of Philip in Acts*, 37; Cho, "Spirit and the Kingdom in Luke-Acts," 189.

[198] Cf. The resurrected Jesus 'opened the... scriptures' for the marginalized Galilean disciples (Lk.24:45).

[199] Barrus, "The Gospel of Luke and the Acts," 150. According to Barrus, the conversion of the Ethiopian does not come into the tale of the colonialist mission narrative because of the unplanned mission strategy, and the desire and query comes from the Gentile Ethiopian. It invokes one's decision to believe in Christ which in effect subverts the two imperial centers of the west-east (Roman-Nubian). Fitzmyer, *Acts*, 414.

[200] The early Christians who were under Roman subjugation try to interpret suffering in terms of the prophet/ the contemporary socio-political suffering under Rome/ the messianic suffering. Polhill, *Acts,* 225.

[201] Johnson, *Acts,* 157.

eunuch story! This probably shows the Lukan style of an open-ended story that would help the marginalized to write their own story to the colonial centers.

Here the Jewish exclusive demand of circumcision to enter the community of God's people is publicly mocked by the author by introducing the ambivalent gender/ethnic/religious identity of the eunuch. The two hybridized characters seem to translate the colonial borders in order to overcome the dominant impositions of culture, space and position.

With the courageous and bold question of the subaltern Ethiopian, 'what prevents me to be baptized (τί κωλύει με βαπτισθῆναι;)?' Philip gives him the baptism by which he enters into the transcultural eschatological community of God. As the eunuch goes back to his 'southern empire,' rejoicing (Ac.8:36-39) probably to disrupt another religio-political center i.e., at the ends of the earth. By converging the proclamation stories of Philip the Hellenist (Ac.8:40; 21:8) and Peter, the Jerusalem Apostle (Ac.9:32-10:1),[202] Luke links the thread of the transcultural hybrid ethnic Christian ecclesia of both Jews and Gentiles through the mission work of the Hellenist Jewish Christians. The *ekklesia* becomes a catalyst in the ground breaking mission of carving the eschatological space for the marginalized through the good news of Jesus Christ.

4.7 Paul's Call/Commission to the Nations, a move from the Center (Ac.9:1-31)

By drawing Paul's call/conversion, Luke depicts the protagonist of the marginalized Jesus movement who becomes instrumental in taking the gospel of Jesus as Son of God, Christ, Lord (Ac.9:20, 22, 27) before 'the nations (ἐθνῶν) and their kings and before the sons [people] of Israel' (Ac.9:15).[203] It is through him that Luke explains the fulfillment of the command of Jesus Christ (Ac.1:8) through crossing the socio-religio-cultural and national boundaries to proclaim the universal gospel of God.[204]

Paul is introduced initially not only giving approval to the death of Stephen but also continuing to destroy the infant ecclesia single handedly. He 'breathes threat and murder' (Ac.9:1) and putting both men and women in jail (Ac.8:3). On the face of persecution, the minority Christian ecclesia is portrayed as powerless, 'scattered throughout Judea and Samaria.' Paul is acting like the emissary of the imperial center to bring back the scattered Lord's disciples (τοὺς

---

[202] Barrett, *Acts*, vol. 1, 421.

[203] The hybridity of Paul is portrayed by Luke through "merging the worlds of Diaspora and Palestinian Judaism"- Tarsus (nativity Ac.9:11; 21:39; 22:3) and Jerusalem. Penner, *In Praise of Christian Origins*, 278. Luke introduces Paul through the Jewish identity of the name Saul in the call/conversion narrations. However, Saul/Paul is interchangeably used even after post-conversion accounts of Luke (Ac.7:58-9:24; 11:25, 30; 12:25; 13:1, 2, 7). Ronald D. Witherup, SS, "Functional Redundancy in the Acts of the Apostles: A Case Study," *JSNT* 48 (1992), 71, FN. 14.

[204] Melbourne, "Acts 1:8 Re-Examined," 12.

μαθητὰς τοῦ κυρίου) by binding them back to the dominant Jewish center at Jerusalem for pseudo trial (Ac.9:1-2).[205] His intention behind this was probably to have genocide without proper trial and repress their voices. This scene also reflects the religio-political collaborated component of Jerusalem for administrating (in) justice to the imperial subjects under the Roman empire.

By giving three repetitive reports of Paul's call/conversion[206] (Ac.9:1-30; 22:3-21; 26:2-23), Luke exhibits how the imperial order has been collapsed by the divine order on the way to Damascus, the "liminal zone, a space of passages."[207] All three accounts of Paul's call/conversion in Acts reflect commissioning motifs of the OT (eg. Isaiah and Jeremiah).[208] Paul moves from the dominated-persecuted native Jewish center to the transcultural space to proclaim the gospel of the resurrected messiah.[209] The religio-political centers have probably been challenged in the commission of Paul, where he must (δεῖ) suffer and 'carry name' [Jesus] before the nations and the kings and the sons of Israel (Ac.9:15-16).[210] This commission of the 'Lord' (κυρίος Ac.9:15, 17) is done through a marginal disciple of the messianic community (Ananias) and this perhaps leads to disrupt the two powerful imperial centers (Jewish-Roman).[211] Moreover, Paul's call narrative of his

---

[205] Luke describes the scattered community who are 'the men and women of the way' (τῆς ὁδοῦ ὄντας ἄνδρας καὶ γυναῖκας Ac.9:2) explain the liminality of the margins.

[206] Alan F. Segal calls Paul's experience as a conversion experience by analyzing the socio-economic and political context of the imperial society, *Paul the Convert. The Apostolate and Apostasy of Saul the Pharisee,* New Haven and London: Yale University Press, 1990, 30-33. Gaventa further emphasizes the transformation in terms of radical change of the conversion perspective by reinterpreting the past (traditions) in the light of the present, *From Darkness to Light,* 10, 12.

[207] Damascus is located in the north-eastern part of Jerusalem. For Luke, the significance of this city probably goes with the liminal space (Arabian Desert border) consists of the Diaspora Jewish population having the Roman influence (*JW* 2.559-561; 7.368). Barrus analyses the liminal zone in terms of the meeting place between Philip and the Ethiopian eunuch, "The Gospel of Luke and the Acts," 150. Spencer, *Acts*, 97; Polhill, *Acts,* 236. The conversion language in Paul's call has been questioned by K. Stendahl, because he did not change his religious affiliation, *Paul among Jews and Gentiles. And Other Essays* (Phialdelphia: Fortress Press, 1976), 7-23.

[208] Charles W. Hedrick, "Paul's Conversion/Call: A Comparative Analysis of the Three Reports in Acts," *JBL* 100/3 (1981), 415.

[209] The move from the imperial center is probably called conversion in Paul's life and not in religious terms. For Barrett, the call and conversion are complementary elements. There is radical change in both religious direction and action, *Acts,* vol. II, 422.

[210] Hedrick finds connection between Ac.9:15 (carry my name) and the programmatic plan of Ac.1:8 in witnessing to the Jews and the Gentiles, "Paul's Conversion/Call," 420-421. Paul witnesses before the Roman administrative officers in Caesarea (Ac.24-26) and waiting to witness Caesar at Rome during the period of his trials. The divine imperative of suffering is emphasized by the word δεῖ in this commission (Ac.9:16; cf.17:3; Lk.9:22; 17:25; 24:7). Witherup, "Functional Redundancy in the Acts," 81.

[211] The call account in Acts 26 narrated by Paul before King Agrippa, the Lord himself commissioned him on the Damascus road (Ac.26:16-18). The identity of 'Lord' is significant (here

standing 'before Gentiles and their kings and before the people of Israel' (Ac.9:15) probably mimics the two political centers (Jewish and Roman) that collaborate together for safeguarding the Roman imperial government.[212] The latter narration shows Paul's witnessing before the religio-political imperial centers in Jerusalem and Caesarea (Ac.21-26; cf.Lk.12:11, 12; 21:12).

The divine initiative of the risen Lord is seen throughout the episode in visions and interactions.[213] The call/conversion/commission of Paul on the way to Damascus transforms him radically, probably a shift from the religious center to the eschatological space of the marginalized, turning from 'the persecutor of the marginalized' to the witnessing 'persecuted of the marginalized.'[214] As soon as Paul stepped into the eschatological space of the marginals, he starts preaching boldly (ἐπαρρησιάσατο) outside of synagogues at Damascus, at the religious center (Jerusalem), to the Jews (center) and the Gentiles (margins) that Jesus is the 'Son of God' (ὁ υἱὸς τοῦ θεοῦ Ac.9:20, 26-28).[215] This proclamation probably mimics to disrupt the dominant center claims of 'Christ/Lords' of the varied religio-political quarters of the first century Greco-Roman world. The later missionary expedition explains, how Paul skillfully affiliates and distances with the Jewish eschatological expectation of the messiah as well as maintains an accommodative-disruptive posture to the Roman colonial centers (Ac.9:19-30).[216]

After Paul's call/conversion, there is a drastic peace (εἰρήνην) to the 'church throughout Judea, Galilee and Samaria' in terms of its growth, the presence of the eschatological Spirit and 'in the fear of the Lord' (Ac.9:31).[217] Here in this context, the Lukan understanding of peace explains the life threatening situation of the marginalized subjects who flee for life in utter fear and trembling.

---

it is the risen Christ) in the light of the religio-political milieu where all the characters are directed to him.

212 Jesus predicts to his disciples about their standing 'before synagogues, rulers and authorities' (Lk.12:11, 12) and he promised the help of the eschatological Spirit to the Christian community. Fitzmayer, *Acts,* 748. Similarly, in the programmatic description of suffering, Paul primarily suffers under the Gentile Roman authorities for witnessing to the name (ὄνομα) of Jesus. Skinner, *Locating Paul,* 96.

213 The "Lord's sovereign orchestration of people and events" are seen in the entire episode to achieve God's purpose. Spencer, *Acts,* 99. Tannehill, *Narrative Unity of Luk-Acts,* vol. II, 115-117.

214 According to Polhill, the vision of the risen Lord radically transformed Paul from the space of the persecutor to the persecuted. Here the radical shift is called conversion, *Acts,* 240.

215 Soon after Paul's Damascus experience, he starts fellowshipping with the Damascene disciples (Ac.9:19), preaching the gospel of Jesus Christ in Damascus (Ac.9:20-22; cf.Gal.1:16,17) and in Jerusalem (Ac.9:26-29). The Son of God title explains the expected royal messiah in the line of David (cf.Lk.1:32). Marshall, *Acts,* 174; Spencer, *Acts,* 100.

216 Paul's witnessing resulted in both acceptance as his disciples (οἱ μαθηταὶ αὐτοῦ Ac.9:25, 19b) and disapproval as enemies. Spencer, *Acts,* 100.

217 The programmatic geographical expansion of witnessing has taken place by this statement 'through out all Judea Galilee and Samaria' (Ac.8:1).

4.8 The Gentile Mission and the Disruptive Discourse of Peter-Cornelius Episode (Ac.10:1-11:30)

Meanwhile, Peter continues his witnessing in Joppa and Lydda through the act of benevolence in raising (ἀνάστηθι) Aeneas the paralytic and Tabitha from death (Ac.9:34, 40), cause many to turn to the Lord (Ac.9:35). In this context, Luke introduces the first female disciple (μαθητρια Ac.9:36) Tabitha, who is reminiscent to the Hellenist Christian leaders act like a patron in charitable service.[218] Moreover, the female patronage is probably brought into the messianic movement which affiliates with the economic patronage of the imperial Rome. Moreover, her house becomes a meeting place for the community of believers (Ac.9:40-42).[219]

Ac.10:1-11:30 is the pivotal point in which the Gentile mission narrative turns by the conversion of Cornelius, a Roman centurion in Caesarea. This cultural hybrid starts crossing the borders through the sharing of his possessions like the Jerusalem rich, and through the social interaction even before becoming part of the eschatological community of God. Paul's Gentile mission is later theologically legitimized through the Jerusalem council connecting the conversion stories of both Peter and Cornelius. Moreover, the Gentile mission which is brought through Peter to the family of Cornelius in Caesarea disrupts the Jerusalem centered Jewish-Christian cultural nationalism. In this context, Luke is presenting the ambivalent nature of this community in finally endorsing the Gentile mission by saying 'God also gave even the Nations/Gentiles repentance to life' (Ac.11:18b).[220]

The imperial background of the Roman centurion (ἑκατονταρχης) and his colonial location in the eastern administrative center at Caesarea are probably portrayed to reflect the Roman colonialist into a positive limelight.[221] On this account, Luke exhibits the religious virtues (praying, devout, generous, righteous and God-fearing) of this Roman official (Ac.10:1, 22) to arouse the sympathy to

---

[218] Spencer, *Acts*, 107. The word female disciple (μαθητρια) comes only here in the NT. Tabitha's social status in the community is narrated through the sympathy by the time of her death. Luke probably shows the ecclesial mimicking of the patronage system of the Greco-Roman world to explain the growth of the messianic community (107-108).

[219] Barrus, "The Gospel of Luke and the Acts," 144. Tabitha's upper room can be compared to the meeting place of the first century Christian believers in Jerusalem. Spencer, *Acts,* 108. Other female benefactors in Acts are Mary, Lydia and Priscilla (Ac.12:12; 16:14-15, 40; 18:18-28). Witherington has the view that the first century ecclesia played a liberation role for women in the patriarchal society of the Greco-Roman world. However, there also finds both the mixed message of both patriarchal and liberation elements in biblical narrations, *Acts*, 334-339.

[220] The Jerusalem centered, Jewish-Christian messianic community reluctantly concedes to the Gentile mission begun by Peter and later supports the Antiochan ecclesia for their mission among the Gentiles (Ac.11:22-26). Polhill, *Acts,* 230.

[221] Rowe, "Luke-Acts and the Imperial Cult," 289. Cornelius holds a special troop of *cohortes Italicae.* T.R.S. Broughton, *The Beginning of Christianity*, vol. v, edited by F.F. Foakes-Jackson, et al., (London: Macmillan, 1933), 441-43.

the Roman colonial administration.[222] Moreover, the Cornelius episode ruptures the socio-political-ethnic and cultural hegemonies through supernatural events (angelic visits, visions and spirit's manifestation; Ac.10:1-6, 9-16, 30-32, 44-48) and finally lead to the table fellowship between Jews and Gentiles (Ac.10:23, 48).[223] Apostle Peter is guided to a new level of conversion experience with the marginalized Gentiles through the heavenly vision, which resulted the breaking of the ethnic-cultural boundaries of common (κοινὸν) and unclean (ἀκάθαρτον Ac.10:14, 15, 28).[224]

Cornelius, the Roman military officer, along with a group of Gentile audience are keen to hear 'all the things having been commanded by the Lord perhaps to mimic the imperial submissive nature of a colonial administrative officer (Ac.10:33). The following speech of Peter is based on the impartial nature of God and this would possibly disrupt the imperial authority of the religio-political power center in Jerusalem (Ac.10:34-43).[225]

The impartial nature of a sovereign God in accepting both the Jews and Gentiles is the opening remark of the transformed Jerusalem Apostle (Ac.10:35; cf.Rom.2:9-11).[226] Similar to the earlier speeches, Peter's speech lauds Jesus as the benefactor (Ac.10:38) and cast the blame of Jesus' execution on the shoulders of Jews in Jerusalem (Ac.10:39). However, the resurrected Jesus receives the authority as an eschatological judge of the universe which would naturally disrupt the dominant centers (Ac.10:42, 43; 17:31; cf.Ac.2:38-39; 3:19-20).[227] In the Caesarean context of Cornelius, Peter preaches the radical themes of repentance and forgiveness to all (Ac.10:43; cf.Lk.24:44-48). He most likely acclaims the lordship of Jesus Christ in the context of conflicting rival claims for universal lordship.[228] Row explains the emphatic declaration of the language force for the

---

[222] Barrus finds similarity between the 'converted centurion' in Acts and the Roman centurion who witnessed Jesus' death and confessed Jesus as a righteous man (Lk.23:47), "The Gospel of Luke and the Acts," 136-137.

[223] Luke explains in this episode how the spirit through visions directing Peter, the representative of the Jerusalem Apostles to have fellowship with the Gentiles. Spencer, *Acts,* 103. Peter's association with Simon the tanner (Ac.9:43, 10:5-6, 17-18, 32) indicate crossing the dominant Jewish religio-cultural boundaries. Simon the tanner's social identity is specified by the location of his house. Haenchen, *Acts,* 347.

[224] Spencer, *Acts*, 110-111.

[225] Haenchen, *Acts,* 351; Bruce, *Acts*, 211-212; Dunn, *Acts,* 141-152; Barrett, *Acts*, vol. I, 519. The dietary boundary markers of clean/unclean, holy/profane have been clarified through this vision.

[226] Rowe, "Luke- Acts and the Imperial Cult," 289-90. 'Having fallen at the feet and worship' shows the deifying nature of Cornelius before Peter the Apostle. And his reply 'I myself am a man' (ἐγω αὐτος ἄνθρωπος εἰμι Ac.10:25, 26) emphatically says the contrasting human nature of Peter.

[227] Tannehill, "The Functions of Peter's Mission Speeches," 412-413.

[228] Rowe, "Luke-Acts and the Imperial Cult," 298.

demonstrative pronoun, 'this one is Lord of all' (οὑτος ισ κυριος παντον Ac.10:36; cf.2:36), in the context of the other imperial lords.[229] Therefore, the imperial deification cult is simultaneously disrupted by the proclamation of the peaceful reign through Jesus Christ, who is Lord of all.

The gentile Cornelius and his family are placed on equal footing in the eschatological space of the messianic community based on the Spirit's manifestation on the Gentiles (Ac.10:44-45). The racial, ethnic, socio-political-cultural barriers have been broken down by the eschatological Spirit pouring out on the Nations/ Gentiles (ἔθνη Ac.10:45, 46). Later, Luke explains the prospect of the new step initiated by Peter to the Jerusalem messianic community as an 'apologetic defense' to legitimize the mission to the Nations/Gentiles (Ac.11:1-3, 15-17).[230] He also explains God's initiative in this process to convince "the native Jewish and Jewish-Christian cultural nationalists in Jerusalem."[231] The Jewish center finally concedes to the plan of God in accepting the nations "into the covenant community" (Ac.11:17, 18).[232] Further, the final decision taken by Jerusalem council (Ac.15) ruptures the imperial ideology of exclusive Jewish ethnicity and incorporates all diverse groups into the transcultural ecclesia of equals.

4.9 The Uninterrupted Proclamation of the word of God in the midst of Persecution and Martyrdom (Ac.12:1-25)

The imprisonment of the Apostles, James and Peter, by the imperial king works as an interlude in the context of the Apostles' (Barnabas and Paul) effort to bring relief fund from the Antiochian Christian community (Ac.11:29-12:1 and Ac.12:25).[233] This demonstrates the *philanthropia* nature of the ecclesia to help the famine affected in Jerusalem. The progress of the Christian movement in Caesarea (Ac.10) and Antioch (Ac.11) must have triggered the dominant Jewish-Roman religio-political centers. In the context of resistant move of the nascent

---

[229] Rowe, "Luke-Acts and the Imperial Cult," 291. In the historical context of Roman colonialism, the narrative impact on the Greco-Roman audience is significant. Row cited Suetonius' indication of Domitians' desires to be called "*dominus et dues noster*," (*Dom.*13.2). Philo refers Caligula as κυρίος (*Leg.Gai.*286; 356), Josephus refers Titus as ὁ κυριος (*JW* 6.134). Luke himself refers to the unknown emperor as τῷ κυριῳ (Ac.25:26) by the reference of Festus' letter to the then Roman emperor (294). Rowe's statistical study on the use of κυρίος in Luke-Acts explains Lordship for Jesus' earthly carrier (Lk.7:13, 19; 12:41-42; 18:41; 22:61; 24:34). In Mary's womb, Jesus is ὁ κυρίος (Lk.1:43; cf.Lk.2:11). In Acts narration, Jesus is the resurrected Lord as well as the 'Lord of heaven and earth (κυρίος οὐρανοῦ καὶ γης Ac.17:24; cf.10:36) (291).

[230] John T. Squires, "The Function of Acts 8.4-12.25," *NTS* 44 (1998), 614.

[231] For a detailed discussion on the trouble caused due to the culture and theology of the Hellenist mission, refer Samuel "*The Acts of Philip,*" 64.

[232] Spencer, *Acts*, 118.

[233] David T.N. Parry, "Release of the Captives-Reflections on Acts 12," in *Luke's Literary Achievement: Collected Essays*, edited by C.M. Tucket (JSNT Sup.116; Sheffield: Sheffield Academy Press, 1995), 157.

ecclesia, Luke portrays the martyrdom of James as well as the deliverance of Peter.[234] The contents of this section may divide accordingly: the persecution of Herod Agrippa against the minority Christians and the death of James (vv.1-2), the miraculous escape of Peter by the Lord (vv.3-19a), the divine retribution to the imperial despondent (vv.19b-23) and the effective witness of the proclamation of the 'word of God' (λογος του θεοῦ vv.24,25).[235]

Luke simultaneously gives the tragic story of the death of James the apostle with the divine retribution to the despot who claims the honor of God. Moreover, there is a shift in the direction for growth of the word of God through the liberation of Peter, the spokesperson of the early Christian ecclesia.[236] Here, Luke has a definite purpose behind placing these two tragic ends as well as the retributive punishment of a political challenge against the minority Christians. The following study shows that the Christian movement is counter-cultural that disrupts the dominant political ideology of deification of the emperor cult as well as discursive in its stand before the Roman collaborated power center at Jerusalem.

4.9.1 The Imperial Persecution against the Minority Christians and the Death of Apostle James

The turning point in the narrative is the illustration of the arrest of 'some members of the church' (τινας τῶν ἀπὸ τῆς ἐκκλησίας) by Herod with no legal accusation against them (Ac.12:1-2). The intention behind their arrest can be analyzed in the context of Agrippa's run to get political loyalty both from the center of the imperial Rome as well as from the collaborated native Jewish center in Judea.[237] It is probable that Agrippa fears the new movement under the Lordship of Jesus would usurp his throne. The capital powers of the king Agrippa points out how the political mechanisms are used to maintain *Roman pax* in the colonial state under his jurisdiction. Herod's move in executing James with a sword shows the political threat over against the Christian marginals.[238] Beheading the prisoners exhibits the cruel action of the imperial rulers to suppress their opponents (cf.Lk.3:20; Mk.6:14-29), and here in this case the Christian

[234] Barrett, *Acts*, vol. 1, 569; Haenchen, *Acts*, 380-92.

[235] Barrett, *Acts*, vol. 1, 569. Roman emperor Caligula honors Herod Agrippa I (10 BCE-44 CE) with the status of 'the King' (*Ant.*19.292-316), reigns northern Transjordan (37CE) with Galilee, Perea (39 CE) and Judea (41 CE). Agrippa's political diplomacies in wooing both the political center and the Jews have been discussed in the background study.

[236] Munoz-Larrondo, *Living in Two Worlds*, 107.

[237] The infinitive 'to harm' (κακῶσαι) used with laid on (ἐπέβαλεν) intends to make physical harm (Ac.7:6, 19; 18:10; cf.1Pet.3:13). Barrett, *Acts*, vol. 1, 574. Agrippa's ambivalent stand towards the Jews shows his political diplomacy (*Ant.*18.126, 131-34, 143-69, 179-204, 228-301; 19.236-44, 274-77, 288, 292-354). Polhill, *Acts*, 278.

[238] Barrett, *Acts*, vol. 1, 574-75.

movement becomes a political threat to the Roman imperial regime.[239] This heinous act also explains how the political tools have been used in the earlier cases where the Apostles and the believers are cruelly persecuted and killed by the dominant Jewish priestly system. Moreover, the narration explains a collaboration of mutually pleasing one another of the dominant Jewish center and the political Roman authorities. The narration also proves that "[s]uffering and death were a real part of the experience of the early church" from the political state but this should be seen in the light of the deliverance.[240]

Contrary to the execution process of James, Herod intends to bring Peter before the people for *'public execution'* (ἀναγαγεῖν) after the festival of Passover (v.4),[241] and Luke does not give any explanation to his readers about this. The background study shows that the Passover festival is the time of political uproar in Jerusalem over against the Roman imperial government. Herod likes to avoid a revolutionary threat by secretly beheading James without any trial. Luke, however, gives the impression from the earlier accounts that the Roman authorities give consent to the Sanhedrin to have power to persecute the minoritarian Christian community.[242] The motif behind Herod's persecution seems to have been a political scheme to please and to gain the favor of the dominant Jewish collaborative nationalists.[243] At this juncture, the Apostles and the Jesus community in Jerusalem do not undertake any public retaliatory actions in the face of persecution. Moreover, the Apostles being under the Lordship of a different authority (Ac.5:29) respond in discursive resistance mode with the religio-political centers (cf.Ac.4:19-20; 5:17-32).[244] They respond to the religious (high priest and Sanhedrin) and political (Herod) centers with forgiveness (Stephen, James) and prayer (for Peter's release).[245]

---

[239] In a parallel way, Herod Antipas beheaded John the Baptist (Lk.9:9). The zealous nature of James (eg. 'sons of thunder') would have made him a political threat to the Roman *imperium*. Polhill, *Acts*, 278-79.

[240] Barrett, *Act*, vol. 1, 569. The suffering motif in this story is perhaps similar to the story world of the Gospels (Lk.9:22-26; 18:31-33; Mk.8:31; Mt.5:10-12; 10:38-39), both in literary and social contexts of the first century. Samuel argues for a postcolonial purpose of the suffering rising Son of Man (Mk.8:31; 9:31; 10:33ff). Samuel, *A Postcolonial Reading of Mark's Story*, 130-34.

[241] For Barrett, "ἀναγαγεῖν can hardly mean here bring him *up for a public trial*," *Acts*, vol. 1, 577 (Italics in the original).

[242] Sanhedrin's activity under Roman rule, refer A.N. Sherwin-White, *Roman Society and Roman Law in the New Testament* (Oxford: Clarendon Press, 1963), 35-43.

[243] Munoz-Larrondo, *Living in Two Worlds*, 243. The same favoritism and collaboration continues during the procuratorship of Felix (Ac.24:27) and Festus (Ac.25:9).

[244] Cassidy, *Society and Politics*, 41.

[245] Cassidy, *Society and Politics*, 38. Sanhedrin acts as a religious legal body which functions within the Roman political jurisdiction. In the midst of the arrest of the Apostles (Ac.4:1-31; 5:17-40; 6:12-7:1), 'loving ones enemies' may be a postcolonial discursive strategy taught by Jesus.

4.9.2 The Deliverance of Peter from the Roman Imprisonment Shatters the Imperial Destructive Strategy

Luke portrays the early Christian community's unity, faith and prayer over against the violent and cruel attack of the Roman client King Agrippa I as a response in a positive manner. God's intervention in the power deal is demonstrated by sending his angel to deliver Peter. This incident also explains the liberative power that works on the basis of unity of the minoritarian community's faith and earnest prayer. The disbelief at the miraculous deliverance of Peter and his position in the Roman jail underscores the probable plight (1-4, 6) of an individual who stands for truth, love and justice. Luke narrates the leader of the Jerusalem Christians as a prisoner between two soldiers and with double chains (v.6; cf.*Ant.*18.196; Seneca, *Ep.*5.7), 'four squads of four soldiers each' (Ac.12:6) at the doors and the Iron Gate explicate the mighty power of the imperial throne used to eliminate the opponents and the deviants.[246]

As Peter is the prominent leader of the Christian minority in the first part of Acts narration (Ac.1-12), his miraculous escape signifies the divine intervention and also ruptures the Roman colonial power.[247] Peter's escape also explains the humble cry of the marginalized Christians as a whole for God's deliverance in the midst of political threat and genocide of their minority leaders. The miraculous deliverance (vv.6-19) brings joy and wonder in the hearts of many marginal figures like servant Rhoda (παιδίσκη Ῥόδη). Luke adds a comic touch by mentioning the presence of the passive Peter in the narration as he lie down in sound sleep between the soldiers; who needed to be pushed on his back like 'a little child' ('get up'; 'put your coat on'; 'tie your sandals'; follow me'); and Rhoda's role in reporting and the community's unbelief. The death penalty for the sixteen soldiers who guard Peter (Ac.12:19) without any trial further explains the intensity of Peter's escape.[248]

---

246 The location where the angel leads Peter towards the city has historical evidence of the Roman military barracked at Antonia tower where Peter is probably kept and "its eastern entrance leads into the streets of the city." Polhill, *Acts,* 281; Barrett, *Acts*, vol. 1, 581.

247 Ac.5:17-25; 16:23-29; 27:1-44; 28:4 describe the imprisonment of the apostles 'in public jail' by either the exclusive political or the priestly combined political authorities. The miraculous deliverance of the apostles by an angel at night explains the divine intervention by the earnest prayers of the Church. Luke's redaction interest in imprisonment is significant in the context of the Roman imperialism. For e.g., the imprisonment of John the Baptist (Lk.3:20); the future imprisonment of the disciples (Lk.21:12) and Peter's readiness to go with Jesus in prison (Lk.22:33). The similarity of language between Peter's deliverance account and the exodus account explain the divine salvation act behind the scene. Polhill, *Acts,* 281; Parry, "Release of the Captives," 159.

248 The Roman law gives the same penalty to the escapee and to the guards in the case of the prisoner's escape. Polhill, *Acts,* 183.

The dislocation of the divinely escaped Peter (Ac.12:17) probably explains the continuing political threat to the minority leader.[249] However, the client King, Herod Agrippa I's dislocation from Judea to Caesarea (v.19; cf.*Ant.*19.343) to conduct the imperial games and festival point to the political nature of the imperial functionaries and their priorities than settling the provincial issues.[250]

4.9.3 The Divine Judgment on King Herod Disrupts the Roman Imperial Strategy

Throughout the history of biblical interpretation, scholars understand this pericope (for various reasons of historical value), as an act of retribution and as a model of 'type' scene.[251] This is the way the reader understands the collaborative work of the Jewish religious centers in Jerusalem and the political center of the Roman client kings. For Luke, King Agrippa represents the Herodian dynasty, the political collaborator of Rome who makes plans to destroy the newly found Christian movement by murdering its leaders.[252] His political anger (θυμομαχεῖν only once in NT) does not end by killing the marginal Christians in Jerusalem probably on the basis of their political stand, but now extends to socio-economic factors and other marginal dependants.

Since the time of the Herod the Great, it is Herod Agrippa I who gained the political glory in its vast Judean territory and power. However, Luke resisted the political ideology of the Roman legal system by pointing out the impropriety in disvaluing the legal system and executing innocent people.[253] Moreover, the life-threatening value systems have been condemned by the sovereign God with whom the minority Christian movement is associated. However, the political

---

[249] There are other interpretation for Peter's dislocation: widespread missionary activity at Antioch (Ac.9:32-10:48) or (Rome?), and transferring the apostolic authority to James. Barrett, *Acts*, vol. 1, 587.

[250] Fitzmyer, *Acts*, 490.

[251] Conzelmann sees this pericope as unconnected and unrelated to the overall plot of Acts narration, *Acts*, 94, O. Wesley Allen Jr., observes this unit as the theological function of retribution, *The Death of Herod: The Narrative and Theological function of Retribution in Luke-Acts* (SBL.158; Atlanta: Scholars Press, 1997), 3; *Marshall, Acts*, 206. For Muñoz-Larrando, "Luke uses Herod's death as a type-scene to represent the destiny of the empire" and its collaborators as punishment and retribution for self-exaltation. Muñoz-Larrondo, *Living in Two Worlds*, 78.

[252] Muñoz-Larrondo, *Living in Two Worlds*, 74. Herod's dynasty from Herod the great (who killed innocent children to annihilate the messiah Mt.2:1-18), to Herod Antipas (who killed the path maker and consented the death of the anointed messiah) and Herod Agrippa epitomized the great persecutors of the new movement (111).

[253] Barrus, "The Gospel of Luke and the Acts," 140. The first century Roman political atmosphere points out to the strategic passivity of the legal defenders for the sake of maintaining the *Pax Romana.* In the gospel account of Jesus' trial also, Luke veils out the ambivalent web of power alliance between the client kings (Herod and Pilate) and the imperial Rome. Luke directly condemns Pilate for his actions by redactionally removing the 'washing of hands' from the trial scene (Lk.27:24).

authorities join hands with the Judean power centers to do away with the work of God.[254] The narrator may be questioning the integrity of the political voice of the client King who beheaded James and imprisoned Peter on political grounds. The story displays both the destructive hand of the Herodian rule as well as the divine power that dispels the human power centers through wonders and miracles.

The people of Tyre and Sidon depend on Palestine because their country is fed/nourished (τρέφεσθαι αὐτῶν τὴν χώραν Ac.12:20) by Palestine from agricultural products.[255] The people jointly appeals the king for a peace-treaty initially by bribing (πείσαντες-'persuation by payment') Balstus, the court official, to intervene on their behalf. This event mimics and mocks the political nepotism under the Roman imperial regime.[256] However, on the second day of the assembly, instead of hearing the cry of the people, Agrippa delivers a public address in 'godly voice' that questions the integrity of his position as a king and the protector of human lives. Luke demonstrates through this discourse that the power is given to 'public servants' not to get their undue glory rather for service to humanity. Luke mocks the King's attire and his public address being seated on the judgment seat (καθίσας ἐπὶ τοῦ βήματος) to show off his popularity by deifying himself. This makes fear and awe in the hearts of the assembly (*Ant.*19.345).[257] The angel of the Lord who delivers Peter from the prison strikes him down because he diverts the power towards him. Luke probably brings this event to disrupt the socio-political system that defies the imperial kings.

The Roman client King Herod Agrippa's death is further portrayed by Luke as a divine judgement of being 'eaten by worms' for deifying by claiming himself equal to god (Ac.12:23).[258] The witnessing of the gospel in Jerusalem ends with the

---

[254] Tannehill finds parallelism in the mode of arrest (to please Jews Ac.12:3; Lk.22:54), and its timing (during the Passover Ac.12:4), *The Narrative Unity of Luke-Acts*, vol. II, 151-52.

[255] In the context of Roman imperial exploitation of money, the King's restriction on Tyre and Sidon (free cities under the province of Syria) to import food grains freely from Judea caused added food shortage in the country (*JW* 3.38-39). Muthuraj, "A Post-Colonial Reading of Acts," 89; Smallhood, *The Jews Under Roman Rule*, 198. The word meaning of τρέφεσθαι, 'nourished' indicates the dependency of these countries to Palestine for their food and the famine in Jerusalem. This may be referred to a later date after the death of Herod. Barrett, *Acts*, vol. 1, 589. Other ancient trade between Judea and Tyre and Sydon (1Kg.5:11, 23; Ezek.27:17).

[256] Barrett, *Acts*, vol. 1, 589.

[257] Muthuraj, "A Post-Colonial Reading of Acts," 89. 'And the assembly was crying out, [it is] God's voice and not of men' ('ὁ δε δῆμος ἐπεφώνει, Θεοῦ φωνὴ). Luke mocks the deifying nature of the imperial propaganda at a festival in honour of Caesar. Josephus gives greater details of the robe worn by the King. Luke places the divine attribution in the praises of the δῆμος (the selected assembly) and not from the delegates (*Ant.*19.345). This may also signify the expectancy of the Roman king to be called as a divine being. Barrett, *Acts*, vol. 1, 590; Howell, *The Imperial Authority and Benefaction*, 43; Fitzmyer, *Acts*, 491.

[258] Barrus, "The Gospel of Luke and the Acts," 137. Luke discursively accuses the policies of Rome by narrating this account in the context of the atrocities against the apostles and the growing Christian movement. In the earlier cases, a direct blame is placed on the Jewish priestly collaborators

death of Stephen but it may be retributed with the death of the great persecutor of the Church, Herod Agrippa I. For Luke, deification of humanity is sinful because for him people are mortal and only God should be worshipped (Ac.14: 14-15; cf.Ac.10:25, 26). For Luke, the retributive miserable death of King Herod might be an appropriate warning to the center politics which tries to attack the minority Christian group.[259]

4.9.4 The Effective Witness by the Proclamation of the 'word of God' (λογος του θεοῦ)

In the midst of political oppression, martyrdoms and miraculous deliverances, famine and political upheavals, the nascent ecclesia is experiencing multiple growth through the effective witness of the proclamation of the word of God/ Lord (Ac.4:31; 6:2; 8:14; 11:1; 13:5,7, 46, 48; 17:13;18:11;12:24).[260] The narrative world of the early Christians in and around Palestine comes to an end by the disappearance of the twelve and by the completion of the famine support (Ac.11:30) of Paul and Barnabas in Jerusalem.[261] A direct shift is taking place for the next phase of the early Christians by the newly developed marginalized Christian community in Antioch (Ac.13:1-3).

4.10 Summary and Theological Reflection

The Acts of the Apostles is considered to be a postcolonial discourse of the minoritarian resistant Jesus community that constitutes its transcultural space in different parts of Jerusalem-Judea-Samaria and towards the colonial provinces of Rome. In the light of the commission of the resurrected Lord to the Galilean marginalized disciples and his ascension to heaven mimic the Roman dominant discourse of the first century CE. The commission to witness to the end of the earth and the boldness of the Apostles in witnessing in the midst of persecution demonstrate the rupturing of the dominant native Jewish center in and around Palestine. The nascent community appropriates the Greco-Roman *politeia*,

---

and the frequent miraculous escape of the Apostles from the arrest, imprisonment and execution (Ac.4:1-22; 5:17-42; 6.8-8.3). There are similar retributive death narrations from the colonial context of the first century are reported in Judith 16.17; Apoclypse of Peter 27; 2Macc.9.5-12, the death of Antiochus IV, *Ant.*17.168 190-the death of Herod the Great; Esuebius, *Hist.Ecc.*8.16.4), Barrett, *Acts*, vol. 1, 591; Fitmyer *Acts*, 491. Howell takes the steps of Joseph Klauch to use this pericope as a Lukan form (σχῆμα) for implicitly criticizing the traits of all the successive emperors from Nero. Howell, *The Imperial Authority and Benefaction,* 43. Josephus gives much explanation to the suffering of the King, "... his privy member was putrified, and produced worms; ...had difficulty of breathing, ...had also convulsions in all parts of his body." (*Ant.*17.169).

[259] Barrett, *Acts*, vol. 1, 576.

[260] In the colonial context of the first century, the word Lord (κυρίου) is a competitive word for the early Christians and they must have used discursively both the words, God and Lord (θεοῦ/ κυρίου) alternatively.

[261] Fitzmyer, *Acts*, 493.

patronage system, imperial ideology of unification, language signs, and Jewish religious traditions in the process of mimicking the imperial expansion. The Jesus movement which is begun as a community of marginal people of 'the way' (ἡ ὁδός) starts its journey from Jerusalem as a Jewish religious sect would disrupt the imperial dominant ideology through the affiliative-contesting dynamism.

The marginalized movement tries to write a resistant discourse of affiliating and distancing to the religio-political centers by making use of mimicry and ambivalence. By using postcolonial strategy, Luke probably writes back to the empire makers through negotiating with the dominant power centers probably with the help of the religio-political sympathizers like Theophilus, Gamaliel the Pharisees and Cornelius, the Roman centurion.

By mimicking the colonial agenda of mapping the nations under the imperial Rome, Luke catalogues fifteen different nationalities who gathered on the day of Pentecost to hear the mighty act of God. It likely ruptures the imperial plan of unifying the nations far and wide through the miracle of language. The newly formed transcultural community does not however enter into a political subversive mood of a direct encounter which would be fatal as history proves in the light of Great War in 68-70 CE. On the contrary, Jesus community tries to live effectively by discursively challenging the dominant socio-religious and political centers through witnessing the Lordship of Christ in the midst of persecutions.

The Roman imperial domination prompts the early Christian community to expect the realization of eschatology and the proclamation of 'Jesus as Lord' instead of Caesar which would disrupt the protocol of the colonial manifesto. Witnessing the entire universe (οἰκουμενη) makes the early Christians to cross the national, ethnic, linguistic and class-cultural boundaries. Through the act of witnessing, the eschatological community pose a challenge to the ideology of 'the eschatological distancing' of the sectarian community like Essenes or the militaristic nationalism of the Palestinian Judaism. The early Christian proclamation of kingdom of God (βασιλεια τοῦ θεοῦ) and the Lordship of Jesus for all (πάντων κύριος) mimic the imperial claims of the emperor which would disrupt the colonial agendas.

The summary descriptions of the early Christians (Ac.2:43-47; 4:32-37) mimic the Greco-Roman *politeia* of a higher social order of 'one soul, everything common' (μια ψυχη and ἅπαντα κόινα) which would disrupts the imperial socio-economic and political structures of the colonial world. The transcultural Christian community is less foreign to the Jewish identity and announces the Christian *politeia* which is more in line with the Roman political ideologies of higher socio-cultural values. However, the ecclesia interrupts the Greco-Roman patronage system through voluntarily renouncing the wealth for the sake of the poor without expecting anything in return. In this discourse, Luke writes back to the dominant centers through accommodating as well as disrupting the Jewish-Greco-Roman traditions.

The early Christians experienced the Roman colonial ethos of *Pax Romana* in more than one way with the purpose of counter it effectively. They, thus, display the ideal model of the Christian *politeia* by selling their possessions and give to the poor with out expecting anything in return. This counters the pattern of Greco-Roman patronage-beneficiary system of maintaining the dominant status quo of the colonial system. The distribution of wealth to the poor among the early Christians breaks the socio-economic hierarchical structural differences to make them as a community of equals. Luke gives significant space for social justice to the poor and the marginalized as he narrates the world of the colonized in and around Palestine.

The speeches of Peter to the Jewish audience in Jerusalem and Caesarea as well as Stephen's speech disrupt the dominant native Jewish center and the Roman colonial periphery. In these discourses, the leaders of the Christian ecclesia use the postcolonial strategy of disrupting the religio-political centers by simultaneously accommodating and contesting to the native Jewish cultural traditions. Furthermore, he affiliates with the Hebraic prophetic traditions to preach with boldness to the power centers. Through Stephen's speech, he challenges the racial-ethnic-cultural exclusive nature of the Jerusalem religious center. The speeches ultimately aim for repentance both in the individual level as well as in the community level for conversion and transformation both to the Jews and to the Gentiles/Nations. The impartial nature of God preached by Peter to the Gentile audience at Caesarea and placing them at the equal footing with the Jewish community through the baptism must have disrupted both the imperial centers at Jerusalem and Rome. Moreover, the preaching of radical move from the 'corrupt generation' through the message of *metanoia* is a challenge to the dominant power centers.

Stephen and James boldly speak to the face of the religio-political leaders and face martyrdom. However, the effective witness of the Apostles, the Hellenist Christian leaders and the transcultural Christians who are scattered due to the persecution in Judea, make the growth of the early Christians to forge a paradigm in the midst of suffering and death. The Christian community enters into an eschatological space as a challenge to the Jewish-Roman religio political centers. The cultural ethnic marginals like the Hellenist Christians, the Ethiopian eunuch, and the Gentile community of Cornelius find their wholistic identity by entering into the eschatological space. The unjust suffering on the basis of class, colour, gender, race and ethnicity has been transformed in the eschatological in-between space of the community of the equals.

The sovereign God works for the subordinate marginal community by miraculously delivering Peter from the Roman prison irrespective of the capital death sentence. In this episode, God is portrayed as subtly disrupting the imperial despotic kings who claim to be gods and sons of gods for their self-gratification. The divine retribution and punishment is given to those who oppose the plan of

God from the beginning of the narration (Judas, Ananias and Sapphira, Simon the magician and Agrippa I). A democratic nature of power structure is displayed in Acts that amounts to distributing the power to all disciples that would disrupt the hierarchical web of power. God's power is bestowed on his disciples not to dominate anyone but for human service. In the programmatic structure of the mission journey, Luke presents the Apostles as the servants of God including King David and Jesus the anointed. Moreover, God cannot be confined in the human-made centers, because there is no power center in the plan of God, the people are the power centers and power resides in the community fellowships.

Luke significantly adds the call/conversion/commission of the hybrid Paul to demonstrate how the eschatological mission started in Jerusalem moves out into the Greco-Roman world outside Palestine through witnessing to the Nations/Gentiles. The call radically transformed him from the center (persecutor) to the liminal space (persecuted) to proclaim the resurrected Lord, Jesus Christ (κυρίος, 'Ιησοῦς χριστός) to the kings-nations and to the people of Israel.

Chapter 5

The Narrative World that Centeres on the Early Christian Witness in the Greco-Roman World Outside Palestine (Acts 13-28)

5.1 Introduction

The transcultural Christian community slowly moved out of Palestine bearing witness to the gospel of the Lord Jesus (Ac.14:3; 15:35; 19:5; 28:30) through Paul and his associates preaching in the Roman provinces of the eastern parts of the colonial world. Through his 'world-wide' missionary journeys along with his co-workers, he planted transcultural communities in the Roman provinces of Asia Minor, Macedonia, and Greece despite the opposition from both the Jewish cultural nationalists and the religio-political authorities.

This chapter reflects on the gospel witness mainly of Paul through the expedition like narrations at Pisidian Antioch, Philippi, Thessalonica, Athens, Corinth, Ephesus, Caesarea and finally, Rome. The study deals with the discourses that portray direct conflict with the dominant religio-political institutions and the Hellenistic cultural centers of power. Further, the trial narratives in Jerusalem and Caesarea (Ac.21-26) before the Jewish-Roman authorities (Felix, Festus and King Agrippa) are read by using postcolonial theoretical concepts of strategic essentialism, mimicry, hybridity and ambivalence. The last section deals with Paul the protagonist's arrival at the Roman imperial center boldly proclaiming and teaching about the kingdom of God and the Lord Jesus Christ, disrupting the imperial kingdom.

5.2 Paul's Speech at Antioch Disrupts Jewish-Dominant Centre (Ac.13:1-52)

In order to fulfill the Lord's commission, Paul and the co-missionaries traveled to the north-western part of the Greco-Roman world as witnesses 'before gentiles and their kings and before the people of Israel' (Ac.13:2; cf.Ac.9:15). The expansion of the gospel to the nations begins through the re-commissioning of the missionaries by the ecclesia at Antioch for a mission expedition (Ac.13:1-3).[1] This commission of the ecclesia apparently mimics the Roman imperial commissioning. As a mission strategy, these Apostles go to the synagogues to preach the gospel in affiliation to the Jewish traditions and when they are rejected they preferentially opt for the Gentiles (Ac.13:5, 14; 14:1-2). In this mission, Paul also confronts the local power centers of deceptive religion (false prophet Elymas Ac.13:6-12) that opposes the gospel preachers from reaching to the political authorities.[2] Further, Luke narrates the significance of the teaching of the Lord (τῇ διδαχῇ τοῦ κυρίου) in the background of the miracles that help the Roman proconsul, Sergius Paulus to believe in the Lord (Ac.13:12).[3] The proconsul's radical shift to the eschatological space would apparently rupture the political power center in Cyprus.

After the mission in Cyprus, Paul and his companions witness to the people of Antioch of Pisidia by meeting them in their synagogue on the Sabbath, and read from the Law and the Prophets (Ac.13:14-16). Paul addresses the mixed audience of both Jews and the God-fearers through retelling the Jewish national story starting from the patriarchs to David (Ac.13:16b-22).[4] Here, Paul accommodates the Jewish diaspora history of prosperity in Egypt which he ironically connects to the present day Roman era. He develops the history through the period of judges and the change in monarchy from Saul to David. It is through David, the promised Israel's saviour that Jesus enters into the scene (Ἰσραὴλ σωτῆρα Ἰησοῦν Ac.13:23, 26; cf.Lk.1:69; 2:11).[5] By bringing John the Baptist as a transitional

---

[1] The ecclesia of Antioch is considered to be a transcultural community which reconstituted people from various strands (Levite/Pharisee), different races (Jews/African), distinct socio-religio-cultural positions (Manean, a court companion of Herod the tetrarch), Spencer, *Acts*, 137.

[2] The presence of Elymas in Cyprus can be seen as an oppositional power center that is in collaboration with the native religious and political powers. However, Paul performs 'sign and wonders' most likely as part of the benevolence of the eschatological era (cf.Lk.4:16-44).

[3] Tannehill explains the functionary style of Jesus and Paul's mission where the miracles and wonders compliment the mission (Ac.13:12; cf.Ac.2:42; 3:1-10; Lk.4:32), *The Narrative Unity of Luke-Acts*, 162.

[4] The God-fearers in the synagogue cross over to the liminal space where they participate with the Jewish community in its fulfillment of the expectation of a messiah. Joseph B.Tyson, "Jews and Judaism in Luke-Acts: Reading as a Godfearer," *NTS*, vol. 41, 1995, 25-32.

[5] Luke brings the comparison between King Saul and David (a man after my own heart) probably to make his point clear to the audience about the messiah who does God's will for Israel (Ac.13:22, 23).

figure, Paul connects a possible accommodative-disruptive link between the Jewish prophetic tradition and the messiah in Jesus (Ac.13:24, 25).[6]

As the speech continues, Paul includes the audience and blames the collaborated religio-political administration in condemning and nevertheless executing the prophecy about Jesus, the messiah.[7] Simultaneously, Paul alleviates the religio-political crime for Jesus' crucifixion, death and burial (Ac.13:26-30; Cf.Lk.22:37; 24:44-46) by stating the Jewish community's ignorance as well as the prophetic fulfillment. Besides preaching the resurrection of Jesus from the dead, the Apostles in all probability disrupt the dominant Jewish power center (cf.Ac.2:24; 3:15; 4:10; 5:30; 10:40). Further, Paul along with Barnabas now becomes witnesses of this good news (Ac.13:31-32).[8] As Paul concludes the speech, he quotes from the scriptures the fulfillment of God's promise to the Jewish nation that Jesus has become the permanent royal messiah in the line of David through his resurrection (Ac.13:33-37; cf.Ac.2:25-28; Lk.1:32-33).[9] The resurrection of the crucified messiah on the colonial cross would obviously bring contestations due to the challenge that makes to the religio-political centers. In the end, Paul calls the audience for repentance (Ac.2:38; 5:31; 10:43; cf. Lk. 3:3; 24:47) in the light of the eschatological era which is inaugurated through Jesus (Ac.13:38-39).[10] Moreover, by quoting another Jewish prophetic discourse (Ac.13:40-41; cf.Hab.1:5), he invites the hearers through an appeal as well as a warning for judgement.[11]

Luke demonstrates a mixed Jewish response of acceptance and yet rejection to Paul's speech. The dominant Jews become jealous of seeing the inflow of the Gentiles ('nearly all the city') to hear the word of the Lord' (τὸν λόγον τοῦ κυρίου Ac.13:42-45). However, the Jewish rejection makes Paul and Barnabas to obey the commandment of the Lord to be 'a light to [the] nations (ἐθνῶν)... salvation until the ends of the earth" (Ac.13:46-47; cf.Ac.1:8). Here Luke brings

---

[6] Polhill, *Acts,* 301. John's announcement of the coming of the messiah possibly accommodates and yet disrupts the religio-political milieu of the time through the challenges he makes (Lk.3:3-20).

[7] Luke ambivalently put the blame on Jewish leaders in handing over the Innocent Jesus to Pilate to execute him even though they did not find proper ground for a death penalty. However, 'having judged they fulfilled the voice of the prophets that being read on every Sabbath' (Ac.13:27).

[8] According to Tannehill, in the process of the gospel witnessing to the ends of the earth (Ac.1:8), the Galilean Apostles take the gospel to the Jews but it is through Paul, the gospel reaches to the nations (Ac.13:47), *The Narrative Unity of Luke-Acts,* 169-170.

[9] The resurrected (Ac.13:33b; cf.Psa.2:7) and the exalted Jesus fulfill the promise which is given to David (Ac.13:34, 35; cf.Isa.55:3c; Psa.16:10). According to Robert O'Toole, Jesus' resurrection plays the thematic unity in Ac.13:13-52, "Christ's Resurrection in Acts 13, 13-52," *Biblica,* vol. 60, 1979, 361-372.

[10] Here in this speech, Paul is speaking the new era of forgiveness of sins, universal gospel ('everyone who believes') over against the Jewish legalism and exclusive cultural bounds.

[11] By using the midrashic interpretation of Habakkuk, Luke probably warns the Jewish-colonial centers to repent and turn to God.

the midrashic interpretation by quoting from the prophetic voice (Isa.49:6) as an affiliative strategy to identify with the native Jewish traditions of their moral obligation to bring the universal salvation to the nations. This is to prove that Lukan Paul's mission is universal but it must start from the Jews (Ac.13:26, 32; cf.Ac.9:15).[12] Moreover, this rejection does not run off the missionaries from witnessing to the Jewish community rather goes to the synagogue on the next phase of ministry in Iconium for a great success (Ac.13:50-14:1; cf.Ac.17:1, 10, 17; 18:4, 19; 19:8).

5.3 The Expedition of Paul and Barnabas and the Jerusalem Council (Ac.14:1-15:35)

By crossing the socio-cultural-religious and geographical boundaries, Paul and Barnabas spread the universal gospel of the Lord Jesus Christ to the nations (both Jews and Gentiles). Signs and wonders have been performed along with speaking boldly for the Lord (παρρησιαζόμενοι ἐπὶ τῷ κυρίῳ) in the neighboring cities of the Roman provinces of Galatia (Iconium, Lystra and Derbe; Ac.14:1-18). This expedition trip is probably imitating the Roman agenda of colonial expansion with a difference. The mixed response from both the Jews and the Gentiles (Ac.14:1-6) and the Jewish rejection lead the missionaries to turn to the Gentiles once again (Ac.14:8-20; cf.Ac.9:16).[13]

In Lystra, the deification is challenged in the light of the healing of the crippled by stating that 'we are of the same nature' (καὶ ἡμεῖς ὁμοιοπαθεῖς ἐσμεν Ac.14:15; cf.Ac.10:26).[14] Moreover, the probable success of mission of Paul and Barnabas is shown through revisiting the nascent transcultural ecclesia in the provinces of Asia Minor through reminding the need to suffer persecution in order to participate in the kingdom of God (Ac.14:22).[15] 'The appointment of the elders' (πρεσβυτέπους) in each church and further they are 'commended them to the Lord' (παρέθεντο αὐτοὺς τῷ κυρίῳ Ac.14:23) to

[12] Tannehill, *The Narrative Unity of Luke-Acts,* 173-174. The repetitive statement Paul makes in the context of Jewish opposition, 'we are turning to the Gentiles/Nations,' (Ac.13:46; 18:6; 28:28) is probably considered as a programmatic movement. C. Kavin Rowe, *World Upside Down. Reading Acts in the Graeco-Roman Age* (Oxford: University Press, 2010), 57.

[13] The Iconium persecution suggests for a combined disruption including the rulers (Ac.14:5; cf.Ac.4:25-27). The Jewish conflict has gone up to the extent of stoning Paul to the point of death and dragging him outside the city (Ac.14:19). This event would reminiscent to the incident of Stephen (Ac.7:58). Tannehill, *The Narrative Unity of Luke-Acts,* 177.

[14] In a Greco-Roman context, deification and the imperial cult have been challenged by the mini speech in Lystra which is in parallel to the Athenian speech (Ac.14:15-18; 17: 22-31). According to Rowe, the divine identity is reconfigured to the Gentile context and the call is to 'turn from... to the living God' (Ac.14:15), *World Upside Down*, 19, 22.

[15] Spencer, *Acts,* 151. The divine imperative (δεῖ) is probably given to explain the Lukan suffering motif both in the context of Jesus (Lk.24:46-47), his disciples (Lk.9:22-27), Paul (Ac.9:15-16) and the new disciples (Ac.14:22).

carry on the task would perhaps mimic the religio-political centers in delegating authority for a particular assignment.[16] By returning back to the ecclesia at Antioch, Paul and Barnabas report the details of the expedition, how God "opened a door of faith (to) the Gentiles" (Ac.14:27).

The mission expansion to the nations brings trouble from the Jerusalem ecclesia (Jewish-Christian cultural nationalist?) in terms of how to fix the space for the Gentiles into the Jewish fold. The ethnic centered circumcision party from Jerusalem brings their agenda of ethnicity, circumcision and dietary laws as a major disruption in Paul's mission practice (Ac.15:1-5; cf.Gal.2:4-5, 11ff).[17] The probable resolution for the disruption comes after hearing the speeches of Peter, Barnabas and Paul (Ac.15:7-12) at the ecclesial council of Jerusalem. Peter speaks of the universal mission practice on the basis of the eschatological spirit's bestowal on the Gentiles just like the circumcised Jews (Ac.15:8-9; cf.Ac.11:4-17). Further, his speech makes clear of God's role in the universal mission plan where God chooses, cleanses the hearts by faith, testifies and accepts all (Ac.15:7-9). At this juncture, James, the leader of the Jerusalem council, in his decision crosses the borders of the Jewish imperial culture to the eschatological middle space of transculturalism and cultural hybridity.[18] Consequently, he accommodates certain Jewish essentials of moral-religious obligations of food sacrificed to idols, blood, strangled animals and fornication devoid of cultural imposition on Gentiles (Ac.15:19-29; cf.Lev.17:8, 10-14; 18:6-23).[19] The Council's letter is well accepted by the budding ecclesia in locations outside Palestine based on the ambivalence of negotiations and contestations with the Jewish dominant culture (Ac.15:30-35; 16:4). Finally, the inside disruption has been resolved and the next phase of the expedition journey of Paul has been started from Syrian Antioch.

---

[16] The Jewish religious authorities in Jerusalem are called by Luke as elders (Ac.4:5, 8, 23; 6:12; cf.Lk.9:22; 20:1; 22:52) and once with the elders of the Jerusalem ecclesia (Ac.11:30). Spencer, *Acts*, 152. Paul and Barnabas appoint elders in the new congregations probably in Affiliation with the Synagogue leadership tradition. Polhill, *Acts,* 319.

[17] Samuel calls the mission engagements from the Christian perspective as 'mission practice,' "Mission Practice," 6. The disruptive elements in the Antiochan mission are called 'the circumcision party,' 'the sect of the Pharisees,' (Ac.15:5; cf.Gal.2:12) who promote Jewish cultural nationalism upon the Gentile converts.

[18] Quoting of Amos.9:11-12 and allusions of Jer.12:15 and Isa.45:21, Luke probably made use of the midrashic interpretation as an affiliative-disrutpive strategy in order to incorporate the Gentiles into the eschatological community of God. A new people have been formed out of the nations for his (God's) name's sake (ἐξ ἐθνῶν λαὸν τῷ ὀνόματι αὐτοῦ Ac.15:14). Spencer, *Acts,* 156; Polhill, *Acts,* 329. James confirms his argument of the Gentile inclusion by using the rebuilding metaphor (Ac.15:16, 17; cf.Ac.2:30-36; 13:32-24) with the restoration of Israel. Tannehill, *The Narrative Unity of Luke-Acts,* 187-189.

[19] Spencer, *Acts,* 152. The official decisions are considered to be collegial unanimous decision (Ac.15:20-22, 24, 25, 28) of the Jerusalem apostles and the assembly. For Polhill, these decisions are moral prohibitions, *Acts,* 331.

5.4 Disruptions to the Jewish and Roman Institutions in the Greco-Roman World (Ac.15:36-21:36)

During the second expedition of Paul, Luke portrays the movement of the gospel witness to new geographical locations and simultaneous conflict with the relgio-political dominant institutions in Philippi (Roman colony), Thessalonica (the capital of the province of Macedonia), Athens (the renowned city in Greece), Corinth (the capital of Achaia) and Ephesus (the capital of Asia). Between Ac. 16-19, Tannehill analyses four scenes of Jew-Gentile public accusation against Paul and Silas in Philippi, Thessalonica, Corinth and Ephesus (Ac.16:19-21/17:5-7; Ac.18:12-13/19:24-27).[20] Moreover, the missionaries are considered to be social deviants, disrupters of the dominant orders, disturbers of the *Pax Romana* and traitors.[21] In this mission trip, Paul encounters "more widespread and more particular opposition."[22] The first public accusation comes from the Greco-Roman business lobby which is in collaboration with the imperial administration.

The second missionary/expedition journey of Paul (Ac.15:36-18:22) starts with a unique vision of a Macedonian call 'to come and help.' This vision explains the new foreign territory Paul is going to cross over.[23] Here, the call to help may be seen as the cry for freedom and *salus* in the context of Roman colonialism and cultural imperialism by the bourgeoisie businessmen who occupy this colony for their own business and profit. Luke probably understands Paul's witness in Macedonia as the next phase in the expansion of the *imperium* of God by mimicking the Roman territorial extension but with a difference in its imitation. They proclaim "salvation and freedom through Christ Jesus."[24] This is the first

---

[20] Tannehill, *The Narrative Unity of Luke-Acts,* 202, 209.

[21] Spencer, *Acts,* 160.

[22] Spencer, *Acts,* 159.

[23] Paul's second mission trip is misinterpreted by many NT scholars as a missionary journey to Europe, being influenced by the modern ideas of geography for supporting the colonial missionary agendas. Dunn, *Acts,* 215; Johnson, *Acts,* 281, 290, 297. However, by the beginning of the 20th Century, Rackham questions the Western colonial interpretation of Macedonia equating with Europe because of the specific call in the narration. R.B. Rackham, *The Acts of the Apostles: An Exposition* (London: Methuen and Company, 1906), 272. For Staley, the common geographic division in the ancient Gracean world was Libya, Asia and Europe. J.L. Staley, "Changing Women: Postcolonial Reflections on Acts 16:6-40," *JSNT* 73 (1999), 114.

[24] S. Samuel, "The Imperial Prison and the Irrupting Gospel as Discursive Symbols of Stewardship," *niyog-* NTC Magazine, 2004, 40. Samuel reads the Roman propaganda machine as disrupted by the claims of the gospel of Jesus Christ in the colonized Rome. Paul's proclamation of the gospel resulted in his imprisonment in the military state of the Roman colony (cf.Phil.1:13). In the first century Roman province, the politically accused prisoner would be guarded by a soldier (cf. *Ant.*18.186-204). The Roman imprisonment was usually severe and varied according to the social class. Stambaugh and Balch, *The Social World of the First Christians,* 35-36.

encounter of Paul and Silas with the Roman administrators and Luke displays the Roman character of a colony for his readers.[25]

5.4.1 The Beginning of the Transcultural Community in Philippi (Ac.16:11-40)

By the ministry of Paul and Silas, a mixed Christian community is formed in Philippi in the house of Lydia in line with the eschatological community formations in other parts of the Roman Empire. Luke seems to have a significant purpose in bringing disruption in the slave trade which is regarded "as the worst sins committed against humanity."[26] It is probable that the slave trade becomes popular in the Roman imperial world outside Palestine. The complex narration which deals with various religio-political issues raises some queries to answer: What is the role of the liminal space for prayer beside a river in the cross-bordering experience of Lydia and the slave girl with regard to the transcultural community of equals? Why did the Apostles not reveal their Roman citizenship early so that they would have avoided the Philippian imprisonment? What does female patronage have to do with the first century Christian movement?

5.4.1.1 The Two Women Characters and the Transcultural Community in Philippi

The two women characters who are culturally hybrid and colonized figures from two different geographical locations, come into contact with the gospel preachers in the 'leading city of the district of Macedonia, and a Roman colony' (v.12). This gives space for threat to the center as well as hope to the margins in the narration.[27] Paul and Silas meet the diaspora subjects including some women on the river bed of Gangites, on the cross borders of the city in the transcultural space. They probably enter into a self-hood of 'non-colonial identity', through 'the new eschatological teaching' on a Sabbath day (Ac.16:13-14).[28] The location of their gathering for prayer and Lydia's household who are worshippers of God (σεβομέ

[25] Staley, "Changing Women," 115. Staley accuses the misrepresentation/misinterpretation of Ac.16:9 to justify the European empire expansion since the sixteenth century. However, Samuel points out the difference in mimicking its agendas (salvation through Jesus Christ) and its imperial power center (the resurrected Christ). Samuel, "The Imperial Prison," 40.

[26] Muthuraj, "A Post-Colonial Reading of Acts," 88.

[27] Barrus, "The Gospel of Luke and the Acts," 152. There is a colonization of the Romans over the native Philippian Greeks. "The full name of the new town was Colonia Julia Augusta Philippensium." Barrett, *Acts*, vol. II, 778. According to the Roman law, the minority Romans ('veterans and the displaced Italians) with the dominant imperial power in administrative enactments (Latin become the official language) and with all privileges of the Roman citizenship can run the government. B. Rapske, "Philippi," in *BAPRC*, vol. 3 (Grand Rapids: Wm. B. Eerdmans Publishing Company, 1994), 116.

[28] The banks of the river Gangites is about three kilometers west of Philippi marking the border crossing of the city where the hybrid God-fearers come for prayer on a Sabbath. In the context of

νη τὸν θεόν) probably demonstrate how the first century women enter into a new phase of life through their fidelity to the Lord Jesus (κύριος ᾿Ιησους).[29]

The colonial atmosphere of the city is well portrayed through the multicultural subjects like that of migrant Asians like Lydia, the slave girl from Delphi, the gospel preachers (Paul and Silas) and the native Macedonian Greeks. Further, their relationship to Rome in this narrative is probably ambivalent and hybrid in nature due to the conflicting status of a Roman colony.[30] The imperial power is portrayed by the political and legal language of Roman hegemony under the pretext of extending the *Pax Romana* of peace and salvation to Macedonia.[31] Luke explains the conflicting status of the colonized people through them.[32] For Staley, the two women "justify and mystify an act of ideological colonization" by portraying them as 'good' and 'bad' women.[33] However, we see something more than a mere juxtaposition of a good and bad dichotomy because nothing is bad in the slave girl except the imputed badness in her. The slave girl's position in a colonized state by her 'Roman' masters is a doubly oppressed position and conveys a broader critique of the Roman colonization.

In this story world, these two women characters meet Paul the preacher of the gospel on a colonial Roman territory with conflicting status.[34] Both of them respond differently to Paul portraying the ambivalence of the colonial subjects to the new message that comes on their way. Lydia welcomes Paul and his message but the slave girl challenges him peripherally even though she longs for her salvation from her colonial masters. Both the women characters in the

---

anti-Jewish sentiments in Philippi, anti-Semitic feelings are flared up from the political centers. Rapske, "Philippi," 120; Conzelmann, *Acts*, 130.

[29] A new phase of life for women to enter into the eschatological community without any barrier in contrast to the temple-centered worship where only men can fully participate in the worship center. This exhibits the privilege of the new community of God in the in-between space. Luke's interest in women characters are explained by the passages-Ac.1:14; 8:3,12; 9:2; 16:1; 17:4, 12, 34; 18:2, 26; 21:5; 22:4. Barrett, *Acts*, vol. II, 782.

[30] Samuel, "The Imperial Prison," 39.

[31] The imperial language shows the Roman hegemony- eg., "(κολωνία [16.12], στρατηγοὶ [16.20,22,35,36,38], ῥαβδοῦχος [Latin, *lector*; 16.35,38], Ῥωμαίους ὑπάρχονας [16.37,38])," Howard C. Kee, *To Every Nation under Heaven: The Acts of the Apostles* (Harrisburg: Trinity Press International, 1997), 197-220; Bruce, *Acts*, 335-36; J.H. Nerey, "Luke's Social Location of Paul: Cultural Anthropology and the Status of Paul in Acts," in *History, Literature, and Society in the Book of Acts,* edited by B. Witherington III (Cambridge: Cambridge University Press, 1996), 263-64; Staley, "Changing Women," 125.

[32] Barrus, "Luke-Acts," 151. Thyatira was a leading trade center of purple dye and its business is a lucrative one. Haenchen, *Acts*, 494.

[33] Staley, "Changing Women," 116.

[34] Staley, "Changing Women," 134. Staley reads the text with the imperialist ideologies but she does not accept fully Luke's use of the discursive mimicking of the imperial agenda as a resistant discourse of the first century Christians. Lydia's diaspora identity places her in the marginal space even though she had a lucrative business.

story cross their geo-cultural–religious borders to embrace a new way of life into the transcultural community of equals.[35] The gospel probably gives the migrant community an identity of their own through the formation of the transcultural group in the Macedonian city of Philippi. This is the first account in Acts where the colonized Greco-Romans rather than the Jewish collaborators become the instigators of opposition.

5.4.1.2 Slavery and Economic Exploitation in Colonial Philippi

It is probable that the Roman slave system and its atrocities are thrown open to the public view. It is challenged by the detailed narration of a transformed business woman who becomes the patron for the Christian community. Slave system has been a socio-historical reality of the first century and minimizing the core message will not do justice to the text. Similar to any colonial context prevalent at any time in the world, the slave trade was a profitable business where the human beings are converted into commodities.[36] The slave girl becomes a commodity to make profit to the Roman businessmen (Ac.16:19) who were probably Roman veterans who held much property in the colony and their legal standing must have supported their wealth.[37] The 'salvation' from the slave trade and from the colonial masters probably makes this pericope as one of the main episode for a postcolonial reading of Acts.

As per the information given by the narrator, the girl is basically a slave (παιδισκη), possessed by a 'pythian spirit' (πνευμα πυθωονα), has several owners (κύριοι) and is making much profit (ἐργασίαν πολλὴν) through her prophetic gift (τέχνη).[38] Luke mockingly mimics the Roman discursive symbol of *Pax Romana* by exhibiting the humiliated and dehumanized nature of the slave system. Moreover, the slave girl is abused and doubly exploited by the Greco-

---

[35] Staley argues for border-crossing of the characters for geographical conquest through inter-textual reading by citing the arguments of Shamanah's bad women and new territory (Rahab-Josh.2:18,21; Cananite woman-Mt.15/Mk.7; Samaritan woman-Jn.5). M.D. Shamanah, *Toward a Post-Colonial Feminist Interpretation of the Bible,* Unpublished PhD dissertation, Nashville, TN, Vanderbilt University, 205-09 cited by Staley, "Changing Women," 126.

[36] Muthuraj, "A Post-Colonial Reading of Acts," 88. The British colonial system also inherited this most profiting slave business from the Portuguese and Dutch.

[37] In Philippi, the land is divided among the pensioned soldiers who probably become big businessmen in the colony who controls the political power on behalf of the native Greeks. Rapske, "Philippi," 119.

[38] I.R. Reimer, *Women in the Acts of the Apostles: A Feminist Liberation Perspective,* translated by L.M. Maloney (Minneapolis: Fortress Press, 1995), 152, 53. In the slave system, human rights are violated by taking away their production, and their lives become like a machine for benefiting their masters. For eg., "[What] they brought in or produced belonged, both legally and factually, to their masters," (153). The 'pythonic' spirit is referred to the Greek cult of the Delphic oracle and represents god Apollo who predicts future events (cf.Herodotus, *Persian Wars* 1:46; 2Kgs.17:17; *Ant.*6.330). Barrus, "Luke-Acts," 151. But during the Roman colonial period, the Greek cult in all its forms becomes collaborator with the imperial system.

Roman collaborated imperial system.[39] The powerless marginals like the unnamed slave girl in the society are the target of the colonial exploitative structures and the Roman government possibly promotes such systemic evil in the society. In Aristotle's term, a slave is an "animate property" (*Politics* 1253b 32) and legally slaves belonged to their owners as *instrumentum* under the Roman imperial period.[40] The imperial government supported the elite businessmen to exploit the poor and the religious-political network for private gain.[41]

The slave girl's cry (ἔκραζεν) about the apostles as 'these men are *slaves of the most high God,* who are proclaiming to you (the) *way of salvation,*' (v.17 Οὗτοι οἱ ἄνθρωποι δοῦλοι τοῦ θεοῦ ὑψίστου εἰσίν, οἵτινες καταγγέλλουσιν ὑμῖν ὁδὸν σωτηρίας).[42] This cry for salvation is probably the expression of her desperate hope as well as the probable disruption of the imperial propaganda of salvation through calling the missionaries as the true messengers of salvation. It is interesting to note that the exorcism done by Paul against the slave girl has legal implications of a socio-political crime.[43] Staley critically analyses the exorcising of the spirit in the context of political oppression that might have caused the demonic possession similar to the case of the Gerasene demoniac (Lk.8:26-39; Mk.5:1-17; 7:24-31).[44] Further, Fiorenza's interpretation explains the act of

[39] In Greco-Roman context, augury and divination become popular enough that the military campaign and the emperor's decrees are given only by consulting an oracle. Polhill, *Acts*, 351. The unnamed slave girl is juxtaposed with the named slave girl Rhoda in Ac.12:13 which probably explain the identity she inherited among the community of equals.

[40] Reimer, *Women in the Acts*, 153. Slaves do not have any rights of their own production and it belongs to their masters. By mimicking the spirit of python (πνεῦμα πύθωνα) in the overall context of the Holy Spirit (ἁγίου πνεύματος Ac.1:8) of the eschatological community, Luke probably speaks with a double vision and forked tongue for challenging the imperial dominance.

[41] Samuel, "The Imperial Prison," 39. Simon, the sorcerer, in Samaria is condemned by Peter for making use of religious power to selfish gain and profit-making (Ac.8:18-23). Luke challenges the socio-religious network behind the exploitation of the marginalized.

[42] Italicized for emphasis. In the first century context, 'the most high God' is used to describe the Jewish God (*Ant.*16.163). However, the context of the dehumanized position of the slave girl who becomes a commodity in the hands of the businessmen shows the 'disturbed' sign of her cry. Her cry ironically mimics the masters voice with a difference. The imperfect word 'ἔκραζεν' points out to the repeated process for an undefined period that annoyed Paul.

[43] A direct legal implication suggests by Reimer for a possible socio-political turmoil that can cause the revealing identity of the apostles as slaves of the most high God (δοῦλοι τοῦ θεοῦ ὑψί στου). Reimer, *Women in the Acts of the Apostles*, 171; Sherwin-White, *Roman Society and Roman Law*, 79. Reimer points out that the slave girl's meeting (ὑπαντῆσαι Ac.16:16) and following (κατακολουθοῦσα Ac.16:17) probably explain her longing for a self identity. The discipleship stems from the phrase 'to follow' (ἀκολουθεῖν) implies her following Paul as a disciple (cf.Lk.23:55), *Women in the Acts*, 156, FN. 39.

[44] "Changing Women," 124. The exorcism is analyzed as anti-colonial expression.

exorcism as a healing and act of liberation.[45] However, she herself is critical of Lukan unfavorable treatment towards women in limiting their roles in a patriarchal society.[46] This discursive element explains the nature of the biblical text that has inscriptions of patriarchal dominancy as well as emancipatory discourses.[47] Here through the narration, Luke probably speaks for the doubly subaltern voiceless subject community through simultaneously approximating the dominant voices and recovers the liberative voices in the context of patriarchy.

Moreover, Reimer presumes the possibility for the liberation for the 'freed girl' through the place of prayer (προσευχη) with which Luke starts the narration (v.16).[48] There is a possibility of the ambivalent genre (novelistic) to give an open space by the narrator so that the reader could construct his/her story (probably to write back to the center) in the context of the newly formed Christian community of equals synonymous to the Jerusalem transcultural community (Ac.2,4).

5.4.1.3 Imperial Persecution and the Penetrating Power of God inside the Roman Jail

The loss of economic profit from the slave trade causes socio-political disturbances and arrest of the missionaries (vv.19, 20).[49] The preachers of the gospel of Christ are brought before the magistrates (τοῖς στρατηγοῖς vv.20, 22, 26, 38) who are generally responsible for maintaining law and order in the Roman colony.[50] The Apostles are accused of civil disturbance by anti-imperialistic, anti-Semitic propaganda of 'being Jews' (Ἰουδαῖοι ὑπάρχοντες v.20) and anti-Roman slants ('they are proclaiming customs which is permitted for us being Romans neither to accept nor to do' v.21).[51] The imperial nationalistic pride flares up in the Roman

---

[45] *In Memory of Her,* 265. Witherington also points out the 'double message' of Lukan portrayal of both women's liberation and subjugation by citing Seim, *The Double Message*, 249 in *Acts,* 334.

[46] *In Memory of Her,* 145-146. Luke gives list of women who actively participated in mission activity of Jesus movement (eg.Ac.1:14; 2:17-18; 12:2; 16:13-15; 18:18-26).

[47] Fiorenza, *Power of the Word,* 129. For Fiorenza, Feminist criticism is a 'collaborative Hemeneutics' where one studies the dominant patriarchal system work along with other colonial systems (race, class and imperialism, *Power of the Word*, 122-129.

[48] Reimer, *Women in the Acts,* 180-84 Reimer argues for the liberation of the slave girl by constructing another story around the in-between space of prayer with the help of socio-historical *mileu* of the first century. The "[M]anumission inscriptions' exhibit the liberative work of the diaspora Jewish communities" efforts in saving the slaves through the prayer and this community become a patron to them (181-82); cf.Deismann, *Light from the East*, 271 ff.

[49] For the Roman businessmen, Paul's action is a legal issue of damaging their property because the slaves were "instruments of production." N. Brockmeyers, *Antike Sklaverei* (EdF 116. Darmstadt, 197[illegible]), 9 cited by Reimer, *Women in the Acts*, 174.

[50] The magistrates "serve as the public prosecutors in both civil and criminal matters in the colony" have the right to use physical or corporal punishment. They are attended by policemen (ῥαβδοῦχοι vv.35, 38). Rapske, "Philippi," 124.

[51] The racial tensions have been created by the business men ('being Jews' and 'being Romans) who divided the society for their personal benefit. Similar racial discrimination has been reflected

colony of Philippi for the economic benefit of certain elites. The business lobby in Philippi holds much of the socio-political web of power with their military service and material wealth. This also give a social-cultural superiority that they could easily create a riot in the city for their selfish gain against the minoritarian preachers of the gospel.[52]

The liberation of the dehumanized slave girl causes disturbance and disruption to the existing *Pax Romana* which is protective of the elite exploiters as it dehumanizes the marginalized (women, slave). They are probably uneducated in the first century. The imperial mechanism makes legal charge against Paul and Silas based on their ethnicity and culture, and creates division in the society.[53] In the light of the dissension between the diaspora community and the business lobby, the former is at the margins due to its socio-political disadvantage. The Roman administration including the magistrates yield to the political pressure created by the Roman businessmen (v.21) to persecute the Apostles instead of administering justice to the Roman subjects.[54]

Luke pictures different shades of the Roman socio-cultural and political life where the decisions of the government authorities have been very decisive to the moral ethics of societal life. This is evident in the following atrocities against Paul and Silas. The Apostle's garments are being stripped off, beaten, flogged and finally imprisoned at the instigation of the colonial masters without any administrative trials. This portrays the cultural hatred and imperial silencing against the minority communities.[55] They are treated as dangerous criminals and are thrown in the inner cell (τὴν ἐσωτέραν φυλακὴν) with their feet fastened in the 'stock' (ξύ λον v.24).[56] The whole incident explains the imperial support to the business

through the edict of Claudius in expelling the Jews (ca.49/50 CE), proconsul Gallio's anti-Semitism in administering Paul's case in Corinth (Ac.18:12-17) and the Jewish-Roman war (66-70 CE). Certain customs followed by the Jews (monotheism, circumcision, Sabbath observance and food regulations) may have negative effect in the Roman colony. The Judeo-Christians are accused of being "atheistic and misanthropic," (Ac.19:23-27; Tacitus, *Ann.*15.44; Dio Cassius, *Ep.*57.14) due to the threat they may have caused to the Greco-Roman religious-cultural and political web of conventions. Rapske, "Philippi," 117-18; Sherwin-White, *Roman Society*, 81. Freedom of religious expression is openly challenged by the business lobby in Philippi.

[52] Rapske, "Philippi," 120. The business lobby is compared to a corporate or business company which held joint partnership.

[53] Anti-Semitic elements have been strong in Philippi. Reimer, *Women in the Acts*, 179.

[54] "The Roman colonial administration portrays itself to be a civilized one with good laws and customs, but at opportune moments it resorts to mob governance and to political opportunism to get its way." Samuel, "The Imperial Prison," 40.

[55] Samuel, "The Imperial Prison," 39. 'Tearing off the clothes' is a Greco-Roman custom of shaming the offender. The chief magistrates... were commanding to beat (Οἱ στρατηγοὶ.... ἐκέ λευον ῥαβδίζειν v.22) show the explicit order of the magistrates to beat and throw them into prison. Barrett, *Acts*, vol. II, 791.

[56] Scourging the innocent subjects by the colonial powers are reported quite repeatedly in the Acts narration (Ac.4:3-21; 5:17-42; 12:1-19; 24-26; cf.Lk.22:63-23:25). The Roman tribunal

elites who operate as the dominant self. And the marginalized minorities are the 'colonial other,' who are totally neglected and deprived of their fundamental rights.[57] Here, Luke is taking the final narration to a transcultural community of equals where the center-margin dichotomy is very minimal.

Luke is probably mimickingly mocking the imperial persecution by the attitude through the prisoners who reflect calmness and joy in the midst of suffering inside the prison (v.25; cf.Ac.12:12:6). The marginalized apostles inside the jail 'praying, singing hymns to God' (προσευυχόμενοι ὕμνουν τὸν θεόν) and the foundations of the prison are opened by the mighty act of God (Ac.5:19-26; 12:5-19). This incident would disrupt the power of the colonial center.[58] God's saving power against the imperial subjugating powers come to the rescue of the imprisoned preachers of the gospel by shaking the prison's foundations, loosing their chains and opening the doors (v.26). This created fear and terror in the heart of the Roman jailor.[59] Moreover, Luke is mocking the imperial imprisonment further by the prisoners' availability ('for we are all here') even though they could have escaped in the middle of the night (v.27).[60] Their act of benevolence ruptures his association with the imperial saving powers and crying for salvation-'what is it necessary for me to do in order that I may be saved? (τί με δεῖ ποῖεν ἵνα σωθῶ; v.30). This cry would mock ironically the imperial situation who could not give the *salus* to the custodians of the *Pax Romana*.[61]

The Apostles move to 'speak to him the word of the Lord' (ἐλάλησεν αὐτῷ τὸν λόγον τοῦ κυρίου v.32) resulting in the baptism of the jailor's family which possibly ruptures the imperial power base. The family of the Philippian jailor's service and hospitality into the house are analogous to the Christian community

---

Lysias' scourging "would have completed (him) if Paul had not spoken up." Cassidy, *Society and Politics,* 100. Christian martyrs are tortured by placing their feet on stocks (Eusebius, *Hist.Ecc.* 5.1.27; 8.10.8).

[57] The severe punishment given to the Apostles as well as their delay in disclosing their Roman identity seem to shed light on the pressure from the business lobby who initiated the riots.

[58] Similar prison escape scenes in Ac.5:17-26; 12:6-19 mimic the disruption of the Imperial forces that curtail the gospel mission by socio-political confinement. However, God's power works in all these scenes either to release the prisoners or to carry on the process of witnessing. M.L. Skinner, *Locating Paul. Places of Custody as Narrative Setting in Acts 21-28* (Atlanta: SBL, 2003), 94.

[59] The open prison ruptures the imperial forces who try to curtail the dissemination of the gospel by imprisoning the messengers and their resistant voices.

[60] The symbolic gesture of the benevolence of Paul and Silas for being available to the trial process rather than being opportunistic which disrupts the imperialistic ideology of eliminating the resistant voices and causing great wonder in the heart of the Roman colonial jailor.

[61] Under Roman imperialism, everyone lives under the fear of death, and a similar parallelism is seen in the killing of the sixteen guards who are responsible for guarding Peter in prison (Ac.12:19). Similar to the other gentile context, here too the jailor fell down before Paul and Silas (προσέ πεσεν τῷ Παύλῳ καὶ Σιλᾷ) mimic the deification of persons which is condemned by Luke (cf. Ac.10:26). He is led to 'the Lord Jesus' (τὸν κύριον Ἰησοῦν v.31).

life in Jerusalem (cf.Ac.4:32). This juxtaposes the hierarchical dominant structures of imperial atrocities against the minority subjects.

5.4.1.4 The Roman Citizenship of the Apostles and the Patronage of Lydia Rupture the Political Power System

While being available for the Roman trial procedure, even though they were freed miraculously from the chains, Paul and Silas wait for the imperial representatives to escort them outside the jail. The imperial magistrates (οἱ στρατηγοὶ) pass on the charge to release the wrongfully arrested prisoners through the enforcement officers (ῥαβδούχους) by the word 'go in peace' (v.36 πορεύεσθε ἐν εἰρήνῃ). This word of peace would mimic the colonial masters' illusory discourse and mocks the false claims of the imperial center.[62] Paul challenges the mistreatment of the colonial center against the uncondemned Roman citizens by stating the public insult through illegal beating (δείραντες v.37) before the trial. The release order from the magistrates without trial (v.36; cf.Ac.22:25, 28) makes Paul to show his discursive resistance and ask for the personal appearance of the magistrate (for an apology?). This would show a rupture in the political system.[63] The discursive claim of Roman citizenship at a strategic moment makes the public apology possible (v.39) from the imperial magistrates. Moreover, this action would rupture the colonial authority over the expansion of the gospel in Philippi.[64]

The Apostle's delayed confessions of their Roman citizenship by which they mimic the center become a potential menace to the colonial authority. However, their hybridity of both Jewish and Roman identity make them to negotiate by staying in the in-between space for the sake of the marginalized Christian community of equals. Their ambivalent identity is construed to shame and disrupt the power of the colonial masters.[65] They strategically postpone their Roman identity in a situation where their hybrid (dual) identity is shifting to

[62] The symbol of the enforcement office is "a bundle of rods with an axe protruding from the middle." Polhill, *Acts,* 352.

[63] Barrett, *Acts*, vol. II, 802. Luke discursively writes back to the center pointing out to their atrocities against the Christian minority and asks the center to have a fair trial before they punish the marginal subjects. The Apostles' socio-cultural hybridity challenges the center by demanding an apology from the center for their wrongs.

[64] The magistrates' public apology to the prisoners before the day light is probably contrasted with the terms 'in public' and 'secretly' (δημοσίᾳ, λάθρᾳ v.37). The imperial authorities gesture would disrupt the deceptive imperial judiciary that favors the business lobby.

[65] Barrus, "Luke-Acts," 152. The Roman-Jewish citizenship is referred by Josephus in the Jewish history (*Ant.*14.228, 232, 234, 237, 240). The name Παῦλος signifies his Roman identity (Ac.22:28b). Fitzmyer, *Acts*, 590. Lentz portrays Paul among the elites of the eastern part of the Roman Empire on the basis of his dual citizenship-Tarsus and Roman (cf.Ac.21:39; 22:25-28). John C. Lentz Jr., *Luke's Portrait of Paul* (SNTSMS 77; Cambridge: Cambridge University Press, 1993), 66.

and fro in a liminal space of collaboration and contestation.[66] It is also true that their Jewishness would have been negatively applied in the Roman colony where Semitism makes conflicting approaches due to the pressure of the business lobby.[67] Moreover, escapism from the suffering margins may have caused the newly formed transcultural community at the risk of questioning the integrity of the Apostles.[68] In this suffering process, they identify with the minoritarian transcultural diaspora marginals who are not Roman citizens in the colony of Philippi.

Luke shows the dual role of resistance by the Apostles, on one side by resisting the Roman civil system by discursively challenging and on the other side by making use of the privilege of the Roman citizenship to exhibit the flaw in the imperial system. Correspondingly, by responding pragmatically to the economic patronage of the first century Roman world, Lydia probably becomes an influential patron who becomes a generous benefactor in the infant church at Philippi.[69] In the imperial cultural context, the elite female patronage has great significance of socio-economic and political influence and the Christian movements pay debt to its culture of adopting the female patroness in Philippi.[70] Finally the story ends by positioning the three main characters, Paul the missionary, Lydia the patron and the liberated slave girl "positioned together (albeit also positioned differently) in a shared borderland."[71]

By emphasizing the widespread influence of the role of female patrons of Greco-Roman urban settings, Luke adopts Lydia's role as a patron in the formation of a Christian movement in Philippi as she opens her home for the transcultural community to experience intervention and creativity where they experience the new identity in the new eschatological space. The house church in Philippi mockingly mimics the imperial system of *pater familias* by discursively

[66] According to Bhabha's terms, Paul and Silas are negotiating for their multiple experiences of 'nationness, community interest, or cultural value.' Bhabha, *The Location of Culture,* 1-2; Samuel, *A Postcolonial Reading of Mark's Story*, 30.

[67] Rapske, "Philippi," 133. The tension creates by the Roman imperial perpetrators between Jews and Romans (Ἰουδαῖοι and Ῥωμαίοις) explicitly reveals the negative evaluation of the magistrates, i.e., in the accusation and the punishment given to the apostles. "The assertion 'I am a Roman citizen' would imply, If not 'I am not Jewish" (133-134)

[68] Rapske, "Philippi," 134.

[69] Barrus, "The Gospel of Luke and the Acts," 144. The other female benefactors in Acts are Tabitha (Ac.9:36-42), Mary the mother of John (Ac.12:12), and Priscilla (Ac.18). Luke portrays in the latter half of the text, the support of the female patrons for the spread of Christian movement outside Palestine. In Thessalonica, the missionaries get the support of the native Greek women of high standing (Ac.17:12).

[70] Barrus, "The Gospel of Luke and the Acts," 143-44. In the first century urban context, women with socio-economic ranking have "highly charged emblems of social power," to become part of the Christian movement.

[71] Barrus, "The Gospel of Luke and the Acts," 152.

challenging it with the community of equals in Lydia's house.[72] Paul's ministry in Philippi mimics the Roman colonization by creating a new community of equals under the patronage of Lydia as well as the family of the Philippian jailor who acts like a patron. This act also challenges the Roman colonization as the ecclesia pursues a different agenda in spreading the gospel of Jesus.

5.4.2 The Affiliative-Disruptive Posturing in Thessalonica (Ac.17:1-9)

As the narration progresses in the expedition, there are widespread oppositions to Paul's mission among the diaspora Jews who worship in the Synagogues. Affiliating himself to the Jewish traditions by going to synagogue on three Sabbath days, negotiating and contesting with the diasporic community from their own scriptures, Paul tries to prove that Jesus is the Christ (Ac.17:2-3). The proclamation focuses on the suffering, death and the resurrection of Jesus the messiah (Ac.17:3; cf.13:16-31; Lk.24:25, 26).[73] The positive response of some Jews as well as 'a large number of God fearing Greeks (σέβομαι) including some prominent women (Ac.17:4; cf.Ac.17:12, 34) probably cause instability to the religious center at Thessalonica.[74]

The jealous Jews collaborate with the colonized native Greeks and drag Jason before the city officials (πολιτάρχας) with 'public accusation' for treason.[75] He was brought before a Roman court. They accuse them politically as trouble makers (ἀναστατόω) of the entire world (Ac.17:6; cf.Ac.16:20) and anti-imperialist because they preach 'another king, saying to be Jesus' (βασιλέα ἕτερον λέγοντες εἶναι᾽ Ιησοῦν Ac.17: 7; cf.Lk.23:2-4).[76] However, the irony is that it is the jealous Jews who bring the people from the market place (ἀγοραί

[72] Reimer, *Women in the Acts*, 126.

[73] The divine imperative (δει) is used to explain Jesus' death and resurrection (Ac.17:3; cf.Lk.24:45-46). Spencer, *Acts*, 170. Moreover, messiah's suffering is given special emphasis in Luke-Acts (Lk.24:26; Ac.3:18; 26:22,23).

[74] Thessalonians were given freedom to have Greek pattern of administration. Polhill, *Acts*, 358. The positive response of 'few prominent women' who joins the Christian ecclesia probably helps the reader to understand the realities of economic patronage by women. Barrus, "The Gospel of Luke and the Acts," 144. The Lukan prominence to women who become part of the ecclesia in Ac.16-19 must be considered seriously in the first century religio-political context of Rome. E.g., Damaris in Athens (Ac.17:32), Priscilla in Corinth (Ac.18:2, 18, 26). Tannehill, *The Narrative Unity of Luke-Acts*, 208.

[75] Tannehill finds "public accusation type scene" in Philippi, Thessalonica, Corinth and Ephesus (Ac. 16-19), *The Narrative Unity of Luke-Acts*, 202. The jealous Jews bring people from the market place (τῶν ἀγοραίων) and 'turn the world upside down.' The first century inscriptions prove the presence of the magistrates (πολίταρχος/ πολιτάρχης) of the Macedonian cities. Bruce, *Acts*, 324.

[76] Tannehill, *The Narrative Unity of Luke-Acts*, 209. The verb 'ἀναστατόω' can mean a political agitator because the following accusation against the missionaries points to that. Through his preaching, Paul seems to mimic the Roman propaganda with a difference of calling Jesus to be the messiah. The opponents pursue the Apostles in other places also (Ac.17:6). According to Barrett,

ος) 'to turn the world upside down.'[77] There is a clear deception from the Jewish opponents in accusing the missionaries politically to get support of the imperial power center (Ac.17:5; cf.Ac.17:13).[78] In addition, Luke portrays the Roman imperial society where the mob governance takes the law in their hands and the administrators are shown as pawn in the hands of the powerful (Ac.17:8). Further, he shows the position of the marginalized in an imperial society where the Jewish religious elites are in collaboration with the political center. Also they silence the marginalized by favoring the orders of the officials (Ac.17:9). However, in the midst of the political opportunism, Luke portrays the miraculous escape of the missionaries through the help of the newly formed eschatological community at the house of Jason (Ac.17:7a) and also explains the defensive mechanism of the patronage system in the Roman colony.[79]

5.4.3 Paul Witnessing before Areopagus in Athens (Ac.17:16-34)

Paul's expedition journey continues as he preaches 'the good news about Jesus and the resurrection' in Athens (Ac.17:18), the renowned city of the Greek culture and philosophy of the first century world (Pliny, *Nat.Hist* 4:24).[80] He dialogues (διαλέγομαι) with the native Greek philosophers, the Jews and the God-fearers in the synagogue and in the market place (ἀγορα/) to carve a space for the eschatological community (Ac17:17, 18).[81] Here, the main target of his visit is probably to encounter the dominant religio-cultural-political center through appreciating the religiosity of the native Greek audience and lead them to the creator God (Ac17:19-21).[82]

The speech at the Areopagus (Ac.17:22-31) portrays how did Paul converse with the dominant Greek/Hellenistic cultural centers of power, contrary to the

---

It is a well calculated charge of sedition, *Acts*, vol. II, 815-816. For Rowe, "King Jesus is juxtaposed beyond doubt the Roman emperor," *World Upside Down*, 99.

[77] According to Spencer, "Paul never aligned his messianic mission with plots to overthrow Roman rule or incite public disturbances," *Acts*, 171.

[78] The cause of Jealousy against the missionaries (Ac.17:5; cf.Ac.5:17; 13:45) may be by seeing the inflow of prominent people (Jews, Greeks and prominent women) to the eschatological space.

[79] Spencer, *Acts*, 172. The city magistrates did not do a proper trial rather avoid the case by taking bail from Jason. Like Lydia, the patron in Philippi, Jason becomes the patron for the assaulted missionaries in Thessalonica and suffers on behalf of them.

[80] Fitzmyer, *Acts*, 600-601; Johnson, *Acts*, 318. The philosophical schools (Stoic and Epicurean) and the great philosophers (Plato and Aristotle) gave fame to this city. Gill explains the 'city full of idols' in the light of the imperial cult, "Achaia," 443-445.

[81] Paul adopts the dialogical teaching similar to the great philosophers (Socrates) of the time. Karl Olav Sandnes, "Paul and Socrates: The Aim of Paul's Areopagus Speech," *JSNT* 50, 1993, 21.

[82] Socrates was accused of rejecting the gods acknowledged by the state and was preaching about other deities (Xen. *Mem.*1.1.1). Dean Zweck, cites in "The Exordium of the Areopagus Speech, ACTS 17.22, 23," *NTS*, vol. 35, 1989, 101, FN. 5.

speeches to a Jewish audience.[83] In his preaching, he seems to accommodate as well as disrupt the native Hellenistic religio-cultural-philosophical beliefs and practices of the time. Moreover, he adopts the traditional rhetoric style ("deliberative rhetorical strategy") of appreciating their religious piety of identifying the 'unknown God' and makes use of a native discourse of a poem of Aratus (Ac.17:28). This disrupts their position of worshipping their creator in the form of idols or other imperial images.[84] Moreover, this creator God of the cosmos is 'the creator of the heaven and the earth,' 'gives everyone life and breath and everything else' (beneficent Lord) and he is the sustainer of the whole universe (Ac.17:24-29; cf.Ac.14:15-17).[85] This self-sufficient God cannot be circumscribed in temples ('does not live in temples built by hands,' Ac.17:24; cf.Ac.7:48) that may logically include the imperial cult. He also brings the concept of universal kinship through this speech by the unification of all nations (πᾶν ἔθνος Ac.17:26). Moreover, our relationship with God ('we are his offspring' γένος) would disrupt the imperial domination of one group of people/race over the others.[86] It is probable that the true knowledge of God not only disrupts the derivations of the images in the form of idols but also the other imperial deities all over the Roman Empire.

Paul's deliberative aim through this speech is to lead 'all men (sic) everywhere to repent' (Ac.17:30; cf. Ac.14:15) because this benevolent God overlooks the ignorance of humanity.[87] In addition, Lukan Paul ironically mimics the Hellenistic religio-cultural centers of power by pointing towards a man who is appointed by God to be the judge of the entire universe (Ac.17:31; cf.Ac.10:42) in justice and righteousness. By hearing this disruptive discourse on judgement, the imperial center arouses curiosity and decision making.[88] As a result, Luke demonstrates a

---

[83] Paul is probably brought before a council in Areopagus (Ac.17:22; cf.Ac.17:33, 34). N. Clayton Croy, "Hellenistic Philosophies and the Preaching of the Resurrection (ACTS 17:18,32), *Nov.T*, xxxix, vol. 1, 1997, 25. The speech at Lystra (Ac.14:15-17) is also based on natural theology in the narrative context of deification of human beings. Witherington, *Acts*, 425.

[84] Sandnes, "Paul and Socrates," 17. Paul leads the audience to the true God from their own worship image of the 'unknown God ('ἄγνωστος θεός).

[85] According to Rowe, Paul's use of 'this one (οὗτος) being the Lord of heaven and earth' (Ac.17:24; Ac.10:36) is juxtaposing the claim of the Roman emperors which is disruptive, *World Upside Down,* 111.

[86] Paul brings the concept of the kinship of humanity by mixing up different traditions and cultures (Jewish-Greek). The quotation, 'we are his offspring' (Ac.17:28b) is from Phaenomena of Aratus (ca.315 BCE) from Cilicia. Johnson, *Acts,* 316. Lukan Paul uses the same arguments in the speech at Lystra (Ac.14:15-17).

[87] The word repentance (μετανοιω) is closer to ἐπιστρεφω which convey a conscious turning. F.Laubach, "ἐπιστρεφω," *NIDNTT,* vol. I, edited by C. Brown, Exeter:Paterson Press, 1975, 354-355.

[88] Paul presents obscurely the judicial role of Jesus as the resurrected one and as the judge. Tannehill, *The Narrative Unity of Luke-Acts*, vol. II, 220.

mixed reaction of mocking (ἐχλεύαζον) and some becoming believers from the audience (Ac.17:32-34).[89]

5.4.4 The Apostles before the Proconsul Gallio in Corinth (Ac.18:1-17)

Luke starts the narrative context of Paul's mission in Corinth of his association with the Jewish family (Aquila and Priscilla) who are expelled from the imperial center by the Roman emperor, Claudius (Ac.18:2).[90] Similar to the other expedition trips, Paul makes affiliation to the Jewish synagogue in preaching the messiahship of Jesus with the mixed community of Jews and God-fearers. He also experiences disruption from the Jewish community in collaboration with the colonial administrators. When Paul finds commotion in the synagogue, he moves to the house of Titius Justus, 'a worshipper of God' (σεβομένος), a liminal space. The mission to the nations widens with so many joining with the eschatological community including the synagogue ruler and his household (Ac.18:7, 8).[91] Paul also receives the commission of the Lord in a vision assuring his presence and protection (Ac.18:9-11). Further, he continues his ministry for eighteen months in Corinth.

Paul faces public accusation of *religio illicita* ('this one is persuading to worship God against the law') before the judgment seat (τὸ Βῆμα) of the proconsul Gallio (Ac.18:12-17).[92] However, this accusation most likely be seen in the context of Paul disrupting the Jewish cultural particularism. The Roman administrator left the case for the Jewish discretion which shows the positive portrayal of the Roman administrator in relation to Paul's mission in Corinth.[93]

In the following narration, Luke shows Paul's affiliation to the Jewish traditions (cf.Numb.6:1-21) as a pious Jew by cutting his hair for fulfilling a vow in obedience to the law (Ac.18:18; cf.Ac.21:23-26). He also demonstrates the favourable position of the proconsul towards the Christian mission through

---

[89] 'The Areipagite, Dionysius and woman by name Damaris and others with them' (Ac.17:34b) portray those who moved to the eschatological space.

[90] The anti-Semitic attitude of Claudius, the Roman emperor is discussed in the background study. The racial discrimination in the colonial Roman provinces are dealt in other occasions (Ac.16:20, 21). The strategic location of Corinth attracted the Romans to colonize it (44 BCE) and made this city as the capital of Achaia (27 CE) and Gallio as the proconsul (52-54 CE). Polhill, *Acts*, 380, FN.104, 387.

[91] The conversion of Crispus and his entire house exhibit a probable disruption to the dominant Jewish religious center at Corinth.

[92] In Philippi and Thessalonica (Ac.16:21; 17:7), the accusation against Paul was against the Roman law, however here in Corinth, there is an ambiguity with regard to the accusation whether Roman law or Jewish regulations. However, for Paul, the minority representative does not get a chance to defend his case (Ac.18:14) which shows the failure of the Roman judicial system.

[93] For Gallio, the accusation is a Jewish dispute of their internal matters of name and law (Ac.18:15). In contrast, Cassidy refers 'τὸν νόμον' as the Roman Law (Ac.18:13), *Society and Politics in the Acts*, 92.

rejecting the case.[94] However, later, Luke illustrates the abusive picture of mob governance of 'beating Sosthenes before the judgement seat' (βήματος Ac.18:17; cf.Ac.16:22) probably for the reason of his affiliation to the messianic movement. Finally, the following proconsul's passivity in administering justice to the minority subject in the colonial province shows the political opportunism of the governing center.[95]

5.4.5 The Disruption to the Imperial Cult in Ephesus (Ac.19:1-41)

Luke summarizes the three year ministry of Paul in the administrative, commercial center and the imperial cultic center of the Roman province of Asia with an aim of expansion of God's *imperium* in Christ.[96] Paul probably affiliates with the synagogues, 'public centers' like the school of Tyrannus (Ac.19:8-10) and the city theater to preach the kingdom of God to the diverse community with ethnic-racial differences. The disruptions in the synagogue did not stop him from preaching the gospel to the Jews altogether, rather he continued it to all the inhabitants of Asia (πάντας τοὺς κατοικοῦντας τὴν' Ασίαν Ac.19:10). Moreover, the extraordinary miracles through Paul exhibits how he exercised the spiritual authority that rested on him (Ac.19:11, 12; cf. Ac.5:12, 15-16; Lk.10:13; 19:37). During this mission trip, Paul reiterates his desire to visit the religious center in Jerusalem and the political center in Rome to reiterate the expansion of Christian mission universally, both to the East and West (Ac.19:21; cf.Ac.9:51).[97]

The mob violence in Ephesus points to the divisive nature of the Greco-Roman society that the imperial administration probably wants to continue wherever they rule. Luke narrates the picture of Roman colonized Asia with the other exploitative structures manifested through the 'practice of sorcery' and exorcism (Ac.19:13-20). However, the humorous display of the spirit's mockery over the deceptive Jewish exorcism run by the sons of Sceva (Ac.19:13-16; cf.Ac.13:6-12; 8:18-24) in invoking the name of Jesus finally resulted in the interruption to their own agenda.[98] The disturbance to the magical power centers causes fear to all and

---

[94] The discursive position of the Proconsul is dealt by Rowe, by discussing divergent views (pro, anti-Roman*), World Upside Down,* 61-62. According to Marshall, Paul makes this vow in the light of the God's blessing upon his life in Corinth, *Acts,* 300.

[95] Tannehill alludes Gallio's anti-Semitic nature where he shows indifference to the attack of the native Greeks against a Jew, *The Narrative Unity of Luke-Acts,* vol. II, 228.

[96] Samuel, "The Imperial Prison," 40. For Samuel this expansion is in the context of Paul's ministry in Philippi.

[97] Paul's two locations of travel comes in the divine necessity (δεῖ). Tannehill, *The Narrative Unity of Luke-Acts,* vol. II, 239. Luke narrates Paul's co-workers (Apollos, Priscilla/Aquilla, Timothy/ Erastus, Gaius/ Aristarchus) who travel to different parts of the empire but functioned independently. Spencer, *Acts,* 182. Priscilla's position before her husband probably shows her as a woman minister (184).

[98] Polhill reports the historicity of Jewish exorcism from the magical papyri discovered from the Greco-Roman world, *Acts,* 403.

'they were exalting (megalu/nw) the name of the Lord Jesus' (Ac.19:17) instead the imperial deities. Here Luke probably mimicking differently the imperial collaborated agenda of expansion through the word of the Lord (Ac.19:20 'the word of the Lord was growing strong' κυρίου ὁ λόγος ηὔξανεν καὶ ἴσχυεν). Moreover, Paul's authority based on the risen Jesus over the exploitative magical web power leads many to repentance (Ac. 19:18-19).[99]

Paul's preaching of the gospel disrupts the 'particularism of the Ephesians' (Artemis cult) which is in collaboration with the first century Roman imperial cult (Ac.19:27-28).[100] The subtle anti-Semitic element erupts when Alexander the Jew tries to quieten the crowd through his defense speech (ἀπολογεῖσθαι Ac.19:32-34).[101] Luke also describes direct conflict with the business lobby in Ephesus (Demetrius, the silversmith) for the loss of profit and the probable conflict between the imperial cult ("Empress's association with the goddess") and the religiously marginalized 'people of the way' (Ac.19:23-24).[102] However, the slippery position of the religio-economic and political allied center is portrayed through the mob's perplexity and their confusion (Ac.19:29, 32; cf.Ac.21:34). Further, Luke also explains the sympathetic elements within the Roman official establishment. Paul the missionary is protected with the timely advice of the Asiarchs (τινὲς δὲ καὶ Ἀσιαρχῶν) and the town clerk (γραμματεύς).[103] The sympathetic figure of the imperial administration is shown through the affiliation of the town clerk. He says, 'these men are neither temple robbers (probably of respect) nor blaspheming our God' (Ac.19:37). Further, he suggests legal advice to the accusers to bring the case either before the provincial court or before the town assembly (Ac.19:38, 39).[104] The 'judicial explanation' given by the town

---

[99] Making religion as a profit making agent is countered by Luke in his narration (cf.Ac.8:20; Lk.9:23-24; 18:18-30) through Paul the protagonist of the new movement (cf.Ac.18:3).

[100] Tannehill, *The Narrative Unity of Luke-Acts*, vol. II, 242. The Asian Greco-Romans accused Paul and his co-ministers in Ephesus for causing civil disturbance based on his teaching that 'gods made with hands are not gods' (Ac.19:26).

[101] Luke demonstrates how did Alexander' gesture quiten the crowd and discloses the racial discrimination in Asia.

[102] There are strong connections amongst the imperial cult, imperial propaganda and the silver temples of Artemis. For the archaeological evidences refer, Trebilco, "Asia," 302-357; Kreitzer, *Striking New Images*, 109-112. The narration explains the significant link between the economy, religion and the imperial politics in the Greco-Roman world.

[103] The Asiarchs, the influential officials of the province of Asia who are associated with the imperial cult restricts Paul from appearing before the crowd. Further, the town clerk officially intervenes to calm the tumultuous situation (Ac.19:30-31, 35-41). Kreitzer, *Striking New Images*, 110-111; Spencer, *Acts*, 188.

[104] Polhill, *Acts*, 413. This incident explains the Lukan politics of apology to Rome. Haenchen, *Acts*, 102.

clerk legitimizes Paul and the new movement, and leaves the blame upon the religio-political establishment in Ephesus.[105]

The narrative addresses the complex socio-political-cultural and religious issues of the Greco-Roman world and how the missionaries responded to it. Luke also explains the web of power that interlinks society-religion-magic-economy-politics and culture for the sake of the dominant Roman collaborated Hellenistic cultural centers of power. However, the propagation of the gospel causes disruption to the religio-political dominant centers.

5.5 Paul's Arrest and Trial before the Roman Religio-Political Figures in Jerusalem and Caesarea (Ac.21:1-26:31)

Luke elaborates the significance of Paul as a true gospel witness by placing him before the Jewish institutions as well as the Roman court as a prisoner under legal custody.[106] Paul's arrest and trial before the Roman authority begins from his final return to Jerusalem after his longer period of ministry in Ephesus (Ac.20:31). The earlier narrations explain the religio-political accusations in the context of Paul breaking the socio-religio-cultural boundaries in preaching the gospel of Jesus Christ before the dominant centers of Jerusalem and Rome.

5.5.1 Paul's Trial before the Jewish Cultural Nationalists and the Religious Institutions in Jerusalem

Before the climax of Paul's arrest in Jerusalem, the narrator signals (through prophecy and human advice) the plot of the unbelieving Jews who try to destroy him (Ac.20:3, 19, 22-24; cf.Ac.21:4, 10-11). However, Paul is bold enough to face challenges probably as the part of fulfilling the plan of God to witness the gospel to the religio-political authorities in Jerusalem.[107] In parallel, Luke also explains Paul's affiliation to Judaism as a pious Jew who closely observes the religious traditions (Ac.20:6, 16; cf.Ac.18:18).

Luke reports the dominant accusation against Paul's universal mission practice by the native Jewish cultural essentialists who hold the Jewish exclusive ethnicity and cultural essentialism. Luke focuses on the involvement of the Asian

---

[105] Fitzmyer, *Acts,* 656. The rare word 'running the risk' (κινδυνεύομεν vv. 27, 40) in two different contexts put the blame for the riot on the 'unruly Ephesians.' Polhill, *Acts,* 414.

[106] Paul's Roman custody and his defense constitute "approximately one half of Luke's story about Paul." Skinner, *Locating Paul,* 59-60.

[107] Tannehill, *The Narrative Unity of Luke-Acts*, vol. II, 266. Tannehill compares Jesus and Paul in their decision to go to Jerusalem for imprisonment, trials, death and in prayer for God's will (Ac.Ac.21:13, 14; Lk.22:42). Both of them appear before the religio-political authorities and declared innocent but the corrupt leadership yield to the political pressures (264-265). In Jerusalem, Paul is probably depicted as a sufferer for the cause of the gospel (Ac.21-28) in bonds (Ac.26:29; 28:20) like Jesus who is pictured in the passion narrations as left alone to suffer at the crucial hour. Tannehill explains the "theology of suffering' in Paul's trials towards the latter parts of Acts, *The Narrative Unity of Luke-Acts*, vol. II, 271.

Jews in making a disruptive scene in Jerusalem accusing of his involvement in 'teaching everyone everywhere against the people [λαός], the law and this place' (Ac.21:28, 30-31; cf.Ac.6:13; 7:48-50) making his mission anti-Jewish.[108] However, the earlier narration of his joining in the purification rites and his paid offering not only for him but also for four other Jews (Ac.21:23, 24) explain his affiliation with the religio-cultural traditions.[109]

Luke reflects the political situation of the city of Jerusalem through the riot that tried to kill Paul (ἀποκτεῖναι Ac.21:31, 36; 22:22; cf.Lk.23:18) and the ambiguity of the Roman commander to perceive the true identity of Paul (Ac.21:37-38).[110] Claudius Lysias' intervention in rescuing Paul from the angry mob (Ac.21:31-36) shows the imperial administrator in a probable positive light. His apprehension of Paul as an Egyptian insurrectionist (*JW* 2.261-263; *Ant.*20.168-172) explains the desolate political situation of Palestine (Ac.21:37-38). Further, Paul discursively disrupts the Jewish mob that comes to kill him through his defense speech (retelling the story) in his ethnic language, Aramaic (Ac.22:1-21).[111] Moreover, he also persuades his audience by narrating his zealous national identity, education (Ac.22:3 5) and the commission of 'the God of our fathers' (Ac.22:14) from the temple to go to the Gentiles/Nations far off (εἰς ἔθνη μακράν Ac.22:21).[112] Lukan Paul is probably making his affiliative-distancing position to witness to the religio-political centers for which God has called him (Ac.22:14, 15; cf.Ac.9:15; 26:16-17).

---

[108] Tannehill, *The Narrative Unity of Luke-Acts*, vol. II, 269. Paul is accused of defiling the holy place by bringing the Greeks (Trophimus) into the temple. Tannehill makes comparison between the episode of Paul and Stephen in the accusations (cf.Ac.6:13), response of the crowd to the point of death (Ac.22:22-23; 21:30-32; cf.Ac. 7:54-58) and the introductory address (Ac.22:1; cf.Ac.7:2) (273).

[109] The leaders of the Jerusalem Jewish ecclesia proposed Paul to follow the temple ritual. This shows that the Jerusalem centered Christian mission promotes the Jewish cultural traditions exclusively. However, Lukan Paul follows an in-between space of negotiation between the cultural particularism and Paul's advocacy of universalism. Samuel, "Mission Practice," 12-17.

[110] Tannehill compares the disruptive Jewish posturing in their demand for the life of Jesus and Paul (Lk.23.18, Ac.21:36; 22:22), *The Narrative Unity of Luke-Acts*, vol. II, 274.

[111] Paul defends the Jewish accusations (Ac.22:3-5, 12-15, 17, 19-20) by making use of the Jewish cultural heritage and also by calling them 'brothers' (ἀδελφοὶ Ac.23:1, 6; 28:17) which shows his affiliation to the Jewish culture. Skinner, *Locating Paul*, 114. The colonial subjugated masses retelling the story in a postcolonial context probably have its transforming effect at the dominant center.

[112] The speech highlights Paul's universal mission and its authority directly comes from the Lord. Tannehill, *The Narrative Unity of Luke-Acts*, vol. II, 277. Tannehill further explains the Jewish affiliation that Paul makes in this speech. For eg., the Jewish name for Saul (Ac.22:7,13), Annanias as a devout Jew (Ac.22:12), Jesus as the righteous one (Ac.22:14; cf.Ac.3:14; 7:52) and the commission he receives in the Jewish temple to witness to the exalted yet persecuted Lord (Ac.22:17-18) (278-279, 281).

At the same time Luke explains the rude method (beating with whips) the commander adopts to find out the truth from the imprisoned Paul (Ac.22:23-24), but with his hybrid position Paul challenges the Roman commander for flogging a Roman citizen (Ac.22:24-28; cf.Ac.16:35-39).[113] Further, he is brought before the Sanhedrin for trial (Ac.22:30) and there he disrupts the order of the high priest Ananias for his unjust treatment (to strike Paul's mouth) by pronouncing divine retribution on the dominant religious authority (Ac.23:2, 3). However, Luke explains Paul's simultaneous affiliation towards the high priest through asking excuse for the outburst which ironically disrupts the corrupt religious leadership (Ac.23:5; cf.Ex.22:28).[114] Moreover, he cleverly makes a wedge into the religious imperial authority by showing his affiliation with the Pharisaic conviction about the hope in the resurrection of the dead (Ac.23:6-10).[115] Hence, some cross the borders (scribes/ Pharisees) to enter into the liminal space to defend Paul the accused (Ac.23:9). Further in Jerusalem, he suffers life threat under the religious authorities but the Roman tribune discursively show his decisive role of saving Paul in the midst of the Jewish power lobby who try to annihilate Paul through trickery (Ac.23:12-22).[116] However, the flawed Roman justice is portrayed through the deceptive letter that Lysias sent to his superior (Ac.23:26-30) while he transfers Paul to Caesarea as a Roman prisoner.[117] According to Haenchen and Wengst, Paul's arrest by the Roman army, the intervention of the imperial authorities and his Roman citizenship, are to be virtually seen as an apologetic measure from the Jewish religious opponents.[118]

The following imprisonment and trials of Paul in Caesarea praetorium raise some basic queries that need to be answered. For what purpose Paul's witness has been shifted from the Jewish religious center in Jerusalem to the political center of Caesarea (Ac.24-26)? Are the trial scenes, apologetic to Rome/Church or do they have some other purpose? Why does Luke construct the last quarter of the narration by the court scenes where Paul stands before the Roman political figures

[113] The privileges of the Roman citizen have been highlighted through the conversation between tribune and Paul (Ac.22:27-29). Roman citizenship in the backdrop of the First century political history and literature, refer Rowe, *World Upside Down*, 65-71

[114] Paul quotes from the Torah (Ex.22:28) to underscore the divine law (honor your leaders) which explains his affiliation to the Mosaic Law.

[115] According to Tannehill, Paul's hope in the resurrection is the real issue of controversy as well as the core factor of his witness that will direct to the fulfillment of Israel's messianic kingdom (cf. Ac.24:15, 21; 26:6-8; 28:20), *The Narrative Unity of Luke-Acts*, vol. II, 285, 291.

[116] The narrator demonstrates the climatic situation of Paul's death threatened life at Jerusalem where the Roman authorities come to the rescue. Moreover, Luke discursively put the blame upon the native priestly aristocracy behind the plot to kill Paul (Ac.23:14, 15).

[117] Tannehill explains the ambivalent nature of Lysias who presents himself as the protector of the colonial interests in saving Paul, without revealing the actual truth of what he has done on him (binding and torturing), *The Narrative Unity of Luke-Acts*, vol. II, 295.

[118] Wengst, *Pax Romana*, 91-92; Haenchen, *Acts*, 650.

like Felix (Ac.24), Festus (Ac.25) and King Agrippa II (Ac.25:13-26:31) and defend his stand through the speeches? In the overall narration of Acts what does Paul's appeal to Caesar mean? Why is Paul accused as an anti-Roman revolutionary who disturbs and causes riots through out the Roman world? What is the purpose behind mimicking the imperial court scene, the legal oratory through the speeches of both the prosecutor and the defendant?

5.5.2 Paul's Trial before the Imperial Governor Felix (Ac.24:1-23)

Towards the end of the narration, Luke brings the forensic speech probably to place Paul, the representative of the marginalized *Christanio* (the people of 'the way') on a defendant platform. Luke prepares the audience to judge the accused justly by hearing the case directly from a political point of view and also by relocating Paul in the Caesarean praetorium, the administrative-judicial center of the Roman Empire.[119] In this courtroom, the Jewish high priest Ananias and the Jewish elders bring their attorney Tertullus to represent the religious power as a legal advocate to prosecute the religio-politically accused Paul. The defending party places Paul, the preacher of the gospel of Christ as the advocate for the transcultural marginalized Christian community.

The Roman commander at Jerusalem informs the procurator Felix through the official letter that conveys the fact of the case.[120] The information given through the letter points to the evil plot of some Jews to kill Paul, but the accusations are nothing serious for a 'death or imprisonment' (Ac.23:26-30).[121] The arrival of Paul at Caesarea with a large military contingent (seventy horse men, two hundred soldiers, two hundred paramilitary) shows the wise decision of a senior Roman tribune who would take the precautionary measures over a prisoner in his care from the probable political uprising on their travel to Caesarea.[122] Paul's position in Herod's praetorium (Ac.23:35) shows that Felix treated him as a political prisoner over against the Tribune's letter and bound him in chains (δεδεμένον Ac.24:27).

[119] In the first century context, Caesarea becomes the administrative center of the eastern part of the Roman Empire and Luke makes the settings of Paul's case in this imperial center.

[120] In this study, the terms 'Procurator' and 'Governor' are interchangeably used as they are the emperor's representatives in the eastern part.

[121] According to Cassidy, the letter to Felix is a political "cover" to hide the manner Lysias handles the meddled up situation in Jerusalem; *Society and Politics*, 100.

[122] Rapske, The *Book of Acts and Paul in Roman Custody*, vol. 3, 153-54.

5.5.2.1 Tertullus and his False Accusations against Paul Mockingly Impersonate the Imperial Proceedings (vv.1-9)

The legal proceedings at Caesarea impersonate the professional legal procedure and the oratory of the Roman legal court of the law.[123] The trial scene seems to be a mocking drill because it is the accusers' demand that makes the trial procedure to take place and not the decision of the procurator (v.1). The religious power center of Jerusalem (the High priest Ananias with elders) imposes its socio-religio-political dominance to accuse Paul based on their credentials.[124] They try to twist the hand of the imperial judiciary before the court by their presence and complaint.

The Roman propaganda mechanism of the law and order (*Pax Romana*) sheds its light through the judicial convention of *Captatio benevolentiae* by Tertullus, the legal advocate of the religio-political center.[125] His speech lauds the governor by the public order and his foresight as a procurator of Judea by stating that 'much peace having attained through you and reforms…to this nation by your foresight' (Πολλῆς εἰρήνης τυγχάνοντες δια σοῦ καὶ διορθωμάτων… τῷ ἔθνει τούτῳ διὰ τῆς σῆς προνοίας v.2). The foresightedness of Felix is praised by the "periodic revision of legal ordinances" probably in the light of 'the spiral of violence' in different parts of the first century Roman Empire or with regard to the religious administration.[126] Whatever may be the acclamation to this political monarch, the reference to 'much peace' (πολλῆς εἰρήνης) has been seen in the light of the imperial imposition on the resistant voices all over the eastern part of the Greco-Roman world. The elite religio-political web of power system supports the Roman imperial strategy ironically mocking the civil law and the public order

[123] Polhill, *Acts*, 479. Winter finds similarities with other first century legal proceedings of the court records; "Official Proceedings and the Forensic Speeches," 315.

[124] B. Rapske, in *The Book of Acts and Paul in Roman Custody*, vol. 3 (Grand Rapids: Wm. B. Eerdmans Publishing Company, 1994), 158. From here onwards the book title will be *BAPRC*.

[125] *Captatio benevolentiae*, is a judicial convention used in legal proceedings to flatter the administrative heads. Here in this court proceeding, the *Captatio benevolentiae* is used not only to flatter the judicial chair but also to direct his attention to the law and order situation in the province. Polhill, *Acts*, 479; B. Winter, "The Importance of the *Captatio Benevolentiae* in the Speeches of Tertullus and Paul in Acts 24:1-21", *JTS* 42 (1991), 521. Tertullus' flattery continues in v.3 by stating him as a great benefactor 'in everyway and everywhere.'

[126] Winter, "The Importance of the Captatio Benevolentiae," 517. According to Winter, the judicial competence of Felix is attested by his position of a judge to assist the Emperor Claudius in some legal matters. By highlighting the relationship between *captatio benevolentiae* and the revision of the law, he proves the historicity of the idea of providence. Reform (Διορθωμα) is discursive in its meaning- the "periodic revision of legal ordinances," with regard to the religious administration (the Temple or Sanhedrin) or with the public administration. Winter finds the probability of the "legislation promulgated by Felix," in the light of the Claudius era of legal notification against the Alexandrian Jews (517-18).

situation during these turbulent periods.[127] Josephus' reports (*JW* 2.252) about the cruel rule of procurator Felix (52-60 CE) that must be read in the light of the 'peace' and 'foresightedness' praised by Tertullus. During the governor's reign, the historically applauded administration of *Pax Romana* has been implemented by silencing the resistant minoritarian voices with the powerful military system.

Tertullus' general comments about Paul as a λοιμόν (pest, pestilence, plague) show him as a trouble maker who can criminally influence the Jewish community. By falsely representing the whole Jewish nationals on the side of the Romans, Tertullus brings three criminal charges in the *narratio* against Paul as a 'rioter among all the Jews throughout the world,' which makes Paul the disturber/ troublemaker of the civic life of the Roman imperial world (v.5b) and a 'ring leader of a Nazarene sect' (v.5a; cf.Ac.28:22).[128] Paul is also accused of profaning the Jerusalem temple by bringing Gentiles into the temple (v.6) based on a false accusation made by the Asian Jews (Ac.21:7,9). This accusation could be seen in the light of the contemporary disturbed socio-political situation which contrasts Tertullus' lauding with regard to the 'peace and reforms' (εἰρήνη and διόρθωμα) of the procurator.[129] The political charge in bringing an anti-Roman insurrection move against Paul may have had its seditious implication on the Christian movement. Moreover, this would obviously invite capital punishment for political rebellion.[130] As Sherwin-White alleges that there is a probable similarity between Claudius' accusation against the anti-Roman resistance of some Jewish nationals from Syria or Egypt in Alexandria for "stirring up a universal plague" and the political charge against Paul by Tertullus for inciting riots throughout the universe

---

[127] Judea experiences less peace during the reign of Felix (52-60 CE). More historical details are given in Chapter, 2. He used to quell the resistance movements ("rebellion of an Egyptian prophet") by the Roman military power (Ac.21:38; *JW*.2.261-63). Winter, "The Importance of the Captatio Benevolentiae," 516. The rebellious anti-Roman resistant movements sprang up due to his anti Semitic feelings and in addition he is removed from the office due to his ineptitude to settle the Jewish-local dispute in Caesarea (Ac.24:27; cf.*Ant*.20.182; *JW* 2.266-70). He is addressed as 'Governor Felix' in the letter of Claudius Lysias (Ac.23:26). The title for the higher rank, used for imperial legate of Syria (Lk.2:2). Polhill, *Acts,* 487, 475 (F.N.90).

[128] Inciting riots (κινοῦντα στάσεις Ac.24:5a) have been a serious political situation in Palestine. The attorney's sedition charges against Paul are serious "to elicit Roman "vengeance." Rowe, *World Upside Down*, 74. The marginal nature of the insignificant Christian movement is politically labeled as 'the sect of Nazarenes' (Ναζωραίων αἱρέσεως).

[129] Winter, "Official Proceedings and the Forensic Speeches," 320. Jewish nationalism and insurrection movements run to its climax. The accusation against Paul is that he stirs up sedition/ agitation (στάσις) and also disturbs the imperial system of *Pax Romana*. The criminal charges made by Tertullus are very apt according to the rhetorical handbooks. Winter, "The Importance of the *Captatio Benevolentiae,*" 518.

[130] Sherwin-White, *Roman Society and Roman law*, 52. The Jerusalem lawyer may be bringing into the court's attention the anti-Roman riot made by the Egyptian prophet.

(κινοῦντα… κατὰ τὴν οἰκουμενην).[131] Tertullus' third false charge against Paul of profaning the temple is a *confirmatio* (vv.6-8) as a proof to the earlier allegations which has serious religio-political repercussions.[132]

By linking the two legal procedures of *captatio benevolentiae* of praising the 'queller of the rebellion' and through the *narration* pointing Paul as the disturber of peace both in Diaspora and Jerusalem, Tertullus seeks justice before the tribunal.[133]

5.5.2.2 Paul's Defense Speech makes him a Strategic Essentialist (vv.10-21)

By standing alone as the defendant, Paul argues his case confidently like Jesus, standing alone in defending his case before the Jewish as well as the Roman courts.[134] Without flattering the procurator by using the *captatio benevolentiae*, Paul starts defending his case by placing evidences (παραστῆσαι) against the political accusation of creating disturbances in the imperial world in pointing out his purpose of visiting the Jerusalem temple.[135] With due respect to the court, Paul discursively challenges the legal prosecutor and the legal system to substantiate their charge with proof (v.13).[136] However, Paul's association with the temple and worship causes interference in the eyes of Jewish religious institutions.

Luke implicitly depicts Paul as the protagonist of the first century Christian community which tries to associate itself with the native religious institution, but the radical Jerusalem based Jewish leaders try to persecute them with their native essentialist ideology.[137] The hybrid identity of Paul as well as his association

---

[131] Winter, "The Importance of the *Captatio Benevolentiae*," 518. An imperial edict from Claudius against the universal Jewish resistant movement (41CE and 49 CE) is deliberately used by the legal prosecutor. Sherwin-White, *Roman Society and Roman law,* 51.

[132] In the oratory speeches, *confirmatio* is the proof brought against the allegations. Winter, "The Importance of the *Captatio Benevolentiae,*" 519. The Jews made their judgement of execution over the false accusation that Paul profaned the temple.

[133] Winter, "The Importance of the Captatio Benevolentiae," 516. Felix the Governor is ironically named as the 'queller of the rebellion' by the Roman *imperium.*

[134] As a relgio-political hybrid, Paul starts to defend his case confidently/courageously.

[135] Paul's purpose of coming to Jerusalem is to 'worship' and not to incite sedition (ἐπίστασις) anywhere in the city (v.12). His limited stay (twelve days) in Jerusalem stated as the first proof of his innocence. He uses rhetorical language to provide proof that turns the table against the attorney. His defense speech also follows the legal conventions of Quintilian iii.9.1 (*exordium, narratio, probatio/ confirmatio, refutatio and peroratio*). Winter, "The Importance of the Captatio Benevolentiae," 522, F.N. 81. According to Quintililian iv.2.4, the *narratio* should be a brief summary of facts, cited by Winter, "The Importance of the Captatio Benevolentiae," 523, F.N. 87.

[136] Winter gives the meaning of the word παραστῆσαι as 'to substantiate the argument with the proof' or 'produce in the court.' Winter, "The Importance of the Captatio Benevolentiae," 524, F.N. 90.

[137] For Samuel the Markan Jesus, "affiliates himself to the religious institutions and customs of Judaism, but at the same time he disrupts the authority of the religio-political leaders and their social space," *A Postcolonial Reading of Mark*, 123.

with the Asiatic Gentiles gives him the role of a strategic essentialist, and in that position of affiliative-antagonistic attitude to act towards the Jewish traditions similar to the first century transcultural Christian marginalized community.[138]

Paul defends (*refutatio*) and clarifies the opponents' religious accusation of being a part of a 'Nazarene sect.' His solidarity with a transcultural hybrid community in the third space (ἡ ὁδος) is in affiliation with the God of their ancestors (v.14) and their scriptures (the Law and the Prophets).[139] By placing himself in the in-between space, he probably affiliates with the tangential faith in Judaism by giving alms to the nation ('my nation' ἔθνος μου) and offering sacrifices at the temple (Ac.24:15-18). Paul argues for the structural empowerment by affiliating with that faith in the same God, which has the same scriptures and shares in the same hope of resurrection, but probably distancing simultaneously with a new vision and reconstruction in building up with the hope of the resurrected Jesus.[140] Paul strategically enters into the cultural space of Judaism with a double vision to challenge the religious center and expand the idea of resurrection as the foundational concept of Christian faith. In this process, he elaborates the resurrection of both the righteous and the unrighteous by associating with the Jewish scriptures during the post-biblical period.

In the context of the alleged desecration of the Temple by the Gentiles, Paul defends the accusation of the Jewish attorney by stating his purification purpose of coming to the Temple. By recalling the Nazirite vow (Ac.21:24) Paul takes along with him four other Jews and proves the accusation of the attorney as falsely made. By stating 'my nation (ἔθνος μου) with regard to the collection Paul brought to the poor in Jerusalem, he may have included the whole Jewish race (cf. Rom 15:26, 31).[141] Paul takes upon himself a position of discursive state of affiliation with the whole Jewish nation (v.17). In this discursive ambivalent position, Paul as a hybrid Jew most likely engages himself negotiating in the in-

[138] The native Jewish leaders are portrayed as "essentials of the native religious customs and cultural traditions." Samuel, *A Postcolonial Reading of Mark*, 126. Samuel's study on Mark shows that Jesus' discursive approach in associating and distancing both to the Jewish-Roman colonial forces make him an enemy to the religious essentialists (eg. Mk.2.6, 16; 3:6; Observance of ritual purity, Sabbath regulations, the temple destruction).

[139] Paul keeps his discursive ambivalent position of being part of the way (ἡ ὁδος), a new space that creates "vision and reconstruction" for a new community that transcends the hierarchical claims in terms of the Jewish ethnicity. Bhabha, *The Location of Culture*, 37; Samuel, *A Postcolonial Reading of Mark*, 30. By placing them in the interstitial pace, the transcultural Christian community designates them as the people of the way and transcends the exclusive Jewish ethnicity. The same designation is used in the Qumran community and Taoist tradition (*tao* –'way'). Polhill, *Acts*, 234, F.N. 10; J.A. Fitzmyer, "Jewish Christianity in Acts in Light of the Qumran Scrolls," in *Studies in Luke-Acts*, edited by L. Keck and J.L. Martyn (Nashville: Abingdon Press, 1966), 240-41.

[140] Bhabha, *The Location of Culture*, 3; Polhill, *Acts*, 483. The resurrection theme continues in the following defensive speeches.

[141] Fitzmyer, *Acts*, 736.

between space where he accommodates and distances simultaneously. This he does by bringing the Gentile Church collection to the native Jews who undergo financial struggles without looking into the Jewish cultural antagonism and their exclusive claims based on the religio-cultural traditions.[142]

Paul points out before the jury about the absence of the 'witnesses' (Asian Jews) who are the prime accusers (v.19). According to the legal procedure, the *prima facie* accusation shall be brought before the court in person for legal validity. The narrator has already informed the readers that the accusation is false as it is based on the hybridity of Paul that makes him to associate with Trophimus who is a Greek (Ac.21:29). By staying at the liminal zone and thus affiliating with the Jewish traditions and distancing from both the religio-political centers, Paul affirms his conviction of the resurrection of the dead (vv.20-21) which is the conviction of the Pharisaic Jews. In this declaration of the resurrection of the dead, he affiliates with his opponents as well as disrupting the religious center (the high priest and elders) in principle from their essential cultural nationalism (v.21; Ac.23:6; 26:8).[143] Paul in his argument proves that he breaks neither the Roman nor the Jewish law but rather affiliates and at the same distances from both.

5.5.2.3 Paul's Implicit Challenge to the *Imperium* by Passively Taking the Imprisonment (vv.22-27)

By joining with the Jewish collaborators, Felix, the Roman colonial agent skillfully adjourned the whole proceedings till the arrival of the Roman commander Lysias to Caesarea even though he had already given his acquittal report about Paul (Ac.23:29).[144] He is also well informed the things concerning the way (τὰ περὶ τῆς ὁδοῦ), but his lack of courage did not allow him to give his final acquittal to the protagonist of 'the way' because he favoured the imperial power center.[145] He

[142] I am placing Lukan Paul's negotiation practice of bringing the Gentile Church collection to the Jerusalem Jews by comparing the early Christian mission practice of the first century by Matthew and Luke of simultaneous accommodative and disruptive action "toward Jewish religio-cultural traditions." Simon Samuel, "Mission Practice: The Early Christian Perspectives," *DTJ* 4.1 (2007), 6. Paul's hybridity is known in his use of language (Greek and Aramaic), religious and cultural traditions of following the Jewish traditions. However, he strategically moves away from the exclusive zealotic nationalism, his nativity (Tarsian Jew but educated in Jerusalem) and nationality (Roman with no specificity).

[143] Paul disassociates with the essentials through his conviction of the resurrection of Jesus, who is the expected messiah. He challenges the Jewish accusation by pointing their inability in connecting the Jewish resurrection hope and the gospel that he preaches. Before the Sanhedrin in Jerusalem, Paul affirms the same conviction by which he disrupts the religious center in his earlier case (Ac.23:6-10).

[144] In Felix's two years reign one does not see any report of him sending for the commander Lysias that shows the legal laxity in postponing the case.

[145] Luke reveals the baseless foundation of the Jewish sedition charges against Paul and the Christian minorities through the statement that 'Felix having known more accurately the things about the way' (v.22). He is probably known about 'the Way' through his third Jewish wife Drusilla

seems to have feared the wrath of the collaborated religio-political power centers for selfish gains by complying with the pressure of the Jewish delegation (v.22). In the fragmented religio-political atmosphere of Caesarea, the Governor seems to have given orders to the Centurion that he may detain his freedom of movement but allow 'his friends to take care of his needs.' This portrays the favourable posture of the Roman official (v.23).[146] The Lukan readers know well about the evil plot of the native Jewish cultural nationalists as well as the unjust role played by the Governor. It would appear that they do not acquit Paul even after they are convinced of Paul's innocence. The delay in executing the investigation after knowing well of the case makes Paul's confinement under the procurator so crucial.

The imperial Governor's family life with the Jewish wife Drusilla sheds light on the religio-political web of power alliance (*Ant.*19.354-55; 20.139-44; *JW* 2.220) that persecutes the new eschatological movement as well as the curiosity of hearing from Paul 'concerning his faith in Christ Jesus' for political reasons (v.24).[147] The messiahship of Jesus who is the true judge of the righteous and the unrighteous are crucial political topics to converse with a Roman prisoner who is detained for political compulsions. Through conversation with the representatives of the colonial powers, Paul mockingly mimics the legal and imperial cultural values like 'righteousness, self-control and of the judgement' (δικαιοσύνης, ἐγκρατείας καὶ τοῦ κρίματος v.25) in the light of the eschatological reign of Jesus the Lord.[148] Luke is placing the ideological framework of the people of 'the

---

as well as learned by his curiosity as a political administrator. The second case is proved by his private conversation with Paul himself. Polhill, *Acts,* 485; Rapske, *Paul in Roman Custody,* vol. 3, 164.

[146] Rapske explains the freedom Paul experienced under the military custody that shows he is treated as an anti-colonial prisoner in chains (cf.Ac.26:29). He cautions the misleading interpretation of the phrase 'to prevent no one' (μηδένα κωλύειν) for having undue freedom as a prisoner because the actual meaning is negative and it denotes restricting access to even to his family members. Rapske, *Paul in Roman Custody,* vol. 3, 169-71. However, certain scholars argue by stating the compassionate approach of the Roman officials. Dean P. Bechard, "The Disputed Case against Paul: A Redaction Critical Analysis of Acts 21:27-22:29," *CBQ* 65/2 (2003), 250; P.W. Walaskay, *'And So We Come to Rome'. The Political Perspective of St. Luke* (Cambridge: Cambridge University Press, 1983), 201; Maddox acclaims the Roman imperial protective system in Acts, *The Purpose of Luke-Acts,* 94. Skinner points out the freedom of Paul in the Roman custody and the opportunity for proclaiming the gospel to powerful figures do not take into consideration the actual prison experience in the first century. Skinner, *Locating Paul,* 135-36.

[147] Drusilla is the youngest daughter of King Herod Agrippa I whose unholy alliance with the political power system takes the life of so many minority Christians including Apostle James (Ac.12). The diplomatic alliance of Felix with the Jews in the east is seen in the unholy marriage with the Jewess Drusilla. In the latter context, Luke brings to the reader's attention king Agrippa II, the ruler of a tetrarch who comes into the Caesarean court with Bernice II, the sister of Drusilla, wife of Felix (Ac.24:24).

[148] The ethical standards of the eschatological kingdom mimic a higher righteousness probably mimicking the legal systems of the Roman imperial government. By fulfilling the order of the

way' in a higher pedestal to mock the political propaganda of the Roman legal system. This is a possible ironic scene where the powerful Roman Governor with an equestrian rank is learning from a chained prisoner who represents the people of the marginalized.[149] Paul becomes a discursive threatening force that disturbs the Roman Empire, ruptures the imperial agenda, even though this challenge is personal and private. He ruptures the imperial throne to such an extent that it panics through the 'kingdom declaration' of righteousness and judgement for the oppressors.[150] This strategic insurgency helps the colonized to enter into the cultural center of the colonizer and disrupts "the dominance of colonial unity and authority."[151]

Paul seems to have mimicked the imperial judgement in the context of the futuristic vision envisioning the eschatological judgement of the resurrected messiah. This creates probably fear in the heart of the imperial governor about another 'Lord' (κύριος). Paul possibly ruptures the power center by staying in the in-between space in creating, recreating and re-imagining a new and just world order in the place of the chaotic present imperialist world order which is ruled by 'mobocracy' and political opportunism.[152] However, in the same mode of conversing with the ethical values of the civic life of righteousness and judgement, Luke is exposing the deceptive greedy picture of the Roman colonial administration by the mean expectation of the Roman governor for a bribe from the prisoner who is under their custody (v.26).[153] Moreover, the probability of the procurator's expectation of the bribe is based on the alms that Paul must have brought for giving to the poor in Jerusalem (V.17).

In addition to the expectation of the bribery from Paul, Luke mentions the primary motivation of Governor Felix's delay in the disposal of Paul's case as it has to do with a political favour to the Jewish center (v.27).[154] However, irrespective of this affiliation with the Jewish power center, he does not quickly handover Paul to the Jews because of the fear of having a public uproar that may shake his position. The ambivalence in Felix's dealings with Paul's case also shows

resurrected messiah, Paul is witnessing before the imperial ruler about the judging values of God's reign which is based on 'truth' and 'righteousness' (cf.Ac. 17:31-32; 13:32-34).

[149] Muñoz-Larrondo, *Living in Two Worlds*, 358, F.N. 749.

[150] In Mark's story of Jesus, the Kingdom declaration of Jesus together with the actions "disrupts the space of the native Jewish leaders." Samuel, *A Postcolonial Reading of Mark's Story,* 128.

[151] Samuel, *A Postcolonial Reading of Mark's Story,* 27.

[152] Wright, *The New Testament*, 370.

[153] Irrespective of stringent legal laws to restrict bribery in the first century, Roman Procurators were infamous for receiving it (cf.*Ant.*20.215; *JW* 2.273).

[154] Felix's political diplomacy in showing favoritism to the Jews delays Paul's case for two years. Finally, he was removed from his office, due to his mismanagement of a civil strife and his anti-Jewish bias (*Ant.*20.182; *JW* 2.266-70). Polhill, *Acts,* 487.

the typical nature of the colonial authority within the Roman administration characterized by "corruption and brutality."[155]

The political opportunism and mob governance get its priority in not giving justice to the imprisoned Paul. Instead of administering justice to the poor colonial subject and ordinary marginal like Paul, the Roman governor Felix silenced the truth for two years and left him under detention. Luke is portraying the true story of the minority groups like the newly formed transcultural community in and around the Greco-Roman world by the representative position of Paul who tries to defend his case all alone. The voice of the powerless individuals and the minority community in the empire are suppressed by the dominant voices of the coalition ruling party in Jerusalem.

5.5.3 Paul before Festus the Imperial Governor in Caesarea (Ac.25:1-12)

Paul's second trial before the newly appointed procurator of Judea comes in the context of the lack of political will from the part of the predecessor Felix. The escalated threat against Paul, the minority Roman citizen is very well depicted by Luke through this second episode. By repeating the trial scenes from the life of Paul, Luke probably teaches his readers how they need to discursively resist the political subjection and surveillance. As Paul is still under Roman custody, the Jewish adversaries plotted another plan to extradite him back to Jerusalem. The wavering position of Festus leads Paul to appeal before Caesar because he learnt that the Roman judiciary sides with the powerful and the wealthy.

5.5.3.1 The Religio-Political Unholy Alliance Duplicates the Roman Imperial Reign (vv.1-9)

Festus, the successor to Felix makes a diplomatic visit to the Judean province on the third day of his accession to his administrative office in Caesarea. The socio-historical situation reveals the need for an immediate personal supervision of his province that is in turbulent waters by the anti-Roman revolutionary popular movements.[156] This journey probably explains the need for a personal encounter with the tumultuous situation as well as to establish good relations with the religious power center in Jerusalem. The native Jewish-political authorities of Jerusalem which includes 'the high priests and the leading men' (οἱ ἀρχιερεῖς καὶ οἱ πρῶτοι cf.*Ant.*20.179) bring their charges against Paul. This shows the collaborated position between the Roman colonial authorities and the native Jewish aristocracy. This mutual unholy alliance before the forensic trial further explains the upper hand of this religious lobby that influences the

[155] Polhill, *Acts*, 487.

[156] The menace of the political separatist movement like the Sicarii was rampant during this period (*Ant.*20.185-87). Festus takes the initiative in dealing with certain impostors who "promised them deliverance and freedom from the miseries they were under" (*Ant.*20.188).

political decisions.[157] In addition to the charges formulated against Paul, they also request a favour of extradition to transfer Paul from Caesarea to Jerusalem. Luke mentions their conspiracy of ambushing Paul en route which unravels the criminal behavior of the powerful lobby and the continuing violence in the Jewish political center which would like to eliminate the deviant voices.[158] The crime of Jewish leadership is evident by the consecutive plot in eliminating Paul without a proper trial. Further in the trial case too, Luke brings the crime of the Jerusalem Jewish leaders in manipulating the Roman governors.

In Paul's case, the Roman administration joins hands with the native dominant Jewish leaders. The initial observation brings to the attention the oscillating nature of the procurator Festus who tries to keep his political position intact by collaborating with the powerful Jerusalem lobby as well as keeping his eye on his judicial position. However, Festus' strong stand in asking the Jewish leaders to come and argue their case before the imperial court in Caesarea show the Lukan portrayal of the positive side of the Roman authorities. He calls the powerful men (the high priests and the dominant leaders) from Jerusalem to come together with him. This reflects the political move of the Roman Procurator (v.5). The two dominant power centers are jointly working against the powerless victim of marginalization and political favouritism.[159] Luke is making a contrast between the powerful (δυνατοι\) of Jerusalem and the powerless Paul in Caesarea who is kept in prison for taking the task of the marginalized Christians.

As soon as Festus takes charge of the judgement seat (τοῦ βήματος cf.Ac.1:21; 18:12, 16f; 25:10, 17) in Caesarea, he calls Paul and the Jewish authorities for trial. The powerful lobby which comes down with him from Jerusalem stands around him in a threatening posture and levels many serious charges (πολλὰ καὶ βαρέα) against him without specifying any of them (v.7). But the dominant native Jewish aristocracy would not prove its charges.[160] Luke demonstrates the disorderly way of the trial in the imperial court. Paul defends his case by declaring his strategic stand by his adherence to the Jewish traditions as well as make use of the amenities of the political center (v.8; cf.Ac.24:16).

The uprightness of the Roman Procurator is questioned by his 'Jewish favouring' as "a diplomatic gift" (χαρίσασθαι) to the Jews by the single phrase

---

[157] The chief priests and the leading Jewish men (cf.Ac.28:17) together make the religio-political alliance of the present Judean mileu.

[158] Forming an evil plot by the religio-political leaders of Judea in the case of Jesus is explained in the gospel account (Lk.20:20-26). Here too, the Jerusalem Jewish leaders were behind the plot but they are not caught by the judiciary. The political conspiracy plans during the latter middle of the first century CE by the cultural nationalists (Zealots, Zicarii and different Prophetic movements) to topple the Roman imperial reign were dealt severely.

[159] Muñoz-Larrondo, *Living in Two Worlds*, 363.

[160] The imperfect usage 'they were not able to prove' (οὐκ ἴσχυου ἀποδεῖξαι) is used by Luke to refer the continuous and unsuccessful attempts from the side of the Jewish opponents.

'to be judged by me' (κριθῆναι ἐπ' ἐμου v.9) in Jerusalem.[161] Festus proves himself to be a Roman colonial opportunist and does not desire "to establish Paul's innocence for fear of the repercussions from the Jews."[162]

As a Roman judge, Festus invites the prominent men of Judea to bring charges against Paul in the judicial court at Caesarea. The Caesarean court is supposed to make the final verdict of either condemnation or acquittal against the accused who waits for justice all these years. However, the political fovouritism does not allow acquittal. Rather, Festus leans towards the political opponents of Paul. The representative of Roman political governing council and the custodian of social justice becomes a victim of cowardice and political favouritism. Ironically it is the Jewish cultural nationalists who plot against Paul in ambushing him that cause civil disturbance in the Jewish religious center of the Roman Empire.

Paul's bold negation of the religio-political accusations makes him a hero of the minority transcultural community, and Festus does not comment on Paul's defense. Is it a proof of the deception of Roman propaganda of giving the entire subjects good and just governance under the guise of judicial legal procedures, showing political favouritism by sitting on the 'bema seat' of judicial decisions? Luke mimickingly mocks the abuse of the court by not making the final verdict but rather yielding to do a favour for the dominant Jewish cultural nationalists who try to kill Paul. Luke depicts Paul as wise in his judgment over against the political judge of Roman judiciary who exercises his judicial authority for the sake of the powerful centers.

5.5.3.2 Paul's Response to Festus' Political Opportunism Ruptures the Imperial Judiciary (vv.10-12)

The response of Paul to the transferring proposal of Festus disrupts the evil plot of the Jerusalem lobby and its political network of the Roman judicial center in Caesarea. He challenges the proposal of Festus expressing his displeasure to the political opportunist and by asserting his right stand with the Jewish law. He also

[161] The relationship between the verb χαρίσασθαι and noun χαρίς in this section (Ac.24:27 and 25:3, 9) reveal the intricate political favouritism between the two religio-political centers. Skinner, *Locating Paul*, 142-43. 'To be judged by me,' probably indicates a Roman court in the Jewish center at Jerusalem. The Sanhedrin as a provincial tribunal which is a life threatening center in the narrative world of Luke-Acts (cf.Ac23:15; 4:5-21; 5:27-41; 6:12, 15; Lk.22:66-23:2). There is an alternative reading by an addition of 'ἤ' before 'ἐπ' ἐμου' that makes some sense in Festus' proposal asking for Paul's opinion in the case of venue for trial i.e., in Jerusalem or before me. Barrett, *Acts* II, 1128. A similar perplexing stage is seen in the trial case of Jesus where he stands before the Governor's tribunal. For the political favouritism refer, J.K. Chow, "Patronage in Roman Corinth," in *Paul and Empire: Religion and Power in Roman Imperial Society*, edited by R.A. Horsley (Harrisburg: Trinity, 1997), 110-13.

[162] Polhill, *Acts*, 491. Political favouritism is being condemned by Luke throughout the narration. In Peter's speech at Cornelius' house, he reiterates the same rule of impartiality because God is not the favor of persons (Ac.10:35).

discursively challenges the fact of "miscarriage of justice" from the side of the procurator who is supposed to stand for the justice of the Roman *oikoumene* as well as the right of a prisoner.[163]

Paul discursively admonishes the procurator for failing in his duty to stand for the truth and demands justice by challenging the extradition move by stating that 'before the judgement seat of Caesar I stood… I appeal to Caesar' (Επὶ τοῦ βήματος Καίσαρός έστώς εἰμι… Καὶσαρα ἐπικαλοῦμαι vv.10, 11).[164] By reiterating his appeal to the Caesar's court, Paul expresses his affiliation with the Caesar's court but ruptures the legal validity of the Roman-appointed authority in the east as invalid by denying the proposal of Festus.[165] He challenges the provincial court in Caesarea for its shortcuts in the administration of justice by distancing himself from the Roman legal process in Caesarea but affiliating with the political symbol of Roman administrative power of the Roman Caesar. His defiant statements show the disruptive prowess of Paul that has the potential to disturb the religio-political collaboration that works together to annihilate Paul. He discursively rejects the plan of a Roman judge but at the same time appeals to the Roman emperor. This seems to have ruptured the imperial agenda of muffling the colonized resistant voices and detaining the minorities for years under the guise of the diplomatic relationship between the religio-political networks centered in Jerusalem.[166]

Paul's strategic decision to appeal to Caesar reveals that he is still negotiating with the Roman political system as a representative of the minority community. By his appeal to the emperor, Paul accommodates and negotiates simultaneously with the amenities of Rome. For Luke, Paul is at negotiable stand and it is significant in

---

[163] Cassidy, *Society and Politics*, 108, E.N.32. The partial and unjust functioning of other provincial Governors (Gallio and Felix) are highlighted by Luke in his earlier reflections.

[164] According to Cassidy, Paul uses his citizenry right "only under considerable pressure," *Society and Politics*, 109. Paul challenges the move of the Procurator by saying no to any political favours. Fitzmayer, *Acts*, 745. Maddox and Conzelmann reflect Paul's appeal to Caesar as Luke's relative appreciation to the Roman imperial order. Maddox, *Purpose of Luke-Acts*, 95; Conzelmann, *Theology of St.Luke*, 144.

[165] Paul's appeal to Caesar has been discussed in its different legal provisions either *provocatio* in which the Roman citizen appeals to a jury of fellow citizens or to the emperor himself over a magistrate's verdict or *appellatio* which gives provision for a Roman citizen to appeal to a different magistrate over an unjust verdict. In Paul's case, he seems to have used a special legal provision of *provocatio* to appeal to the emperor. Sherwin-White, *Roman Society and Roman Law*, 68-70; Polhill, *Acts*, 491; Rapske, *Paul in Roman Custody*, vol. 3, 186-87. "This right was confirmed by Augustus in the *Lex Iuliade vi publica seu privita,* which protected Roman citizens through out the empire from highhanded decisions of provincial governors, summary punishment, execution, or torture." Fitzmayer, *Acts*, 746.

[166] Rapske, *Paul in Roman Custody*, vol. 3, 187. In the backdrop of the Lukan story, the reader is well aware of the political opportunism of the Roman governor Pontius Pilate who crucified the innocent, Paul's messiah due to the popular outcry (Lk.22:66-23:25).

the context of political resistance against the dominant center (Ac.25:12, 21, 25; 26:32; 28:19). Luke places Paul in the in-between space of keeping his affiliation with the Jewish faith traditions but distancing himself from the ethnic exclusive nationalistic Judaism centered in Jerusalem. He affiliates himself with the imperial Rome by making use of the amenities of his Roman citizenship and appeal for trial before the Caesar's court.

Over against the lack of self-will from the side of the Roman Procurator, Paul is bold in his appeal hoping to be acquitted from death penalty by the Roman Caesar (v.11). His public declaration seems to be another challenge to the imperial judiciary from the defiant voices to act immediately for the cause of justice. When Festus is seated at the bema seat of the judiciary by favouring the opponents of the marginalized, Paul is considered to be faithful to his call and task for justice. He is portrayed as a powerful defender for the cause of justice even if his life is being sacrificed. His heroic stand before the wavering judges of the Roman Procurator reflects the symbolic ideology of the marginalized Christian community. He proves himself to be not like the Roman colonial opportunist but an unwavering leader of the marginalized in the midst of severe political pressures.

Festus' final verdict of granting Paul's appeal to Caesar is made by consulting the administrative council for judicial discretion when he loses his own political ground based on favouritism and political opportunism (v.12).

5.5.4 Paul's Trial before King Agrippa in Caesarea (Ac.25:13-26:31)

Luke brings in King Agrippa and a grand political audience to break the impasse of finding a solution in the case of Paul in his account. Paul's defense speech before King Agrippa is the main feature of the narrative. Festus makes use of the political visit of King Agrippa as a boon in his hour of crisis because he needs to form an official report (dossier) of the legal charges against Paul who is imprisoned in Caesarea for more than two years. Luke is mimickingly mocking the typical embarrassed position of Festus who is caught between two dominant centers (political and religious).[167] Moreover, he tries to keep his official power from losing by a logical report to the emperor which will justify the Roman court.

5.5.4.1 The Conversation between Festus and Agrippa Mockingly Impersonate the Roman Judiciary (Ac.25:13-22)

The Roman political scenario of obeisance to the higher positions in their assumption to the office is to establish political benefaction relationships. In addition, their family relationships are mentioned by Luke to give the readers a clear picture of the political plan which is widely known as the 'alliance politics.' By referring to different Herodian descendants, Luke probably connects their political positions with the Roman colonial era and their political aspiration as a political strategy of being welcomed by the East. The conversation between

[167] Polhill, *Acts,* 493. The political favouritism of Festus complicates the decision making.

Festus and the Herodian King Agrippa II probably fills in the gap of his implicit authority on Jewish matters in the legal trial of Paul.

The reporting session of Festus with Agrippa mimics and mocks the whole legal case against Paul to show how truth is reported by a Roman Governor. Festus pretends himself to be the champion of Roman judiciary by commenting on the Roman standard of justice and by presenting both the cases of the defendant and the accuser face to face before the judiciary.[168] The *Aequitas romana* that praises Roman fairness in the legal procedures are mimickingly mocked by the reply of Festus that 'it was not the custom for Romans' to hand over an accused before the legal trial (v.16).[169]

Festus admits the total failure of the accusers in their inability to prove their charges against Paul except the charges based on the Jewish faith that Paul had already made in his defense before the court (v.19a). The resurrection of the dead man Jesus is another interesting charge Festus reports to King Agrippa (v.19b; cf.Ac.1:3, Lk.24:5, 23) which is not a trickery from the side of Paul but "the centerpiece of his mission and a hallmark of his defense until the end of Acts."[170]

The incompetence of Festus in dealing with the Jewish religious matters explains the flaw in the Roman judiciary of claiming themselves as the just rulers of the Roman world. Luke mocks the action of Festus by hiding in the report the whole action of injustice that he has done in favouring the Jewish lobby (Ac.25:1-12). The reader knows well that the proposal made by Festus has already taken place in Jerusalem before the Sanhedrin under the leadership of the Commander of Judea, Lysias (Ac.22:31-23:10). By informing Agrippa of the present position of the case of remitting Paul's case to Caesar, Festus may be seeking the professional help from the Judean King in framing charges against Paul (dossier) as well as "an indirect plea for sympathy."[171] He presents "himself in the role of Paul's protector" as well as a responsible Roman administrator, by maintaining the Roman jurisprudence of calling the court on time and making the court procedure to run in its course.[172] This may be an ambivalent Lukan portrayal of a positive posture of the Roman Procurator.

---

[168] Appian, *Civil War*, 3.54; Conzelmann, *Acts*, 206. The basic right of equality in legal presentation is challenged by early Christians (Justin, *Apology* 1.3; Tertullian, *Apology*, 1.3; 2.2); Polhill, *Acts*, 494.

[169] Equality for both the accused (κατηγορούμενος) and the accusers (κετηγόροι) are mentioned in the case. Fitzmayer, *Acts*, 750.

[170] Skinner, *Locating Paul*, 122, FN. 33. The resurrection of Jesus brings the Lordship of Jesus and thus challenges the Roman imperial reign of Caesar.

[171] Cassidy, *Society and Politics*, 111. The terms Σεβαστοῦ and Καίσαρα are used in reference to the Emperor of Rome.

[172] Polhill, *Acts*, 493. A similar case of twisting the truth is seen in the case of Lysias' letter to Governor Felix that 'there was no charge against him that deserved death or imprisonment' (Ac.23:29). However, he is chained like a criminal/ traitor (Ac.21:33). Cassidy, *Society and Politics*, 111.

5.5.4.2 The Setting of the Court Room Replicates the Imperial Pomp (Ac.25:23-27)

Luke depicts the setting of a professional court for Paul's final defense before the representative Jewish-Roman political rulers of the time.[173] This includes the Roman political leaders (Governor of Judea, high ranking offices and prominent Gentiles of Caesarea) and Jewish religious representative figures including the last Herodian king, Agrippa II with Bernice (v.23).[174] The pageant parade of the notables 'great pageantry' (πολλῆς φαντασίας) in the court room discursively mimics the pomp and glory of the "opportunistic and self-serving situation" of the administrative and military center at Caesarea.[175] The politically accused is brought into the court room (in chains?). This probably explains the status of the suffering Christian community, but Paul boldly defends his case before the high-ranking political leaders of the imperial east.[176] This parade also mimics the *modus operandi* of the imperial rulers' ostentatious display of who keeps their hegemonic way of life.[177] The trial of Paul before King Agrippa becomes a mockery because Paul's appeal to the Supreme Court makes the trial in lower court null and void.

Bringing the feminine presence of Bernice also mimics the flawed influence of women in Roman politics that probably challenges the Roman judicial system.[178] The accompaniment of the 'high ranking officers and the leading men of the city' mimics the dominant and elitist cultural categories that simply follow the unjust imperial rule of Rome without questioning the Roman political center. In reality the marginalized are crushed under the feet of the glittering glories of the Roman political system of the elitist propaganda. Paul, the representative of the marginalized, is brought in by the command of Festus after the procession is over.

---

[173] For Skinner, the setting of the court room does not make it as a trial account rather a time of hearing/ investigation (ἀνάκρισις, v.26) to help in getting a sensible report, *Locating Paul*, 145.

[174] The family history of Agrippa II connects him with his Jewish mother, the Hasmonean princess Mariamme and Agrippa I (Ac.12:1-11, 20-23; *JW* 2.220). Bernice II's liaison with her brother Agrippa II (*Ant.*20.145; *JW* 2.217) and later becomes the mistress of Roman Emperor Titus (Dio Cassius, *Roman History* 65.15.4; Tacitus, *Histories* 2.2) implicitly portray the private life of the Roman political leaders. Fizmayer, *Acts*, 749.

[175] Muñoz-Larrondo, *Living in Two Worlds,* 363. Skinner explains this scene as a "star-studded episode" which points to the magnificent political position of King Agrippa, *Locating Paul*, 145, 147.

[176] A similar parade is reported already in the case of Agrippa I who addresses the crowd with pomp and glory. Finally the divine punishment came upon him so that he is eaten by worms (Ac.12:19-23).

[177] Skinner, *Locating Paul,* 145.

[178] A similar case of Felix and Drusilla who is a Jewess is brought in the earlier chapter (Ac.24:24-27). This may reflect the political stage of the first century politics.

The suffering of Paul under the native Jewish leaders and the Roman colonial leaders can be equated with the suffering motif in Luke (Lk.9:43-45; 18:31-34; 22:1-23:56).[179] It is predicted by prophets like Agabus that he would be bound and killed by the Gentiles in Jerusalem (Ac.21:10-14). The bold witness of Paul challenges the prediction which is a disruptive move of the protagonist of the transcultural community under the Roman Empire.

By bringing the flawed report of Paul's arrest in Jerusalem and his appeal before the Roman court (vv.24-25) mimics the deceptive picture of the imperial Roman judiciary. The repeated reports also explain to the readers the opportunistic figure of the Roman judge and the delayed imprisonment of Paul in Roman custody. Festus generalizes the petition of a scanty essentialist cultural nationalist in representing 'the whole Jewish community' (τὸ πλῆθος τῶν Ἰουδάων) that mimic the unjust way of presenting the case against the oppressed minoritarian community (v.24).[180] There is parallelism between the statement of Festus which repeatedly declares the political innocence of Paul ('he has done nothing deserving of death' v.25) and the innocence of Jesus being declared repeatedly by Pilate the governor of Judea in the passion narratives (Lk.23:4, 14-15, 22). Here, Festus keeps his Roman position by distancing himself from his earlier favouring position with Paul's accusers in Jerusalem. He defends his official position by blaming Paul for appealing to Caesar his Lord (ku/rioj).[181]

Luke further mocks the lost position of Festus, when he contradicts himself by stating Paul's innocence yet positions his inability of framing charges to the Lord (τῷ κυρίῳ) when there is no charge against Paul (v.26a).[182] Luke also shows the opportunistic nature of Festus to keep his office with manipulation and political favouritism (v.27). Proper attention for legal framing of charges against Paul has come only in the wake of threatening of the Governor's official position.

---

[179] Tannehill, *The Narrative Unity of Luke-Acts,* vol. II, 253-274. The suffering motif in Mark is analyzed by many including Samuel in his postcolonial reading of Mark. Samuel, *A Postcolonial Reading of Mark,* 128-135. The suffering of Paul in the trial narrations of Acts is from the native Jewish leaders of Jerusalem. Implicitly he was in chains in the colonial imprisonment for more than four years. Luke is considered to use the theology of glory at this juncture but these trial passages point to the suffering of the first century Christian protagonist.

[180] This could be a misrepresentation of a report, i.e., 'the whole Jewish community' or only a Lukan hyperbole in the light of the usage of multitude (πλῆθος Ac.6:2, 5; 15:12; Lk.23:1). *Skinner, Locating Paul,* 146, F.N.97; Fitzmayer, *Acts,* 752.

[181] There are inscriptions referred to Nero as κύριος and Domitian as *dominus et dues noster.* Polhill, *Acts,* 496, F.N.148.

[182] Similarity can be seen between the imperial governors' (Pilate and Festus) for their juridical investigation and their political opportunism to safeguard the imperial interest, even after making the verdict that 'nothing worthy of death' (μηδὲν ἄξιον ... θανάτου Ac.25:25; cf.Lk.23:13). Luke probably mocks the colonial centers for the ambivalent titles used for Caesar as Lord (τῷ κυρί ῳ Ac.25:26) as well as for the client procurator as King Agrippa (Ἀγρίππα βασιλεῦ Ac.25:24, 26).

Luke portrays the ambivalent position of Festus for a third investigation from the part of Agrippa II so that he will specify the charges against the accused for the reason to appeal to the emperor, and the delay in Roman confinement.

5.5.5 Paul's Defense before King Agrippa (Ac.26:1-31)

Paul tells the story of his earlier essentialist stand as a Jewish cultural nationalist who persecuted the Christian disciples (vv.4-11; cf.Ac.22:3-5). His later stand in Judaism as a strategic essentialist who changes his exclusive essentialist position based on his commission by the risen Lord on the way to persecute the run away minority Christians in Damascus (vv.12-23; cf.Ac.22:6-11, 17-21). He substantiates the changes based on the transformation, commission and his commitment to the risen Christ (vv.6-8, 23). He explains his suffering as an obedient servant in fulfilling the 'Lord's commission' (probably mimicking Caesar, the imperial Lord) to be a witness before the entire *oikoumene* (both to the Jews and the nations). This witnessing according to Paul will lead people from darkness to light and to repentance from their sins (vv.18, 23), implicitly pointing to the corrupt practice of the two empire makers, the exclusive ethnic Jewish nationalism and the Roman colonialism. Luke brings the final declaration statement at the end of the speech that mimics the affirmation of acquittal on behalf of the Caesarean court. This account may fulfill the commission of the risen Lord (Ac.9:15; cf.Lk.21:12-15) to be a witness before governors, kings (Ac.25:23-26:22) and the children of Israel (Ac.13:5, 14-27; 14:1; 17:1, 10, 17; 18:4,19; 19:8; 23:6) and explain the persecution of the first century minority Christians. The culmination of Paul's speech before King Agrippa is the climax of his defense where he states his religious experience within Judaism and his affiliation with it as a Pharisaic Jew.

5.5.5.1 Paul's Affiliation with the Jewish Culture Disrupts the Religious Center (vv.1-5)

Paul who is a hybrid reared in a multicultural socio-religious context defends his case as a Roman prisoner in chains by logically arguing his life as a minority Christian. Luke treats Agrippa in a favourable light and highlights his discursive affiliation with the Jewish traditions as a Judean king on behalf of the imperial government.[183] This positive insight of a Roman authority must be seen in the light of Herod Agrippa I (Ac.12:20-25) and other Herodians who are antagonistic to the marginalized Christians (cf. Herod Antipas; Lk.3:19-20; 9:7-9; 13:31; 23:7-12). It is more or less a narration of his story/ a running commentary of his transformation to a political person who is in a better position with the Jewish socio-cultural systems. Besides, the speech reflects the transcultural community's witnessing to the resurrected Christ.

---

[183] Polhill, *Acts,* 499. King Agrippa is 'half Jewish' (*Ant.*14.403) from his Idumean background. Fitzmayer, *Acts,* 756.

By using the judicial convention of *Captatio benevolentiae*, Paul seems to mimic the earlier cases where Tertullus unjustly praises the then Governor (cf. Ac.22.2-4). He is brief in his opening remarks and truthful to his opinion about King Agrippa that he is confident in a fair hearing that 'you being especially well expert (μάλιστα γνώστην) with all the Jewish customs and controversies' (v.2f).[184]

By giving proper attention to the accusations brought against him by the Jews, Paul is slowly dismissing it by his strong affiliation with his ancestral Jewish faith (vv.4-6). Paul's stating of his Jewish birth, rearing, education under the strict Pharisaic Judaism and his present position of continuing as a Jew show his postcolonial position of being in the in-between space of having both affiliation and distancing simultaneously from his ancestral faith.[185] However, he probably mimics the imperial position of the Jewish cultural nationalists who persecute the reconstituted people of God by making a distinction between his present position of being in the interstitial space and his earlier position in Judaism as a persecutor.

5.5.5.2 Paul's Belief in the Resurrection of Jesus and his Experience in Christ Interrupts the Cultural Center (vv.6-8)

Faith in the resurrection of Jesus implicitly disrupts the colonial execution as well as the affiliation with the liberative power. This idea of resurrection lies in the Jewish cultural strand which is implicitly tied to apocalyptic traditions. By centering on the fulcrum of resurrection, Paul accommodates and disrupts the native Jewish and colonial discourses of Power. His affiliation with the Pharisaic sect and the common cultural traditions like the observance of the law, the messianic hope and the resurrection of the dead (cf. *JW* 2.162-63; *Ant.*18.14; Dan.12:2-3; Isa.26:19; Hos.6:2; Ezek.37:1-14), give him the space to negotiate with the native Jewish leaders. Paul considers the totality of the Jewish race with the concept of 'the twelve tribes' who place their hope in the resurrection of the dead which ruptures the present position of the diversified Judaism.[186] Luke

[184] Paul's remarks about King Agrippa may be analyzed in the context of the earlier trials where the Roman Governors are not well acquainted with the Jewish religious systems. Agrippa's multifaceted life situation of both the Jewish King as well as his Roman political position may bring a just and true evaluation of the case. Luke designates Agrippa's authority in Judaism (Ac.25:26; 26:3, 27).

[185] The terms 'my nation', 'our religion', and 'god of our father' (vv.4-6) show his affiliation with the Jewish traditions. Luke gives a positive picture of the Pharisaic sect in the Acts of the Apostles (Ac.5:34-40) and Paul claims himself still as a Pharisee (Ac.23:6). In an earlier context, Luke portrays Gamaliel, the first century Jewish teacher (*Ant.*20.213) in a positive light by defending the Jerusalem Apostles before the Sanhedrin (Ac.5:34-39). By keeping his position among one of the main religious sects of the first century Judaism, he confirms his Jewish affiliation.

[186] The twelve tribes reflect the totality of the whole Jewish race and their hope in God's promises of the resurrection. Lukan Paul disrupts the position of the native cultural essentialists for

makes resurrection of the dead a personal challenge to King Agrippa as well as a public challenge by using the plural personal pronoun (ὑμῖν v.8). By placing himself at the 'Third Space of enunciation,' Paul revisions and reconstructs the resurrection strand of Judaism where he approximates, translates, re-historicizes and reads anew that which seems to rupture the colonial authority of the Jewish cultural center.[187] His hybrid position makes him to negotiate and contest at the borders of cultural differences to disable the monolithic dominance of the Jewish cultural nationalism. He also disrupts the dominant religious center by stating his solidarity with the marginalized Christian community as a strategic essentialist.

5.5.5.3 The Transformed Paul Mockingly Imitates the Ideology of Jewish Cultural Nationalism (vv.9-19)

Paul shows his earlier position of opposing 'the name of Jesus of Nazareth' by mimicking the present Jewish cultural nationalists who are aggressive in their essentialist cultural agenda.[188] In his flash back, Paul mimics the similar persecuting activities of his past life as a member of Sanhedrin by imprisoning 'many of the saints.'[189] This mimicking is possibly used by Paul for the purpose of postcolonial mockery for disrupting the colonial dominance of the Jewish nationalists. Paul admits that his persecution habits have gone to the extent of not only being limited to Jerusalem synagogues but also to the foreign cities in pursuing the embarrassed Diaspora minoritarian Jewish Christians (v.11).[190]

Paul elaborates his shift from the dominant native Jewish ideology of cultural nationalism to the interstitial space of the transcultural Christian community through the Damascus road experience of the commission received from the risen Jesus (vv.12-18; cf.Ac.9:1-30; 22:5-21).[191] In this commission dialogue, the

their exclusive stand which divides the community.

[187] Paul seems to creatively re/construct the cultural traits of resurrection from the transcultural minoritarean perspective which would "elaborate strategies of selfhood…that initiate new signs of identity, and innovative sites of collaboration." Bhabha, *The Location of Culture,* 1-2.

[188] It is probable that the Lukan use of δεῖ as a divine mandate acquits the native Jewish cultural nationalists from their criminal actions. The gospel writer of Mark acquits the Roman colonialists by stating the divine mandatory (Mk.8.31; 9:33; 10:33) in the study of Samuel, *The Postcolonial Reading of Mark*, 134.

[189] Paul mimics the persecuted minority Christians by calling them as 'saints' (cf Ac.9:1). The persecution is by killing (ἀναιρεῖν-19 times in Acts, twice in Luke; three in the rest of NT; eg. Stephen and James) and casting vote against the Christian witnesses. Barrett, *Acts*, vol. II, 1155.

[190] Paul narrates his 'persecution' nature by putting the saints in prison, consenting vote for their death, and punishing them in their synagogues to blaspheme, probably by the name of Jesus the messiah as a curse (eg.1Cor.12:3 ἀνάθεμα Ἰσοοῦ). Luke narrates the persecution of Paul in the case of Stephen's death (Ac.6:8-8:3). Historically Christians were forced to blaspheme the name of Christ during the persecutions (Pliny the Younger, *Ep*.10.96.5; cf.1Cor.12:3). Fitzmayer, *Acts,* 758; Barrett, *Acts*, vol. II, 1156.

[191] Hedrick analyses Acts 26 as a commissioning narrative from the risen Lord. Hedrick, "Paul's Conversion/Call," 426f.

risen Lord's question in native Aramaic dialect 'Saul, Saul, why do you persecute me? (cf.Ac.9:4; 22:7)' most likely mimics the native cultural nationalism of its exclusive stand of fighting against the Lord of the marginalized. Further using a Greek proverb, 'It is hard for you to kick against the goads' in the Aramaic language, he ruptures the exclusive cultural nationalism of the Jewish leaders.[192] The climax of Paul's speech is centered on the commission from the resurrected Christ to be a 'servant witness' (v.16; cf.Ac.22:15; 23:11) of the gospel (the *imperium* of God) to bring them 'from darkness to light, and from the power of Satan to God,' forgiveness of sins to the Jews and the Nations/Gentiles alike (v.18).[193] Kim finds a parallelism in Paul's commission account between him and the commissioner, the resurrected Jesus.[194] The colonial cultural dualistic imageries (light/darkness, 'under power of sin' Satan/ God' and sanctification by works/faith) shatter the cultural categories of ideological and moral comparisons of the collaborated imperial center by probably critiquing their socio-religio-political life of deception, unjust rule, political favouritism, idolatry, and colonial domination.[195] Witnessing to the risen Lord is the first commission given to the minoritarian community (Ac.1:8) and this commission discursively disrupts the colonial (Jewish and Roman) socio-religious-cultural and political center.

[192] In the colonial context this phrase comes from the Lord of the marginalized who challenges the authority of the actions of Paul and disrupts the actions of the Jewish colonial center in Jerusalem by the action of kicking against the master's goads, will be severely punished. For Fitzmayer, the proverb talks about the futile resistant move against the "divine influence in the future conduct" and so nothing to do with Paul's past experience, *Acts,* 759.

[193] Paul's story in Acts show that he becomes a faithful 'servant witness' (Isa.42:7, 16) of the past (εἶδές) and of the future revelations (ὤφθήσομαί) to the Jews and Gentiles, Greeks and Romans, Governors and Kings. Luke seems to have discursively disrupt the apostolic centers by countering the servant title (cf.Lk.1:2- servants of the Lord- ὑπηρέται…τοῦ λόγου). The gospel of Jesus is described as the light in the midst of darkness, opening the eyes towards truth, explaining the deceptive religio-political rule in which the first century community is placed. Moreover, the reign of God may be viewed in the context of the collaborated colonial centers (Jerusalem-Roman) where the demand is to repent. E.S. Fiorenza, *Jesus and the Politics of Interpretation* (New York: Continuum, 2000), 168-74. Servant leadership is what Jesus teaches his disciples as they start mimicking the leadership style of the nations /Roman colonial leadership (Lk.22:24-27).

[194] Kim studies Paul's apostolic commission in parallel to the Jesus' maiden sermon (Lk.4:18-19) in the context of Isianic servant passages (Isa.42:7,16; 61:1-3), but only in terms of redemption from the bondage of Satan, *Christ and Caesar,* 129-131.

[195] The dualistic phraseology (darkness/light, Satan/God) is used among the Qumran writings (1QS 1:9-10; 1QM1:1; 1QS1:18,23; 2:19;1QM 1:1; 1QS 2:2,5; cf.Isa.42:16; LK.2:32). Fitzmyer, *Acts,* 760. Luke probably uses the cultural language to mockingly mimic the imperial reign that is under darkness and is in alliance with the dominant Hellenistic religious culture. The Jewish cultural imagery of sanctification received by faith in the resurrected Christ is used to mimic the Jewish sanctification of sacrificing animals in the religious center.

5.5.5.4 Witnessing Christ both to the Jews and Gentiles Discursively Disrupts the Coalition Colonial Rule (vv.20-23)

Paul reveals his absolute submission to the commission of the risen Lord and starts his ministry from Damascus (cf.Ac.9:20-25), Jerusalem (cf.Ac.9:28f) Judea and to the nations (τοῖς ἔθνεσιν) preaching the gospel of repentance (meta/noia) to both Jews and Gentiles so that they may turn to God (v.20).[196] The proof of their repentance is the good works that challenge the deceitful dominant power system.[197] This brings anger in the heart of the exclusive dominant Jewish fundamentalists who make their attempts to eliminate Paul (v.21). The whole imperial system is challenged to call for repentance from the abusive-exploited power system for their private gains, and moreover calls all of them to turn to the creator God.

Witnessing the gospel of Christ to the 'small and great alike' (v.22b) mimics the probable social hierarchy that the colonial rule creates. Paul's final reference to the gospel is related to his commission to the prophetic fulfillment (Moses and the prophets) of the suffering and the resurrection of Christ (22c-23) where he affiliates with the Jewish cultural traditions of the midrashic interpretation of the Old Testament prophecies.[198] Preaching the gospel of repentance directly to the King of Judea will of course disrupt the imperial authority because the preaching of the gospel challenges the abuse of religion and politics.

5.5.5.5 Paul's Appeal to King Agrippa Replicates the Christian Proclamation (vv.24-29)

Paul's appeal to Agrippa imitates the Christian proclamation to rupture the imperial center. Luke probably shows the emotional outburst of the judiciary against the minoritarian voices by interrupting Paul's speech. However, he boldly offers defense by showing full respect to the 'most excellent Festus' and claims that

---

[196] The gospel writers announces the arrival of the reign of God on earth so the hearers may repent from their sins and produces the fruits of repentance (Mk.1:15; Mt.4:17; Lk 4:16-19). Repentance and turning toward God are Lukan concepts used in the speeches (Ac.2:38; 3:19; 14:15; 17:30).

[197] The preaching of John the Baptist also calls for repentance of their evil ways and produces 'fruits worthy of repentance' (Lk.3:8).

[198] The suffering motif of Luke is reflected by using suffering (παθητός), a cognate of πάσχω used in Jesus' passion narrations in Luke-Acts (Ac.26:23; cf.Ac. 1:3; 3:18; 9:16; 17:3; Lk.22:15; 24:26, 46). Skinner, *Locating Paul,* 96-97. Luke probably uses the midrashic interpretation of the messianic suffering, death and resurrection. They are the core of the gospel teaching that seems to disrupt the Jewish-Roman colonial authorities of its power. The suffering of Jesus has a redemptive purpose (Lk.24:7, 17-26) as it is designed by God (Moses and prophets). The midrashic interpretation of the OT passages (Isa.35:5; 42:7; 61:1; Jer.1:8; Ezek.2:1-6 and Psalms) are used both in the Gospels and Epistles which has affiliative and disruptive dynamics.

his statements are true and reasonable.[199] This is also a dubious intervention of Festus when Paul is directly addressing Agrippa (vv.2, 7, 19) which may defy the position of the Roman judiciary.

Paul affiliates himself with the Judean king, complimenting him about his knowledge of the Jewish scriptures and the formation of the Christian community (v.26-29).[200] Paul openly challenges the dominant political centers for considering the Christian movement not as a separate religious sect, rather tracing its conformity with the Roman imperial history as well as with the Jewish religious traditions of the resurrection of the dead and its faith in a messiah as foretold by the prophets.[201] Luke shows the slippery position of King Agrippa's fear of moving away from the political center and drawing closer to the transcultural space with the convincing witness of Paul.[202] However, he fears a threat to his official position at the center if he associates with the marginalized and the persecuted Christians (v.28).[203]

The bold witnessing position of the minoritarian community is portrayed by Luke through Paul in the midst of imprisonment and suffering. He invites the entire audience who are associated with the colonial centers to become part of the position of the transcultural eschatological space, 'except for these chains.' This discourse probably brings interruption at the colonial center (v.29; cf.Ac.20:34; 28:20).[204] The forceful assertion of Paul that 'all who are listening to me today

---

199 Justin defended his position over against the accusation from Trypho (Justin, *Dialogue* 39.4). Polhill, *Acts,* 507, F.N. 175.

200 Speaking freely (Παρρησιαζόμενος) probably means the free and bold conversation between the Jewish King and Paul the Roman prisoner.

201 'It was not done in a corner,' expresses the open display of the trajectory of Christian movement narrated by Paul.

202 Paul ruptures the hypocritical position of the Judean King by asking a question of his true identity ('do you believe the prophets?') and locates him in an embarrassing stage by favouring the colonial position than moving away from the political center (vv.27, 28). In the gospel narration, the Roman leaders question the politically accused Jesus about his true identity (Lk.22:70; 23:3), but here Luke mimics the scenario of Paul asking questions to the leader of a religio-political authority.

203 In a short while (ἐν ὀλιγω) probably explains the discursive position of king Agrippa's slippery position from moving away from the colonial centers to enter into the in-between position of the colonial subject. The complexity of the meaning of 'in a short time' or 'almost' explains the embarrassed position of King Agrippa. However, the following answer given by Paul makes the second meaning possible. Fitzmyer, *Acts,* 765. It is a mockery on the part of Luke to show the slippery position of King Agrippa. There is a political note in the translation given by Bruce, i.e., "you would persuade me to play the role of a Christian," *Acts,* 496. The term Χριστιανὸν is named for the persecuted transcultural community by a religio-political Roman official in a trial context (cf.Ac.11:26; 1Pet.4:16).

204 The chain explicitly shows the colonial zeal in the hands of the prisoner. In a little and in great (ἐν ὀλίγῳ καὶ ἐν μεγάλῳ) give the probable meaning of the whole group in the oppositional side (small and great). Barrett, *Acts,* vol. II, 1172. Rapske explores honour and shame in Roman imprisonment by highlighting the imperial prison conditions and custodial severity. Rapske, *Paul in*

might become what I am,' implicitly mimics the universal concept of bringing all under the umbrella of the transcultural community of God.

5.5.5.6 The Jewish-Roman Combined Declaration of Paul's Innocence Ruptures the Colonial Center (vv.30-32)

Paul's innocence is reiterated by the presence of the whole judiciary of King Agrippa and his advisory council and their declaration to one another that 'this man is not doing anything that deserves death or imprisonment' (Ac.26:31; cf.Lk.23:14, 15).[205] The culmination to the repeated declaration of Paul's innocence by the Roman administrators that they 'could have set him free' (v.26b; cf.Ac.23:9; 23:29; 25: 18f, 25) may muddle up the deceptive picture of a 'just' Roman governance. The proposal to release Paul from the imprisonment comes from a Jewish client King Agrippa II. This verdict probably disturbs the imperial center at Caesarea who formulates a dossier to Caesar against Paul.[206] This pronouncement would make political ripples in the entire colonial world that could finally dislocate the imperial reign of Caesar. This open declaration of Paul's innocence may question the earlier position of both the Procurators (Felix and Festus) who prolonged the imprisonment of Paul for private gain or for political favoritism. Moreover, irrespective of the open declaration of Paul's innocence before the Roman court of the law, Luke pictures Paul still as a prisoner in chains (Ac.27:1; Ac.28:20). This picture in all probability interrupts the position of Roman justice.[207]

Luke shows the Jewish king in a positive light till the end of the episode by casting the entire burden of charting deceptive legal charges (dossier) against Paul

---

Roman Custody, vol. 3, 283-98. The literal meaning of the word 'chains' (δεσμά) in this context is questioned because of the gesture of defense by stretching his hands in v.1. However, the word refers to the severity of a prisoner in Roman custody. Skinner, *Locating Paul,* 148, FN. 106.

[205] Polhill, *Acts,* 510.

[206] Writing a report of innocence to the emperor naturally questions the whole judicial procedures at Caesarea.

[207] R.J. Cassidy, *Paul in Chains: Roman Imprisonment and the Letters of St.Paul* (New York: Crossroad, 2001), 37-43. The custodial setting of Roman imprisonment points out the cruelties of "arbitrary corporal punishment, torture, painful chaining, cruel guards, overcrowding, darkness, poor hygiene, malnutrition, psychological distress, humiliation and social stigmatization." Skinner, *Locating Paul,* 180. The ambiguous binding (δέω, δεσμά, and ἅλυσις) also makes the discursive position Luke portrays over against the Roman imprisonment due to the diabolic expression Luke gives in certain contexts (Ac.24:27; 26:29-31; 28:20) (181). Rapske, *Paul in Roman Custody,* vol. 3, 20-35.

over the imperial Procurator Festus.[208] However, he preserves the imperial interest by endorsing the appeal, a process created by Festus by sending Paul to Rome.[209]

5.6 Paul's Arrival to the Colonial Center Mimics the Re-colonizing Pattern of the Transcultural Community (Ac.27:1-28:31)

Luke's reports of Paul's journey to Rome on the sea voyage (Ac.27:1-44) under the watchful custody of Julius the Centurion of the Emperor's cohort seems to mimic the implicit conquering journey to Rome similar to the colonial successful patterns. In this voyage the centurion, Julius of the Augustan Cohort shows his affinity towards Paul by saving his life when they plan to kill all the prisoners from escaping at the time of ship-wreck. This kindness portrays the Lukan positive posture of the Roman establishment towards Paul at the end of the narrative. Paul takes the commanding position during this voyage as a 'saviour' of the imperial forces because of his faith in God. Moreover, the perilous situations during the sea voyage cause disturbances in the Roman commanding position.[210] Paul's Roman custody makes him to witness through warning in the midst of dangers, giving comfort and hope, providing food to the Roman prisoners including the commander, and showing compassion and healing on the island of Malta (Ac.27:1-28:15). Specially, kindness shown to Paul and the co-travelers by the chief of the Island of Malta also possibly explains the Lukan portrayal of the optimistic position of the Roman establishment.

Paul the protagonist of the eschatological community comes to the geopolitical space of Rome as a prisoner of the gospel. He implicitly signifies his discursive affiliation to the political center as a Roman citizen. Simultaneously, he disturbs the center through his proclamation of the gospel of Jesus.[211] He seems to

---

[208] Luke gives the imaginary hypothesis of the *litterae Dimissoriae* to the readers. As a diplomatic Roman official, the weakness of the case would be covered deceptively by putting the entire blame on the Jewish leadership without mentioning the political favouritism that caused Paul to appeal to Caesar. Rapske, *Paul in Roman Custody,* vol. 3. 185.

[209] Cassidy, *Society and Politics in the Acts*, 115. Festus does not want to offend the Emperor and his eastern province which is under the threat of colonial resistance by acquitting Paul. He acts like Pilate who got rid off his responsibility by passing the ball into the Emperor's court (Lk.19:1-16).

[210] Paul the prisoner affirms the authoritarian position of God (AC.27: 23-25) over the imperial position of the Roman jurisdiction by giving directions for safe voyage in the midst of natural calamity that works against them. The narration shows that Paul acts more responsibly and becomes the 'saviour' (σωθῆναι, Ac.27:31; διασωθῆναι, Ac.27:44) to the co-travelers and the co-imperial captors (Ac.27:33-37; 28:3-9; cf.20:9-12). This ironically mimics the cowardly sailors, the captain and the owner of the ship. Skinner, *Locating Paul*, 154-55. In the island of Malta, Paul's miraculous deliverance makes him to be a god (Ac.28:6) because "God himself has now ratified the verdict that Paul had done 'nothing to deserve death' (Ac.23.29; 25.25; 26.31)." Alexandru Neagoe, *The Trial of the Gospel: An Apologetic Reading of Luke's Trial Narratives* (SNTSMS 116; Cambridge University Press, 2002), 296.

[211] Skinner, *Locating Paul*, 31. Alexander compares Paul's voyaging narrations with the Greek romance for the invasions of distinctly Greek culture, "In Journeying Often," 17-49; Scott, "Luke's

march towards the center as the one who is approved by God through supernatural aid and prophetic endorsements (Ac.21:10-15; 23:11). He travels through the sea dispelling all the odds that come against him as a hero mimicking the Greek epic (Ac.27:1-28:13).[212] Luke affirms the theological position of God as the saviour of both the margins and the center. However, this does not bring out a position of triumphalism in the overall narration of Acts rather in the complex conditions of a mixture of victory and denunciation.[213]

Contrary to the Caesarean setting of Paul's political custody where the Jewish-Christian community of Jerusalem do not accompany him, Paul's arrival at the colonial center is narrated as one who comes as a dignified person, welcomed by the Roman believers.[214] Luke seems to have minimized the severity of the imprisonment conditions of Paul as he comes to the colonial center at Rome. He discursively narrates the probability of his social status including the Lukan strategy of bringing the witnessing power of the gospel that triumph over the imperial Rome.[215] Contrary to the public shame as a Roman under imprisonment with "physical and emotional anguish,"[216] Luke portrays Paul in his libertine spirit proclaiming and witnessing the gospel both to the Jews and to the Gentiles at Rome.

Geographical Horizon," 483-544.

[212] Skinner, *Locating Paul*, 72. In his journey, Paul stands in the in-between space of liminality as one approved by God affiliating and distancing from his companions both Jewish and Gentile audiences. R.L. Brawley, "Paul in Acts: Lucan Apology and Conciliation," in *Luke-Acts: New Pespectives from the Society of Biblical Literature Seminar*, edited by C.H. Talbert (New York: Crossroad, 1984), 134-43. Luke partially minimizes the blame of the Roman colonial masters by showing the divine plan behind Paul's witness in the colonial center (the use of δεῖ in Ac.19:21; 23:11; and 27:24) and through the supernatural hand behind his transportation to Rome. Charles H. Cosgrove, "The Divine ΔΕΙ in Luke-acts: Investigations into the Lukan Understanding of God's Providence," *Nov.T* 26 (1984), 179-83; Squires, *The Plan of God in Luke-Acts*, 182-85.

[213] Skinner, *Locating Paul*, 190.

[214] Skinner, *Locating Paul*, 162-63. Brothers from the Forum of Appius and Three Taverns come to meet him and explain the participatory support to the Christian sufferer (Ac.28:15). The Christian presence in Rome shows the non-colonial feature of the gospel witnessing in the early centuries.

[215] The social status and political connection make the possibility of a rented house arrest with the freedom of inviting guests. C.S. Wansink, *Chained in Christ: The Experience and Rhetoric of Paul's Imprisonments* (JSNT Sup.130; Sheffield: Sheffield Academy Press, 1996), 23, 44-46; Rapske, *Paul in Roman Custody*, vol. 3, 13-14, 33. Luke seems to have discursively hidden the dangers and misery of the Roman imprisonment of Paul to strategically avoid the Roman custodial dangers. Examples of imprisoned mortality due to physical and psychological factors are shown by Rapske, *Paul in Roman Custody*, vol. 3, 206-9.

[216] Skinner, *Locating Paul*, 84, 86; Rapske, *Paul in Roman Custody*, vol. 3, 284-98.

5.6.1 Paul makes use of the Interstitial Space of a Rented House to Proclaim and to Judge the Center

As soon as Paul reaches the imperial center, he is brought under house arrest with the imperial guard but with certain privileges (vv.16, 23, 30).[217] He is not able to see the Roman Emperor for which he travels all through because the absolute center will be no more if there is individual freedom for the subjects. Moreover, Luke diplomatically avoids mentioning the name of the present Roman Emperor at the center (eg. Claudius; Ac.11:28; 18:2; cf. Augustus and Tiberius; Ac.2:1; 3:1).

Luke presents Paul's stay in an interstitial space as a prisoner restricted to a limited space but having the freedom to entertain guests in the process of contestation and appropriation (v.20).[218] He witnesses to them 'the hope of Israel,' which is fulfilled in Jesus the messiah. He makes use of the liminal space of 'in the guest room' and 'in his own rented house' (εἰς τὴν ξενίαν, v.23; ἐν ἰδίῳ μισθώ ματι, v.30) for discourse and interaction with the prominent Jews (Ἰουδαίων πρώτους) of Rome irrespective of his constraint in chains (ἅλυσις; Ac.20:23; 26:29, 31).[219] He does not place a direct blame upon the Jewish nation for his present fate rather asserts his innocence as a prisoner. In addition, he affirms his loyalty to the nation ('of my nation' τοῦ ἔθνους μου) and his commitment to the messianic hopes (vv.17-20). The rupturous movement of the transcultural community is pointed out by the phrase, 'everywhere spoken against' (πανταχοῦ ἀντιλέγεται) as a sect (αἵρεσις) gives momentum to the Jewish leaders of the political capital to know about (v.22).[220]

Luke prepares a trial scene at the political center by setting a day where both the parties (accuser and defendant) agree to come. This event most likely

---

[217] The freedom Paul enjoys in Roman imperial custody by staying by himself (καθ ἑαυτὸν) in his own rented house (vv.16, 30) probably due to his social status or based on the procurator's report about Paul as the prisoner. He needs to find his own resources for his survival during the house arrest. Rapske, *Paul in Roman Custody,* vol. 3, 34, 209-13.

[218] According to Skinner, the translation of the word ξενία as 'guest room' is imposed because this meaning is given only at a later date, *Locating Paul,* 164. Irrespective of the difficulty in translating the phrase ἐν ἰδίῳ μισθώματι 'in his own rented house' or *"payment of rent,"* Paul pays for his stay (164-65) (Italics in the original); Rapske, *Paul in Roman Custody,* vol. 3, 178-79; Haenchen, *Acts,* 724. The financial position of Paul is a debatable one, but Lukan depiction of his social status (Ac.16:38; 22:25-27; 24:26; cf.20:33-34) makes him to pay his rent. It is also probable that Paul enjoys the benefaction from the churches which he planted. G.A. Krodel, *Acts,* ACNT (Minneapolis: Augsburg, 1986), 507; Dunn, *Acts,* 356.

[219] Rapske, *Paul in Roman Custody,* vol. 3, 181. ἅλυσις gives the meaning of handcuffing. The prominent Jews seem to be the elders of the Roman synagogue. Polhill, *Acts,* 539.

[220] The lack of knowledge about the Christian community is probably due to the political reasons of Claudius' edict of expulsion of Jews from Rome (c.49 CE; Ac.18:2) or may be due to the diplomatic reason of distancing or Lukan plan of making Paul as the founder of the Christian community in Rome. Bruce, *Acts,* 530; Polhill, *Acts,* 540; Barrett, *Acts,* vol. II, 1242.

disrupts the center in the absence of the emperor who is supposed to judge the case. By confining himself to this interstitial space of two centers (Rome and Jerusalem), Paul the Jew tries to elaborate the Jewish conviction of the hope of Israel about the Kingdom of God and bears witness to it (διαμαρτυρόμενος). The restoration of a religio-political 'kingdom' through the proclamation of Jesus as 'the Lord'/'the messiah' which authenticates through 'the law of Moses and the prophets' would disorder the wishes of both the centers (v.23; cf.Ac.26:22-23).[221] Paul's ambivalent nature is portrayed as a Roman citizen of 'two worlds,' both Jewish and Roman, most likely by accommodating and disrupting the political center simultaneously. He makes use of the citizen's privileges yet disrupts the political propaganda through his claim of the lordship of Jesus Christ and the kingdom of God. Similarly, he accommodates himself with the Jewish center at Jerusalem by continuing his identity as an apostle to both Jews and Gentiles yet disrupts the center by preaching their hope of a messiah fulfilled in the resurrected Jesus.

Skinner compares Paul's position in the Roman center as a judge in the imperial court room that seems to mimic the awaited hearing of Paul before Caesar.[222] Instead of Paul being tried under the imperial center according to the narrative progression, the climax of the story makes Paul an imperial judge who mocks the imperial centers by a scene of calling the hybrid Roman Jews to hear his verdict.[223] Paul's speeches disrupt the religious center by making a probable wedge (οἱ μέν; οἱ δέ) into the stubborn-hearted Jews who refused the gospel and the one who heeds to the reign of God (v.24). The collaborated empire cannot stand when it is divided based on the openness to the truth. The expansion of the *imperium* of God in Christ has been fulfilled by the faith of some Jews in the kingdom of God resulted in the implicit collapse of the collaborated religio-political kingdom of Caesar.

A discursive symbolic judgement is made upon the hard-hearted Jewish religious center by quoting the Isianic prophecy (Isa.6:9, 10) for their obduracy in perception by closing their heart for truth, ears and eyes to the gospel of salvation through Jesus which would disrupt the religio-political alliance of Rome.[224] By adopting the usual Jewish midrashic method of the first century Jewish context,

[221] The apologetic stand of the narration of Acts is dismissed by the lack of political defense in Rome. Neagoe, *The Trial of the Gospel*, 212.

[222] Paul implicitly pronounces the judgement at the imperial confinement and it mimics the court room. Skinner, *Locating Paul,* 166-67.

[223] The words used in the narration like testifying and dismissal (διαμαρτυρόμενος, ἀπελύοντο Ac.28.23, 25), mimic the court scene.

[224] Paul distances himself from the Jewish center in this context by stating 'your fathers' (v.25b). Marguerat analyses the second scene of hearing between Paul and the Jewish leaders at Rome as a court of reversal order. Here, in this process Paul becomes the judge and the religious center becomes the accused, on the basis of the prophetic word that comes through the Holy Spirit (vv.25-27). Daniel Marguerat, "The Enigma of the Silent Closing of Acts (28:16-31)," in *Jesus and the*

Luke makes use of the interpretive method of affiliative-disruptive dynamism of the sacred scripture. By making use of the native discourses he affirms the Jewish traditions and implicitly disrupting the Jewish center for their callousness.[225] When the 'official Judaism' rejects this 'salvation of God' (σωτήριον τοῦ θεοῦ v.28; cf.Ac.13:42-47; 18:6-8; 19:9), the message has been sent to the periphery nations who have been deceived by the collaborated web of religio-political power centers.[226]

5.6.2 Preaching and Teaching the Kingdom of God: Foreseeing a New World through Revision and Re-imagination

The unhindered bold preaching about the kingdom of God and about its Lord Jesus (κύριος Ἰησους) in the imperial center to a universal community ('all' πάντας) seems to disrupt the deceptive imperial kingdom built by the Roman Caesars with the collaboration of the Jewish leaders and the leaders of the nations.[227] The custodial and moral freedom Paul receives at the center may be the Lukan irony for mocking the imperial power center for its deceptive imprisonment of the colonial subjects who resist the colonial ideology. For Luke, the end of the story is the effective preaching and teaching of the *kingdom of God* (Ac.1:3, 6; 8:12; 14:22; 19:8; 20:25; 28:23) and the gospel of the *Lord Jesus Christ* (Ac.4:18; 5:28, 42; 18:25) by 'welcoming all' the nations in the liminal zone of the

Heritage of Israel: Luke's Narrative Claim upon Israel's Legacy, edited by D.P. Moessner and D.L. Tiede (Harrisburg: Trinity, 1999), 295-96.

[225] Luke uses a proof text from Isa.6:9-10 and authenticates the spoken word of the Holy Spirit. The discursive move of Paul in rejecting and accepting the Jewish people in his missionary endeavor and his move to the Gentiles cause difficulties of interpretation. Some suggests for complete rejection J.T. Sanders, *The Jews in Luke-Acts* (Philadelphia: Fortress Press, 1987); D. Slingerland, " 'The Jews' in the Pauline Portion of Acts,' " *JAAR* 54 (1986), 305-21. However, the internal evidences show the Jewish acceptance of the gospel in the synagogues (Ac.13:42; 17:4; 28:24; cf.14:1; 18:4; 19:10; 28:30).

[226] The Lukan statement of 'turning to the Gentiles' (Ac.13:46; 18:6; 28:28) does not imply the outright rejection of the gospel by the Jewish nation rather the discursive way of negotiating with the Jewish center even after they reject the gospel. Jose.L, *Luke's Description of the Gentile Mission in the Book of Acts*, Unpublished thesis submitted to the Senate of Serampore, 2001, 62-112. A probable transition of verses 28 to 30 is missing from the major Greek MSS. The missing link is about the wedge that Paul creates among the Jewish religious leaders, as there is a vigorous dispute among them. Fitzmyer, *Acts*, 796. Polhill uses the term 'official Judaism,' *Acts*, 545.

[227] Loveday Alexander, "Reading Luke-Acts from Back to Front," in *The Unity of Luke-Acts*, edited by Joseph Verheyden (Leuven: Leuven University Press, 1999), 419-46. The boldness of Paul's preaching is compared with the preaching of Jesus and John the Baptist in the Gospel of Luke (430-431). There is a probable progression in the universality of the proclamation started with the Romsn Jews (Ἰοδαίων πρῶτοι v.17): many (πλείονας) ordinary Jews (v.23) and Gentiles/nations (ἔθνοι v.28). Rapske, *Paul in Roman Custody*, vol. 3, 363.

colonial confinement.[228] Here the transcultural community envisages/re-imagines a project with revision and reconstruction.[229] This 'space of enunciation' where all gather without any socio-political-cultural differences, reflect the first century Christian locale.[230] The apocalyptic concept of the restoration of the kingdom (cf.Ac.1:6) gives the critical re-imaginative power of postcolonial hybridity to the marginalized community to see future prospects through a just rule of the messiah who reigns the universe with humble service.[231]

The in-between space is being built through the disruption of the center. This space creates the possibility for negotiation while rejecting the imperial colonial ideology of silencing the resistant voices. The freedom of speech at the Roman political center is something that Luke reflects at the end which would disrupt the absolute authority of the Roman imperialism. However, the explicit anti-colonial Zealotic move can be fatal at the Roman political center. The political dimension of the two terms that are used by Luke, 'boldness and without hindrance' (παρρησίας and ἀκωλύτως), in witnessing the gospel of the kingdom and the Lord Jesus Christ to the assembled audience interrupt the imperial ideology of persecuting the marginal Christians.[232] The liberative voice

---

[228] Margueret analyses the syntactical construction with imperfect, i.e., 'was welcoming' (ἀπεδέχετο v.30) expresses the continuous and ideal pattern of preaching and teaching about 'the kingdom of God and the Lord Jesus Christ (τὴν βασιλείαν τοῦ θεοῦ και τοῦ κυρίου Ἰησοῦ Χριστοῦ cf.Ac.2:42, 45-47;5:16;8:3; 12:25; 15:35;18:11; 19:8-10; 28:23), "The Enigma of the Silent Closing of Acts," 302.

[229] Italics for emphasis. By connecting the passages of Ac.10:36 and Ac.28:30-31 with the *inclusio* of Lk.2:1-14, Kim shows Lukan intention of bringing the universal Lordship to Jesus. Kim, *Christ and Caesar*, 83-84.

[230] The inclusive nature of the proclamation of the gospel is further strengthened by the Western manuscripts by adding "Jews and Greeks." Polhill, *Acts*, 546, FN. 96. The imaginative power of Luke is highlighted by Rapske's house church formula where Paul could preach and teach. Rapske, *Paul in Roman Custody*, vol. 3, 365-67; B.B. Blue, "Acts and the House Church," in The *Book of Acts in its Graeco-Roman Setting*, vol. 2, edited by D.W.J. Gill and C. Gempf (Grand Rapids: Eerdmans, 1994), 119-222. The 'third space of enunciation,' where the vision, revision, creativity, imagination, and re-imagination take place without claiming hierarchical difference and cultural purity. Bhabha, *The Location of Culture*, 37.

[231] The re-imaginative skill in countering the Roman imperial ideology is applied in Paul's letter to Galatians which gives much input for Lukan re-imagination of the kingdom of God for a just reign. Imaginative power in the apocalyptic and prophetic writings, refer W. Brueggemann, *The Prophetic Imagination* (Minneapolis: Fortress Press, 2001).

[232] The political dimension of the term boldness (παρρησίας Ac.9:27, 28; 13:46; 14:3; 18:26; 19:8; 26:26) could be analyzed by the work of Robert A. Wild, "The Warrior and the Prisoner: Some Reflections on Ephesians 6:10-20," *CBQ* 46 (1984), 290-94; Skinner, *Locating Paul*, 169; D.L. Mealand, "The Closing of Acts and Its Hellenistic Greek Vocabulary,' *NTS* 36 (1990), 583-97. The tradition of Paul's fatal death by the hand of the emperor would be an anticlimax for the purpose of his narration as well as the progress of the marginalized Christian community in resisting the colonial center.

of the gospel is given at the center by a faithful witness of Paul where there is both affiliation and resistance while being imprisoned.[233]

Paul the protagonist of the transcultural Christian community is considered to be discursive in the witnessing approach of the gospel. Thus, the exclusive apologetic reading of the earlier interpreters probably did not give sufficient attention to Paul's ambivalence towards the empire where the gospel witness is affiliative and antagonistic, accommodative and disruptive simultaneously. The open-ended conclusion of Acts mimics the postcolonial novelistic pattern of creating/rewriting a visionary history with special displacement for the marginalized similar to the persecuted Christians of the first century.[234]

5.7 Summary and Theological Reflection

The expedition of the missionaries for the purpose of witnessing to the nations bring direct conflict with the dominant Jewish constituency and Roman colonial constituency in Asia Minor, Macedonia, Greece and further to the imperial capital. The narratives deal with conflict-disruptive posturing with the diaspora Jews and the natives where Paul discursively presents the gospel in affiliation with the Greco-Roman religio-cultural-political traditions. He also addresses the socio-economic issues in these provinces that exploit the marginalized with an alternative culture of the gospel of Jesus.

The first expedition mimics the expansive dynamism of the eschatological community by disrupting the dominant Jewish discourse and the Greco-Roman religio-cultural discourse in the provinces of Galatia (Ac.13, 14). Further, the Jerusalem council is called to negotiate and carve a space for the nations by accommodating certain moral-religio-cultural obligations of Jewish traditions yet simultaneously distancing from the ideologies of Jewish ethnicity and cultural nationalism.

The second expedition of Paul brings disruption to the Jewish-Roman imperial constituency of the Greco-Roman provinces of Macedonia, Greece and Asia (Ac.16-21). In Thessalonica, Athens, Corinth and Ephesus, Luke adopts the postcolonial traits of ambivalence to the native dominant Jewish discourse and to the Greco-Roman cultural discourse. The early Christian communities have been formed in the Roman world outside Palestine in the environment of persecution which has direct encounters with the Roman officials. Women's participation (Lydia and her household, slave girl) in the new eschatological community

[233] The 'allegiance and witness' theory proposed by Cassidy seems to be a feasible alternative to the political and ecclesial apologetic proposals. However, the exclusive Christian readership and the radical subversive position of Paul make Cassidy one among the modern interpreters who find it difficult to understand the ambiguous discursive political stance of Luke. Cassidy, *Society and Politics*, 158-67.

[234] Barrus points out the mimicking of the imperial expansionism by the Lukan story of the first century Jesus' movement and its expansion through the hybrid imprisoned Paul, "The Gospel of Luke," 146-147; Ashcroft, et. al, *The Empire Writes Back*, 33.

challenges the 'temple' centered worship services where men control the whole worship affairs. Also the dehumanized nature of slave trade of the first century which mimics the imperial exploitation policy is severely condemned through the Philippian slave episode. By pragmatically affiliating and distancing to the Greco-Roman system of female patronage and benefaction, the first century Christian community transforms its meaning for creating a new community of equals.

In the Roman imperial context of Philippi, Thessalonica and Corinth the diaspora marginals receive their self-identity at 'the eschatological space of emancipation.' Paul challenges the religio-political network behind the 'pythian spirit' used by the Roman businessmen for economic exploitation by saving the poor slave girl from their clutches.

Luke gives significant space (Ac.21-28) for Paul's arrest, custodial imprisonment, political defense, and his witness to the gospel to show the political importance of Paul as a Roman prisoner. Luke brings at the end of his postcolonial resistant discourse a thematic climax to show the position of writing back to the allied religio-political forces through open discourse as a challenge to their atrocities against the Christian minorities.

Paul's physical confinement in the Caesarean-Roman detention under military guard for the minimum of four years mimics the strategy of the dominant politics to control the resistant voices as well as to maintain the diplomatic relationship with the Jerusalem centered Judaism.[235] The Roman propagandized world-wide peace, and the life-security of the marginalized 'others' are mocked by Paul's imprisonment in Caesarea and his defense speeches.

Since the beginning of the imprisonment, the framing of charges and the examination of the accused are mostly done unmindfully of the consequences in mechanical manner. The accusers conciliate the political separatists in considering Paul as a criminal and treat him as a 'political commodity' who has to be weighed on the web of power rather than as a worthy citizen of the Roman empire.[236] The long repeated trial of Paul before the Caesarean court mockingly mimics the functioning of the Roman officials because the Roman legal system is deceptively projected as a system of justice and impartiality. For avoiding a serious tumult and protest against the imperial reign, the Procurators including the Judean King Agrippa II favourably takes a devious stand. The 'saviour of the east' makes justice to be flayed in the air to keep the political positions of the Governors.

[235] Skinner, *Locating Paul,* 197. Imprisonment as the political strategy of 'official censure,' refer B.J. Malina and J.H. Neyrey, "Conflict in Luke-Acts. Labelling and Deviance Theory," in *The Social World of Luke-Acts: Models of Interpretation*, edited by J.H. Neyrey (Peabody: Hendrickson, 1991), 120. The martyrdom and persecution of Christians in the latter part of the first century refer Judith Perkins, *The Suffering Self: Pain and Narrative Representation in the Early Christian Era* (London: Routledge, 1995).

[236] The phrase 'political commodity' is used by Skinner, *Locating Paul,* 197.

The native Jewish leaders as well as the Roman colonialists wield their power over the subject masses through their unholy family alliances. Subsequently, the political and religious centers work together in collaboration with each other for getting political favours (χαρίζομαι) for their parties.

The defense speeches of Paul portray him as a bold witness to the gospel. His speeches mimic the first century oratory which is adopted by the hybrid protagonist of the subaltern that evasively challenges the imperial centers. He becomes a strategic essentialist. The theological impulses of God as the liberator of the colonized seem to have given Paul the moral empowerment to defend the gospel under Roman detention.[237] The fear in the heart of Procurator Felix and Agrippa's slippery direction towards the transcultural community explicate the disruptive power of the gospel which can transform the centers.

The apocalyptic language challenges the religio-political centers by envisioning a different new world order with justice and equality. Luke discursively upsets the center through the use of visionary and symbolic apocalyptic language and creates new avenues to the subjugated marginal.

Paul's freedom of proclamation and speech are curtailed by the Roman imprisonment which indicates the Roman strategy of silencing the resistant voices. Luke shows Paul not as a silent subaltern who does not speak but as a subaltern cultural hybrid who strategically 'speaks back' to the center with negotiation and resistance.[238] The multiple identity of the hybrid Paul is portrayed on many occasions through the 'trial scenes' by negotiations and contestations due to the "ever-shifting borders of cultural difference articulated on the field of colonial resistance."[239]

Luke describes the discursive stand of the transcultural community which affiliates with the Jewish traditions but is antagonistic to the zealotic national movement of exclusivism on the basis of racial purity. Paul plays the role of an obedient Roman citizen but expresses his counter voices whenever is necessary. He distances himself by challenging its colonial evil policies but strategically adheres to the political center at strategic points. However, he is ready to obey the voice of God which would inevitably disrupt his affiliation with Rome but stands in "outright rebellion against the imperial order [which] will be ruinous."[240] Paul's

---

[237] Skinner, *Locating Paul,* 188.

[238] Luke portrays Paul as a hybrid Hellenistic Jew who associates himself with the Jewish traditions as well as speaks for the marginalized early Christians as a Hellenistic philosopher because the pure subaltern cannot speak. Spivak, "Can the Subaltern Speak?', 271-313. On the basis of Roman citizenship, legal procedures and moral virtue, Lentz places Paul at a high social standing, *Luke's Portrait of Paul.* Neyrey analyses Paul's social status from the point of view of his association with the elites and his performance in the society, "Luke's Social Location of Paul," 251-79.

[239] Barrus, "The Gosepl of Luke," 153.

[240] Samuel, *Postcolonial Reading of Mark,* 140-41. Samuel explains the strategic distancing of the colonial marginal like Jesus who live in-between Caesar and God in the context of the entrapping question of the Jewish political lobby, 'Is it lawful to pay tax to Caesar or not?' (Mk.12:14).

strategic space with the transcultural community helps him to move away from the Jewish cultural nationalistic center but adhere to the God of Israel.

Paul's challenging call to the political center to repent from their evil ways of darkness to light, turning towards God of the universe mimics the call of the transcultural community who moves towards a strategic space of re-visioning a just and egalitarian world that would challenge the existing power centers.

The hybrid Paul makes use of the liminal space in judging the centers for their stubborn heart and calls them for repentance. The authority that Paul receives from the resurrected Jesus to be a witness to the gospel makes him to stand above the Roman custody. The liminal space of confinement both in the prison at Caesarea and at the confined house arrest in Rome makes Paul to intersect the political centers and the Jewish religious leaders of Jerusalem and Rome. He disrupts and ruptures the imperial web of colonial power based on bribery, partiality, favouritism and unjust political imperial reign. Paul's functioning in the liminal space gives him the opportunities to wield its power, based on the God-given commission to witness the gospel to both Jews and to the Nations/ Gentiles.

Luke depicts Paul ambivalently as a super hero like Caesar, who judges and saves both the imperial rulers and the subjects under him despite the danger of death hovering over his head from the religio-political colonial centers. The trust in God makes him to show valour in hostile situations and become a saviour to the colonial masters. Paul's witnessing and the power of God work together in unsettling the colonial plan of imprisonment, detention, confinement, and the imposed silencing the resistant minoritarian voices.

Chapter 6

A Postcolonial Reading of the Acts of the Apostles
Implication for Theological Education and Action in India

6.1 Introduction

A postcolonial analysis of the passages in the Acts of the Apostles reveals the magnanimity of the theological as well as the political stance of Lukan discourse in the context of Roman imperialism and Jewish cultural nationalism. The divergent viewpoints on behalf of the first century Christian ecclesia reveal discursiveness and the postcolonial ambivalence of the subjugated group that leads to the liberation praxis. Therefore, the aim of this chapter is to draw guidelines to the present day readers of the third millennium in their socio-political-cultural-economic and religiously imposed position of neocolonialism and religious fundamentalism because Postcolonial discourse has been used as a liberative tool in the context of neocolonialism and cultural nationalism.

6.2 Church and the State in the Acts of the Apostles

For many centuries, Acts of the Apostles has been traditionally seen as a missionary document with an apologetic motif for defending the first century minority Christians on behalf of the imperial Rome.[1] However, the postcolonial reading

[1] Many political encounters were read traditionally as the pro-Roman stand of the Christian Church- e.g., Claudius Lysias, Roman procurator's conviction of Paul's innocence (Ac.23.29, 24:23; 25:18-19; 26:31-32), Paul's claim of Roman citizenship (Ac.16:37-40; 22:25-29), and his political appeal to Caesar (Ac.25:11-12). According to Conzelmann, "Christian preaching does not impinge the power of the empire," *Acts*, xlvii; Powell, *What are they Sayingabout Acts?*, 72-73. The other apologetic stands are: Apologia for Paul in reconciling between the Petrine-Pauline groups- W.W. Gasque, *A History of the Interpretation of the Acts of the Apostles* (Peabody, MA: Hendrickson, 1989), 27-30; apologia *pro ecclesia* (political apologetic) (F.J. Foakes-Jackson and K. Lake, eds., *The Beginning of Christianity*, Part 1, vol. II, (London: Macmillan, [1922], 1979), 177-87; Cadbury,

accentuates the reader to see the Acts as a resistant discursive discourse of the Christian ecclesia. The minority subjects who face the socio-cultural-religious and political domination from the dominant Jewish cultural nationalists and the imperial Rome responded with postcolonial characteristics. Their resistant voices are not altogether rebellious or revolutionary in nature similar to the Jewish cultural nationalists who faced severe set backs during the Jewish-Roman war (64-70CE; 132-35CE). By staying in the in-between space, the first century Christian subalterns strategically challenged the dominant colonial structures through postcolonial concepts of hybridity, mimicry and ambivalence. They used these tools to challenge the religio-political power structures that destroy human values and dominate the marginals. Also, Luke probably chooses the term ecclesia as an assembly (Ac.11:26) to denote the growth of the minority Christians as a counter-cultural liberative movement.[2]

The study analyzes the origin and development of the transcultural Christian community's witnessing role from Jerusalem-Judea-Samaria and to the ends of the *oikoumene*. As a result, there are socio-religio-cultural marginals like the transgender Ethiopian eunuch, the Hellenist Christians, and the Gentile household of Cornelius who crossed the national, ethnic, linguistic and class-cultural borders to enter into the eschatological in-between space of the community of equals. However, the imperial state administration, collaborated with the native Jewish leaders used the military and judiciary function to discharge the Roman imperial order to curb the growth of the infant ecclesia. Moreover, Luke reports that Herod Agrippa, the Roman client King was responsible in directly persecuting the minority Christians, as he killed one of the leaders and imprisoned Peter (Ac.12:1-25). The final account of Acts shows a clear hand of the state in collaborating with the Jerusalem priests and their allies in persecuting Paul the protagonist of the infant ecclesia (Ac.21-28).

The Making of Luke-Acts, 299-316; Haenchen, *Acts*, 106, 116; Conzelmann, *Theology of Luke-Acts*, 138-40; Bruce, *Acts*, 22-25); confirmation of the Gospel (Marshall, *Acts*, 17-22); apologia *pro imperio* to his church (Walasky, *'And so we came to Rome,'* 64.); apologia *pro paulos* (Rapske, *BAPRC*, vol. 3, 313-422); the theory of political apology is questioned by Barrett for the incomprehensive theological and ecclesiastical material for a Roman official to understand, C.K. Barrett, *Luke the Historian in Recent Study* (London: Epworth, 1961), 63; *pro evangelio* (L. Alexander, 'The Acts of the Apostles as an Apologetic Text,' in M. Edwards, *Apologetics in the Roman Empire: Pagans, Jews, and Christians*, edited by M. Goodman and S. Price (Oxford: Oxford University Press, 1999), 15-43; Neagoe, *The Trial of the Gospel*, 187-218); and anti-apologetic (Cassidy, *Society and Politics*, 148-55).

[2] Roger Gaikwad, "Towards a New Ecclesia: Re-Reading the concept of 'Ecclesia' in the Bible: A Few Pointers," *Religion and Society*, vol. 52/2 (June, 2011), 14-18. The word 'ἐκκλησία' is ambiguously used in the earlier part to mean a community/communities (Ac.5:11) and generously used in the latter part of the Luke's narration of the growth of the people of God. The second usage in the mouth of Stephen (Ac. 7:37-38) refers to the oneness this word has to make with the people of God in the past, and the community of people in the wilderness/ the liminal space. The ambivalent terms used for this community are ἅγιοι, ἀδελφοί, and μαθηταί.

The portrayal of Roman state administration is depicted as corrupt, dishonest, partial and politically motivated and not siding with the poor marginals, especially the minority Christians. The collaborated business network (Ac.16:16-19) and the unholy alliance of the popular religion with the imperial cult (Ac.19:23-41) exhibit the first century exploitative political structure of the state. Luke also exposes the greedy face of the state administration in terms of bribe expected from a mere political prisoner (Ac.24:26). The political propaganda of Pax Romana deceptively offers political unity and peace to the Greco-Roman provinces. On the contrary, in affiliation to the state, the Apostles seem to have best used the travel facilities of the state like better roads and sea routes.

Luke develops a praxis-oriented postcolonial discourse for the first century Christian community on how to respond to the colonial forces by weaving together the theological as well as political strands of thought. The dichotomy between political/spiritual, theological/secular, Church/State do not find place in the postcolonial reflection on Acts. Luke narrates the origin and development of the colonial resistant communities in/around/outside Palestine that radically challenge the socio-religio-cultural-political imperial reign with a clear vision of a just world order. The early Christian community makes their interstitial space in framing a counter-cultural discursive strategy. In this process they have entered into negotiation, resistance, affiliation and antagonism, accommodation and disruption with the religio-political policies of the time.

The Indian ecclesia who has been in practice of dichotomizing between the spiritual and the secular needs to develop a postcolonial discursive strategy of negotiation and resistance. The compartmentalized attitude will never help the present day majoritarian community who suffer persecution from the hand of the religio-political centers. The outbreak of religious fundamentalism reflects the outrageous attack of the dominant native Jewish cultural nationalists against the newly formed Christian community in collaboration with the imperial state politics. Moreover, the persecuted Christian community in India being under the neocolonial reign of liberalization, globalization, privatization and religious fundamentalism, need a theology of ecclesia from the neocolonized majoritarian point of view. The Lukan portrait of the resistant discourse is the best paradigm for the present day neocolonial Indian ecclesia. The church of the new millennium must be a people's church that seeks justice and peace for the subalterns in the context of neocolonialism.[3]

At the threshold of the new millennium, the Lukan postcolonial discourse helps to construct critically a theological education and action in India in view of the socio-political-cultural issues that lead to "transformative politics of human plurality, of justice and equality, and of responsibility and solidarity, which counters

[3] Aram I, *For a Church Beyond its Walls* (Antelias, Lebanon: Armenian Catholicosate of Cilicia, 2007), 31.

and moves beyond a colonial mentality of domination."[4] Besides, Postcolonial methodology critically dismantles, de-centers and deconstructs all types of dominant relations of power in everyday life situations of humanity and liberates the colonized subjects from the power centers by envisioning a transformative humanity with equality and justice.[5]

6.2.1 The Neocolonial Capitalist-Religious Fascism Reflects Roman Imperialism and Cultural Nationalism

No one can run away from the political web of neocolonialism of the European nations through neo-liberal capitalism, privatization and globalization resulted in widespread poverty, displacement of the tribal community and the underprivileged, political favouritism, destruction of the environment, and militarism.[6] Above all, terrorism created by religious fundamentalism moves in a faster pace than the neocolonial move of the Western nations.[7] Roman imperialism and colonialism are replicated today by the new world orders of globalization through World Bank, IMF, and WTO in the present era of Indian life. European colonialism makes a division in the world history dividing the nations into first world and third world nations on the basis of economic and political power. The new international world order created by the developed nations constructs India under the colonial reign of the new world empire with free market economy. The socio-cultural and political identity is analyzed by her partnership with the developed nations and thus the Roman colonial structure is probably reincarnated in new

---

[4] Namsoon Kang, "From Colonial to Postcolonial Theological Education. Envisioning *Postcolonial* Theological Education: Dilemmas and Possibilities," in *Handbook of Theological Education in World Christianity. Theological Perspectives-Regional Surveys-Ecumenical Trends*, edited by D. Werner, et al (Bangalore: ATC, 2010), 31-32. Instruction and learning have been a part of the whole Lukan discourse of the origin and development of first century ecclesia. Hence, the implication drawn from the postcolonial reading of Acts should be incorporated in the Indian theological instruction and learning.

[5] Kang, "From Colonial to Postcolonial Theological Education," 36. Kim suggests for a 'postcolonial theological education.' Postcolonial methodology guides theological education to be an instrument in challenging the web of power centers that colonize the theological discourses. It helps to reconstruct strategically the politics of essential identity that decides the race, ethnicity class and sexuality (31-32).

[6] The economic policies of LPG in neocolonial India and corruption in the bureaucracy increase the gulf between the rich and poor on a daily basis. S. Das, "Witnessing to Christ in India: Problems and Challenges," in *Edinburgh 2010: Witnessing to Christ today in India*, edited by J. Massey and W. Longchar (Bangalore: BTESSC/SATHRI & SCEPTRE, 2011), 23-25. In neocolonial India, the benefit of the development extensively as demonstrated through the technical revolution reaches finally in the hands of the powerful industrial owners, the rich land holders and the elite professionals. Different issues of poverty due to the socio-political structure, refer F. Franco S.J, "The Structural Nature of Poverty in India," in *Poverty in India. Challenges and Responses,* edited by J. Murickan S.J (Bangalore: A Xavier Board Publication, 1988), 37-85.

[7] For religious fundamentalism, refer, Sharma, *Hidutva,* 17-175.

phases. In this postmodern world, colonialism has changed its face in other areas of Western imperialism over the impoverished nations through their economic and military power. Thereby the poorer nations get into the trap of consumerism, job opportunity to the intellectual elite and urbanization. The business class of the Indian society makes their alliance with the colonial markets creating the gap wider between the colonial rich and the colonized poor. The rural community gets into slavery and displacement in the name of development due to land acquiring programme of the multinationals for accumulation of resources.[8] Subsequently, they lose their human identity and become the subjected community in the form of debt trap. It is estimated that through the decades that approximately 40% of the Indian masses live in poverty due to the non-affordability of the essential food commodities.[9] The grave face of Indian reality shows the staggering dimensions of poverty where farmers commit suicide in Karnataka, Maharashtra and Gujarat due to the debt burden.[10] Postcolonial critics in India like Ajith Roy, Ashis Nandi and R. Guha talk of a counter-culture to neo/colonialism in neocolonial India.[11]

The Roman institutionalized imperial slavery is reincarnated into new forms of slavery in the form of human trafficking by the multinational companies which has resulted in the marginalized ending up as slaves in the global market.[12] In addition, sexual slavery continues due to poverty, hunger and debt in the neocolonial India due to the unethical promotion of neo-liberal capitalism, privatization and globalization.

The Roman imperial cult is reincarnated into many forms of the dictatorial reign of the Western nations in the socio-political sphere of the third world nations by thinking that they are 'the police' to the entire *oikoumene*. Similarly, the cultural

---

[8] Kurian explains the reason behind the poverty in India. It is as an institutional problem where the ownership of resources and market are in the hands of the elites (privatization) who controls the natural resources. Moreover the institutionalized racial discrimination added the burden on the poor masses in India. C.T. Kurian, "Why the Poor are Poor… And are Likely to Remain So," in *Journal of Social and Economic Studies*, vol. 1/2 (April-June 1984), 103-116.

[9] Magnitude of poverty is analysed by Paul de la Gueriviere, S.J, "Social Analysis," in *Poverty in India. Challenged and Responses*, edited by J. Murickan S.J (Bangalore: A Xavier Board Publication, 1988), 107-113; John Dayal, "Poverty of Ideas In Tackling Hunger and Deprivation. BPL Formula Mock the Poor," *Indian Currents*, vol. XXIII/42 (Oct. 10-16, 2011), 26-31.

[10] *India Today* reports suicide and starvation in Vidarbha villages in Maharashtra due to debt burden from the bank and money lenders. It is estimated that 29,000 farmers ended their lives between 1997-2005 in M.P and every 30 minutes a farmer ends his/her life in India. Damayanti Datta and Kiran Tare, "Rahuls Lost Widows. Suicide and Starvation haunt Vidarbha Villages," *India Today* (Nov. 7, 2011), 18-24.

[11] Ranajit Guha, *Dominance without Hegemony. History and Power in Colonial India* (Delhi. Oxford University Press, 1998), 13-20; Ajith Roy, *Monopoly Capitalism in India* (Culcutta: Naya Prokash, 1976).

[12] E.S. Fiorenza argues for freedom not in a metaphorical sense but in a social-material sense, "Slave Wo/men and Freedom: Some Methodological Reflections," in *Postcolonial Interventions. Essays in Honour of R.S. Sugirtharajah*, edited by T.B. Liew (Sheffield: Phoenix Press, 2009), 124.

nationalists' demands a totalitarian imperial reign, which imposes a majoritarian culture on others resulting in social disintegration. The resistant discourse of the first century portrayed in Acts gives hope to the suffering community in India through the new vision, re-imagination of a new kingdom and a new world order. Repentance from the 'corrupt generation' and turning to God explains the blessed experience of a new humanity at the threshold of the third millennia.

6.3 A Postcolonial Ecclesiology in the Acts of the Apostles

The Acts of the Apostles begins the story of Jesus and his followers who have constituted the Christian minority community in Jerusalem-Judea-Samaria and to the Greco-Roman colonial world. They have empowered with the eschatological Spirit to witness the crucified and the resurrected messiah to the end of the universe. The subjected community started witnessing the risen Christ and his kingdom as part of the commission of the risen Lord (Ac.1:8). They positioned themselves in-between the dominant colonial and the native nationalistic spaces and witnessed from the Jewish religious center (Ac.1-12). In their witnessing, they crossed the geographical borders of Judea, Samaria, and Syria to incorporate both the Jewish and Gentile audience. They were finally led to the Greco-Roman world (Ac.13-28) to mimic the imperial propaganda of a universal ideology to rule the end of the *oikoumene* with a counter culture. Moreover, theological education and learning was part of the life and worship of the early ecclesia (Ac.2:42-47; 4:32-37; 5:42; 16:40; 18:24-28).[13]

Luke establishes the true significance of the community of people, the 'new people of God' which is inclusive of all human races irrespective of the racial privilege claimed by the Jewish community.[14] According to Seccombe, it is a revolutionary transformation from the exclusive cultural nationalism to the wide open declaration of the acceptance of all human races in this ecclesial community of the nations.[15] In this context, Luke elaborates the theme of universality by bringing the fifteen different nationalities to witness the arrival of the eschatological Spirit on the day of Pentecost (Ac.2:9-11). He also demonstrates the full acceptance of the Ethiopian eunuch (Ac.8:26-39) into the ecclesia who is both a gentile as well as a transgender in the formation of the new people of God. Moreover, the gift of the Holy Spirit is given to unite the various communities of people (Jews, Samaritans, and Gentiles) through different phases of entry into the ecclesia (Ac.2:1-4; 8:14-

[13] In the present day Indian context too, theological education is part and parcel of most of the church's ministry. Hence, Indian churches seek the help of theological seminaries for intellectual responses to the contextual issues they face at present. John Joshva Raja, "Relevant and Effective Theological Education in the Twenty First Century India," in *Ministerial Formation*, vol. 100 (2003), 9.

[14] David P. Secombe, "The New People of God," in *Witness to the Gospel: The Theology of Acts*, edited by I.H. Marshall and D. Peterson (Grand Rapids/Cambridge: Eerdmans, 1998), 358.

[15] Seccombe, "The New People of God," 350-372.

17; 10:44-46). Similarly, at the end of Luke's narration of the development of the ecclesia, Paul welcomes 'all who come to him' to preach and to teach about the Kingdom of God and about the Lord Jesus (Ac.28:30, 31). Transcending ethnicity, gender, tribalism and nationalism creates multiculturalism, transnationalism and transculturalism resulted in new identity and an alternative envisioning in the process of crossing the borders to create the spirit of universality.

Further, the first century Christian community is not identified with strictly defined borders of a community ('the established center'), rather it is equated with 'the people of the way' (Ac.9:2; 19:9, 23; 24:14), ecclesia or a movement of the in-between space.[16] Thomas suggests the fluid nature of the ecclesia in the Indian context where the new community of believers continues to follow their cultural Indian traditions and their community.[17] In this juncture, Kappen's proposal for a 'global community of humans' to transcend the exclusive national identity is very significant in the context of the colonial nature of the hyper nationalism.[18] Accepting all human races as equal (cf.Ac.17:24-28) will inspire the *transcending magnitude of theological education and praxis* for the present day ecclesia.[19] The Western type ecclesial hierarchy that borrowed the imperial model of white collar ministry for the leaders is against the model that emanated from the first century ecclesia.[20]

---

[16] During the formative period of Christian community life, it crossed boundaries of Jewish ethnic frontiers, and chronology (imminent parousia). Wilfred, "Introduction," x-xi. Thomas criticizes the stagnant nature of the institutionalized and organized nature of the Indian Church. In postcolonial terms this refers to the religious center that needs to be challenged. Thomas, *To the Ends of the Earth,* 90.

[17] Religious conversions in the Indian context become a serious issue based on the over emphasis of the western culture and the 'number politics' that causes communal disharmony. Thomas challenges the mode of Christian baptism for the new converts in Indian context where religious conversion is seen with suspicion'; for instance, some Indian Christians (K.C. Sen and Kandi Swamy Chetty) who were Christian disciples did not take baptism, *To the Ends of the Earth (The Acts of the Apostles),* translated by T.M. Philip (Thiruvalla: CSS & BTTBPSA, 2005), 70.

[18] S. Kappen, "Hindutva-Emergent Fascism," in *Understanding Communalism,* edited by M. Muralidharan, P.K.M. Tharakan & S. Kappen (Bangalore: Visthar, 1993), 99. According to him, "while valuing our national identity, we must also recognize and respect *the right to otherness* of other peoples," because the earth unites us all (99).

[19] Felix Wilfred, "Introduction: The Art of Negotiating the Frontiers," *Concilium* 2 (1999), vii. Wilfred suggests the process of building up the spirit of universality by "negotiating the frontiers and communing across them, Christians will continuously discover new dimensions of their own faith identity," (xii). (Italics for author's emphasis).

[20] Manohar criticizes the feudalistic and hierarchical western model that has been adopted by the Indian church. M.P. Manohar, "Christian Witness in India Today. Travails of a Feudal Church in a Democratic Polity," in *Edinburgh 2010: Witnessing to Christ today in India,* edited by J. Massey and W. Longchar (Bangalore: BTESSC/SATHRI & SCEPTRE, 2011), 102. He criticizes the signs of feudalism in the titles of the office bearers of the church (Rt. Rev., Most. Rev., Archbishop) which would be similar to the 'human gods' in India who are called in similar terms like 'thiru', 'abhivandya', and 'pujya.'(109).

6.3.1 The Ecclesial Liberation Praxis of Witnessing - A Paradigm for Neocolonial India

Witnessing Christ in the poverty-stricken imperial society and multi-religious context is a significant task.[21] Luke highlights an alternative Christian *politeia* with cardinal virtues of *koinonia* and *philanthropia* in the colonial context of stratified socio-economic system by making them as community of equals of one mind and soul. The community confronts the social inequality by instructing the rich to sell off their possessions and give to the poor (Ac.2:44-45). The economic disproportion is addressed by an alternative structure with the Greco-Roman friendship tradition where they enjoyed the community life of 'one in heart and mind' and 'everything in common' (Ac.2:42-47; 4:32-37). The first century ecclesia quickly learnt the Christian ideals of mutual love and mutual responsibility by disrupting the imperial economic systems of the day in the process of sharing their possessions.[22] They enjoyed the reign of God in their midst by their sacrificial giving and *koinonia* (Ac.2:43-45; 4:34).[23]

The early ecclesial community witnessed through the proclamation of the gospel and through their community life.[24] The subjected community at Jerusalem functioned as a liberation movement which resisted the colonial move of the Jewish cultural nationalists. As the present day Indian ecclesia boasts of its two millennium tradition, she cannot act as a separatist movement/isolated community like the Qumran community of the first century. Rather, the Indian ecclesia needs to address the present day socio-economic-religious and political challenges of bankruptcy and poverty by speaking truth to the dominant religio-political centers. This can be done by educating the leaders of the ecclesia and by structuring a new social order and constructing a new humanity with the ideal principles based on God's love.[25]

---

[21] When the few rich elite accumulate great wealth through big market economy (MNC and TNC), the 40% of the Indian population suffer poverty through the after effects of the policies of Liberalization, Privitization and Globalization. Religious fundamentalism leads to "extremism, violence, destruction and death." Das, "Witnessing to Christ in India," 22-23.

[22] Thomas, *To the Ends of the Earth,* 72. Luke places service (διακονέω) to the poor and the needy to be the basic function of Christian ecclesia.

[23] The practical expression of this new counter-culture made the community to share their material blessings. Davis Peterson, "The Worship of the New Community," in *Witness to the Gospel. The Theology of Acts,* edited by I.H. Marshall and D. Peterson (Grand Rapids/Cambridge: Wm. B. Eerdmans Publishing Company, 1998), 391.

[24] Thomas, *To the Ends of the earth,* 59. Kappen advocates for 'basileic communities' united by the bond of divine love that transcends the human boundaries of caste, colour, race, culture and creed. S. Kappen, *Jesus and Culture,* vol. 1 (Delhi: ISPCK, 2002), 1-72.

[25] Thomas, *To the Ends of the earth,* 72-73. According to Thomas, Christian theologians should address the present day social issues and not to identify with Western imperialism. M.M. Thomas *The Christian Response to the Asian Revolution* (London: SCM Press, 1980), 315-16.

First century Christian witnessing must be understood in the light of political adversity. Witnessing with 'boldness and without hindrance' (Παρρησί ας and ἀκωλύτως Ac.28:31) are in concurrence with the right of a citizen to speak with forthrightness even in the light of political oppositions. Similarly, mapping an eschatological transcultural community through witnessing one soul and heart will disrupt the religious fundamental forces in India.

The Apostles and the newly formed Christian community did not participate with the exclusive cultural nationalism of the Zealots and the militancy of Sicarii. Rather, they embraced the multi-religious-lingual-cultural and national colonized subjects, envisioning hybridity as a resistive movement and simultaneously affiliating-distancing with the dominant centers.[26] By doing it, the imperial religio-political centers stands disrupted. The Christian community did not try to build an alternate kingdom by the revolutionary way of subverting the religio-political kingdoms, rather gave the humanity a new vision for bringing healing and wholeness in a discursive move of affiliation and distancing with the dominant centers.[27]

The Christian witness in India helps the underprivileged to cross the borders of their socio-religio-cultural boundaries in order to find their human identity.[28] However, this witnessing probably brings misconception of the colonized nature of Western Christianity.[29] So, one should disrupt the dominant colonial cultural legacy that the western Christianity has imposed through theological institutions by imposing their socio-cultural legacies. It is also possible to witness Christ in a manner which is not antagonistic to the other faiths, but both in affiliation to the ancestral faith of our land as well as through fight against the oppressive elements of religious fundamentalism. So, proclamation of the gospel as a means of civilizing the uncivilized by the imposition of Western culture needs to be resisted by turning towards God for holistic transformation.

---

[26] Thomas challenges the Indian Church structures that adopted the Roman imperial tradition instead of receiving the first century ecclesial tradition of following the multicultural and multilinguistic traditions. Thomas, *To the Ends of the Earth*, 61.

[27] According to Clarke and Peacock, theology is humanization for action by reflecting on reality, S. Clarke and P.V. Peacock, "Constructive Vision for Action," in *Dalits and Religious Conversion. Slippery Identities and Shrewd Identifications*, edited by S. Clarke, D. Manchala and P.V. Peacock (Oxford: University Press, 2010), 191

[28] C.P. Martin, ed., *Religious Liberty in Peril-The Indian Churches' Experience* (Nagpur: NCCI, 1999), 53.

[29] The Portuguese and British colonialism has made Indian Christian theology in a Western jacket. Indian Christian theologian, Thomas made his attempt in this regard in reconstructing a Christian theology from the Indian context. Thomas, *The Christian Response*. According to Ariarajah, gospel message is not a 'package deal' by which we bring people to a religious fold, rather it is a way of life. S.W. Ariarajah, *The Bible and People of Other Faiths* (Geneva: World Council of Churches, 1985), 56.

6.3.2 The Counter-Cultural Ecclesia in the Context of Religious Fundamentalism

The empire building political parties in India through the modern phenomenon of religious fundamentalism tries to build 'majority religious fascism' which is reminiscent to the Jewish cultural nationalism. The first century ecclesia counters the religio-political claim of the imperial ideology of exclusive nationality, culture, language by mimickingly mocking the imperial agenda. They crossed the language, gender, culture and ethnicity in witnessing to God's love, justice and peace to the entire *oikoumene* through the Kingdom proclamation. The first century ecclesia created an alternative paradigm that recreated re-imagined the deceptive political propaganda of *Pax Romana*. The language signs of the ecclesia in their counter-cultural move (eg., kingdom, Lord, Saviour, Gospel, Peace) transcended and disrupted the imperial hegemony of Caesar. A communitarian life atmosphere around the table of having food together, sharing common property, and praising God were formulated to disrupt the hegemonic Jewish-Roman collaborated imperialism.[30]

Jewish cultural nationalists however, collaborated with the first century imperial Rome and colluded in persecuting the minority Christians in the Roman colonial world (Ac.4:1-21; 7:1-8:3; 12:1-23; 16:16-40; 21-28) which caused socio-religio and political disintegration. Today the majoritarian Christian community in India is struggling to survive in hostile and intolerable circumstances of political oppression. In this context the Indian ecclesia must take a postcolonial stand of simultaneous negotiation and resistance similar to what Luke has portrayed.

In some of the Indian states (Orrisa, Gujarath and Karnataka) of the post-independent era, religious fundamental ideology of fascism has started persecuting the marginalized community.[31] Studies have been done by social activists reveal the threatening facts of cruelties against the Christian minorities over the last two decades over the issue of religious conversion among the tribal belt.[32] Since

---

[30] Kappen suggests this counter-cultural community as 'open communities,' 'beyond Churchist theology' of committed disciples, 'from customary to essential morality,' 'parting with dead symbols,' 'critical approach to all religious traditions,' 'aesthetic creation,' and 'letting Jesus appear in person.' Kappen, *Jesus and Culture,* 66-72.

[31] India has witnessed a sudden shift from a socio-political secular administrative structure to the fascist ideology propagated by the hyper cultural nationalists in different walks of life. Peter van der Veer, "Writing Violence," in *Making India Hindu: Religion, Community, and the Politics of Democracy in India*, edited by D. Ludden (New Delhi: OUP, 1996), 253-60.

[32] The fascist aggressive approach to religious minorities in India is proved by the murder of the Australian missionary Graham Staines and his two sons on 22 January 1999, the death of Catholic Priest Arul Das in Mayurganj of Orissa in the same year, the destruction of Babri Masjid at Ayodhya on December 1990 and the recent violent assault against Christians in Kandahamal in 2007. These incidents show the shift from a religious ideology to a political ideology of cultural nationalism. Sebastian Kim, *The Debate on Conversion, 1998-1999*, http://www.ocms.ac.uk/docs/sebastian%20 kim%20lecture 20040921. pdf (18th March, 2011). The term conversion has a wrong meaning

there is no evidence given by the religious fundamentalists for the conversion on the basis of force or allurement, the purpose of their attack is possibly due to the challenge made by the minority Christians against the fascist ideology of exclusive cultural hyper nationalism and their intolerance towards the 'pluralistic cultural heritage.'[33] Moreover, their colonizing process has made inroads in the educational system, the media, and administrative bureaucracy in order to capture political power.[34] In the fascist nature of cultural nationalistic ideology, the ethnocultural minorities (Dalits and Tribals) do not have any identity of their own; rather they are compelled to be a part of the homogenized majoritarian culture. The minority communities who are on the socio-cultural periphery are asked to restore the essentialist identity by joining with the religious center. In a homogenized exclusive cultural nationalism, Hindu/Christian/Muslim is a colonial concept that disturbs the integrity of the nation. The cultural nationalists in India formulate monolithic essentialist views in order to create tension in socio-cultural equilibrium so that they could divide the society.

Anti-imperialistic and anti-Semitic propaganda practiced in the Greco-Roman world, especially in the colonized Philippi (Ac.16:21) and Rome (Ac.18:2) reflect the minoritarian feelings propagated by the imperial religious fundamentalists in the Indian scenario. The socio-cultural-religio-political superiority of the business lobby in the Roman outposts of Philippi, Thessalonica, and Ephesus exhibited the imperial dominancy of the business-religious political network. Similar dominancy continues in the neocolonial era to deprive the fundamental rights of the subaltern minorities. This probably reflects quite well with the present Indian scenario where the politicians link themselves with the elite religious lobby. The minority communities are accused of being non-Indians and less patriotic.[35] In this context, witnessing Christ to people of other faiths must be undertaken with utmost care and in association and affiliation with appreciating the cultural traditions of India.

Theological education in India must integrate the contextual realities of the offshoots of colonialism-communalism, religious fundamentalism, caste system, class, gender discrimination, implicit slavery, poverty, displacement and the

---

according to the traditional understanding but for Luke conversion has socio-economic-cultural and political meaning (Ac.2:40; cf.Lk.3:1-14).

[33] Kim, *The Debate on Conversion*, 4. Sociological study shows the reason for religious conversion among the tribals. It is based on socio-cultural protest rather than religious activity. According to Kappen, "the fear that this mighty religious-secular build-up might engulf and eventually eliminate a tottering Hinduism and that it may be used to lure the backward classes into the Christian fold." S. Kappen, *Divine Challenge and Human Response* (Thiruvalla: CSS, 2001), 80.

[34] M.E. Prabakar, "Saffronization of Education," in *Religion and Society* 46/4 (Dec, 1999 & 47/1 March 2000), 36-43.

[35] Since the demolition of the Babri Masjid in 1992 religious fundamentalism has divided the country. Inter religious/faith dialogue processes have been affected by the development of cultural nationalism and fascist ideology. Prabhakar, "Saffronization of Education," 19-30.

struggles of the colonized minoritarian masses into the syllabus.[36] In the Indian context the transculturalism can prove to be a resistant move against the colonial move of the religious fascist and other hyper cultural nationalist forces.[37]

6.3.3 The Ecclesial Nature of Transcultural Hybridity and Strategic Essentialism

The postcolonial study on the Acts of the Apostles has elucidated the significance of transcultural hybridity and strategic essentialism as the way to cross the borders of caste discrimination in India. In the narrative world of the expansion of the ecclesia, Luke brings the culturally marginalized Hellenists (Ac.6:8-7:60), the Samaritans (Ac.8:5-23), the transgender Ethiopian eunuch (Ac.8:26-40), the gentile Cornelius (Ac.10:1-11:18), the migrant Asian Lydia and the Philippian slave girl (Ac.16:16-40) and the Gentiles in Lystra and Athens (Ac.14:8-18; 17:16-34) who have entered into the in-between space. The Indian churches must learn thereby how to disrupt the colonial wall of separation on the basis of ethnicity, cultural exclusivism, nationality and accept all the marginalized into the full humanity in the interstitial hybrid space. The marginalized subalterns can enter into the transcultural community of equals by crossing the colonial borders and liberate them from the injustice done by the colonial centers.

The neocolonial India where the minority civilians are bonded on socio-cultural-religious and nationalistic essential identities, could cross the borders which come to the rescue for a new beginning. "The act of border crossing opens up new locations for conversion and new alliances" to the marginalized.[38] In the resistant discourse of Acts, Philip the Hellenist, the Ethiopian eunuch, the purple dealer Lydia, the slave girl at Philippi and Cornelius the Roman centurion break the structural boundaries to cross the geographic-socio-religious-cultural, racial, ethnic, and gender borders in search of their human identity. Subsequently, they enter into the transcultural space to interpret the Jewish religious scriptures (Philip-

---

[36] J. Massey, "Preface," in *Edinburgh 2010: Witnessing to Christ today in India*, edited by J. Massey and Wati Longchar (Bangalore: BTESSC/SATHRI & SCEPTRE, 2011), vii-vii. Massey discusses the subaltern struggle, especially the Dalit and tribal resistant movements (for land, forest, Water resources, and identity) for a life with dignity and respect. He discusses the constitutional rights, reservation rights, fundamental and human rights for the Dalit Christians in the Church and Government bodies. J. Massey, "Prophetic Witness and Subaltern Struggle for Justice," in *Edinburgh 2010: Witnessing to Christ today in India*, edited by J. Massey and W. Longchar (Bangalore: BTESSC/SATHRI & SCEPTRE, 2011), 67-69.

[37] Sathianathan Clarke suggests a contextual resistance-liberation movement in India among the ethno-cultural minorities, "Hindutva, Religious and Ethnocultural Minorities, and Indian-Christian Theology," htt://www.religion-online.org/showarticle.asp?title=2449 (18 March 2011).

[38] D.N. Premnath, ed., *Border Crossings. Cross-Cultural Hermeneutics* (New York: Orbis Books, 2007), 2. M. Thomas Thangaraj finds the possibility of understanding the border crossing as a theological practice in his essay "Let God be God. Crossing Boundaries as a Theological Practice," in *Border Crossings. Cross-Cultural Hermeneutics*, edited by Premnath (New York: Orbis Books, 2007), 89-102.

Ethiopian eunuch) constructively through mutual engagement of theological dialogue.[39] The transcultural hybrid identity has much potential for convergent matrices for mimicking the religio-political center where the margins break the binary structure of antagonism and homogeneity.[40] Paul's hybridity as a Hellenist Jew with Roman citizenship who is multilingual, multicultural and transnational help him to speak back to the centers and ruptures the colonial power structures (Ac.22:1-21; 24:10-21; 25:8-11).

The Ethiopian eunuch's story portrays the racial and gender discrimination that excludes people from fully participating in the imperial socio-cultural and religious life. The caste system in India is similar to the racial discrimination in other parts of the world where birth determines the societal status. The religious center decides the caste on the basis of birth and subsequently fixes the socio-cultural-religious status of the population. The subaltern struggles continue in India searching for a just society "with fuller redeemed dignity and recovered humanity."[41] Moreover, the caste discrimination continues in Christian ecclesia through the caste oriented theology.[42] Discrimination based on caste engulfs all aspects of life from birth to death and even after death to the burial ground. The minority Indian Dalit Christians who have crossed the borders of caste Hinduism for human dignity and respect, for socio-economic-cultural and religious status in the society, are not spared from the evil practices of the caste system within the Church.[43] There are other discriminative issues like the physically challenged, the

---

[39] Rajkumar, *Dalit Theology*, 171. "Dalit theology through its ideology of binarism has the potential to replicate-in-reverse the attitudes it seeks to subvert," (171).

[40] Rajkumar, Clarke and Abraham criticize the bipolar methodology of Dalit theology due to the societal intersection between different communities in socio-economic and political matters. Rajkumar, *Dalit Theology*, 169-171; S. Clarke, "Dalit Religion as a Resourceful Symbolic Domain: A Critical Review of Theories of Religion and a Constructive Proposition to Glean the Richness of Dalit Subjectivity," in *Religion and Society* 49, 2 /3 (June-September 2004), 38; K.C. Abraham, "Dalit Theology: Some Tasks Ahead," *BTF* XXIX, 1/2 (March-June 1997), 36-47.

[41] J. Massey, *Dalits-Issues and Concerns. India 50 Years of Independence. 1947-97. Status, Growth and Development* (Delhi: BR Publishing, 1998), 195.

[42] Peniel R. Rajkumar, *Dalit Theology and Dalit Liberation: Problems, Paradigms and Possibilities* (Surrey: Ashgate, 2010), 36. Dalit theologians challenge the traditional Indian Christian theologies. Gnanavaram, "'Dalit Theology,' 59-83; P. Mohan Larbeer, "Deconstruction of Academic Theology and Reconstruction of Dalit Theology," In the Twenty First Century India," in *Ministerial Formation*, vol. 100 (2003), 17-24.

[43] The present Indian Churches where the two-thirds are Dalit Christians experience caste discrimination inside the church at the time of celebrating the Eucharist, making separate queues, having different leadership, churches, seating places, burial grounds and denied the reservation benefits for Dalit Christians. Rajkumar, *Dalit Theology*, 21. The Indian Church needs to take up the steps of affiliative-distancing mode of resistance towards building up a transcultural community of equals with a hybrid culture of new identity.

HIV cases, the sex workers and the transgender that must be addressed by the Indian ecclesia through theological education and liberation praxis.[44]

The minority subaltern community must use strategic essentialism as a powerful tool over against cultural essentialism which is eternally defined as a monolithic conception.[45] The hybrids in the Lukan narration make use of this theoretical concept of strategic essentialism as a powerful political tool in their consensual-conflictual and affiliative-distancing mode of resistance. In the Indian context too, by claiming strategically the essential characteristics of a Dalit or a transgender would probably help to re/construct a necessary liberation praxology in the process of colonial resistance.[46]

6.3.4 The Eschatological Hope for Ecclesia

During the context of imperial persecutions against the minority Christians since the period of Emperor Caligula, Nero and Domitian, apocalyptic discourses gave endurance and resistance to the persecuted subalterns. Acknowledging the sovereignty of God in the context of imperial powers gave reason for endurance and power for resistance. The visions and imagination of the 'God-world-human' configurations had a greater role to play in constructing a theology of hope in a postcolonial context.[47] Moreover, the ecclesial theology of hope in the interstitial space transforms and disrupts the colonial structure.[48] The creative and transforming power of imagination is very well a part of the religious cultural formation from time immemorial. In that vein, the eschatological spirit empowered and enabled the Christian community to envision/dream for the future (Ac.1:8; 2:17-21), at the in-between space.

The hope of a futuristic judgement and a just reign of God disrupted the political centers in the process of apocalyptic imagination (Ac.24:24-26). As

[44] Longchar exposes the wider context of theological education as it challenges and give opportunities (cf.Acts 8 deals with gender and racial issue). Wati Longchar, "Engaging Theological Education in Context: Focus on Persons with Disabilities," in *Ministerial Formation*, vol. 109 (July 2007), 28-33.

[45] The postcolonial theoretical concept of strategic essentialism is already discussed in the methodology chapter. For further details, on 'Strategic Essentialism,' Laura Arnold, http://academic.reed.edu/english/courses/English558/Week2.html (18 March 2011).

[46] Franklyn J. Balasundaram, Dalit Struggle and its Implication for Theological Education," in *BTF*, vol. 29/3-4 (1997), 69-91.

[47] According to Clarke, "theology has an emerging vision for the trajectories of possible worlds pledged to human beings by God." S. Clarke, "Dalit Theology. An Introduction and Interpretive Theological Exposition," in *Dalit Theology in the Twenty-first Century. Discordant Voices, Discerning Pathways*, edited by S. Clarke, D. Manchala and P.V. Peacock (Oxford: University Press, 2010), 28; L.R. Bryant, *Imagination and the Life of the Spirit* (California: Scholars Press, 1981), 3.

[48] The term 'Theology of Hope' was coined by J. Moltman for the "promise of a declaration which announces the coming of a reality that does not yet exist." J. Moltmann, *The Theology of Hope: On the Ground and the Implications of a Christian Eschatology*, translated by J.W. Leitch (New York: Harper & Row, 1965), 103.

a strategic essentialist, Paul approximates the idea of resurrection which offers future hope to the persecuted ecclesia. By staying in the interstitial space between the colonial center and the periphery, Paul envisions an eschatological kingdom for transformation with ethical values of justice and righteousness. He makes use of *this liminal space* to accommodate and disrupt the religio-political leaders in revisioning and reconstructing their perceptions of power. This may be a feasible platform to discuss and evaluate the socio-political scenario with the consent of both the centers. In this process the colonizer will be able to expose the deceptive picture of the colonial regime to the general public. It may be possible that the moral empowerment can transform the political centers like the fear created in the heart of Governor Felix. Moreover, the slippery position of King Agrippa is shown by Luke who feared for moving towards the transcultural space (Ac.26:28, 29) of Christian ecclesia.

Luke proposes a *re-imaginative* world order through his discursive creative counter discourses by analyzing the historical reality of Roman imperialism. In this process, a critical re-imagination is possible for a new world order. The Lukan Paul re/visions, re/constructs, re/imagines at the interstitial space for viable opportunities for a just world order under the eschatological reign of God. He calls both the religious and political centers for a call to repentance and turning towards the God of the universe who liberates humanity from their colonized situation. Luke narrates the freedom of speech to Paul at the imperial center and the emperor moves away from the center in view of the colonial disruption where the transcultural hybrids have freedom to express freely their futuristic hopes. Similarly, Paul makes use of the privilege of a Roman citizen to have access to the political center but potentially abrogates the political center by preaching the reign of God with justice and righteousness. This explains the consensual-conflictual nature of postcolonial ecclesiology.

Envisioning a new age of the reign of God, resurrection of the dead, and judgement of the unrighteous would potentially challenge the existing imperial ideology (Ac.8:12; 28:31; 24:21, 25; 28:30-31). Paul's imprisonment in the Caesarean praetorium and in Rome (Ac.24-26; 28:16-31) explicitly plays a greater role in the life of the deceptively and wrongly persecuted Christians in India. Challenging the colonial centers might bring suffering for the marginalized similar to the first century Christian ecclesia who suffered persecution and imprisonment. Some experienced death (Stephen and James) during the persecution. The socio-cultural and political similarities make this narration potential for responses. When the colonial centers take the support of the hyper cultural nationalists to torture the subaltern Christian ecclesia, the modus operandi can be the method Paul adopted during his imprisonment (Ac.22-28).

6.4 Ecclesia Amidst Imperial Threat of Imprisonment and Martyrdom

Luke narrates the arrest, detention, persecution and martyrdom of the minority Christian community, especially their leaders by the religio-political allied forces in the eastern part of the Roman colonies. The beheading of James the Apostle with a sword by Herod Agrippa explains the political threat of the Roman Empire against the marginalized Christians (Ac.12:1-25). The newly formed subjected minority movement probably became a threat to the Jerusalem-Roman centers as they set their feet outside Palestine started disrupting the imperial world (Ac.13-28). They brought false charges against the Apostles which were defended by them (Ac.5:29-32; 7:2-53; 16:19-39; 17:6; 18: 12-13; 19: 25-27; 22:1-21; 24:10-21; 25:10-11; 26:1-23). Luke gives special significance for Paul's Roman imprisonment and custody in Caesarea and Rome on the basis of falsely accused civil disturbance in the Roman world. The Roman imperial powers used to persecute them as a repressive strategy. In addition, Luke displays the political favoritism of the Roman imperial governors (Felix and Festus) and their partisan spirit with the Jewish religious center at Jerusalem (Ac.24:27; 25:1-2, 9). This became a threat to the first century minority community. The political web that mutually benefits from the collaboration of the Jewish cultural nationalists and the Roman imperial structure mirrors the Indian context where the hyper cultural nationalists get the support of the political power system.

The prolonged imperial custody of the Apostles and their trials in the provincial capitals of Judea and Rome bring probable guidelines for educating the minority Christians how to respond to the religious imprisonment in India. The accommodative and disruptive strategy towards the colonial powers explains the way the Indian ecclesia may respond to the present day imperial reign. In India, the minority Christians go through trials under the neocolonial reign of the fundamental forces who strategically plan for a genocide and ethnic cleansing.[49] The subjected community must use the postcolonial characteristics of hybridity, mimicry and ambivalence in strategic essentialist terms as the situation demands.

As a political strategy of appropriation, the present day ecclesia must confront the legal prosecution with charges of proof (cf.Ac.24:13). She ought to appropriate the amenities of the political privileges of her country in defending her Christian minority position and witnesses in the midst of imprisonment and suffering. She must strategically make use of her Indian citizenry privileges to appeal her case before the political centers (cf.Ac.25:6-12). Paul the protagonist is a perfect example for the minority Christian ecclesia who did not waver from

[49] The cultural nationalist movement and its influence in Indian politics, refer, Jyothirmaya Sharma, *Terrifying Vision: M.S.Gowalkar, the RSS and India* (Viking: Penguin Books, 2007), 67-88; for the formation of hyper Nationalism, the convergence of the cultural nationalist strategies, refer, Christopher Jeffrelot, *Hindu Nationalist Movement and Indian Politics, 1925-1990* (Viking: Penguin Books, 1996), 11-75, 314-446.

his Christian minority position in the midst of persecution and suffering from the religio-political centers. Rather, he defended his faith and became a bold witness to the gospel before both the Jewish religious institutions and Roman legal administrators. He speaks back to the colonial centers through a consensual-conflictual, accommodative and disruptive dynamism on socio-religious-cultural and political issues.

6.4.1 Ecclesia Strategically Affirms the Constitutional and Minority Human Religious Rights

The strategic portrayal of Paul's Roman identity as a citizen in Philippi disrupts the colonial master's authority over the marginalized Apostles (Ac.16:37-39; 22:25-29; cf.Ac.25:11, 12). Over against the essentialist ideology of cultural nationalism, Paul strategically uses the essentialist religio-political characteristics of affiliating himself with his own people, nation, with faith in the same God, scriptures and hope in the resurrection (Ac.26:1-29). However, he preaches the kingdom of God and teaches about the crucified-resurrected Jesus at the Roman colonial center as a resistant move against the colonial ideology of the Roman propaganda that Caesar is the Lord of the universe (Ac.28:30-31). He strategically appropriates the Roman citizenship (Ac.24-25) in disrupting the Roman legal powers by questioning the flogging of an ordinary subject and pronounces judgement upon the High Priest Ananias (Ac.22:22-29).

The difficulties faced by the first century ecclesia in a colonial empire are well portrayed by Luke through his resistant discursive discourse and how they resolved the majority religio-political oppression. Luke also portrays the positive side of the religio-political authorities and the favours he received from them. Further, a parallel colonial structure can be viewed in the Indian context where the minority community has been targeted by the majority fascist ideology of cultural nationalism. In the socialist-secular-democratic India, secular values have been upheld through the constitution in the context of a pluralistic society for the wellbeing of all citizens of the nation, where every citizen has the freedom of conscience and profession to practice and propagate one's own religion.[50] The Indian Constitution has given special consideration for the religio-cultural minorities by giving them minority rights.[51] Moreover there is no preferential

[50] Religious freedom to the minorities is given under the Indian Constitution (article 25, 26, 27 and 28) which gives 'freedom to profess, practice and propagate religion.' A secular nation envisioned by M.K. Gandhi and Jawaharlal Nehru had equality for all religions, not creating colonial centers of religious fundamentalism. A detailed discussion on the topic on Constitution and religious freedom, refer M.T. Cherian, *Hindutva Agenda and Minority Rights: A Christian Response* (Bangalore: Centre for Contemporary Christianity, 2007), 143-54.

[51] For a discussion on minority rights (Articles 15, 1, 25 and 26) refer, Cherian, *Hindutva Agenda and Minority Rights*, 268-82. The Universal declaration of Human Rights by UNO (Article 18) also supports the freedom of religion in his/her belief, practice, teaching, and proclamation (290).

status to any religion for developing a colonial center that would cause danger to the safety of the minorities. When these rights have been denied, the responsible citizen has the privilege of approaching the judiciary to fight for his/her rights similar to Paul's appeal to Caesar over against the partisan position shown by governor Festus.

History proves that exclusive politicization of religion (eg. Afganistan, Lybia, Iraq, Iran, Yemen, Nepal) is a threat to the stability of a nation-state due to the polarization it creates among the citizens. Witnessing of one's faith is constitutionally a right to freedom of conscience. However, in the present Indian context, the freedom to witness is questioned by the hyper cultural nationalists through their imperialistic- mobocratic ideology. Thus, it is advisable for theological education to integrate the study of human, constitutional, minority and religious rights in the curriculum.

6.4.2 The Ecclesial Dialogical Discourse with the People of Multi Religio-Political Faiths

The universal nature of the gospel urges the Christian ecclesia to call for a dialogue and witness with the people of other religio-political faiths. Paul's model of witnessing the gospel at the political center in an interstitial space provides guidance for a call for dialogue with the other religio-cultural and political communities on a common platform. This must be done with a liberative spirit working for justice and peace for the entire *oikoumene* irrespective of Paul's imprisonment at the colonial center. Luke narrates the idea of an inter-religio-political dialogue by narrating Paul's trial speeches where he strategically appropriates the Jewish concept of resurrection, the forthcoming judgement, justice from OT passages and faith in prophets (Ac.24-26).[52] There is no aggression in the dialogic process rather Paul acts with humility and solidarity with a call to witness to 'all' in love.[53] In this process, Paul affirms his religio-political (Jewish-Roman) loyalty and reassures the messianic hopes (Ac.28:17-20). He affiliates with the Jewish essentialist understanding of a messianic kingdom fulfilled in Jesus, yet disassociates with the exclusive cultural nationalism and the dominant political empire. Interestingly, the dialogical process starts in the beginning of Acts narration between the resurrected Jesus and his disciples about the nature of Kingdom of God (Ac.1:6-8).[54] One of the subject matters in this dialogue is about the counter-cultural 'Gospel of the Kingdom,' the topic Apostles discussed in

---

[52] D.H. Milling, "Dialogue with People of other Faiths: Some NT Evidences," in *Bible Speaks Today: Essays in Honour of Gnana Robinson* edited by D.J. Muthunayagom (Delhi: ISPCK, 2000), 267-68.

[53] M.N. Behera, "Edinburgh-2010 Mission Conference Issues and Challenges for Mission and Unity," in *Edinburgh 2010: Witnessing to Christ Today in India,* edited by J. Massey and W. Longchar (Bangalore: BTESSC/SATHRI & SCEPTRE, 2011), 119.

[54] Thomas, *To the Ends of the Earth*, 48.

Jerusalem (religious center), Philip discussed in Samaria (Hellenist center), Paul discussed in the eastern part and finally at Rome (political center).

We must take Lukan postcolonial discourse as a model for the 21st century theological education and action in India where witnessing includes not only proclamation, but also dialogue, "worship, inculturation, contextualization," with an aim to build a harmonious community.[55] Here, the emphasis is on multi-religious community dialogue which brings the 'colonized subjects' to wholeness and healing to a *cosmo-theo-anthropic* relationship.[56] In the pluralistic religio-cultural Indian context of multiple colonial centers which exercise power through religion, theological education in India should facilitate for an inter/multi-religious community dialogue by bringing them on to an interstitial space where the centers will come with openness for affiliation and rejection.[57] The task is to "bring a socio-political lens" to identify the power structures that are deep-rooted in the religio-political web for power that marginalizes twenty percent of the population.[58] Moreover, the 'dialogue ministry' would bring both caste Hindus and Dalits on the same platform to listen to the socio-political life issues of one another with justice concerns.[59] In this context, the purpose of the dialogue between gospel-culture-politics, and the agenda must be mutual transformation and liberation from the oppressive structures in the

---

[55] W. Longchar, "Introduction," *Edinburgh 2010: Witnessing to Christ Today in India,* edited by J. Massey and W. Longchar (Bangalore: BTESSC/SATHRI & SCEPTRE, 2011), 10. In the dialogue process, one can include intra/er faith dialogue with other religions (9). Martey proposes some feasible advantages for inter-religious dialogue in the African context- for peaceful and harmonious co-existance of humanity, enriching mutually in search for the truth, and mission of the Christian church. Emmanuel Martey, "Interfaith Dialogue in Theological Education. The Challenge of Inter-Religious Dialogue and Praxis for African Theological Education," in *Handbook of Theological Education in World Christianity: Theological Perspectives-Regional Surveys-Ecumenical Trends,* edited by D. Werner, et al (Bangalore: ATC, 2010), 207-08.

[56] P.J. Rajkumar, "Public Ministry and Communication Studies in Theological Education. Public Ministry, Ethical Formation and Theological Education in India-An Exploration of Key Issues," in *Handbook of Theological Education in World Christianity. Theological Perspectives-Regional Surveys-Ecumenical Trends,* edited by D. Werner, et al (Bangalore: ATC, 2010), 166.

[57] Religion plays a significant role in both aggravating a conflict between communities as well as "channeling them into the service of justice, love, peace, and reconciliation." S. Wesley Ariarajah, *Axis of Peace. Christian Faith in Times of Violence and War* (Geneva: WCC Publications, 2004), 69-78. Ariarajah suggests a certain theology to focus in the context of religious pluralism and interfaith dialogue-'a theocentric approach,' 'rethinking Christology,' and 'God's reign and God's mission.' Ariarajah, *The Bible and People of Other Faiths,* 64-69.

[58] Rajkumar, "Public Ministry and Communication," 166; S. Wesley Ariarajah, *Not Without My Neighbour. Issues in Interfaith Relations* (Geneva: WCC Publications, 1999), 79. According to Ariarajah, religious pluralism is "not as a threatening reality to be rejected, but as a reality to come to terms with." Ariarajah, *The Bible and the People of Other Faiths,* 63.

[59] Ariarajah, *Not Without My Neighbour,* 82-83.

form of healing and reconciliation.[60] In a multi-religious context of India, Wilfred suggests three important tasks to do Christian mission-taking the universality of the Spirit's overwhelming grace (cf. Lk.13:32) which leads to a dialogical encounter with other faiths with love, and respectful relationships to promote and cultivate a culture of tolerance and peace with other faiths, and explore the ways of understanding the mystical in nature.[61] In the process of dialogue, there is a possibility for a change/transformation of faith which emerges from/for/by the people and for the benefit of the *oikoumene*. In lieu of the emerging fascist hyper cultural nationalism, a pedagogical device of 'dialogical social context,' must be a counter cultural strategy to tackle the emergent religious fascism.[62] Moreover, a relevant theological education and praxis is possible through the dialogue where the ecclesia 'welcomes all' for a new world order with justice and righteousness.

---

[60] Ariarajah finds "the close relationship between religion, culture and identity," and he proposes three ways to attain peace, 'justice: the condition for peace', 'reconciliation: the way to peace,' and 'nonviolence: the hope for peace," *Axis of Peace*, 67, 114-137. Ariarajah calls for a number of goals in dialogue- 'listening and learning together,' 'community development,' 'way of humility,' 'caring and sharing,' and 'witnessing.' S. Wesley Ariarajah, *Dialogue* (C.C.A Concern Series 1; Singapore: Christian Conference of Asia, 1980), 15-23.

[61] F. Wilfred, " A New way of Being Christians to Encounter Neighbours of Other Faiths," in *Unanswered Questions*, edited by C. Theobald and Dietmar Mieth (London: SCM Press, 1999/1), 40-44. For Ariarajah, dialogue is a way of love, the way of the cross, self giving message of the gospel. Ariarajah, *The Bible and the People of Other Faiths*, 30-38. Samartha who pioneered the process of religious dialogue suggests a theology of love for our neighbors that will help us to listen with friendliness, a theology of support in all the human struggles with hope for transformation, and theology of impregnability for readiness to change. S. Samartha, *Courage for Dialogue. Ecumenical Issues in Inter-Religious Relationships* (Geneva: WCC, 1981), 58-62.

[62] Kappen, "Hindutva-Emergent Fascism," 98. Kappen suggests a dialogical community in creating a pluralistic nationalism where the multireligious community develops a bond irrespective of caste, color or creed. The members come together to share their life experiences and generate communitarian life with shared symbols.

Conclusion

Luke's narration of the origin and growth of the early Christian ecclesia in the Greco-Roman Jewish cultural world is so complex that biblical interpreters have taken centuries to identify the interstitial space from where the colonized subject community discursively responded to the religio-political imperial reign. The postcolonial reading of the Acts of the Apostles tries to identify the first century transcultural community's ambivalence towards Roman imperialism and the Jewish cultural nationalism, though the traditional interpreters have understood it in either pro or anti-colonial form. The multiple stances taken by Luke enabled one to think the possibility of the incongruous responses used by the colonized subject community.

Luke presumably, the protagonist of the infant ecclesia, resists to two colonial forces-the Jewish cultural nationalism and Roman imperialism. The colonial situation was encountered by the hybrid, mimetic, ambivalent posturing.

The discursive world of Acts is uncovered by critically analyzing Roman imperialism and its colonialism in the East that become the framework for the birth and growth of the Christian ecclesia. The colonial East reacted differently to the imperial design of colonizing the entire οἰκουμένη through empire expansion, its socio-economic strategies to extract wealth through imperial taxation and the religio-cultural-political impositions to unite the subjects under its reign. While ambivalently responding to the imperial cult and other colonial impositions, there were political reprisals to the revolutionary movements who protested against the supremacy of Rome.

The popular movements during the first century CE have brought out the revolutionary involvement of the peasants in the national liberation movements. However, while recognizing the involvement of the Jewish peasantry for a call for national independence, the thesis analyses the discursive position of the subalterns including the Jesus' movement and the Christian community who engaged simultaneously in consensual-conflicting political strategy to the native Jewish religio-cultural world and the alien Roman discourses of power.

The Lukan discourse of the transcultural Christian ecclesia's formation in Jerusalem-Judea and its spread to the Greco-Roman world characterize the postcolonial strategy of mimetic, ambivalent and hybrid features with strategic appropriation of Jewish essentialist ideas and Roman imperial concepts. In this process, Luke narrates the discourse of a resistant community by strategically adopting the scribal medium to witness the Lordship of the crucified Jesus and his kingdom with the help of the Roman patronage (Ac.1:1). The transcultural community mimics and mocks the imperial kingdoms in mapping the geographical locations (Jerusalem to Rome), religio-political proclamation agendas (βασιλεί ας, εὐαγγελιον, εἰρήνη, Κύριος, σωτήρ, Χριστος), cataloguing the nations and adopting the Christian *politeia*. The centers have been challenged by the distributive power system of the eschatological δυναμίς on all the disciples because for Luke the power resides in the community of equals.

The first century ecclesia of a hybrid community enters into 'the transcultural enunciatory space' of ἡ ὁδός by wedging into the socio-political centers with an alternative vision of a new world order for social justice to the poor and the marginalized. Moreover, the significance of the term μάρτυρεω (I bear witness) cannot probably comprehend without acknowledging the socio-religio-political context of the first century. The ecclesia witnessed with boldness to the entire οἰκουμένη in the light of severe persecution. Their witnessing life of a higher social order of μια ψυχή, ἄπαντα κοινά, κοινονια, τῃ κλάσει τοῦ ἄρτον to confront the dehumanized imperial socio-cultural structures naturally disrupts the colonial centers. The Hellenist Philip, Ethiopian Eunuch, Peter, Cornelius, Lydia, the slave girl were selected characters who crossed the class-cultural-racial-ethnic-gender-geographic colonial boundaries to the eschatological hybrid space to have their 'non-colonial' identity. The persecution of King Agrippa against the infant ecclesia, the death of Apostle James and the imprisoning of Peter have been the reflection of a subject community who have become the target of the Jewish-Roman religio-political colonial centers. However, the imperial strategy is disrupted by the discursive portrayal of the divine judgement upon the Roman client King and the deliverance of the Peter from the Roman imprisonment.

The political witness in the Roman world comes in the second part through the proclamation of the gospel by Paul and his associates before the colonial authorities (Ac.13-28). This section reflects the first century ecclesia that was persecuted by the colonial centers and did not get much attention in the theological discussions. However, the postcolonial reading of Acts unravels the potentiality of a resistant discourse used by the transcultural hybrids who strategically employ the essentialist ideals. In this respect, Paul's missionary journeys are probably considered to be Lukan mimicking of the territorial expansion to form a counter cultural community of equals in the context of slavery, imperial persecution and racial-ethnic hatred. In turn, Paul and Silas' hybrid identity helped them to contest the corrupted Roman civil system at Philippi, but negotiate it by claiming the privilege of Roman citizenship.

Paul's arrest, trial and defense before legal courts in the company of Roman political figures discursively disrupt the colonial agendas of the first century. In all the trial scenes, it is probable that Paul is the protagonist of the first century marginalized Christian ecclesia. The display of Paul's strategic essentialist position of a subaltern cultural hybrid speaks back to the colonial centers with affiliation-accommodation yet simultaneously distancing-disrupting the imperial agendas. This provides a paradigm for the Indian neocolonial subject communities to imitate.

The postcolonial reading of the Acts of the Apostles has a greater relevance for the present day ecclesia in the context of neocolonialism and religious fundamentalism. Thus, the implication part of the research tries to develop a postcolonial ecclesiology to address the issues that the ecclesia faces today. The research brings guidelines and practice for the third millennium marginalized ecclesia in India to be active witnesses in the οἰκουμένη which will be taught through theological education and action in India. The socio-economic-religio-cultural issues of the state, especially neocolonialism by the developed nations and religious fundamentalism by the native cultural nationalists must be addressed with postcolonial strategy of negotiation-resistance and accommodation-disruption. There is no dichotomy between religion/politics and state/church in the postcolonial reading of Acts.

The first century ecclesia is formed as a strategic resistant hybrid moved to a 'third space' where she accommodates 'all' irrespective of caste/race, gender, nationality, religious status by following the postcolonial methods of mimicry, hybridity and ambivalence. The counter-cultural ecclesia witnesses kingdom values of God's love, righteousness and justice in word and deed as a discursive resistive paradigm. The postcolonial ecclesiology dismantles all types of colonial relations of power by prophesying righteousness-justice and constructs a theology of hope through vision and imagination.

The imperial arrest, trial scenes, persecution, death and imprisonment bring guidelines for the present day ecclesia how to address similar situations in the present day India. Political witnessing can be done by strategically making use of the essentialist religio-political rights with postcolonial methods. Lukan Paul's model of dialogical discourse with the postcolonial discursive strategy will be a feasible paradigm in the context of imprisonment and threat to the Indian Christian minorities.

The prospect of the postcolonial reading of the emerging Jerusalem-centered Jewish-Christian tradition is not given serious attention in this thesis because of its limited scope and target. In addition, the researcher has not made a serious attempt in challenging the traditional commentaries for its religious colonization because of the overemphasis on the modern day European colonialism without taking into account the Greco-Roman colonial cultural context of the text.[1] The other possibility of analyzing the novelistic genre of Acts that has been popularly used in the first century *milieu* as a postcolonial literature needs to be ventured in the future.[2]

---

[1] Sugirtharajah, *Postcolonial Reconfiguration*, 17-23, 103-04; idem, *Postcolonial Criticism and Biblical interpretation,* 24-28; Muthuraj, "A Postcolonial Reading of acts," 84-86.

[2] The shift from the traditional to the novelistic genre of Acts probably opens scope for the postcolonial reading in a new perspective. Pervo, *Profit with Delight*; Barrus, *Luke-Acts,* 144-147.

Appendix I

The Major Imperial Centers in the East and the Impact of Colonialism

After a series of wars in the eastern part of the Roman Empire, Rome slowly subdued and brought Asia Minor into her political system in 133 BCE which made a great transformation in the socio-political-economic matters of the province.[1] Even the Roman governors and soldiers of the pre-Augustus era made use of the provinces in east (Asia Minor) as a treasury to extort money during the civil wars of Rome.[2] In the first century, the emperor cult united the cities of Greece and Asia Minor in their power relations by constituting them through images, shrines, temples and festivals.[3] The imperial cult in the east became enormously large with separate festivals, sacrifices and imperial priests from the elites.[4] In the Roman world, the emperor's birthday (probably Augustus) became an annual festival in the *Koinon* (union of cities in Asia Minor).[5] Rome became the center of attachment for the subjects of Asia Minor due to the few administrative staff under the governor to handle the legal cases and to maintain order in these provinces.[6] It was not only the emperor, but also the Roman citizens of the equestrian and senatorial class

[1] Trebilco, "Asia," 292.

[2] Stambaugh and Balch, *The New Testament in its Social Environment*, 151. Antony demanded ten year taxes together in the light of civil war following the death of Julius Caesar.

[3] Horsley, *Paul and Empire*, 11.

[4] Prince, "Rituals and Power," 49. There were big processions involving the whole community with donations from the elite benefactors.

[5] G. Walter Hansen, "Galatia" in *The Book of Acts in its Graeco-Roman Setting*, vol. 2, edited by D.W.J. Gill and Conrad Gempf (Grand Rapids: Wm. B. Eerdmans Publishing Company, 1994), 384.

[6] Prince, "Rituals and Power," 48.

who found Asia Minor as a colony to make investments on land.[7] Hence, they probably acted like multinational companies of the present day world economy. The major cities in the east which would be discussed are Syrian Antioch, Ephesus, Galatia, the provinces of Macedonia (Philippi and Thessalonica) and Corinth.

Syrian Antioch

Antioch became an imperial power center which continued to receive patronage and protection of the emperors due to the strategic position of the city in terms of commercial road access to Asia Minor and the natural resources for commercial purpose.[8] Romanizing policies of Emperor Augustus started the building projects for the purpose of making the city an imperial administrative center and the eastern Roman military headquarter.[9] The imperial reign (Augustus, Tiberius) with the help of the client King Herod the Great built miles long colonnaded street to show the pride of the Roman province (*JW* 1.425; *Ant.*16.148) with visual power images of Romulus and Remus.[10] The political significance of this city became prominent during this period as an administrative center to govern the judiciary, implementing taxation, supervising the local governments and to defend the eastern borders (Parthia, Judea and Galilee).[11]

In addition, Roman imperialism had been enforced on the subjects by imprinting emperors' images on the coins and their accomplishments at Antioch to display her sovereignty.[12] This will offend the cultural ethos of the Jews in Palestine because imprinting the image of '*Judea capta* coins' were unlawful for Jewish customs.[13] The Jewish presence in Antioch made the province more significant (*Against Apion* 2.39) due to their ambivalent approach to the imperial system. The Romans gave the Jews (about fifty thousand *JW* 7.43) the religious privileges of exemption from military service and the right of observing the Sabbath (*Ant.*12.119; *JW* 7.43).[14] However, there were occasions of anti-Semitic feelings spread with the point of total extinction of the race in this region (*JW* 7.46-62). For the purpose of humiliating the Jews in Antioch as well as a warning

[7] The governor of Cyprus, Sergius Paulus seemed to have accumulated extensive landholding in Asia Minor region of Pisidia. Stambaugh and Balch, *The New Testament in its Social Environment*, 154.

[8] L.M. McDonald, "Antioch (Syria)," in *DNTB*, edited by C.A. Evans & S. Porter (Leicester: IVP, 2000), 34; Stambaugh and Balch, *The New Testament in its Social Environment*, 146-47. Antioch became the largest city under the Roman Empire during the first century. The city became the Roman governors' residence and ranked third among the Roman cities (*JW* 3.2.4).

[9] Stambaugh and Balch, *The New Testament in its Social Environment*, 146.

[10] Carter, *Matthew and the Margins*, 37.

[11] Carter, *Matthew and the Margins*, 37. The visit of the Roman emperors like Augustus, Tiberius (20 BCE), Vaspasian (66 CE), and Titus (71 CE) show the political importance of the city.

[12] Carter, *Matthew and the Margins*, 38.

[13] '*Judea capta coins*' was issued by Vespasian. Carter, *Matthew and the Margins*, 38.

[14] McDonald, "Antioch (Syria)," *DNTB*, 35.

to the resistant forces, Emperor Titus made a victorious parade displaying the treasures of the destroyed temple over the streets of Antioch (*JW* 7.96-111). Further, the Jewish society was provoked by rejecting the Sabbath privileges and forceful impositions of offering sacrifices at Gentile altars.[15]

The Christian community was rooted in Antioch among the mixed group of both the Jews and the Greeks (Ac.11:19-20). Later, the hybrid transcultural ecclesia sent missionaries to other parts of the Roman Empire (Ac.13:1-3). They grew in numbers and in wealth so that they could send help for the famine affected Jerusalem church (Ac.11:27-30).

Ephesus

Ephesus was strategically positioned due to the land and sea routes. This made her elevated to the status of being the capital of the Asiatic province since the Actium victory of Augustus. The economic growth led this city to become one of the largest cities of the Roman Empire.[16] The great building projects ('the Temple of Artemis, the Magnesian Gate, the Augustan basilica, the temples of Dea Roma, Divus Iulius and the Temple of Apollo') portray the great political significance in terms of administration and economy.[17] The Artemis cult of Ephesus (fertile goddess) made its significance through the construction of the temple which was considered to be one of the Seven Wonders of the ancient world.[18]

The strategic importance of Ephesus in terms of communication network, information center, treasury for the tax collectors, and courier routes to all the provincial administrative centers of Asia made it as the capital city of Asia for the Roman administration.[19] The emperor cult became integral to the imperial system by erecting an altar at the center of the temple.[20] The renaming of Ephesus to *neokoros* ('warden of the emperor's temple') by Domitian and Hadrian would display the political strategy of collaborating with the regional cult.[21]

---

[15] Stambaugh and Balch, *The New Testament in its Social Environment*, 148.

[16] L.M. McDonald, "Ephesus," in *DNTB*, edited by C.A. Evans & S. Porter (Leicester: IVP, 2000), 318. Augustus made Ephesus as the capital in the place of Pergumum due to the strategic location of great high ways and sea routes.

[17] Trebilco, "Asia," 307. After Rome and Alexandria, Ephesus probably could claim to be the third largest city in terms of population (ca.2000,000-250,000). "The city also calls itself "the first and greatest metropolis of Asia' in inscriptions," (eg., I.Eph.647, 1541, 1543) cited by Trebilco, "Asia," 306.

[18] McDonald, "Ephesus," *DNTB*, 319. 'Artemis' was considered as the Saviour (*Geog.* 14.1.22).

[19] Trebilco, "Asia," 309.

[20] Horsley, *Paul and Empire,* 20.

[21] Stambaugh and Balch, *The New Testament in its Social Environment*, 151. There is a possibility that the *Asiarchs* of Ephesus were associated with the imperial cults as high priests. Bruce, *Acts*, 418; Barrett, *Acts,* vol. II, 930.

The Christian community seemed to be in frequent disruption with the religio-political authorities (Ac.19; cf.1Pet.2-4; Rev.2-3).

In the imperial temples, the emperor became the center of attention replacing the traditional deities of the Asiatic region. And in Ephesus, the imperial presence came to permeate the public space through the new temples to the emperors, and by erecting images in the center of the cities.[22]

Galatia

The imperial power and the provincial wealth of the agricultural products were overwhelmingly exhibited through the "triple-arched gate way" of the emperor Claudius and the temple of Augustus.[23] The formation of Galatia as the Roman client kingdom and its expansion to its borders to the south-east marked the time of their support to Roman general Pompey in his march against Mithridates V.[24] Under the emperorship of Augustus, Galatia became a province in 25BCE with additions of other cities and villages (Antioch of Pisidia, Iconium, Lystra, and Derbe).[25]

By knowing the great importance of the province, Emperor Augustus built *Vie Sebaste* to link the Roman colonies of the west and planted a number of military colonies in southern Galatia in order to establish political control over the territory.[26] While retaining the Hellenistic administrative institutions of council and assembly, Rome introduced property qualifications for membership in the council.[27]

The political strategy of establishing the imperial cult through emperor worship in Ancyra and Apollonia (Galatia) made a new culture of praising the emperor through festivals and many other visible objects.[28] Hellenistic Asiatic temples appropriated Roman gods and goddesses explaining the impact of Roman colonialism in the eastern part of the first century CE.[29]

The Province of Macedonia (Philippi and Thessalonica)

Before the final settlement of the Macedonian province before the Roman imperial rulers at the battle of Actium (31BCE), the province was already incorporated into

[22] Horsley, *Paul and Empire,* 21. "[Imperial] temples made the emperor the centre of attention in cities such as Corinth and Ephesus" (22-23).

[23] Hansen, "Galatia," 395. Agricultural crops of wheat and barley, wool industry, wine made Galatia an economic province which benefited the imperial Rome.

[24] Hansen, "Galatia," 381.

[25] Hansen, "Galatia," 382.

[26] Hansen, "Galatia," 384, 387.

[27] Hansen, "Galatia," 388.

[28] Hansen, "Galatia," 395. Augustus *Res Gestae* have been found at the Galatian temples.

[29] Hansen, "Galatia," 392. "Zeus was the most widely worshiped god in Galatia; temples to Zeus were ubiquitous." Zeus was linked with Hermes in Lystra (Ac.14:12).

the Roman Empire for quite some time (179-168BCE).[30] However, Macedonia came under the emperor's direct control since 15 CE.[31]

The city was renamed after the name of the father of Alexander the Great (Philip II of Macedon) in the process of colonizing and defeating Thracians.[32] The strategic military route from Rome through Neapolis-Philippi-Amphipolis-Apollonia-Thessalonica to the east was seen in the primary war for the imperial power by Caesar Augustus and the triumvirate.[33] Later Philippi was given the colonial status (cf.Ac.16:12), a miniature of Rome by the imposition of the imperial language (Latin) which was proved by the Latin inscriptions discovered from the first century period.[34] 'The Roma' reconstituted the colonial center by giving equal status for the subjects with the Italian communities in political freedom and tax exemption for their lands.[35]

The official religion of Rome was forced upon people from the time of the inception of the colony irrespective of minor roles played by the Greek gods and the other local Thracian-oriental cults.[36] The Macedonian natives were incorporated into a Roman army for the purpose of making the state into a colonial regime.[37] In order to maintain peace and order, the Roman administration instituted a judicial authority of the 'Politarch' which also explains the colonial impact in the eastern part of the Roman Empire.[38]

The Augustus era made the imperial cult to become supreme over the Hellenistic and the oriental cults.[39] The Macedonian region (Thessalonica) was slowly pressed out of the Hellenistic influences by the settlers of the Roman colonial

---

[30] D.W.J.G ill, "Macedonia," in *TheBook of Acts in its Graeco-Roman Setting*, vol. 2, edited by D.W.J. Gill and Conrad Gempf (Grand Rapids: Wm. B. Eerdmans Publishing Company, 1994), 402-04. "The acquisition of Macedonia for Rome brought its benefits, some 300,000,000 sesterces into the treasury." Pliny, *Nat.Hist.* 33.17 (402).

[31] Gill, "Macedonia," 406.

[32] L.M. McDonald, "Philippi," in *DNTB*, edited by C.A. Evans & S. Porter (Leicester: IVP, 2000), 787. Philip II started building his kingdom by seeing the rich gold mines in Philippi and he made it a free city.

[33] McDonald, "Philippi," *DNTB,* 787. Both Antony and Augustus Caesar made Philippi a Roman colony by bringing the triumviral soldiers from Rome and settling them by providing colonial status (*Geog.*7.41; *Nat.Hist.*4.42). Paul seemed to have mimicked the imperial strategy during his missionary journeys (Ac.16:12; 17:1).

[34] Gill, "Macedonia", 413. The majority of inscriptions (i.e., Latin 361, Greek 60) were in Latin. The colony was renamed as *Colonia Augusta Julia Philippensis.*

[35] McDonald, "Philippi," *DNTB,* 787-88.

[36] Stambaugh and Balch, *The New Testament in its Social Environment,* 156.

[37] Gill, "Macedonia," 406.

[38] G.H.R. Horsley, "The Politarchs" in *TheBook of Acts in its Graeco-Roman Setting*, vol.2, edited by D.W.J. Gill and Conrad Gempf (Grand Rapids: Wm. B. Eerdmans Publishing Company, 1994), 419-431.

[39] Gill, "Macedonia," 406. Archeological evidences proved an alter dedicated to Augustus.

veterans. This becomes a serious issue with the local people's legal identity.[40] The typical Greek city with the local administration was colonized by the Roman imperial culture.[41]

Achaia/Corinth

The international crossroad between the west and east make Corinth a strategic commercial center of the east and a port city of great wealth (Strabo *Geog.*8.6.32). The Greek cultured Corinth was reconstituted as a Roman colony in the socio-religio-political life. The ancient Achaean league was interfered by the colonial plan of Rome and the whole region of Greece was taxed as a province even before the emperorship of Octavian.[42] The second century Roman colonial expansion into Greece destroyed its male members, enslaved its women and children in 146 BCE.[43] It was Julius Caesar who took initiative in reconstituting the strategically important region in the whole of Greece (44 BCE) to be a Roman colony. The Roman influence in Corinth was felt in language (Latin instead of Greek), administration and structure. This was emphasized by the Latin inscriptions and the Latin names.[44] Caesar made it the capital of the province of Achaia and later it came to the peak of its prominence during the Augustan period.[45]

The dominating imperial presence was all over the city of Corinth including the public spaces by constructing imperial temples, shrines, and images of the successive emperors from Augustus.[46]

[40] Gill, "Macedonia," 411. Thessalonica was on the periphery of Greece founded by the king of Macedonia and named it after the name of his wife who was a half sister to Alexander the Great. It was Antony who founded this colony for the Roman veterans.

[41] Stambaugh and Balch, *The New Testament in its Social Environment,* 156.

[42] D.W.J. Gill, "Achaia," in *TheBook of Acts in its Greco-Roman Setting*, vol. 2, edited by D.W.J. Gill and Conrad Gempf (Grand Rapids: Wm. B. Eerdmans Publishing Company, 1994), 434-435.

[43] Gill, "Achaia," 448. The significance of Corinth was among the cities of Greece from 8th to 2nd Century BCE, till the mass destruction by the Romans.

[44] J.R. McRay, "Corinth," in *DNTB*, edited by C.A. Evans & S. Porter (Leicester: IVP, 2000), 230. For eg. The influence of Latin is seen in the names of the Corinthian Christians (Aquila, Fortunatus, Gaius, Tertius, and Titius Justus).

[45] Gill, "Achaia," 448. "A new colony, Colonia Lalus Julia Corinthiensis, was established in 44 BC by Julius Caesar."

[46] Horsley, *Paul and Empire,* 21. A huge temple structure for the imperial cult in the beginning of the first century CE shows the imposition of the ruler cult on traditional worship of Greek gods (Athena, Olympian). McRay, "Corinth," *DNTB*, 228.

Appendix II

The Major Jewish Resistance against the Roman Imperial Reign (66-70 CE)

The four-year long Jewish-Roman War (66-70 CE) had sought socio-economic-religious-cultural and political independence.[1] According to Josephus, the Jewish-Roman war was considered to be 'the greatest of all recorded wars' (*JW* i.1), fought with the expectation of an imminent messianic kingdom (*JW* 4.312-13).[2] There may have been various actions that ignited the Jewish-Roman war including the cessation of the daily sacrifices for the emperor (*JW* 2.409-10). Similarly, the Jewish insurgents caused fear in the hearts of the Priestly-Herodian aristocracy in Jerusalem who sought the military help from Florus and Agrippa (July, 66 CE).[3] The Jewish resistance strengthened by the inflow of the insurgents in Jerusalem had taken possession of the political strongholds of the upper city. They destroyed the debt records by burning the archives for the sake of the poor, massacred the high-priestly leaders (Ananias and his brother) and the Roman garrison (*JW* 2.430).[4] They also captured the Antonia fortress, Herod's palace, and massive towers; massacred the Roman army and established control over Jerusalem in 67 CE.[5]

By taking hold of the full strength of the Roman army in Antioch (thirty thousand men in Antioch), other auxiliaries from Syria and Agrippa's large contingents, Cestius Gallus arranged for a great retaliatory march to reinvade Judea.

[1] Smallwood, *The Jews under Roman Rule,* 293.

[2] Smallwood, *The Jews under Roman Rule,* 293.

[3] Smallwood, *The Jews under Roman Rule,* 294.

[4] Smallwood, *The Jews under Roman Rule,* 294. The two thousand Roman cavalry sent by Agrippa could not resist the Jewish resistant forces. Menahem's men captured and killed Ananias and his brother.

[5] Smallwood, *The Jews under Roman Rule,* 294-95.

However, he faced a surprise resistance from the Jewish side upon abandoning the Feast of Tabernacle.[6] Meantime there were negotiations from the side of the Jews and the Romans (Josephus and Agrippa) in order to avoid a disastrous military action.[7] The Jewish resistance became more severe by the appointment of Vespasian and his son Titus as the military commanders by the Emperor Nero.[8] In the early 68 CE, Vespasian planned a political strategy of isolating Jerusalem and subjugated the rest of the province which would be considered as a strategic genocide in eliminating one racial group similar to the Hitler's political strategy of eliminating the Jewish race.[9] He recaptured Galilee and most of the Jewish strongholds of the northwestern Judea and prompted the Jews to find refuge in Jerusalem or somewhere in the fortresses in Judea (Herodion, Machaeros and Masada).[10]

The Jewish nationalistic feeling had gone to the extent in which autonomous silver coins of Jewish denominations were declared in anticipation of the freedom of the nation.[11] There were Messianic movements and popular rebellions from among the Judean peasantry under the leadership of Simon bar Giora, "son of the proselyte" in Jerusalem.[12] He proclaimed socio-economic justice for the poor and the slaves (*JW* 4.508), similar to the messianic expectations of a leader (Jer.23:5; Isa.11:4).[13] By this time, John of Gischala from the northern part of Galilee, became a national leader with his associates (four hundred brigands) and came to

[6] Smallwood, *The Jews under Roman Rule,* 296. Agrippa personally led his contingents and client kings of Antiochus IV of Commagene and Sohaemus of Emesa to participate in the Roman military attack against Judea.

[7] Smallwood, *The Jews under Roman Rule,* 296, 300.

[8] Smallwood, *The Jews under Roman Rule,* 306-7. Titus had gone to Alexandria, and Vespasian to Antioch to bring the Roman army to Palestine (*JW.*2.558; 3.1-8, 29). The army strength went up to sixty thousand (*JW* 3.29, 64-9) by bringing cavalry from Syria, Egypt and Antioch.

[9] Smallwood, *The Jews under Roman Rule,* 310.

[10] Smallwood, *The Jews under Roman Rule,* 310-16. The Roman armies systematically devastated the villages and attempted genocide by slaughter or by enslavement (*JW* 4.130; cf.4.419-439). Vespasian established Roman garrisons throughout Galilee (*JW* 4.442).

[11] Smallwood, *The Jews under Roman Rule,* 300.

[12] Horsley & Hanson, *Bandits, Prophets and Messiahs,* 119-120. He "cut up a large part of their rearguard, and carried off many of their baggage animals" from a Roman army which advances to Jerusalem in October, 66 CE (*JW* 2.521). Giora took refuge in Masada when the Roman army was dispatched against him (*JW* 2.652-53). In Nain, he constructed wall for his protection, used caves as storehouses for his treasures and booty. He was preparing the corps for an attack on Jerusalem (*JW* 4.507-13). He had forty thousand followers and had a sizable army. He invaded Idumea and Hebron (*JW* 4.529-34).

[13] Smallwood, *The Jews under Roman Rule,* 301; Horsley & Hanson, *Bandits, Prophets and Messiahs,* 122. Simon acted as the king of the Jews and accused him for triumphal procession that he was planning in Rome (*JW* 7.29-31, 36). "As with the great messianic prototype, the initial ones to join his band were the "worthless" and discontented (*JW* 4.509-513). Eventually, however, with the people as a whole groping for effective leadership against foreign domination, large numbers of

Jerusalem. He joined hands with Eleazar, the son of Simon and laid siege to the temple (*JW* 5.528).[14]

In the light of the Roman re-conquest of northwest Judea in late 67 CE, the brigand groups infiltrated Jerusalem and formed a coalition of resistant movements to fight against Roman imperialism.[15] In this re-conquest of the Judean countryside (Gerasa), the Romans assaulted, killed, plundered the property and destroyed houses (*JW* 4.488-89). The atrocities of the Roman General Vespasian and his officers made a systematic colonization possible through slaughter and enslavement of peasants from the towns and villages (*JW* 4.443-51; 4.551-54).[16] Similar atrocities under Vespasian's delegate Placidus (500 cavalry and 3000 infantry) were carried out which ransacked the houses and torched the villages of Gadara, Jordan and other towns and villages (*JW* 4.419-20, 429-33, 437-39). The systematic slaughter and devastation of the villages caused the escalation of banditry to flee to the nearest fortress city of Jericho or of Jerusalem.[17] These devastations snowballed into panic in the surrounding villages.

By the end of 68 CE, the popular groups joined under the messianic leadership of Simon (*JW* 4.508, 510) and the Zealots including some of the invaded Idumeans (*JW* 4.353, 509-37), who took control of the wall of Jerusalem in order to establish an alternative government.[18] In the third year of the war, Simon took control over the whole of Judea and became the master over Jerusalem in April-May 69 CE (*JW* 4.574-578).[19] Simon killed Matthias and his three sons,

people, including some of the notables, came to recognize him "as a king." R.A. Horsley, "Popular Messianic Movements around the Time of Jesus," *CBQ* 46 (1984), 489.

[14] Smallwood, *The Jews under Roman Rule,* 312; Horsley & Hanson, *Bandits, Prophets and Messiahs*, 84, 123. Since the Zealots attained control of the city, there were tensions between the leadership, mainly between John of Gischala and Simon bar Giora. Horsley & Hanson, *Bandits, Prophets and Messiahs,* 218-19; Hengel, *The Zealots*, 373.

[15] Smallwood, *The Jew under Roman Rule,* 312-16; Horsley & Hanson, *Bandits, Prophets and Messiahs,* 220. The scattered brigand bands from the countryside formed a single unit as they entered Jerusalem and started to take part in any heinous crime (*JW* 4.135-38). R.A. Horsley, "Ancient Jewish Banditry and the Revolt against Rome, A.D. 66-70," *CBQ* 43 (1981), 409-432; *idem,* "Popular Messianic Movements," 471-495; *idem,* "'Like One of the Prophets of Old,' 435-463; *idem,* "The Zealots: Their Origin, Relationships and Importance in the Jewish Revolt," *Nov T* 27 (1986), 159-192.

[16] Horsley & Hanson, *Bandits, Prophets and Messiahs,* 221; E.N. Luttwak, *The Grand Strategy of the Roman Empire* (Baltimore: John Hopkins, 1976), 25-26, 32-33, 41-42, 46-47.

[17] Horsley & Hanson, *Bandits, Prophets and Messiahs,* 222-23.

[18] Smallwood, *The Jews under Roman Rule,* 313-15; Horsley, *Jesus and the Spiral of Violence,* 56. The Zealots summoned the support of the Idumeans (twenty thousand) and siege the walls of Jerusalem. The Zealots killed two ex-High priests Annas and Jesus (*JW* 4.305-17). Hengel, *The Zealots*, 373-75.

[19] Horsley & Hanson, *Bandits, Prophets and Messiahs*, 123-125. John and his followers (Zealots) were seized by Simon's followers. However, when the Romans seized the temple in April 70 CE, Simon and John's forces together resisted the Roman force for five months.

the other prominent priests and distinguished citizens for favoring Romans (*JW* 5.530, 532-33).

The final military operation of Vespasian started in the summer of 69 CE through a siege on the city of Jerusalem and later he handed over the key responsibility to his son Titus once his emperorship was confirmed (*JW* 4.588-629, 656-658).[20] At that time, there were various war strategies used by the Romans to intimidate the Jews, like crucifying their own prisoners and amputating some on the streets (*JW* 5.420-423, 439-459).[21] Simon had ceremonially surrendered before the temple by wearing the royal robes. His ritual execution by considering him as a sacrificial victim displayed the religio-cultural mind of a Jewish nationalist waiting for the intervention of God.[22] In spite of the Jewish resistance, Titus with his mass army demolished the walls around the temple and the siege, causing famine to the Jewish inmates inside the walls (*JW* 5.491-511). The final entry to the temple courts was closed by demolishing the Antonia fortress (*JW* 6.81-94).[23] The prolonged sieges by the resistant groups made the life of the Jews in the city miserable. They thought of fleeing to the desert or giving themselves up to the Romans.[24] Finally the Roman imperial might proved itself by burning the inner courts of the temple which resulted in a holocaust and made the army of Titus to loot the treasure of the sanctuary in September 70 CE (*JW* 6.249-261; 265, 281-85).[25] The Jewish rebels were executed. Able bodied men were sent to serve in the mines or used in shows as gladiators or amphitheaters (*JW* 7.18-20, 23-24, 37-40) and children were sold as slaves (*JW* 4.414-20).[26] The chief leaders were taken to Rome to show before the public and they were ceremonially executed as a mark of Titus' triumph (*JW* 6.370, 433; 7.26-36).[27] He ordered the razing of the temple and the city walls which gave way to a deserted look as a mark of

[20] Smallwood, *The Jews under Roman Rule,* 317.

[21] Smallwood, *The Jews under Roman Rule,* 321.

[22] Horsley & Hanson, *Bandits, Prophets and Messiahs,* 126-27.

[23] Smallwood, *The Jews under Roman Rule,* 321-32. The military action of Titus' siege of the Antonia fortress and the lack of supply of lambs stopped the temple sacrifices.

[24] Horsley & Hanson, *Bandits, Prophets and Messiahs,* 124. The siege caused famine and strife to both Jews and Romans (*JW* 5.421).

[25] Smallwood, *The Jews under Roman Rule,* 324; Horsley & Hanson, *Bandits, Prophets and Messiahs,* 80-82, 125; Farmer, *Maccabees, Zealots, and Josephus,* 114-15. The Jews could watch the tragedy with "lamentations and wailing" (*JW* 6.274).

[26] Smallwood, *The Jews under Roman Rule,* 327. Josephus gives the number of 97,000 as the total prisoners taken in war.

[27] Smallwood, *The Jews under Roman Rule,* 327-29. Simon was ceremonially executed as the leader in effect as well as the King of the Jews (*JW* 7.26-36, 116-157) and John for life imprisonment (*JW* 6.433). The booty of the war was displayed in its procession from the Jerusalem temple to the temple of Jupiter (the seven branched candelabrum, the shrew bread table, the trumpets, the copy of the law).

humiliating the Jewish city.[28] It took another three more years for the Romans to accomplish the siege of the Masada (73CE).

A second massive popular peasantry with the resurrected hope of Jewish nationalism revolted against the military forces of Rome under the leadership of Bar Kochba Revolt (132-135CE).[29] Simeon bar Kosiba had taken the royal messianic title, 'the king' and his followers proclaimed the liberation of Israel.[30] The first century CE ended with greater messianic expectations of a new anointed David expressed through apocalyptic literature such as 2 Baruch and 4 Ezra.[31] The sixty years between the two great wars destroyed many sectarian groups but gave birth to Rabbinic Judaism and Christianity.[32] Apocalyptic visions and revelations gave new spirit for God's intervention among the intellectuals.

---

[28] Smallwood, *The Jews under Roman Rule*, 327.

[29] Horsley & Hanson, *Bandits, Prophets and Messiahs*, 45. The apocalypse of 4 Ezra "produced more vivid and highly developed expectations of "The Messiah" than those expressed in earlier literature" (45).

[30] Horsley & Hanson, *Bandits, Prophets and Messiahs*, 128-29. Simeon and his forces exercised guerilla warfare against the Roman forces for a prolonged time. The royal-messianism is connected by identifying Bar Kochba with the star prophecy (Num. 24:17). Rabbi Akiba identified Bar Kochba, the leader of the renewed revolt as the messianic king as the fulfillment of the oracle of Balaam (Num 24:17): "a star shall go forth from Jacob," (J.Ta'anit 4.8 [68d 48-51]).

[31] Horsley, "Popular Messianic Movements," 492.

[32] Horsley & Hanson, *Bandits, Prophets and Messiahs*, 44-45. Yohanan ben Zakkai along with a group of rabbis laid foundations for Rabbinic Judaism in Yavneh.

Bibliography

Abraham, K.C. "Dalit Theology: Some Tasks Ahead." *BTF* xxix, 1/2 (March-June 1997): 36-47.

Agua, A.D. "The Lukan Narrative of the Evangelization of the Kingdom of God: A Contribution to the Unity of Luke-Acts." In *The Unity of Luke-Acts.* Edited by J. Verheyden. Louvain: Louvain University Press, 1999, 639-61.

Alexander, L. *The Preface to Luke's Gospel: Literary Convention and Social Context in Luke 1.1-4 and Acts 1.1.* Cambridge: Cambridge University Press, 1993.

________. "'In Journeying Often': Voyaging in the Acts of the Apostles and in Greek Romance." *Luke's Literary Achievement: Collected Essays.* Edited by C.M. Tucket. Sheffield: Sheffield Academic Press, 1995, 17-79.

________. "Fact, Fiction and the Genre of Acts." *NTS* 44/3 (1998): 380-99.

________. "The Acts of the Apostles as an Apologetic Text." In *Apologetics in the Roman Empire: Pagans, Jews, and Christians.* Edited by M. Edwards, et.al. New York: Oxford University Press, 1999,. "Reading Luke-Acts from Back to Front." In *The Unity of Luke-Acts.* Edited by Joseph Verheyden. Leuven: Leuven University Press, 1999, 419-46.

Allen Jr., O.Wesley. *The Death of Herod: The Narrative and Theological Function of Retribution in Luke-Acts.* SBLD 158, Atlanta: Scholars Press, 1997.

Angus, S. & A.M. Renwick. "Roman Empire and Christianity." The International Standard Bible Encyclopedia, vol. 4 Q-Z. Edited by Geoffrey W. Bromiley. Michigan: Wm. B. Eerdmans Publishing Company, 1988, 208-222.

Aram I. *For a Church Beyond its Walls.* Antelias, Lebanon: Armenian Catholicosate of Cilicia, 2007.

Ariarajah, S. Wesley. *Axis of Peace: Christian Faith in Times of Violence and War.* Geneva: WCC Publications, 2004.

________. *Not Without My Neighbour: Issues in Interfaith Relations.* Geneva: WCC Publications, 1999.

________. *Dialogue.* C.C.A Concern Series 1; Singapore: Christian Conference of Asia, 1980.

________. *The Bible and the People of Other Faiths*. Geneva: World Council of Churches, 1985.

Arlandson, James Malcolm. *Women, Class and Socity in Early Christianity. Models from Luke-Acts.* Massachusetts: Hendrickson Publishers, 1997.

Arnold, Laura. "Strategic essentialsm." Laura Arnold, http://academic.reed.edu/english/courses/English558/Week2.html (18 March 2011).

Ashcroft, B., G. Griffiths and H. Tiffin. *The Empire Writes Back: Theory and Practice in Postcolonial Literatures.* London: Routledge, 2002.

Ashcroft, B., G. Griffiths and Helen Tiffin. *Key Concepts in Post-Colonial Studies.* London/New York: Routledge, 2004.

________ and P. Ahluwalia. *Edward Said.* London/New York: Routledge, 2007.

Aune, David.E. *The New Testament in its Literary Environment.* Cambridge: James Clarke & Co., 1998.

________. *Revelation 6-16*, WBC 52B. Nashville: Thomas Nelson Publishers, 1998.

Bakhtin, M.M. *The Dialogic Imagination: Four Essays.* Translated by Caryl Emerson and Michael Holquist. Edited by Michael Holquist. Austin: University of Texas Press, 1990.

Balasundaram, Franklyn J. Dalit Struggle and its Implication for Theological Education." In *BTF*, vol. 29/3-4 (1997), 69-91.

Barnett, P.W. "The Jewish Sign Prophets-A.D. 40-70-Their Intentions and Origins," *NTS* 27 (1980-81), 679-97.

Barrett, C. K. *A Critical and Exegetical Commentary on The Acts of the Apostles*, vol. II. Edinburgh: T & T Clark, 1994, 1998.

________. Luke the Historian in Recent Study. London: Epworth, 1961.

Barrus, Virginia. "The Gospel of Luke and the Acts of the Apostles." In *A Postcolonial Commentary on the NT Writings*. Edited by Fernando F. Segovia and R. S. Sugirtharajah. London: T & T Clark, 2007, 133-155.

Bauckham, R. "The Economic Critique of Rome in Revelation 18." *Images of the Empire*. Edited by L. Alexander. Sheffield: JSOT Press, 1991, 47-90.

________. "James and the Jerusalem Church." In *The Book of Acts in its Palestinian Setting*, vol. 4. Edited by R. Boukham. Grand Rapids: Wm. B. Eerdmans Publishing Company, 1995, 415-450.

Bayer, Hans F. "The Preaching of Peter in Acts." In Witness to the Gospel. The Theology of Acts. Edited by I.H. Marshall and David Peterson. Grand Rapids, Michigan: Wm. B. Eerdmans Publishing Company, 257-274.

Beasley-Murray, G.R. "Revelation, Book of." *DLNTD*. Edited by R.P. Martin & P.H. Davids. Leicester, England: IVP, 1997, 1025-38.

Bechard, Dean P. "The Disputed Case against Paul: A Redaction Critical Analysis of Acts 21:27-22:29." *CBQ* 65/2 (2003), 232-250.

Behera, M.N. "Edinburgh-2010 Mission Conference Issues and Challenges for Mission and Unity." In *Edinburgh 2010: Witnessing to Christ today in India.* Edited by J. Massey and W. Longchar. Bangalore: BTESSC/SATHRI & SCEPTRE, 2011, 112-125.

Bhabha, Homi K. *The Location of Culture.* London/ New York: Routledge, 1994.

Blue, B.B. "Acts and the House Church." In The *Book of Acts in its Greaco-Roman Setting*, vol. 2. Edited by D.W.J. Gill and C. Gempf. Grand Rapids: Wm. B. Eerdmans Publishing Company, 1994, 119-222.

Bolt, Peter G. "Mission and Witness," In *Witness to the Gospel: The Theology of Acts.* Edited by I.H. Marshall and D. Peterson. Grand Rapids: Wm. B. Eerdmans Publishing Company, 1998, 191-214.

Bowley, J.E. "Pax Romana." *DNTB.* Edited by C.A. Evans & S.E. Porter. Leicester, England: IVP, 2000, 771-75.

Bradstock, A. and C. Roland, eds. *A Radical Christian Writings: A Reader.* Oxford: Blackwell Publishers, 2002.

Brannigen, K. "Images-or Mirages-of Empire." In *Images of Empire.* Edited by L. Alexander. Sheffield: JSOT Press, 1991, 91-105.

Brawley, R.L. "Paul in Acts: Lucan Apology and Conciliation." In Luke-Acts: New Perspectives from the Society of Biblical Literature Seminar. Edited by C.H. Talbert. New York: Crossroad, 1984, 129-47.

Brett, Mark G. "The Ethics of Postcolonial Criticism," *Semeia* 75 (1996), 219-28.

Brinkman, J.A. "The Literary Background of the 'Catalogue of the Nations' (Acts 2:9-11)." *CBQ* 25 (1963), 418-27.

Brodie, T.L. "The Accusing and Stoning of Naboth IKgs.21:8-13 as One Component of Stephen Text [Acts 6:9-14; 7:58a]." *CBQ* 45 (1983), 417-432.

Brown, R.E. "The Messianism of Qumran." *CBQ* 19 (1957), 53-80.

Broughton, T.R.S. "The Roman Army." In *The Beginning of Christianity*, vol. v. Edited by F.F. Foakes-Jackson, et al. London: Macmillan, 1933, 427-45.

Bruce, F. F. *The Acts of the Apostles: The Greek Text with Introduction and Commentary.* England: IVP, 1976.

________. *The Book of the Acts.* Revised by NICNT. Grand Rapids: Wm. B. Eerdmans Publishing Company, 1988.

Brueggemann, W. *The Prophetic Imagination.* Minneapolis: Fortress Press, 2001.

Bryant, L.R. *Imagination and the Life of the Spirit.* California: Scholars Press, 1981.

Cadbury, H.J. *The Making of Luke-Acts*, 2nd ed. London: SPCK, 1968/72.

Cancik, H. "The History of Culture, Religion, and Institutions in Ancient Historiography: Philological Observations concerning Luke's History." *JBL* 116 (1997), 673-95.

Capper, B. "The Palestinian Cultural Context of Earliest Christian Community of Goods." In *The Book of Acts its Palestinian Setting*, vol. 4. Edited by R. Baucham. Grand Rapids: Wm. B. Eerdmans Publishing Company, 1995, 323-355.

Carr, Dayanchand. "A Biblical Basis for Dalit Theology" in *Indigenous People: Dalits; Dalit Issues in Today's Theological Debate.* Edited by James Massey. Delhi: ISPCK, 1994, 231-249.

Carter, Warren. *Matthew and Empire: Initial Explorations.* Harrisburg: Trinity Press International, 2001.

________. *Matthew and the Margins. A Sociopolitical and Religious Reading.* Bangalore: Theological Publications in India, 2007.

________. *John and Empire Initial Explorations.* New York: T & T Clark, 2008.

________. "Paying Tax to Rome as Subversive Praxis: Matthew 17:24-27." *JSNT* 76 (1999), 3-31.

Cassidy, R.J. *Society and Politics in the Acts of the Apostles.* Mary Knoll, N.Y: Orbis, 1987.

________. and P.J. Scharper, *Political Issues in Luke-Acts.* New York: Orbis Books, 1983.

________. *Paul in Chains: Roman Imprisonment and the Letters of St. Paul* (New York: Crossroad, 2001).

Charlesworth, M.P. *The Roman Empire.* London: Oxford University Press, [1951], 1961.

Charlesworth, J.H. *Jesus within Judaism: New Light from Exciting Archeological Discoveries.* New York: Doubleday, 1988.

Cherian, M.T. *Hindutva Agenda and Minority Rights: A Christian Response.* Bangalore: Centre for Contemporary Christianity, 2007.

Chilton, Bruce, ed., *The Kingdom of God in the Teaching of Jesus.* London: SPCK, 1984.

Cho, Youngmo. "Spirit and the Kingdom in Luke-Acts: Proclamation as the Primary Role of the Spirit in Relation to the Kingdom of God in Luke-Acts," *AJPS* 6.2 (2003), 173-197.

Chow, J.K. "Patronage in Roman Corinth." In *Paul and Empire: Religion and Power in Roman Imperial Society.* Edited by R.A. Horsley. Harrisburg: Trinity, 1997, 104-125.

Clarke, Andrew D. "Rome and Italy." In *The Book of Acts in its Greaco-Roman Setting*, vol. 2. Edited by David W.J. Gill and Conrad Gempf. Grand Rapids, Michigan: Wm. B. Eerdmans Publishing Company, 1994, 455-81.

Clarke, Sathianathan. "Dalit Religion as a Resourceful Symbolic Domain: A Critical Review of Theories of Religion and a Constructive Proposition to Glean the Richness of Dalit Subjectivity." *Religion and Society* 49/2-3 (June-September 2004), 30-48.

________. "Hindutva, Religious and Ethnocultural Minorities, and Indian-Christian Theology." htt://www.religion-online.org/showarticle.asp?title=2449 (18 March 2011).

________. "Dalit Theology. An Introduction and Interpretive Theological Exposition." In *Dalit Theology in the Twenty-first Century. Discordant Voices, Discerning Pathways*. Edited by S. Clarke, D. Manchala and P.V. Peacock. Oxford: University Press, 2010, 19-37.

________ and P.V. Peacock. "Constructive Vision for Action." In *Dalits and Religious Conversion. Slippery Identities and Shrewd Identifications*. Edited by S. Clarke, D. Manchala and P.V. Peacock. Oxford: University Press, 2010, 178-95.

Colins, J.J. *The Apocalyptic Vision of the Book of Daniel.* Missoula: Scholars, 1977.

________. *The Apocalyptic Imagination*. New York: Crossroad, 1984.

Cook, S.A., F.E. Adcock and M.P. Charlesworth, eds. *The Cambridge Ancient History, vol. x, The Augustan Empire 44BC-AD.70*. Cambridge: Cambridge University Press, [1934], 1985.

________. *The Cambridge Ancient History, vol. XI. The Imperial Peace A.D. 70-192*. Cambridge: University Press, [1936], 1980.

Conzelmann, H. *Acts of the Apostles.* Translated by J. Limburg, et al. Edited by E.J. Epp and C.R. Matthews; translated by J. Limburg, et.al. Philadelphia: Fortress Press, 1987.

________. *Theology of Luke*, translated by Geoffrey Buswell (London: Faber and Faber, 1960).

Cosgrove, Charles. H. "The Divine ΔΕΙ in Luke-acts: Investigations into the Lukan Understanding of God's Providence." Nov.T 26 (1984), 168-190.

Cotter, Wendy. "The Collegia and Roman Law. State Restrictions on Voluntary Associations, 64 BCE-200 CE." In *Voluntary Associations in the Greco-Roman World.* New York: Routledge, 1996, 74-89.

Crossan, J.D. *The Birth of Christianity: Discovering what Happened in the Years Immediately after the Execution of Jesus.* San Francisco: HarperOne, 1998.

________. "Paul and Rome: The Challenge of a Just World Order." *USQR* 59/3-4 (2005), 6-20.

________. *The Historical Jesus: The Life of a Mediterranean Jewish Peasant.* Edinburgh: T & T Clark, 1991.

Croy, N. Clayton. "Hellenistic Philosophies and the Preaching of the Resurrection (Acts 17:18,32)." *Nov T* xxxix (1997), 21-39.

Das, S. "Witnessing to Christ in India: Problems and Challenges." In *Edinburgh 2010: Witnessing to Christ Today in India.* Edited by J. Massey and W. Longchar. Bangalore: BTESSC/SATHRI & SCEPTRE, 2011, 15-26.

Datta, Damayanti and Kiran Tare. "Rahuls Lost Widows. Suicide and Starvation haunt Vidarbha Villeges." *India Today* (Nov.7, 2011), 18-24.

Devasahayam, V.V. *Doing Theology in Biblical Key.* Madras: Gurukul, 1997.

David.L. Balch. "Rich and Poor, Proud and Humble in Luke-Acts." *The Social World of First Christians: Essays in Honor of Wayne Meeks.* Edited by L.M. White and O.L. Yarbrough. Minneapolis: Fortress, 1995, 214-33.

Davies, P.R. "Daniel in the Lions' Den." *Images of Empire.* Edited by L. Alexander. Sheffield: JSOT Press, 1991, 160-178.

Dayal, John. "Poverty of Ideas in Tackling Hunger and Deprivation. BPL Formula Mock the Poor." *Indian Currents*, vol. XXIII/42 (Oct.10-16, 2011), 26-31.

Deissmann, Adolf. *Light from the Ancient East: The New Testament Illustrated by Recently Discovered Texts of the Graeco-Roman World.* Translated by L.R.M. Stoughton. London: Hodder and Stoughton, 1910.

Dibelius, M. *Studies in the Acts of the Apostles.* Edited by H. Greeven. New York: Charles Scribner's Sons, 1956.

Dodd, C.H. *The Parable of the Kingdom* (Rev. ed) New York: Scribner's, 1961.

Downing, F.G. "Theophilus's First Reading of Luke-Acts." In *Luke's Literary Achievement: Collected Essays.* Edited by C.M. Tucket. Sheffield: Sheffield Academic Press (1995), 91-109.

________. "Redaction Criticism: Josephus' Antiquities and the Synoptic Gospels." I, II, *JSNT* 8 (1980): 46-65, and 9 (1980): 29-48.

Duling, D.C. "The Promises to David and their Entrance into Christianity-Nailing Down a Likely Hypothesis," *NTS* 20 (1973-74), 55-77.

Dunn, J.D.G. *Baptism in the Spirit.* London: SCM, 1970.

________. *The Acts of the Apostles.* London: Epworth Press, 1996.

________. "ΚΥΡΙΟΣ in Acts." In *The Christ and the Spirit.* Collected Essays of James D.G. Dunn, vol. 1. Edinburgh: T & T Clark, (1998), 241-53.

________. "Spirit and Kingdom." *The Christ and the Spirit.* Vol. 2 Pneumatology. Collected Essays of J.D.G. Dunn. Grand Rapids/Cambridge: Wm. B. Eerdmans Publishing Company, 1998, 133-141.

Edwards, D.R. "Surviving the Web of the Roman Power: Religion and Politics in the Acts of the Apostles, Josephus, and Chariton's *Chaereas and Callirhoe.*" *Images of Empire.* Edited by L. Alexander. Sheffield: JSOT Press, 1991, 179-201.

Elliot, John H. "Patronage and Clientage." In *The Social Sciences and the New Testament Interpretation.* Edited by Richard L. Rohrbaugh. Peabody: Hendrickson, 1996, 144-156.

Esler, P.F. *Community and Gospel in Luke- Acts*. SNTS Monograph 57. Cambridge: Cambridge University Press, 1989.

Farmer, William Reuben. *Maccabees, Zealots, and Josephus: An Inquiry into Jewish Nationalism in the Greco-Roman Period.* New York: Columbia University Press, 1956.

Feldmann, Louis H. *Josephus and Modern Scholarship (1937-1980).* Berlin/New York: Walter de Gruyter, 1984.

________. "Josephus: Interpretive Methods and Tendencies," *DNTB*. Edited by C.A. Evans & S.E. Porter. Leicester, England: IVP, 2000, 590-96.

________. "Josephus (Person)." *ABD,* vol. 3. H-J. Edited by D.N. Freedman. New York: Doubleday, 1992, 981-998.

Ferguson, E. *Backgrounds of Early Christianity.* Michigan: Wm. B. Eerdmans Publishing Company, 1987.

Fiensy, David. "Leaders of Mass Movements and the Leader of the Jesus Movement." *JSNT* 74 (1999), 3-27.

Finley, M.I. *The Ancient Economy.* London: The Hogarth Press, 1985.

Fiorenza, E.S. *The Power of the Word: Scripture and the Rhetoric of Empire.* Minneapolis: Fortress Press, 2007.

________. "Transforming the Margin-Claiming Common Ground: Charting a Different Paradigm of Biblical Studies." In *Still at the Margins. Biblical Scholarship Fifteen Years after Voices from the Margins.* Edited by R.S. Sugirtharajah. New York: T & T Clark, 2008, 22-39.

________. "Slave Wo/men and Freedom: Some Methodological Reflections." In *Postcolonial Interventions: Essays in Honour of R.S. Sugirtharajah.* Edited by T.B. Liew. Sheffild: Phoenix Press, 2009, 123-146.

________. *In Memory of Her: A Feminist Theological Reconstruction of Christian Origins.* New York: Crossroad, 1983.

________. *Jesus and the Politics of Interpretation.* New York: Continuum, 2000.

Fitzmayer, J.A. *The Acts of the Apostles: A New Translation with Introduction and Commentary.* New York: Doubleday, 1998.

________. "Jewish Christianity in Acts in Light of the Qumran Scrolls." In *Studies in Luke-Acts.* Edited by L.E. Keck and J.L. Martyn. London: SPCK, (1966), 233-257.

Ford, J. Massyngbaerde. "Reconciliation and Forgiveness in Luke's Gospel." In *Political Issues in Luke-Acts.* Edited by Richard J. Cassidy and Philip J. Scharper. Maryknoll, New York: Orbis Books, 1983), 80-98.

Franco S.J, F. "The Structural Nature of Poverty in India." *Poverty in India. Challenges and Responses.* Edited by J. Murickan S.J. Bangalore: A Xavier Board Publication, 1988, 37-85.

Freissen, S.J. *Twice Neokoros: Ephesus, Asia and the Cult of the Flavian Imperial Family*. Leiden: Brill, 1993.

Freyne, Sean. *Galilee from Alexander the Great to Hadrian 323 BCE to 135 CE.* Edinburgh: T & T Clark, 1980.

________. *Jesus, A Jewish Galilean: A New Reading of the Jesus-story*. London/New York: T & T Clark International, 2004.

Friedrich, "The Prophets and Prophecies in the NT." *TDNT*, vol. vi. Edited by Gerhard Friedrich. Grand Rapids, Michigan: Wm. B. Eerdmans Publishing Company, 1969, 828-61.

Gaikwad, Roger. "Towarda a New Ecclesia: Re-Reading the concept of 'Ecclesia' in the Bible: A Few Pointers." *Religion and Society* 52/2 (2011 June), 12-20.

Gandhi, Leela. *Postcolonial Theory: A Critical Introduction.* Edinburgh: EUP, 1998.

Garnsey, Peter and Richard Saller. *The Roman Empire: Economy, Society, and Culture*. Berkeley: University of California Press, 1987.

Gasque, W.W. *A History of the Interpretation of the Acts of the Apostles.* Peabody, MA: Hendrickson, 1989.

Gaventa, B.R. *The Acts of the Apostles.* ANTC. Nashville: Abingdon Press, 2003.

________. *From Darkness to Light: Aspects of Conversion in the New Testament.* Philadelphia: Fortress Press, 1986.

________. "You will be my Witness": Aspects of Mission in the Acts of the Apostles." *Missiology: An International Review* X (1982/4), 413-425.

Gilbert, Gary. "The List of Nations in Acts 2: Roman propaganda and the Lukan Response." *JBL* 121/3 (2002), 497-529.

________. "Luke-Acts and Negotiation of Authority and Identity in the Roman World." In *The Multivalence of Biblical Texts and Theological Meanings.* Edited by C. Helmer. Boston: Brill, (2006), 83-104.

________. "Roman Propaganda and Christian Identity in the Worldview of Luke-Acts." In *Contextualizing Acts. Lukan Narrative and Greco-Roman Discourse.* Edited by Todd Penner and C.V. Stichele. Atlanta: SBL (2003), 233-256.

Gill, D.W.J. and Bruce W. Winter. "Acts and Roman Religion." *The Book of Acts in its Graeco-Roman Setting.* Edited by D.W.J. Gill and Conrad Gempf. Vol. 2. Grand Rapids, Michigan: Wm. B. Eerdmans Publishing Company, 1994, 79-93.

Gill, D.W.J. "Macedonia." *The Book of Acts in its Graeco-Roman Setting,* vol. 2. Edited by D.W.J.Gill and Conrad Gempf. Grand Rapids: Wm. B. Eerdmans Publishing Company, 1994, 79-92.

________. "Achaia." *The Book of Acts in its Graeco-Roman Setting,* vol. 2. Edited by D.W.J. Gill and Conrad Gempf. Grand Rapids: Wm. B. Eerdmans Publishing Company, 1994, 433-53.

________. "Taxation, Greco_Roman." *DNTB.* Edited by C.A. Evans & S. Porter. Leicester, England: IVP, 2000, 1161-63.

________. "Roman Political System." *DNTB.* Edited by C.A. Evans & S.E. Porter. Leicester, England: IVP, 2000, 995-999.

Gnanavaram, M. *Treasure in Heaven and Treasure on Earth: Attitudes towards Poverty and Wealth in the New Testament Communities and in the Early Church.* Delhi: ISPCK, 2008.

________. " 'Dalit Theology' and the Parable of the Good Samaritan." *JSNT* 50 (1993), 59-83.

Gnuse, Robert. "'Vita Apologetica': The Lives of Josephus and Paul in Apologetic Historiography." *JSP* 13/2 (2002), 151-69.

Goodman, Martin. *Rome and Jerusalem: The Clash of Ancient Civilizations:* New York: Vintage Books, 2007.

Gottwald, Norman K. "Early Israel as an Anti-Imperial Community." *In the Shadow of the Empire: Reclaiming the Bible as a History of Faithful Resistance.* Edited by R.A. Horsely. Louisville/London: Westminster John Knox Press, 2008, 9-24.

Grant, F.C. *The Economic Background of the Gosepl.* Oxford: Oxford University Press, 1961.

Green, J.B. "Acts of the Apostles." *DLTD.* Edited by R. Martin and P.H. Davids. Illinois: IVP, 1997, 7-24.

Griffin, M. "*Urbs Roma, Plebs and Princeps.*" In *Images of the Empire.* Edited by L. Alexander. Sheffield: JSOT Press, 1991, 19-46.

Gueriviere, S.J, Paul de la. "Social Analysis." *Poverty in India: Challenged and Responses.* Edited by J. Murickan S.J. Bangalore: A Xavier Board Publication, 1988, 89-114.

Gupta, Sobhanlal Datta. "Imperialism and Colonialism: Towards A Postcolonial Understanding," vol. xv, Part I. In *Science, Technology, Imperialism and War.* Edited by Jyoti Bhusan Das Gupta. New Delhi: Pearson Longman, 2007, 423-465.

Haenchen, E. *The Acts of the Apostles: A Commentary.* Translated by B. Noble, et.al. Philadelphia: Westminster John Knox Press, 1971.

Hansen, G.Walter. "Galatia." In *The Book of Acts in its Graeco-Roman Setting,* vol. 2. Edited by D.W.J. Gill and Conrad Gempf. Grand Rapids. Wm. B. Eerdmans Publishing Company, 1994, 377-95.

Hanson, K.C. and D.E. Oakman. *Palestine in the Times of Jesus: Social Structures and Social Conflicts.* Minneapolis: Fortress Press, 1998.

Harkness, G. *Understanding the Kingdom of God.* New York: Abingdon Press, 1974.

Hayes, John H. and S.R. Mandell. *The Jewish People in Classical Antiquity: From Alexander to Bar Kochba.* Louisville, Kentucky: Westminster John Knox Press, 1998.

Heard, W.J. and C.A. Evans. "Revolutionary Movements, Jewish." *DNTB*. Edited by C.A. Evans & S.E. Porter. Leicester, England: IVP, 2000, 936-47.

Hedrick, C.W. "Paul's Coversion/Call: A Comparative Analysis of the three Reports in Acts." *JBL* 100 (1981), 415-432.

Hengel, M. *Was Jesus a Revolutionalist?* Philadephia: Fortress Press, 1971.

________. *Zealots. Investigations into the Jewish Freedom Movement in the Period from Herod I until 70 AD.* Translated by D. Smith. Edinburgh: T & T Clark, 1989.

________. (Appendix) "Zealots and Sicarii. The Question of the Unity and Diversity of the Jewish Freedom Movement in 6-74 A.D." *The Zealots. Investigations into the Jewish Freedom Movement in the Period from Herod I until 70 A.D.* Edinburg: T & T Clark, 1989, 380-404.

________. *Acts and the History of Earliest Christianity.* Translated by J. Bowden. Philadelphia: Fortress Press, 1979.

________. Between Jesus and Paul. Studies in the Earliest History of Christianity. Translated by J. Bowden. Philadelphia: Fortress, 1983.

Holmberg, B. *Sociology and the New Testament.* Minneapolis: Fortress Press, 1990.

Horrell, D.G. "Introduction." *JSNT* 27/3 (2005), 251-255.

Horsley, G.H.R. "The Politarchs." *The Book of Acts in its Graeco-Roman Setting,* vol. 2. Edited by D.W.J. Gill and Conrad Gempf. Grand Rapids: Wm. B. Eerdmans Publishing Company, 1994, 419-31.

Horsley, R.A. *Jesus and the Spiral of Violence. Popular Jewish Resistance in Roman Palestine.* San Francisco: Harper and Row, 1987.

________. *Jesus and Empire: The Kingdom of God and the New World Disorder.* Minneapolis: Fortress Press, 2003.

________, ed. *Paul and Empire: Religion and Power in Roman Imperial Society.* Harrisburg: Trinity Press International, 1997.

________. "The Slave Systems of Classical Antiquity and their Reluctant Recognition by Modern Scholars." *Semeia* 83/84 (1998), 19-66.

________. "Slave Resistance in Classical Antiquity." *Semeia* 83/84 (1998): 133-151.

________. "Popular Messianic Movements around the Time of Jesus." *CBQ* 46 (1984): 471-495.

________. "Jesus and Empire." *The Shadow of the Empire: Reclaiming the Bible as a History of Faithful Resistance*. Edited by Horsley. London: Westminster John Knox Press, 2008, 75-96.

________. "Ancient Jewish Banditry and the Revolt against Rome, A.D. 66-70." *CBQ* 43/3 (1981), 409-432.

________. "Like on of the Prophets of Old': Two Types of Popular Prophets at the Time of Jesus." *CBQ* 47 (1985), 435-63.

________. "The Sicarii: Ancient Jewish 'Terrorists." *JR* 59 (1979), 435-58.

________. "The Zealots: Their Origin, Relationships and Importance in the Jewish Revolt." *Nov T* 27 (1986), 159-192.

________. "Jesus and Empire." *USQR* 59/3-4 (2005), 44-74.

________. "Josephus and Bandits." *JSJ* 10 (1979), 37-63.

________. *The Liberation of Christians: The Infancy Narrative in Social Context.* New York: Crossroad, 1998.

________. *Paul and Politics: Ekklesia, Israel, Imperium, Interpretation: Essays in Honor of Krister Stendahl.* Harrisburg: Trinity International, 2000.

________ and N.A. Siberman. *The Message of the Kingdom: How Jesus and Paul Ignited a Revolution and Transformed the Ancient World.* New York: Crossett/ Rutnam, 1997.

________ & J.S. Hanson. *Bandits, Prophets and Messiahs. Popular Movements in the Time of Jesus.* New York: Harper & Row Publishers, 1988.

Howell, J.R. "The Imperial Authority and Benefaction of Centurions and Acts 10: 34- 43: A Response to C. Kavin Rowe." *JSNT* 31/1 (2008), 25-51.

Huddart, David. *Homi K. Bhabha.* London/New York: Routledge, 2007.

Isaac, Benjamin. "Banditry." *ABD,* vol. 1. Edited by D.N. Freedman. New York: Doubleday, 1992, 575-580.

Jackson, F.J. Foakes and K. Lake eds. *The Beginning of Christianity*, vol. 4, *The Acts of the Apostles.* London: Macmillan, [1920-33], 1979.

Jagersma, H. *A History of Israel from Alexander the Great to Bar Kochba.* Philadelphia: Fortress Press, 1985.

Jeffrelot, Christopher. *Hindu Nationalist Movement and Indian Politics, 1925-1990.* Viking: Penguin Books, 1996.

Jeremias, J. *Jerusalem in the Time of Jesus.* Translated by F.H. and C.H. Cave. Philadelphia: Fortress Press, 1969.

Johnson, L.T. *The Literary Function of Possessions in Luke-Acts.* SBLDS 39; Missoula, Mont.: Scholars Press, 1979.

________. *The Acts of the Apostles.* SP 5; Collegeville, Minneapolis: Liturgical Press, 1992.

Johnson, T.S. "Roman Emperors." *DNTB.* Edited by C.A. Evans & S. Porter. Leicester, England: IVP, 2000, 968-74.

Jones, Donald L. "Roman Imperial Cult." *ABD,* vol. 5. Edited by David Noel Freedman. New York: Doubleday, 1992, 806-809.

Joy, C.I. David. "Mark 10:17-27 in the Light of the Issues of Poor and their Representation: A Postcolonial Reading."*BTF* (June, 2006), 157-171.

________. *Mark and Its Subalterns: A Hermeneutical Paradigm for a Postcolonial Context.* London: Equinox, 2008.

________. "Re-visioning God and Re-conceiving God's Mission in the Postcolonial Indian Context." Paper presented on UTC Alumnae Association, 6th Oct, 2009.

________. "The Social and Religious Origins of the Gospel of Mark and its Hermeneutical Implications: A Post-Colonial Critique". *BTF* 33/1 (2001), 1-24.

Kang, Namsoon. "From Colonial to Postcolonial Education. Envisioning Political Theological Education: Dilemmas and Possibilities." In *Handbook of Theological Education in World Christianity: Theological Perspectives-Religious Surveys-Ecumenical Trends.* Edited by D. Werner, et.al. Bangalore: ATC, 2010, 30-41.

Kappen, S. "Hindutva-Emergent Fascism." In *Understanding Communalism.* Edited by M. Muralidharan, P.K.M. Tharakan & S. Kappen. Bangalore: Visthar, 1993, 79-100.

________. *Divine Challenge and Human Response.* Thiruvalla: CSS, 2001.

________. *Jesus and Culture.* Vol. 1. Delhi: ISPCK, 2002.

Karris, R.J. "Poor and Rich: The Lukean *Sitz im Leben.*' In *Perspectives on Luke-Acts.* Edited by C.H. Talbert. Danville, VA: Association of Baptist Professors of Religion, 1978, 112-25.

Kee, H.C. *Good News to the End of the Earth: The Theology of Acts.* Philadelphia: Trinity Press International, 1990.

________. *To Every Nation under Heaven: The Acts of the Apostles.* Harrisburg: Trinity Press International, 1997.

Keener, Craig S. "Power of Pentecost: Luke's Missiology in Acts 1-2." *AJPS* 12.1 (2009), 47-73.

Kelber, W.H. "Roman Imperialism and Early Christian Scribality." In *The Postcolnial Biblical Reader.* Edited by R.S. Sugirtharajah. Oxford: Blackwell Publishing, 2006, 96-111.

Kennedy, David. "Roman Army." *ABD,* vol. 5. Edited by David Noel Freedman. New York: Doubleday, 1992, 789-798.

Kim, Sebastian. *Christ and Caesar. The Gospel and the Roman Empire in the Writings of Paul and Luke.* UK/Michigan: Wm. B. Eerdmans Publishing Company, 2008.

________. *The Debate on Conversion initiated by the Sang Parivar, 1998-1999.* http://www.ocms.ac.uk/docs/sebastian%20kim%20lecture20040921.pdf (18 March 2011).

Kim, Uriah Y. *Decolonizing Josiah: Toward a Postcolonial Reading of the Deuteronomistic History*. Sheffield: Sheffield Phoenix Press, 2008.

Klauck, Hans-Josef. "The Roman Empire." In *The Cambridge History of Christianity. Origins to Constantine,* vol. 1. Edited by Margaret M. Mitchel and Frances M. Young. Cambridge: Cambridge University Press, 2006, 69-86.

________. "Des Kaisers schone Stimme. Herrscherkritik in Apg 12,20-23," in *Religion und Gesellschaft im fruhen Christentum.* WUNT, 152; Tubingen: Mohr Siebeck), 251-67.

Koester, Helmut. *History, Culture and Religion of the Hellenistic Age.* Philadelphia: Fortress Press, 1982.

Kreitzer, L.J. *Striking New Images: Roman Imperial Coinage and the New Testament World.* JSNT Sup. 134; Sheffield: Sheffield Academic Press, 1996.

Krodel, G.A. *Acts.* ACNT. Minneapolis: Augsburg, 1986.

Kurian, C.T. "Why the Poor are Poor… And are Likely to Remain So." *Journal of Social and Economic Studies,* vol. 1/2 (April-June 1984), 103-116.

Laato, Antti. *A Star is Rising. The Historical Development of the Old Testament Royal Ideology and the Rise of the Jewish Messianic Expectations.* Atlanta, Georgia: Scholars Press, 1997.

Landry, Donna and G. MacLean, eds. *The Spivak Reader: Selected Works of Gayatri Chakravorty Spivak.* London: Routledge, 1996.

Larbeer, P. Mohan "Deconstruction of Academic Theology and Reconstruction of Dalit Theology," in the Twenty First Century India," in *Ministerial Formation*, vol. 100 (2003), 17-24.

Lauback, F. "ἐπιστρεφω." *NIDNTT,* vol. I. Edited by C. Brown. Exeter: Paterson Press, 1975, 354-355.

Lentz Jr., J.C. *Luke's Portrait of Paul.* SNTSMS 77; Cambridge: Cambridge University Press, 1993.

Lewis, N. & M. Reinhold, eds. *Roman Civilization. Source Book II: The Empire.* New York: Harper & Row, 1966.

Liew, T.B. 'Margins and (Cutting)-Edges', in *Postcolonial Biblical Criticism: Interdisciplinary Intersections.* Edited by S.D. Moore and F.F. Segovia. London: T & T Clark International, 2005, 114-65.

Link, H.G. "ἔσχατος." *NIDNTT*, vol. 2. Edited by Collin Brown. Exeter: The Paternoster Press, [1971], 1976, 55-59.

Livingstone, Jose. *Luke's Description of the Gentile Mission in the Book of Acts.* Unpublished thesis submitted to the Senate of Serampore, 2001.

Longchar, W. "Introduction." In *Edinburgh 2010: Witnessing to Christ today in India.* Edited by J. Massey and W. Longchar. Bangalore: BTESSC/SATHRI & SCEPTRE, 2011, 1-14.

________. "Engaging Theological Education in Context: Focus on Persons with Disabilities." In *Ministerial Formation*, vol. 109 (July 2007), 28-33.

Lopez, D.C. *Apostle to the Conquered. Reimagining Paul's Mission*. Minneapolis: Fortress Press, 2008.

Lotz, Carsten Timothy. "A Critical Evaluation of Youngmo Cho: Spirit and Kingdom in the Writings of Luke and Paul: An Attempt to Reconcile these Concepts." *EQ* 82.2 (2010), 124-141.

Ludemann, G. *Early Christianity according to Traditions in Acts*. Translated by J. Bowden, Minneapolis: Fortress Press, 1987.

Luttwak, E.N. *Grand Strategy of the Roman Empire*. Battimore: John Hopkins, 1976.

Maddox, R. *The Purpose of Luke-Acts*. Edinburgh: T & T Clark, 1985.

Malina, Bruce J. *The Social Gospel of Jesus. The Kingdom of God in Mediterranean Perspective*. Minneapolis: Fortress Press, 2001.

________ and J.H. Neyrey. "Conflict in Luke-Acts: Labelling and Deviance Theory." In *The Social World of Luke-Acts: Models of Interpretation*. Edited by J.H. Nerey. Peabody, Mass.: Hendrickson, 1991, 97-122.

Manohar, M.P. "Christian Witness in India Today: Travails of a Feudal Church in a Democratic Polity." In *Edinburgh 2010: Witnessing to Christ today in India*. Edited by J. Massey and W. Longchar. Bangalore: BTESSC/ SATHRI & SCEPTRE, 2011, 101-11.

Marguerat, Daniel. "The Enigma of the Silent Closing of Acts (28:16-31)." In *Jesus and the Heritage of Israel: Luke's Narrative Claim upon Israel's Legacy*, vol. 1. Edited by D.P. Moessner and D.L. Tiede. (Harrisburg: Trinity, 1999), 284-304.

Marshall, I.H. *The Acts of the Apostles: An Introduction and Commentary*. TynNTC; Grand Rapids, 1980.

Martin, C.J. "A Chamberlain's Journey and the Challenge of Interpretation for Liberation." In *The Bible and Liberation: Political and Social Hermeneutics*. Edited by N.K. Gottwald & R.A. Horsley. Maryknoll: Orbis Books, 1993, 485-503.

Martin, C.P., ed. *Religious Liberty in Peril-The Indian Churches' Experience*. Nagpur: NCCI, 1999.

Martey, Emmanuel. "Interfaith Dialogue in Theological Education. The Challenge of Inter-Religious Dialogue and Praxis for African Theological Education." In *Handbook of Theological Education in World Christianity: Theological Perspectives-Regional Surveys-Ecumenical Trends*, edited by D. Werner, et al. Bangalore: ATC, 2010, 203-212.

Mason, S. "Josephus: Value for New Testament Study." *DNTB*. Edited by C.A. Evans & S.E. Porter. Leicester, England: IVP, 2000, 596-600.

________. *Josephus and the New Testament*. Peabody, MA: Hendrickson, 1992.

Massey, J. "Prophetic Witness and Subaltern Struggle for Justice." In *Edinburgh 2010: Witnessing to Christ today in India*. Edited by J. Massey and W. Longchar. Bangalore: BTESSC/SATHRI & SCEPTRE, 2011, 62-79.

________. "Preface." In *Edinburgh 2010: Witnessing to Christ today in India*. Edited by J. Massey and W. Longchar. Bangalore: BTESSC/ SATHRI & SCEPTRE, 2011, vii-viii.

________. *Dalits-Issues and Concerns. India 50 Years of Independence: 1947-97. Status, Growth and Development*. Delhi: BR Publishing, 1998.

McDonald, L.M. "Antioch (Syria)." *DNTB*. Edited by C.A. Evans & S. Porter. Leicester, England: IVP, 2000, 34-37.

________. "Philippi." *DNTB*. Edited by C.A. Evans & S. Porter. Leicester, England: IVP, 2000, 787-89.

________. "Ephesus." *DNTB*. Edited by C.A. Evans & S. Porter. Leicester, England: IVP, 2000, 318-321.

McKechnie, Paul. *The First Christian Centuries: Perspectives on the Early Church* England: Apollos, IVP, 2001.

McRay, J.R. "Corinth." *DNTB*. Edited by C.A. Evans & S. Porter. Leicester, England: IVP, 2000, 227-31.

Mealand, D.L. "Community of goods and Utopian Allusions in Acts II-IV." *JTS* 28 (1977), 96-99.

________. "The Close of Acts and Its Hellenistic Greek Vocabulary." *NTS* 36 (1990), 583-97.

Meeks, W. *The First Urban Christians*. London: Yale University Press, 1983.

Menzies, R.P. *Empowered for Witness: The Spirit in Luke-Acts*. Sheffield: Sheffield Academic Press, 1994.

________. "Spirit and Power in Luke-Acts: A Response to Max Turner." *JSNT* 49 (1993), 11-20.

Metzger, B.M. "Ancient Astrological Geography and Acts 2:9-11." In *Apostolic History and the Gospel: Biblical and Historical Essays Presented to F.F. Bruce on His Sixtieth Birthday*. Edited by W.W. Gasque and R.P. Martin. Grand Rapids: Wm. B. Eerdmans Publishing Company, 1970, 123-33.

Meyer, R. "προφηης." *TDNT*, vol. VI. Edited by Gerhard Friedrich. Grand Rapids, Michigan: Wm. B. Eerdmans Publishing Company, 1969, 812-28.

Milling, D.H. "Dialogue with People of other Faiths: Some NT Evidences." In *Bible Speaks Today: Essays in Honour of Gnana Robinson*. Edited by D.J. Muthunayagom. Delhi: ISPCK, 2000, 266-70.

Mitchell, Alan C. "The Social Function of Friendship in Acts 2:44-47 and 4:32-37." *JBL* 111 (1992), 255-72.

Moltmann, J. *The Theology of Hope: On the Ground and the Implications of a Christian Eschatology*. Translated by J.W. Leitch. New York: Harper & Row, 1965.

Moore-Gilbert, B.J. *Post-Colonial Theory: Contexts, Practices, Politics.* London: Verso, 1997.

Moore, Stephen D. Questions of Biblical Ambivalence and Authority under a Tree outside Delhi; or, The Postcolonial and Postmodern." In *Postcolonial Biblical Criticism. Interdisciplinary Intersections.* Edited by Stephen D. Moore and F.F. Segovia. London and New York: T & T Clark, 2005, 23-78.

________ and F.F. Segovia. "Postcolonial Biblical Criticism: Beginnings, Trajectories, Intersections." In *Postcolonial Biblical Criticism. Interdisciplinary Intersections.* Edited by Stephen D. Moore and F.F. Segovia. London and New York: T & T Clark, 2005, 1-22.

Moreland, M. "The Jerusalem Community in Acts: Mythmaking and the Sociorhetorical functions of a Lukan Setting." In *Contextualizing Acts: Lukan Narrative and Greco-Roman Discourse.* Edited by T. Penner and C.V. Stichele. SBL, 20; Atlanta: SBL, 2003, 285-310.

Morton, Stephen. *Gayatri Chakravorty Spivak.* New York: Routledge, 2003.

Moxnes, Halvor. *Economy of the Kingdom*. Philadelphia: Fortress Press, 1988.

________."Patron-Client relations and the new Community in Luke-Acts." In *The Social World of Luke-Acts. Models of Interpretation.* Edited by J.H. Neyrey. Peabody: Hendrickson, 1991, 241-68.

________. "The Meaning of ἔθνος and ἔθνη and its Significance to the study of the New Testament." *BTF* 29/34 (1997), 3-36.

Muñoz-Larrondo, Ruben. *Living in Two Worlds-A Postcolonial Reading of the Acts of the Apostles.* Ph.D Dissertation submitted to the faculty of the Graduate School of Vanderbilt University, 2008. MuñozLarrondo.pdfetd.library.vanderbilt.edu/…/PhdDissertationRuben (5th Oct 2010).

Muthuraj, J.G. "A Post- Colonial Reading of Acts." In *Interweaving Methodology and Praxis-Exploring Disciplinary Options in Today's World.* Edited by I. J. Mohan Razu. Bangalore: BTESSC/ SATHRI, 2007, 75-99.

Nasrallah, Laura. "The Acts of the Apostles, Greek Cities, and Hadrian's Panhellenion." *JBL* 127/3 (2008), 533-566.

Neagoe, Alexandru. *The Trial of the Gospel: An Apologetic Reading of Luke's Trial Narratives.* SNTSMS 116; Cambridge: Cambridge University Press, 2002.

Neudorfer, Heinz-Werner. "The Speech of Stephen." In *Witness to the Gospel: The Theology of Acts.* Edited by I.H. Marshall and David Peterson. Grand Rapids, Michigan: Wm. B. Eerdmans Publishing Company, 1998, 275-294.

Neusner, J. *From Politics to Piety: The Emergence of Pharisaic Judaism.* Englewood Cliffs: Prentice Hall, 1973.

________. *Messiah in Context: Israel's History and Destiny in Formative Judaism.* Philadelphia: Fortress Press, 1984.

Neyrey, J.H. "Luke's Social Location of Paul: Cultural Anthropology and the Status of Paul in Acts." In *History, Literature, and Society in the Book of Acts.* Edited by Ben Witherington III. Cambridge: Cambridge University Press, 1996, 251-79.

Nickelsburg, G.W.E. *Ancient Judaism and Christian Origins: Diversity, Continuity and Transformation.* Minneapolis: Fortress Press, 2003.

O'Toole, Robert F. "Christ's Resurrection in Acts 13,13-52." *Biblica* 60 (1979), 361-372.

Pahl, Michael W. "The 'Gospel' and The 'Word': Exploring Some Early Christian Patterns." *JSNT* 29.2 (2006), 211-227.

Palatty, Paul. "The Ascension of Christ in Luke-Acts. An Exegetical Critical Study of Luke 24, 50-53 and Acts 1, 2-3, 9-11." *Bible Bhashyam* 12 (2, 1986), 100-17.

Palmer, D.W. "Acts and the Historical Monograph." In *The Book of Acts its Ancient Literary Setting,* vol. 1. Edited by B.W. Winter and A.D. Clarke. Grand Rapids: Wm. B. Eerdmans Publishing Company, 1993, 1-29.

Panikkar, K.N. *Colonialism, Culture, and Resistance.* Oxford: University Press, 2007.

Parry, David T.N. "Release of the Captives-Reflections on Acts 12," in *Luke's Literary Achievement: Collected Essays.* Edited by C.M. Tucket. JSNT Sup.116; Sheffield: Sheffield Academy Press, 1995, 156-164.

Penner, Todd. "Madness in the Method? The Acts of the Apostles in Current Study." *CBR* 2/2 (2004), 223-293.

________. "Civilizing Discourse: Acts, Declamation, and the Rhetoric of the *Polis.*" In *Contextualizing Acts. Lukan Narrative and Greco-Roman Discourse.* Edited by T. Penner and C.V. Stichele. SBL, 20. Atlanta: SBL, 2003, 65-104.

Perkins, Judith. *The Suffering Self. Pain and Narrative Representation in the Early Christian Era.* London: Routledge, 1995.

Perrin, N. *The Kingdom of God in the Preaching of Jesus.* London: SCM Press, 1963.

________. "Jesus and the Language of the Kingdom." *The Kingdom of God in the Teaching of Jesus.* Edited by Bruce Chilton. London: SPCK, 1984, 92-106.

________. *Rediscovering the Teaching of Jesus.* London: SCM Press, 1967.

Pervo, R.I. *Profit and Delight: The Literary Genre of the Acts of the Apostles.* Philadelphia: Fortress Press, 1987.

Peterson, Davis. "The Worship of the New Community." In *Witness to the Gospel: The Theology of Acts.* Edited by I.H. Marshall and D. Peterson. Grand Rapids/ Cambridge: Wm. B. Eerdmans Publishing Company, 1998, 373-95.

Plummer, A. *A Critical and Exegetical Commentary on the Gospel According to Luke.* Edinburgh: T & T Clark, 1922.

Polhill, J.B. *Acts*, NAC vol. 26. Nashville: Broadman Press, 2001.

Powell, M.A. *What are they Saying about Acts?* New York: Paulist Press, 1991.

Prabakar, M.E. "Saffronization of Education." In *Relgion and Society* 46/4 (Dec, 1999 & 47/1 March 2000), 17-45.

Premnath, D.N. "Introduction." In *Border Crossing. Cross-cultural Hermeneutics.* Edited by D.N. Premnath. Maryknoll, New York: Orbis Books, 2007, 1-12.

________, ed., *Border Crossings: Cross-Cultural Hermeneutics.* New York: Orbis Books, 2007.

Price, S.R.F. *Rituals and Power: The Roman Imperial Cult in Asia Minor.* Cambridge: Cambridge University Press, 1984.

________. "Rituals and Power." In *Paul and Empire: Religion and Power in Roman Imperial Society.* Edited by R.A. Horsley. Pennsylvania: Trinity Press International, 1997, 47-71.

Prior, Michael. *The Bible and Colonialism: A Moral Critique.* Sheffield: Sheffield Academy, 1997.

Pui-lan, Kwok. "A Thelogy of Border Passage." In *Border Crossings.* Edited by D.N. Premnath. Maryknoll, New York: Orbis Books, 2007, 103-117.

________. "A theology of Border Passage." In *Border Crossings: Cross-Cultural Hermeneutics.* Edited by D.N. Premnath, New York: Orbis Books, 2007, 103-117.

Puskas, Charles B. *An Introduction to the New Testament.* Peabody: Hendrickson, 1989.

Rackham, R.B. *The Acts of the Apostles: An Exposition.* London: Methuen and Company, 1906.

Raja, John Joshva. "Relevant and Effective Theological Education in the Twenty First Century India." *Ministerial Formation*, vol. 100 (2003), 5-16.

Rajak, T. "Friends, Romans, Subjects: Agrippa II's Speech in Josephus' Jewish War." In *Images of Empire.* Edited by L. Alexander. Sheffield: JSOT Press, 1991, 122-134.

Rajkumar, Peniel J. *Dalit Theology and Dalit Liberation. Problems, Paradigms and Possibilities.* Surrey: Ashgate, 2010.

________. "Public Ministry and Communication Studies in Theological Education. Public Ministry, Ethical Formation and Theological Education in India-An Exploration of Key Issues." In *Handbook of Theological Education in World Christianity. Theological Perspectives-Regional Surveys-Ecumenical Trends.* Edited by D.Werner, et al. Bangalore: ATC, 2010, 161-69.

Rapske, B.M. "Roman Governors of Palestine." *DNTB.* Edited by C.A. Evans & S. Porter Leicester, England: IVP, 2000, 978-84.

________. "Philippi." In *The Book of Acts and Paul in Roman Custody*, vol. 3. Grand Rapids: Wm. B. Eerdmans Publishing Company, 1994, 115-134.

________. "Acts, Travel and Shipwreck." In *The Book of Acts in its Graeco-Roman Setting*, vol. 2. Edited by D.W.J. Gill and Conrad Gempf. Grand Rapids: Wm. B. Eerdmans Publishing Company, 1994, 1-48.

________. "Caesarea." In *The Book of Acts and Paul in Roman Custody*, vol. 3. Grand Rapids: Wm. B. Eerdmans Publishing Company, 1994, 151-58.

Reimer I, Richard. *Women in Acts of the Apostles: A Feminist Liberation Perspective.* Translated by L.M. Maloney. Minneapolis: Fortress Press, 1995.

Riches, John. *The World of Jesus: First-Century Judaism in Crisis.* Cambridge: Cambridge University Press, 1990.

________. *Jesus and Transformation of Judaism.* London: Longman and Todd, 1980.

Robbins, V.K. "The Social Location of the Implied Author of Luke-Acts." In *The Social World of Luke-Acts. Models of Interpretation.* Edited by J.H. Neyrey. Peabody: Hendrickson Publishers, 1991, 305-332.

Roland, Christopher. *Christian Origins: An Account of the Setting and Character of the most Important Messianic Sect of Judaism.* London: SPCK, 1985.

________. and M. Corner. *Liberating Exegesis: The Challenge of Liberation Theology to Biblical Studeis.* Cambridge: SPCK, 1990.

Rosner, B.S. "Acts and Biblical History." In *The Book of Acts in its Ancient Literary Setting*, vol. 1. Edited by B.W. Winter and A.D. Clarke. Grand Rapids: Wm. B. Eerdmans Publishing Company, 1993, 65-82.

Rowe, C. Kavin. "Luke- Acts and the Imperial Cult: A Way through the Conundrum." *JSNT* 27/3 (2005), 278-300.

________. *World Upside Down. Reading Acts in the Graeco-Roman Age.* Oxford: University Press, 2010.

Roy, Ajith. *Monopoly Capitalism in India.* Culcutta: Naya Prokash, 1976.

Ruthven, J. "'This is my Covenant with them': Isaiah 59:19-21 as the Programmatic Prophecy of the New Covenant in the Acts of the Apostles (Part I)." *JPT* 17 (2008), 32-47.

Said, Edward. *Orientalism.* New York: Vintage, 1978.

________. *The World, the Text and the Critic.* Cambridge, MA: Harward University Press, 1983.

________. *Culture and Imperialism.* London: Vintage, 1993.

Saldarini, Anthony J. "Pharisees." *ABD*, vol. 5. Edited by David Noel Freedman. New York: Doubleday, 1992, 289-303.

Saller, Richard P. "Roman Empire." In *The Oxford Companion to the Bible.* Edited by B.M. Metzger & M.D. Coogen. New York: Oxford University Press, 1993, 657-659.

Samartha, S. *Courage for Dialogue: Ecumenical Issues in Inter-religious Relationships.* Geneva: WCC, 1981.

Samuel, S. "Postcolonialism as a Critical Practice in Biblical Studies," Part I. *DTJ* 2/2 (2005), 97-119.

________."Postcolonialism as a Critical Practice in Biblical Studies," Part II. *DTJ* 3/1 (2006), 5-20.

________. *A Postcolonial Reading of Mark's Story of Jesus.* London: T & T Clark, 2007.

________. "The Imperial Prison and the Irrupting Gospel as Discursive Symbols of Stewardship." *niyog*- New Theological College Magazine, 2004, 38-41.

________. "The Acts of Philip and the Τινες Ανδρες (Certain Men) of Cyprus and Cyrene: A Remapping of Early Christian Mission Frontiers." In *Remapping Mission Discourse: A Festschrift in Honor of the Rev.George Kuruvila Chavanikamannil.* Edited by S. Samuel and P.V. Joseph. NTC-ISPCK, 2008, 42-71.

________. "Remapping Mission Discourse: Mission Amidst affluence and Affliction." In *Remapping Mission Discourse: A Festschrift in Honor of the Rev. George Kuruvila Chavanikamannil.* Edited by S. Samuel and P.V. Joseph. NTC-ISPCK, 2008, 160-184.

________. "The Imperial Prison and the Irrupting Gospel as Discursive Symbols of Stewardship," *niyog*- New Theological College Magazine, 2004, 38-41.

________. "Mission Practice: The Early Christian Perspectives." *DTJ* 4.1 (2007), 5-21.

Sanders, E.P. *Jesus and Judaism*. London: SCM Press, 1985.

________. *Judaism: Practice and Belief 63 BCE-66 CE.* London: SCM Press, 1992.

Sanders, J.T. *The Jews in luke-Acts.* Philadelphia: Fortress Press, 1987.

Sandnes, Karl Olav. "Paul and Socrates: The Aim of Paul's Areopagus Speech." *JSNT* 50 (1993), 13-26.

Sarkar, Sumith. "The Conditions and Nature of Subaltern Militancy: Bengal from Swadeshi to Non-Co-operation, c.1905-22." In *Subaltern Studies III. Writings on South Asian History and Society.* Edited by Ranajit Guha. Delhi: Oxford University Press, 1992, 271-320.

Schlier, Heinrich. "παρρησια." *TDNT*, vol. v. Translated and edited by Geoffrey W. Bromiley. Grand Rapids: Wm. B. Erdmans Publishing Company, 1967, 871-86.

Schmidt, K.L. "βασιλεια," *TDNT*, vol. 1. Translated and edited by Geoffrey W. Bromiley. Wm. B. Eerdmans Publishing Company, 1993, 579-90.

Schmidt, T.E. "Taxation, Jewish." *DNTB.* Edited by C.A. Evans & S. Porter. Leicester, England: IVP, 2000, 1163-66.

Schürer, E. *The History of Jewish People in the Age of Jesus Christ*, vol I & II. Edited by G.Vermes, et.al,. Peabody: Hendrickson, 1998.

Schwartz, D.R. "The End of the ΓΗ (Acts 1:8): Beginning or End of the Christian Mission." *JBL* 105 (1986), 669-76.

Schwartz, Seth. *Josephus and Judean Politics.* Columbia Studies in the Classical Traditions 18; Leiden: Brill, 1990.

Scott, James C. *Domination and the Arts of Resistance.* New Haven: Yale University Press, 1990.

Scott, James M. "Luke's Geographical Horizon." In *The Book of Acts in its Graeco-Roman Setting*, vol.2. Edited by D.W.J. Gill and C. Gempf. Grand Rapids: Wm. B. Eerdmans Publishing Company, 1994, 483-544.

Secombe, D.P. "The New People of God." In *Witness to the Gospel: The Theology of Acts.* Edited by I.H. Marshall and D. Peterson. Grand Rapids/Cambridge: Wm. B. Eerdmans Publishing Company, 1998, 349-72.

Segal, Alan F. *Paul the Convert. The Apostolate and Apostasy of Saul the Pharisee.* New Haven and London: Xale University Press, 1990.

Segovia, F.F. "Biblical Criticism and Postcolonial Studies: Toward a Postcolonial Optic" In *The Postcolonial Bible.* Edited by R.S. Sugirtharajah. Sheffield: Sheffield Academic Press, 1998, 49-65.

________. "Mapping the Postcolonial Optic in Biblical Criticism: Meaning and Scope." In *Postcolonial Biblical Criticism. Interdisciplinary Intersections.* Edited by S.D. Moore and F.F. Segovia. London: T & T Clark, 2005, 23-78.

________. "The Gospel of John." In *A Postcolonial Commentary on the New Testament Writings.* Edited by F.F. Segovia and R.S. Sugirtharaja. London: T & T Clark, 2007, 156-193.

________. *Decolonizing Biblical Studies: A View from the Margins.* Maryknoll, New York: Orbis Books, 2000.

________. "Postcolonial and Diasporic Criticism in biblical Studies: Focus, Parameters, Relevance." *Studies in World Christianity*, 5/2 (1999), 177-195.

________. "Notes Toward Refining the Postcolonial Optic." *JSNT* 75 (1999), 103-114.

________. "And They Began to Speak in Other Tongues": Competing Modes of Discourse in Contemporary Biblical Criticism." In *Reading from this Place. Social Location and Biblical Interpretation in the United States*, vol. 1. Edited by F.F. Segovia and M.A. Tolbert. Minneapolis: Fortress Press, 1995, 1-32.

________. "Toward a Hermeneutics of the Diaspora: A Hermeneutics of Otherness and Engagement." In *Reading from this Place. Social Location and Biblical Interpretation in the United States*, vol. 1. Edited by F.F. Segovia and M.A. Tolbert. Minneapolis: Fortress Press, 1995, 57-73.

________. "Tracing Sugirtharajah's Voice from the Margin: From Liberation to Postclonialism." In *Postcolonial Interventions: Essays in Honor of R.S. Sugirtharajah*. Edited by T.B. Liew. Sheffield: Phoenix Press, 2009, 215-239.

Sharma, Jyothirmaya. *Hindutva. Exploring the Idea of Hindu Nationalism*. Viking: Penguin Books, 2011.

________. *Terrifying Vision: M.S.Gowalkar, the RSS and India*. Viking: Penguin Books, 2007.

Shauf, S. "Locating the Eunuch: Characterization and Narration Context in Acts 8:26-40." *CBQ* 71 (2009), 762-775.

Shelton, Jo-Ann. *As the Romans Did. A Sourcebook in Roman Social History.* Oxford: University Press, 1998.

Sherwin-White, A.N. *Roman Society and Roman Law in the New Testament.* Oxford: Clarendon Press, 1963.

Skinner, Matthew L. *Locating Paul. Places of Custody as Narrative Setting in Acts 21-28* Atlanta: SBL, 2003.

Slingerland, D. "'The Jews' in the Pauline Portion of Acts.'" *JAAR* 54 (1986), 305-21.

Smith, M. "Zealots and Sicarii: Their Origins and relations." *HTR* 64 (1971), 1-19.

Spenser, F.S. *The Portrait of Philip in Acts: A Study of Roles and Relations.* JSNT Sup 67; Sheffield: Sheffield Academy Press, 1992.

Spivak, G.C. *A Critique of Postcolonial Reason: Towards a History of the Vanishing Present.* Cambridge, MA: Harwvard Univeristy Press, 1999.

________. "Can the Subaltern Speak?'" In *Marxism and the Interpretation of Culture*. Edited by Cary Nelson and Lawrence Grossberg. London: Macmillan, 1988, 271-313.

________. *In Other Worlds: Essays in Cultural Politics.* New York: Methuen, 1987.

________. *Outside in the Teaching Machine*. New York: Routledge, 1993.

Squires, J.T. The Plan of God in Luke-Acts. SNTSMS, 76; Cambridge: Cambridge University Press, 1993.

________. "The Function of Acts 8:4-12:25." *NTS* 44 (1998), 608-617.

Staley, J.L. "Changing Women: Postcolonial Reflections on Acts 16:6-40." *JSNT* 73 (1999), 113-135.

Stambaugh, J. and D. Balch, *The Social World of the First Christians* (London: SPCK, 1986).

Stanton, G.N. *Jesus and Gospel.* Cambridge: Cambridge University Press, 2004.

Stegemann, E.W. & W. Stegemann. *The Jesus Movement: A Social History of its First Century.* Translated by Stegemann and O.C. Dean, Jr. Minneapolis: Fortress Press, 1999.

Stendahl, K. *Paul among the Jews and Gentiles: And Other Essays.* Philadelphia: Fortress Press, 1976.

Sterling, G.E. *Historiography and Self Definition: Josephus, Luke-Acts and Apologetic Historiography*. Nov.TSup 64. Leiden: Brill, 1992.

Storkey, Alan. *Jesus and Politics. Confronting the Powers*. Grand Rapids: Baker Academy, 2005.

Strelan, R. "The Running Prophet (Acts 8:30)." *Nov T* 43.1 (2001), 31-38.

Sugirtharajah, R.S. *Postcolonial Reconfigurations: An Alternative Way of Reading the Bible and Doing Theology.* London: SCM Press, 2003.

________. *The Bible and the Third World: Precolonial, Colonial and Postcolonial Encounters.* Cambridge: University Press, 2001.

________. "The First, Second and Third Letters of John." In *A Postcolonial Commentary on the New Testament Writings*. Edited by F.F. Segovia and R.S. Sugirtharajah. New York: T & T Clark, 2007, 413-423.

________. "Muddling Along at the Margins." In *Still at the Margins. Biblical Scholarship Fifteen Years after Voices from the Margins*. Edited by R.S. Sugirtharajah. New York: T & T Clark, 2008, 8-21.

________. *Asian Biblical Hermeneutics and Postcolonialism: Contesting the Interpretations*. England: Sheffield Academic Press, 1998.

________. *Postcolonial Criticism and Biblical Interpretation.* Oxford: Oxford University Press, 2002.

________. *Vernacular Hermeneutics*. Sheffield: Sheffield Academic Press, 1999.

________. *Voices from the Margins: Interpreting the Bible in the Third World.* London: SPCK, [1991, 1995], 2006.

________. *The Postcolonial Bible.* Sheffield: Sheffield Academic Press, 1998.

________. "A Brief Memorandum on Postcolonialism and Biblical Studies." *JSNT* 73 (1999), 3-5.

________. "From Orientalist to Post-Colonial: Notes on Reading Practices." *AJT* 10/ 1, (1996), 20-27.

________. "Cultures, Texts, Margins: A Hermeneutical Odyssey." In *Asian Biblical Hermeneutics and Postcolonialism*. Maryknoll, New York: Orbis Books, 1998, 123-39.

________. *Troublesome Texts. The Bible in Colonial and Contemporary Culture.* Sheffield: Phoenix Press, 2008.

Swartley, William M. "Politics of Peace (Eirene) in Luke's Gospel." In *Political Issues in Luke-Acts*. Edited by Richard J. Cassidy and Philip J. Sharper. Maryknoll, New York: Orbis Books, 1983), 18-37.

Talbert, C.H. *Literary Patterns, Theological Themes, and Genre of Luke-Acts.* Missoula: Scholars Press, 1974.

Tannehill, R.C. *The Narrative Unity of Luke-Acts: A Literary Interpretation. vol. I: The Gospel according to Luke*. Philadelphia: Fortress Press, 1994.

________. *The Narrative Unity of Luke-Acts: A Literary Interpretation. vol. II. The Acts of the Apostles.* Philadelphia: Fortress Press, 1994.

________. "The Functions of Peter's Mission Speeches in the Narrative of Acts." *NTS* 37 (1991), 400-414.

Taylor, N.H. "Palestinian Christianity and the Caligula Crisis. Part.I. Social and Historical Reconsideration." *JSNT* 61 (1996), 101-124.

________. "Palestinian Christianity and the Caligula Crisis. Part.I. The Markan Eschatological Discourse." *JSNT* 62 (1996), 13-41.

Thangaraj, M. Thomas. "Let God be God. Crossing Boundaries as a Theological Practice." In *Border Crossings: Cross-Cultural Hermeneutics.* Edited by Premnath. New York: Orbis Books, 2007, 89-102.

Theissen, G. *Social Reality and the Early Christians.* Edinburgh: T & T Clark, 1993.

Thomas, M.M. *To the Ends of the Earth (The Acts of the Apostles).* Translated by T.M. Philip. Thiruvalla: CSS & BTTBPSA, 2005.

________. *The Christian Response to the Asian Revolution.* London: SCM Press, 1980.

________. "Introduction." In *Towards an Indian Christian Theology: Life and Thought of Some Pioneers.* Edited by M.M. Thomas and P.T. Thomas. Thiruvalla: New Day Publications of India, 1992, 1-12.

Thomson, G.L. "Roman East." *DNTB.* Edited by C.A. Evans & S.E. Porter. Leicester, England: IVP, 2000, 962-68.

________. "Roman Military." DNTB. Edited by C.A. Evans & S.E. Porter. Leicester, England: IVP, 2000, 991-95.

Trebilco, P.R. "Asia." In *BAGRS,* vol. 2. Edited by D.W.J. Gill and Conrad Gempf. Grand Rapids: Wm. B. Eerdmans Publishing Comapany, 1994, 291-365.

Trites, A.A. *The New Testament Concept of Witness.* Cambridge: Cambridge University Press, 1977.

Turner, M. *Power from on High: The Spirit in Israel's Restoration and Witness in Luke-Acts.* Sheffield: Sheffield Academic Press, 1996.

________. "The 'Spirit of Prophecy' as the Power of Israel's Restoration and Witness." In *Witness to the Gospel. The Theology of Acts.* Edited by I.H. Marshall and D. Peterson. Wm. B. Eerdmans Publishing Company, 1998, 327-48.

Tyson, Joseph B. "Jews and Judaism in Luke-Acts: Reading as a Godfearer." *NTS* 41 (1995), 19-38.

Veer, Peter van der. "Writing Violence." In *Making India Hindu: Religion, Community, and the Politics of Democracy in India.* Edited by D. Ludden. New Delhi: OUP, 1996, 253-60.

Vermes, G. *The Dead Sea Scrolls: Qumran in Perspective.* Philadelphia: Fortress Press, 1981.

Young, Robert. *Postcolonialism: An Introduction.* Oxford: Blackwell, 2001.

________. *White Mythologies: Writing History and the West.* London: Routledge, 1990.

Walaskay, P.W. *"And So We Come to Rome'. The Political Perspective of St. Luke* Cambridge: Cambridge University Press, 1983.

Walton, Steve. "Acts. Many Questions, Many Answers." In *The Face of NT Studies. A Survey of Recent Research.* Edited by S. McKnight and G.R. Osborne. Grand Rapids: Backer Academic Press, 2004, 229-250.

Wansink, C.S. "Roman Law and Legal System." *DNTB.* Edited by C.A. Evans & S.E. Porter. Leicester, England: IVP, 2000, 984-991.

________. "Primitive Community in Acts? Does Acts Present the Community of goods (2:44-45; 4:32-35) as mistaken?." *EQ* 80/2 (2008), 99-111.

________. "The Acts-of God? What is he 'Acts of the Apostles' all about." *EQ* 804 (2008), 291-306.

________. "The State They were in: Luke's View of the Roman Empire." In *Rome in the Bible and the Early Church.* Edited by Peter Oakes. Grand Rapids: Baker Book House, 2002, 1-41.

Watson, D.F. "Roman Social Classes." *DNTB.* Edited by C.A. Evans & S.E. Porter. Leicester, England: IVP, 2000, 999-1004.

Wedderburn, A.J.M. "Traditions and Redaction in Acts 2.1-13." *JSNT* 55 (1994), 27-54.

Wells, Colin M. "Roman Empire." *ABD,* vol. 5. Edited by D.N. Freedman. New York: Doubleday, 1992, 801-806.

Wengst, Klaus. *Pax Romana and the Peace of Jesus Christ.* Translated by J. Bowden. Philadelphia: Fortress Press, 1987.

Wienstock, S. "The Geographical Catelogue in Acts 2:9-11." *JRS* 38 (1948), 43-46.

Wild, Robert A. "The Warrior and the Prisoner: Some Reflections on Ephesians 6:10-20." *CBQ* 46 (1984), 284-98.

Wilfred, Felix. "Introduction: The Art of Negotiating the Frontiers." *Concilium* 2 (1999), vii-xiii.

________. "A New way of Being Christians to Encounter Neighbours of Other Faiths." In *Unanswered Questions.* Edited by C. Theobald and Dietmar Mieth. Concilium; London: SCM Press, 1999, 39-44.

Wilson, S.G. *The Gentiles and Gentile Mission.* SNTSMS 23; Cambridge: Cambridge University Press, 1973.

Winter, B. "The Importance of the *Captatio Benevolentiae* in the Speeches of Tertullus and Paul in Acts 24:1-21." *JTS* 42 (1991), 505-31.

Winter, B.W. "Official Proceedings and the Forensic Speeches in Acts 24-26." In *BAATS* vol. 1. Edited by B.W. Winter and A.D. Clarke. Grand Rapids: Wm. B. Eerdmans Publishing Company, 1993, 305-336.

________. "The Imperial Cult." In *The Book of Acts in its Graeco-Roman Setting*, vol. 2. Edited by D.W.J. Gill and Conrad Gempf. Grand Rapids, Michigan: Wm. B. Eerdmans Publishing Comapany, 1994, 93-103.

Witherington III, Ben. *The Acts of the Apostles: A Socio-Rhetorical Commentary*. Grand Rapids, Michigan: Wm. B. Eerdmans Publishing Company, 1998.

Witherup, S.S. Ronald D. "Functional Redundancy in the Acts of the Apostles." *JSNT* 48 (1992), 67-86.

Wozniuk, Vladmir. "In Pursuit of a Politics of Holiness: Reconciling Hellenic and Hebraic Political Wisdom in the Acts of the Apostles." *Journal of Church and State* 45/2 (Sept. 2003), 283-304.

Wright, N.T. *The New Testament and the People of God*. London: SPCK, 1992.

________. *Jesus and the Victory of God*. London: SPCK, 1996.

Zanker, P. "*The Power of Images*." In *Paul and Empire: Religion and Power in Roman Imperial Society*. Edited by R.A. Horsley. Pennsylvania: Trinity Press International, 1997, 72-86.

Zeitlin, S. "Zealots and Sicarii." *JBL* 81 (1962), 395-98.

Zweck, Dean. "The Exordium of the Areopagus Speech, Acts 17.22,23" *NTS* 35 (1989), 94-103.

Zwiep, A.W. *The Ascension of the Messiah in Lukan Christology*. NovT Sup 87; Leiden: Brill, 1997.